D1066970

DELINQUENCY:
The Problem and Its Prevention

DELINQUENCY:
The Problem and
Its Prevention

By
DENIS STOTT

Professor Emeritus
Department of Psychology
University of Guelph
Canada

SP

SP MEDICAL & SCIENTIFIC BOOKS
a division of Spectrum Publications Inc.
New York • London

SPECTRUM PUBLICATIONS, INC.
175-20 Wexford Terrace, Jamaica, NY 11432

Library of Congress Cataloguing in Publication Data

Stott, Denis Herbert.
    Delinquency: the problem and its prevention.

    1. Juvenile delinquency. 2. Juvenile Delinquency—
Prevention. 3. Juvenile delinquency—United States.
4. Juvenile delinquency—United States—Prevention.
I. Title.
HV9069.S764   1979   364.3'6   80-25928
ISBN 0-89335-172-5

Printed in the United States of America

FOREWORD

The law-and-order issue in society is, justifiably, always a cause for concern. It was among the very first reasons for the development and organization of society as we know it. Consideration of the issue is heightened at times of social change, and today we are confronted with changes in the order of society at an unprecedented rate. The extent of current concern is vividly illustrated by the fact that at a time when Britain is prepared to arrest the development of, and in some cases reduce, the provision of health and caring services, we are prepared to spend more on law and order.

It is easy to understand such attitudes. What profit is there for a community if it looks to the care and welfare of its citizens yet they are in fear for the safety of themselves and their property? But what does an investment in law and order buy? Certainly cash can buy more policing, and good salaries can ensure the recruitment of intelligent police officers of good standard. But what of the core elements in law and order? Community attitudes, the concept of self and society induced at school, the correction of those children who find themselves in trouble and from whom our adult criminals develop: these are areas where, if a definable amount of money could buy solutions, such resources would be readily forthcoming.

Yet these are the very areas which are surrounded by vague thinking, inept practice, and confusion.

Perhaps the community deserves no better, for although the law-and-order issue is such an area of concern, rhetoric is frequently substituted for thinking whenever this subject is raised. It does not seem to matter whether it is in a factory cafeteria, at a suburban coffee klatch, in debates by so-called experts, or even in the pronouncements of eminent jurists—an absence of effective thinking characterizes comment on these issues.

In recent years leading political personalities have seriously advocated, in addition to the popular call for birching, the use of electric shock, the reintroduction of the stocks, and even branding. On the other hand there are those who wish only to explain away all offending and criminal behavior, who talk only in terms of treatment, who ignore the deep-seated resentment felt by ordinary members of the community when confronted with the waste of vandalism and the pain of violence.

Clearly, one of the greatest contributions which can be made to law and order in this context is to raise the level of debate. Professor Stott in this book makes a singular contribution in this direction. He does so against a background of over thrity years' research in the field of juvenile delinquency. He has complemented this research with a keen understanding of the framework of social administration on both sides of the Atlantic Ocean, and the changing pattern of such over the years.

One does not have to agree with Professor Stott to appreciate the value of his work. The family-centered approach based on direct observation of families with delinquent children has led to the development of a system of diagnosis and action which, at the very least, provides a point of departure for constructive thinking about juvenile delinquency. This book represents a singular contribution to the pursuit of effectiveness in thinking about juvenile delinquency and represents a constructive alternative to the rhetoric of the hawks and the doves.

F. E. Edwards
Director of Social Work,
Strathclyde Regional Council

INTRODUCTION

This book is written at a time when thinking and policies about juvenile crime are in disarray, and the prevailing mood on both sides of the Atlantic is one of defeat. There is a general recognition that the present hodgepodge of arrangements for dealing with delinquent youth have failed. Since the humanitarian philosophy has been in the ascendency during the past generation, it has been blamed for our failure to halt the sharp increase in juvenile crime. Out of a sense of desperation there is now a reversion to punitiveness.

The doves and the hawks are equally ingenuous. Juvenile crime will not go away just by kind admonishment, nor will reliance on deterrence be effective, short of measures too harsh for a modern civilization to countenance.

I argue in this book that the humanitarians have failed for lack of a technology. They have not known how to translate their compassion into preventive and remedial policies that work. In truth they have been without a policy except a wishful optimism not based on any balanced view of the causes of juvenile crime. It is little wonder that many people have become impatient with the ineffectiveness of our juvenile justice system and have demanded tougher measures.

Understanding of causes is the crux of the problem. In this age, when we have worked through nearly all that eclectic skills can offer, little can be achieved in any sphere without understanding of the processes involved. Space travel would have been impossible without the knowledge provided by the theoretical sciences. Advances in medicine depend upon research into the functioning of the body and the nature of diseases. Likewise the prevention of delinquency depends upon an insight into its causes.

Today, as Judge Bazelon has observed, we hear nothing about the causes of crime. What are the reasons for this irrational avoidance? The most fundamental is that crime touches at the heart of our emotional and instinctive make-up in a way that impedes scientific study and the acceptance of such contributions as social scientists have been able to make. The latter have added to the confusion by their academic departmentalization. Sociologists have tried to account for crime in purely sociological, and psychologists in purely psychological, terms. The biological determinants have been largely ignored. I at least had the advantage of not being committed to a single discipline (having come to psychology via delinquency rather than the other way around). The synthesis I have attempted is outlined in the last chapter, and developed in greater detail as particular issues are discussed and theories of others reviewed. It is based, first, upon my five-year study of the reasons for the delinquent breakdown of 102 youths, the details of their personal histories and social backgrounds being available in my report to the Carnegie United Kingdom Trust.* The recent issue of a second edition of this work has enabled me to save space in the present one by reference to these case histories. Second, the synthesis rested on a series of controlled studies of juvenile delinquents within the community, and the follow-up of some 700 of them for ten years into adulthood. Third, I have profited from the excellent empirical work that has been carried out over the past generation on the study of cultures and the effects of cultural disintegration. Lastly, recent events have afforded us natural experiments in how ordinary humans react to the removal of constraints.

Notwithstanding the need, as I saw it, to put the theoretical picture in proper balance, my chief aim has been to present a working guide to delinquency prevention. The core of this book is therefore the provision of effective casework and community techniques which can render enlightened approaches viable and stem the tide of emotional and ineffective punitiveness.

On the other hand I face the paradox that without effective law enforcement and the punishment of those found guilty, no progressive system of delinquency prevention is possible. Social workers are mainly concerned with those juveniles who flout the deterrents. Make lawbreaking and vandalism no longer punishable offenses and we destroy the touchstone which distinguishes the self-interest of the ordinary citizen from the desperation of the individual who casts his self-interest aside.

For the caseworker investigating the motives for the offense of a particular young person and his family background, I have compiled Diagnostic Worksheets. These systematize available information on the character of the offense, the young person's own justification for it, and his behavior in the home and community. For the

---

Delinquency and Human Nature. Sevenoaks: Hodder and Stoughton (Britain and the Commonwealth, excluding Canada). Baltimore: University Park Press (North American Continent). 2nd edition, 1980.

convenience of the social worker, they are available as a separate instrument.

The measures of prevention and treatment that I propose are based on an integration of community and individual casework approaches. Alongside the counseling of the offender's parents, I see the social worker as influencing the life of the neighborhood in order to make life more bearable for its adult population. In doing so they lessen the risk of emotional breakdown among parents which all too often forces the juvenile members of the family into delinquency. A large part of the book has been taken up with the appraisal of various community approaches that have been tried in the United States and Great Britain.

Since readers will have differing priorities in their reading of the chapters, I have provided summaries of the content and argument of each below.

My use of the first person in this book runs counter to contemporary academic usage. In an earlier version I wrote in the third person, but repeated references to myself as "the present writer" and similar tertiary subterfuges became increasingly tiresome. They could no longer be maintained when I had to draw from my own experiences with delinquent youths. I finally decided to write the book with the unashamed admission that I was myself.

Acknowledgments are due for the help I have received: from my wife, for her perceptive suggestions upon reading the various drafts of this book; from my secretary, Mrs. Audrey Street, for the meticulous care which she devoted to the typing and the organization of the manuscript; from my old friend, Donald Wilson, who found time to contribute a chapter on recent developments in Scotland despite his demanding court duties and being concurrently the victim of two street accidents; and from Fred Edwards, Director of Social Work for the Strathclyde Region of Scotland, for his reading of the manuscript and the encouragement I received from him during its writing. I am indebted to David Worth for editing my account of the Ontario Victim-Offender Reconciliation Project and for making it possible for me to draw freely on the report of the Mennonites' Central Committee on social work.

For information on recent developments in England, I am indebted to Paul Cavadino, of the National Association for the Care and Resettlement of Offenders and to the Center for Information and Advice on Educational Disadvantage; and for information on various U.S. projects, to Odell Nord, of the Neighborhood Alternative Center in Sacramento; to Harvey Treger, of the Jane Adams

College of Social Work in the University of Illinois; to James A. Cousins, of the Police-Socialwork program in Niles; and to Mark W. Breuer, of the Social Services Section of the Wheaton Police Department.

CONTENTS

DELINQUENCY:
The Problem and Its Prevention

PART ONE
The Present State of Knowledge

Chapter One
The Sorts of Knowledge Needed
for Delinquency Prevention

The planning of delinquency prevention measures requires two sorts of knowledge. First, we need enough understanding of the causes to know which are within our power to eliminate and how we should set about doing so. Second, we have to be able to identify our patients—that is to say, those children who are delinquency-prone.

In the older sciences the quest for understanding has taken the form of meticulous observation of the nature of the material world—of how its elements interact with each other, of the structure of matter, and of organisms and of processes of development. As each science progressed, it became possible to say that, given certain conditions, if something happens a particular result will follow. It was the exactness of the understanding gained (embodied in so-called laws of science) that provided the basis for the technologies of the internal combustion engine and space travel, both of which demand a high degree of certainty as regards cause and effect.

Unfortunately, in the mainstream of delinquency research this stage of seeking understanding was skipped in favor of statistically oriented studies. The investigators played safe by taking as their variables those broad social and familial conditions which, from general experience, were known to be associated with delinquency. Thereby they obtained statistically significant results, but without much furthering knowledge. Issues which demanded more intimate study remained unresolved. Notably the statistics could not explain why, even though delinquency is associated with poverty, the majority of young people from impoverished homes do not become delinquent. At the time when my study of how 102 youths had become delinquent was published (Stott, 1950/80), there was so little appreciation of the need for first-hand studies of processes that the work was widely criticized for failing to conform to traditional research design using a control group. Those who insisted on jumping in at the deep end without being able to swim could not understand why anyone should first want to test the depth of the water.

One of the drawbacks to the choice of these broad social and familial variables is that they are difficult to define or to relate to recordable phenomena. Thus we find, in the well-known studies of the Gluecks (1950, 1962, 1968) and of the McCords (1958), the chief variables to be affection of the parents for their children, the type of discipline they exercise, and the cohesiveness of the family. Such general impressions about family relationships will of course have some relation to the chances of a child's becoming delinquent. The difficulty lies in objectifying them.

ASSESSING PARENTAL AFFECTION

There is particular difficulty in defining and rating affection. In popular usage it refers to the quality of feeling that one person has for another, a concern for his welfare, and a wish for a permanent attachment. But how do we score its manifestations? If we judge by the number of gestures and words of endearment, we come up against the difficulty that such are freely used in some cultures and sparingly in others. It was against the tradition in Scottish families with a Puritan background for parents ever to kiss their children, yet delinquency among them was exceedingly low. If we go by the amount of physical care, we find the anomaly of the type of culture in which the family is close-knit, but no effort is made to protect children from common dangers. Wilkinson (1955) noted this anomaly among the Eskimos, but it is also found among certain traditional European cultures. In Glasgow some 30 children—at least until recently—used to be drowned each year in the canals which run through certain working-class neighborhoods of the city, yet the parents took no effective steps to keep their children away from them or to insist that they be fenced off.

One of the case studies in West and Farrington (1973, p. 62) contains an excellent example of the practical difficulty in assessing parental affection. The social worker employed in his project discounts the mother's endearments as "putting on a loving act," and rates her as "A thoroughly unloving violent mother" because she "sloshes" her boy for being disobedient. On the other hand, the probation officer reported that the mother, despite her desertions of the family, "always showed some concern about her children." Even professional social workers cannot agree on how to assess affection.

PARENTAL DISCIPLINE

The assessment of parental discipline is equally problematical, for two reasons. The first is one of cross-cultural misunderstanding. A mother like the one cited above, who, with a work-shy husband, is forced to work long hours to support her family, would not have the time or the resources of patience to practice "effective parenthood" techniques. With no conscious goal of training or schedule of punishment for disobedience, such parents are occasionally induced, for their own protection, to react irritably or angrily against their children. To the middle-class observer who has seen their habitual easygoing manner such outbursts seem out of keeping. To describe such discipline as "erratic," as in the conventional ratings, is to misunderstand this instinctive sort of discipline, which really consists in marking out for the child the limits beyond which he runs into danger. The danger he has to face is a temporary withdrawal of parental love; but it would be a mistake to rate the parent as unaffectionate on the basis of occasional outbursts of anger, even though this may be expressed in verbal rejection or physical assault.

Given its objectives, this form of discipline usually works. In many cultures parents try to be as kind and indulgent as they are able, even to the extent of being reluctant to deny anything or to impose restrictions (deriving from their concern about establishing close intergenerational supportive bonds necessary for the parents' old age). This tradition is still extant in the working-class cultures of Europe and America. To those with middle-class concepts of child rearing it looks like spoiling, and neglect of the child's longer-term interests or even safety.

The second source of our misunderstanding is to give primacy to discipline is a variable without enquiring what may lie behind its occasional lack or excess. First-hand study of family relationships reveals that notable failures of discipline are secondary to more general defects in the affectional bond between parent and child.

I began my studies prepared to find a certain number of youths whose delinquency was due merely to their having been spoiled; that is, they were brought up to believe they could do what they wanted and that everything was theirs for the taking. In the earlier stages of my study I even thought I had identified a number of such youths. But as I got to know their family circumstances better, and learned to appreciate the kinds of affectional breaches that had generated delinquency in other cases, it struck me that the failure of the parents to control their sons was itself the outcome of the estrangements, fears, uncertainties, or hostilities which also impelled them into delinquency. One by one these youths were taken out of the "spoiling" category, until the category itself disappeared.

Yet spoiling there had been, and inability to control was almost the rule. None of the spoiled boys committed delinquent acts so long as the spoiling parent was there to continue to spoil them. They occurred when a parent died or otherwise became unavailable, and the boy was left with the other parent, or with a relative, who had disapproved of the spoiling or had been incapable of giving affection (see Sharp, p. 194; Thorn, p. 190; Ross, p. 263).* Others were thrown back on parents from whom they had become estranged because they had been brought up by indulgent grandparents (Percival, p. 136).

When a child is under a compulsion to seek consciousness-filling excitement in order to defend himself against the reality of his loveless or precarious situation (described in Chapter 7 under the heading of avoidance-excitement as one of the most powerful delinquent motivations), he cannot be deterred even by severe discipline and punishment (Norman, p. 73; Finch, p. 318). Attempts by parents to control such children resulted in their running away or committing obvious offenses in order to get legally removed from home (Whitehead, p. 97; Leggett, p. 291). When the discipline applied was harsh and unfeeling to an extreme degree, the outdoor delinquency was diminished, but at the cost of the development of hysterical incapacities, neuroses, or incipient psychosis (Mackintosh, p. 299; Drew, p. 329; Metcalfe, p. 298). The effectiveness of discipline lies not in physical hurt or restriction, but in the temporary negation of a loving relationship which is symbolizes. If a child has written off any expectation of affection from a parent, that parent is impotent as regards the exercise of control. Discipline without love breaks down just as surely as love without discipline. The parent who has lost a child's love has nothing to appeal to. The child also finds such a state of affairs intolerable, and seeks to break free from it by hostility. The punishments by which the parents try to curb the bad behavior, however harsh, are unavailing and likewise usually result in the child's running away or committing wanton offenses in order to get sent to a correctional school (Faulkner, p. 274).

It is therefore not surprising that the extremes of faulty discipline and lack of control should have shown a high correlation with

*All page references in this chapter are to Stott (1950/80).

delinquency. Cyril Burt (1925) and the Gluecks (1962) found that this this was so, whether it was lax, oversevere, or erratic. The West-Farrington study (1973) related delinquency to harshness but not to laxity; the McCords (1958) inculpated laxity. For an effective prevention program that must discover and treat the basic causes, such findings lay a false scent. We need to be able to diagnose those faults in parent-child relationships which are responsible both for the breakdown of discipline and for the delinquency.

In the final chapter I speculate about some cultural aspects of discipline, suggesting that a child-rearing practice which places little emphasis on training in restraint may render the children less able to face their anxieties and contain their emotions, so that they become more vulnerable to behavioral breakdown. But the indulged child normally has few, one might say, insufficient anxieties about parental loyalty and affection. He has no incentive to jeopardize his position in the family and his job prospects by self-destructive acts, when he can get all he wants by imposing on his parents. As an adult he may be unable to meet the demands of life, but as a child, other circumstances being favorable, he will not become a serious or persistent delinquent.

FAMILY COHESIVENESS

As a concept, family cohesiveness has a sound basis in reality in the same way as have affection and discipline, but it shares the same problem of assessment. The indications thereof proposed by the Gluecks represent very much an outsider's view. As an example of lack of cohesiveness they instance the mother who "spends most of the day away from home, giving little if any thought to the doings of the children." Against this popular notion of the working mother, West and Farrington found that the children of mothers in full-time jobs were actually somewhat less delinquent than those of other mothers, and this is in accordance with studies showing that the children of working mothers do somewhat better in school than those whose mothers do not go out to work (Fraser, 1959; Stott, 1965).

BROAD BACKGROUND FACTORS

The research of West and Farrington was so impeccably designed, and their conclusions were so fairly drawn, that it will no doubt rank as the study to end all studies which relate delinquency to broad background factors. It covered all the boys attending six primary schools in a working-class London borough with a high population density. Their parents were interviewed by social workers when the boys were aged 8–9, and by different social workers when they were 10–11 years old. In addition teachers rated their behavior in school, and the boys made evaluations of one anothers' behavior and popularity. Their contacts with the law were recorded between their tenth and eighteenth birthdays. During this period some 20 percent of them had had convictions for offenses which, among adults, would rank as crimes.

As early background factors hypothesized as conducive to delinquency, West and Farrington found the most significant to be the criminality of the parents, low family income, large family, poor parental behavior, and "low intelligence." The first difficulty encountered in assessing them as causes was that they were all closely interrelated. Whereas each of the factors was present on average in about twice as many of the delinquents as in the non-delinquents, the associations tended to disappear once other factors were taken into account. For example, large family size was associated with delinquency only when the home was overcrowded; and poor parental supervision (as an aspect of poor parental behavior) was of little significance after allowing for low family income and parental criminality.

Because of these large overlaps West and Farrington combined their five early-background factors, and used the presence of any three of them as a criterion of delinquency-proneness. But for the needs of a delinquency-prevention program, this still afforded a very blunt instrument of detection. Whereas 49 percent of those boys meeting the criterion became delinquent, 63 percent of the actual delinquents were missed.

With characteristic honesty West and Farrington faced up to the limitations of the traditional methodology that they followed. Their statistical treatment of the data led them to realize that each of their early background factors stood for a complex situation. Beyond this they were unable to go, because the method contained no logic beyond the statistical associations. They thus made no claim to have identified causes. Whatever background factor or combination of them that they found more prevalent among the delinquents was also found among a significant number of nondelinquents.

The methodology of West and Farrington had at least the merit of laying a number of etiological ghosts. Apart from finding that the children of working mothers are not delinquency-prone, they showed that it was not broken homes as such, but those broken by failure of the marriage, that made delinquency more likely. When the loss of a parent was by death, the amount of delinquency was hardly greater than that in two-parent families. Their conclusion was that "the factor which counts most is not so much the separation (from a parent) itself as the underlying family-problems." This points the direction research should take; namely, the identification of the particular family problems which are responsible for delinquent breakdown.

THE MYTH OF THE WELL-ADJUSTED DELINQUENT

By their investigation of the relative popularity among their peers of delinquents and nondelinquents, West and Farrington lay a favorite academic ghost. It had long been a tenet of sociology both on the American continent and in Britain that the typical delinquent was a normal, well-adjusted boy conforming to the behavior pattern of his subculture. West and Farrington found that only 13.5 percent of the future delinquents were in the most popular quarter of their class, while 24.7 percent of them were in the least popular quarter. As far as the age groups studied are concerned, it does not therefore appear that the delinquents were typical members of their age group, or generally well-adjusted young people who would get on well with their classmates. This is confirmed by the teachers' ratings for troublesomeness referred to below.

Of the West-Farrington findings, those on the personal characteristics of the delinquents are of the greatest interest for prevention programs. They asked teachers to rate the boys who constituted their sample on school behavior, which included work habits, ability to concentrate, relations with other children, cleanliness and tidiness, acceptance of discipline, regularity of attendance, and whether the boy might be considered a credit to his parents. From this questionnaire was derived a general rating for troublesomeness. It proved to be the best single predictor of delinquency. The most troublesome third contained 38.1 percent future delinquents, compared with 11.9 percent in the remaining two-thirds. Only 4.1 percent of the least troublesome third became delinquent. Thirty of the 37 future recidivists were in the most troublesome third, and only one in the least troublesome third. Troublesomeness by itself was a better predictor of delinquency than a combination of the earlier-mentioned five early-background factors, and even among the boys who suffered from three or more of these five delinquency-associated factors, it was the more troublesome who tended to become delinquent. Undesirable school behavior was thus the most important means of identifying the future delinquent. Nevertheless it must be noted that the indications of undesirable behavior used in that study were very broad, and for this reason of very little help in specifying the types of behavior disturbance likely to lead to delinquency.

In their ten-year follow-up study in the New York School Board, Craig and Glick (1968) likewise showed that the Gluecks' Social Prediction Table was inferior to the teachers' reports of behavioral problems as a means of identifying future delinquents. If the record of behavior problems in the first three grades only (ages six to eight) is taken, 80 percent of the future delinquents would have been spotted, which is 16 percent better than the prediction of the Gluecks' scale when calculated correctly as the proportion of the total of delinquents correctly selected. If behavior problems beyond the first three years of school had also been taken into account, all but one of the 44 delinquents (97.7 percent) would have been spotted. In sum, behavior disturbance in school is a far better predictor of delinquency than the broad familial factors used by the Gluecks.

The next question to be asked, therefore, is which specific manifestations of behavior disturbance might help most in identifying the delinquency-prone. Since, in the 1950s, the Bristol Social Adjustment Guide (BSAG) was the only instrument aiming at a comprehensive classification of behavior disturbance, I used its first edition (Stott and Sykes, 1956) for a study of all Glasgow boys on probation for the first time during 1957. They were about one-third of all boys found guilty in Glasgow courts during that year (Stott, 1960). Since, as was subsequently established (Stott, 1963), those put on probation were neither more nor less maladjusted than those fined, admonished, or otherwise dealt with, the probationers were representative of boys between the ages of 8 and 15 who were either casual offenders or at the beginning of a delinquent career. In fact 77 percent of them were first offenders, and the sample contained no serious recidivists. Thus, if there is an association between delinquency and maladjustment, the design of this study understated it.

The edition of the Bristol Guides used contained an array of 210 descriptions of behavior, attitude, or mood such as could be observed by the teacher. An allowance of up to four such indications was made in order to cover misreadings or misinterpretations, so that scores of 0-4 would be those of very stable children. Forty-six percent of the nondelinquent controls but only 10.6 percent of the delinquents met this criterion. When it came to maladjustment, signaled by a score of 20 or over, the proportions were reversed: 45.6 percent of the delinquents but only 7.7 percent of the controls met the criterion.

Various authorities (Shaw and McKay, 1942; Kvaraceus and Miller, 1959) have predicted that those living within neighborhoods where delinquency is part of a way of life would usually be found to be well-adjusted normal young people, while those living in well-to-do, low-delinquency areas would be delinquent by reason of their individual maladjustment. To test this theory, the mean BSAG scores were calculated for the delinquents and controls attending schools in four types of neighborhoods, having low, fairly low, fairly high, and high delinquency rates. No significant differences were found. Contrary to the foregoing prediction, the mean BSAG score for those delinquents living in the "high" areas was fractionally higher than that for those living in the "low" areas. Delinquents from all classes of neighborhoods showed a remarkably similar level of maladjustment. As a rigorous test of this finding, the mean maladjustment score was calculated for those delinquents living in so-called "black spots"; that is, where five or more of the delinquents lived within a quarter of a mile of each other. Once again it was only fractionally different from the mean for the delinquents living in well-to-do neighborhoods (Stott, 1960).

It remained to be asked whether the high maladjustment scores of the delinquents were a cultural artefact reflecting social-class differences in behavioral norms and an inability of the disadvantaged child to conform to the expectations of middle-class teachers. If this explanation of social-class differences in the prevalence of maladjustment is correct, we would expect all or nearly all children living in underprivileged neighborhoods, who presumably experience the same cultural conflicts, to get similarly spurious ratings for maladjustment from their teachers. But in fact the mean score of the nondelinquents living in the high-delinquency neighborhoods was less than half that of their delinquent counterparts, and was much nearer to the mean for the nondelinquents in general.

The extent to which delinquents represent a special minority of disturbed individuals, irrespective of the neighborhood in which they live, is demonstrated by a ten-year follow-up study (Stott and Wilson, 1977). To the previously mentioned sample of Glasgow probationers was added a group of all children convicted in Glasgow courts over a period of five months, giving a study sample of 700 (Stott, 1963). The original controls could not be followed up because their anonymity had been a condition of the project, but new controls were chosen in a way that produced a closer matching for social background. Through the register of births each delinquent was paired, so far as possible, with another child born in the same street or one of similar social status within two weeks of his or her own birth date. When these criteria could not be met the delinquents were left unmatched. The 615 controls thus obtained represented a sample of individuals scattered over the city but predominantly drawn from high-delinquency areas. At the time of their selection from the birth register it was not known which of them had become delinquent. Data as to the convictions of both the former juvenile delinquents and of the controls between the ages of 18 and 24 were obtained from the Central Criminal Records for Scotland.

It has been claimed by Mays (1954) in Britain that delinquency is a normal phase of the growing up of well-adjusted youths in certain inner-city areas, and by Martin (1961) in the United States that "most delinquents, who are generally without emotional disturbance . . . reflect the patterned deviancy so often found in their lower-class neighborhoods." Such a view presupposes that the minority who are caught and convicted are merely the unlucky ones. If this is true, the skimming off from a youth population of a sample of delinquents who had been convicted over a comparatively short period would hardly affect the number among the remainder, who would be caught over the years of their childhood and adolescence. In the Glasgow study only about a third of the delinquents were removed over one year, and the second sample took out those over a mere five months. The controls thus had the equivalent of some six years of being at risk, during which they could have been caught and convicted. It would therefore be expected, on the foregoing assumption that the great majority of delinquents are typical members of their subculture, that a good proportion of the controls would have suffered convictions, and that, among the juvenile delinquents and the controls who grew up with them in the same streets, the proportions of those convicted as adults would have been similar. In fact remarkably few of the controls committed offenses as adults. Between the ages of 18 and 21, only 4.4 percent of them were convicted, compared with 38 percent of the former juvenile delinquents; between the ages of 21 and 24, the proportions were respectively 2 and 15 percent. Thus the removal of juvenile samples had the effect of screening out nearly all the future adult offenders, which suggests that the continuance of their delinquencies was due to something more than bad luck in being caught. Moreover, the pattern of recidivism among such adult offenders as there were among the controls counted against the bad-luck theory. The 27 individuals in question had a total of 48 convictions between the ages of 18 and 21. If their 21 repeated offenses had been spread randomly over the whole of the 615, less than one individual would have received a second conviction; in fact 13 of the 27 did, and of these, two had three and three had four convictions (the random chance of a third being less than 1 in a 1000, and of a fourth, infinitesimal). In short, this group of 13 represented the small number of serious adult criminals missed by the removal of the juvenile samples.

The factor, apart from their offenses, which chiefly distinguished the juvenile delinquents from their age-matched peers who were the original controls was a high level of maladjustment. It is therefore a reasonable inference that the continuance of this personal instability, rather than the bad luck of being apprehended, was responsible for the juvenile delinquents having between seven and eight times more convictions as adults than the controls brought up in the same surroundings.

Moreover, the severity of maladjustment among the sample as juveniles is reflected in the number of their convictions as adults. Those with none had had a mean BSAG score of 16.7, compared with 21.0 for those with one or more convictions, the difference being significant at the .0001 level; and the means rise with a remarkable degree of consistency with each additional adult offense. Considering that there was an interval of up to 12 years between the teachers' ratings for maladjustment and the occurrence of the offenses, it can be surmised that a continuing instability of character originating in childhood is a typical characteristic of the adult criminal. It follows also that, even among those living in disadvantaged surroundings, the truly vulnerable are those who were maladjusted as children.

The findings of the Glasgow follow-up study are paralleled by those of Robins (1966) in the United States. Whereas her study was directed chiefly to the study of the origins of sociopathic (deviant or socially maladjusted) personality, nearly three-quarters of the male juveniles in her child-guidance population referred for antisocial behavior suffered at least one arrest as adults, and 49 percent of them three or more arrests. Her finding thus established a strong presumption that antisocial behavior is the precursor, and the earlier form of adult criminality. Conger and W. C. Miller (1966) likewise found an excess of behavior disturbance among delinquents in Denver, when compared with controls who had grown up in similar neighborhoods and had faced similar socioeconomic problems.

As in West and Farrington's study, Conger and Miller found that their Denver delinquents were less well-liked and accepted by their peers than others their age. If the delinquent within the inner city were the pace-setter among local youth, it would have been expected that he would be popular among them. The fact that he was not popular suggests that the teachers' ratings of delinquents as in great part maladjusted is an accurate assessment and not an epiphenomenon of cultural conflict.

In sum, there is an authoritative body of evidence from two continents—which contrasts with the unsupported assertions to the contrary—that on the whole delinquents mark themselves as children who are maladjusted both in school and in their neighborhood milieu. Moreover this applies irrespective of social class, and tends to persist at least until early adulthood.

THE LINK BETWEEN SOCIAL DISORGANIZATION AND MALADJUSTMENT

The foregoing conclusion, psychologically oriented as it may seem, does not exonerate social disorganization as a root cause of delinquency. The breakdown of the traditional community and family structures entails a lessening of safeguards against stress and a lapse of standards of personal conduct. As Harriett Wilson (1962) put it, extreme culture loss reduces the human being to the hazards of animal existence. The danger points are multiplied even by a degree of cultural disintegration such as often occurs when immigrants from nonindustrial communities are injected into city life. With the increase in the number of stress manifestations among adults—shortness of temper, quarreling, violence and violent words, depression, chronic sickness—it is understandable that the prevalence of maladjustment among children will increase. The reality of this link between social conditions and child maladjustment apart from delinquency was confirmed in the Glasgow study. Although nondelinquents in all quarters of the city were on average much better adjusted than delinquents, those living in the worst delinquency— that is, the disadvantaged areas—had BSAG mean scores over one and a half times as high as the nondelinquents living in the low-delinquency areas. Thus, when we identify behavior disturbance as a characteristic of delinquents, we are not deemphasizing social factors, but uncovering the mode of transmission through which social disorganization tends to produce delinquency. We are focusing attention on the mental and emotional states which are the immediate antecedents of delinquent acts. Which types of adverse social influence in turn produce these delinquency-conducive states of mind are the subject of later discussion. Suffice it to note in this context that irrespective of the neighborhood within which they live, delinquents represent by and large a special group of disturbed individuals.

Chapter Two
The Delinquent and His
Social Environment

THE THEORY OF SOCIAL DISORGANIZATION

Clifford Shaw and Henry McKay (1942) formulated a valuable sociological law when they drew attention to the high rate of delinquency in socially disorganized inner-city areas. Nevertheless, for full understanding of the phenomenon we need to know exactly how social disorganization makes certain young people delinquent. The various attempts to fill this explanatory gap are reviewed in this chapter. It will be seen that each school proffers different explanations. These have, however, one tenet in common which is not fortuitous. In order to be able to account for delinquency by a sociological logic, they have had to emphasize the normality of the delinquent and to deny or ignore the relationship between delinquency and personal maladjustment. Shaw and McKay concluded: "Within the limits of his social world and in terms of its norms and expectations, [the group delinquent] may be a highly organized and well-adjusted person." Mays (1954) maintained that the delinquency of inner-city youth "is not so much a symptom of maladjustment as of adjustment to a subculture in conflict with the culture of the city as a whole." He even claimed, without supporting evidence (1962), that 90 percent of offenses by juveniles are committed by those of stable temperament. Kvaraceus and W. B. Miller (1959) were somewhat more moderate in estimating that "the preponderant portion of our 'delinquent' population consists of essentially 'normal' lower-class youngsters," and that not more than 25 percent of all delinquents suffer from "demonstrable emotional disturbance" (pp. 54-55). They claimed that the percentages they gave were "based on the best estimates from past and current delinquency research projects" but, typically, no sources are given. A feature of these statements claiming the normality of the delinquent is that they are entirely theory-conceived and not the outcome of empirical studies. No attempt was made to ascertain the personal stability of delinquents compared with nondelinquents. The only datum upon which the theories were founded was the greater prevalence of delinquency in certain lower-class areas; but this did not preclude a relationship between delinquency and maladjustment.

THE RATIONALE OF THE CHICAGO AREA PROJECT

The theoretical position taken by Clifford Shaw and Henry McKay as chief figures in the famous Chicago Area Project has been succinctly summarized by Kobrin (1959, p. 21), who was himself the Project's supervising sociologist for the best part of two decades: "Where growing boys are alienated from the institutions of their parents and are confronted with a vital tradition of delinquency among their peers, they engage in delinquent activity as part of their groping for a place in the only social groups available to them." This was seen as a striving in a social rather than an antisocial direction. It was adaptive behavior, and not indicative of pathology or malfunction of personality. Indeed, it was assumed that apart from his delinquent behavior, the youngster would remain unaffected as a normal, well-adjusted individual. The delinquency was a matter of social learning, "a reversible accident of the person's social experience" (p. 22). Kobrin refers to this as a conception of human nature which was optimistic as regards the prevention of delinquency and the rehabilitation of the delinquent. If this optimism had been justified we should not still be confronted with a volume of juvenile delinquency which threatens to get out of hand. And there is now a consensus of findings that whatever influences make a young person delinquent also affect his nondelinquent behavior. Typically he is by no means well adjusted, either to the adults who have dealings with him or to his peers, nor is he able to cope with the economic demands of life in his own best interests.

Despite Kobrin's reference to "the institutions of their parents," (p. 21) the Chicago group attached surprisingly little importance to the family. The word is actually seldom used. The family is indeed seen only as one of the primary social groups which control young people's behavior and enforce the conventional mores—in other words, a vehicle of social discipline. There is no recognition that the family means anything more to the child, that it meets the child's need for permanent and unquestioned attachment to protective parent figures. Hence there is no attention to family problems. If among "the instituions of their parents" is included the family, the Chicago group does not elaborate. It does not explain why so many youths do not fear grieving their parents or making them angry by resorting to delinqency. Clifford Shaw's genius, according to Kobrin, was that he was able to perceive delinquency as the natural or inevitable reaction of the youngster "who, whether singly or in groups, is neglected, despised, or ignored as a person" (p. 28). This has the sound of truth—but who does the neglecting, and so on? If it is the family, why not be more explicit about it, and why not include the improvement of parent-child relationships in a preventive program? If it is someone else, who? We are back again at the hiatus: we need to be clear about the exact nature of the emotional deprivations which drive the youngster of the inner-city area to delinquency.

WHAT BASIC NEED IS THWARTED?

In summarizing the theory of Shaw and McKay, Kobrin does at least hint at one basic need, the deprivation of which leads the youth of a disorganized area into crime. He refers to "the efforts of a person to find and vindicate his status as a human being," (p. 21) and, a few lines later, notes that "man tends always to organize his behavior in the service of his human identity" (p. 22). I suspect that the concept in their minds was similar to the "competence" of White (1959) and mine of effectiveness-motivation (Stott, 1961a; Stott and Albin, 1975)—the notion that human beings derive dignity and self-worth from being able to establish and maintain relationships of competence and effectiveness between themselves and their environment. This need is basic in that its nonfulfillment is associated with feelings characteristic of a deprivation state, and prompts behavior to reestablish effective functioning. If such efforts fail, the individual has a number of alternatives open to him. He may mentally belittle the importance of the unrealized goals as "sour grapes," or reduce the insult to insignificance by placing it against his other sources of self-worth; that is, by exercising a sense of humor or seeing things in proportion. The ability to use such deflecting strategies depends upon the individual's being sufficiently sure of himself not to feel compelled to react against every petty attack on his ego. If he is already on the edge of effectiveness deprivation, he is likely to compensate by bragging and showing off, destroying something, or hurting or humiliating someone else. If he is a low-status individual he may achieve a vicarious effectiveness by identifying himself with a prestigious leader, group, or team. Or he may inhibit his need for effectiveness by lapsing into cynicism, lethargy, or depression. There are, in sum, more ways of coping with a deprivation of effectiveness without undue sacrifice of one's long-term interests than there are of rectifying a state of attachment deprivation.

IS DELINQUENCY THE ONLY CHANNEL OF FULFILLMENT?

In discussing below the nature of social frustration and its possible delinquent outcome in relation to the theories of Cohen and of Cloward and Ohlin, I quote a report of the typical behavior of a street-corner group which illustrates this constant exploitation by low-status individuals of minute-to-minute opportunities for effectiveness. Nevertheless, the striving for identity and status as a human being (to use Kobrin's phraseology) does not inevitably steer the youth of a disorganized area toward delinquency. This is well seen in a report by Kobrin himself (1961). He lists as follows the five principal elements in the behavior of a street gang which are shared by the other adolescent gangs of the neighborhood: (1) flouting of adult authority in general, notably by outbreaks of rowdiness and annoying members of an upper-middle-class neighborhood; (2) readiness for physical combat, with a reckless disregard for pain or punishment; (3) rejection of school discipline and dropping out of school; (4) group sharing of a prostitute; (5) delinquency in the form of shoplifting, larceny, strong-arm robbery of other teenagers, occasional burglary, vandalism directed against schools and the settlement house, and assaults. At the same time the gang took part in competitive sports, and attracted new gang members on this count. It is also significant that, "in the elite group delinquency seemed to have a limited and controlled character. Such relatively serious offenses as burglaries of homes and stores, robbery with gun, strong-arm robbery of adults, auto theft, and rape were diligently and quite consciously avoided. The more extreme forms of delinquency were committed by the marginal members of the dominant groups, usually with one or two companions and occasionally alone, and by groups of lower status" (p. 693).

Kobrin distinguished three factions within the gang: the dominant one, "less active in the moderate forms of delinquency and other acts of aggression making up the conduct pattern of the group"; the intermediate group, "distinctive for its toughness and skill in combat and delinquency"; and the faction of lowest status, which was also the smallest, led by a marginal member, a latecomer "who sought, almost desperately, to establish his position by suggesting and trying to organize support for delinquencies rejected by the other leaders as foolhardy" (p. 700).

This rejection of serious delinquency by the group leaders as a whole supports the view that, even in a disorganized area, those youths who can keep their best interests in mind undergo experiences which lead them in an opposite direction to that postulated by Kobrin in his 1959 assessment of the Chicago Area Project. In this gang it was not delinquency, but the avoidance of delinquency, that was "the product of the simple and direct processes of social learning" (Kobrin, 1959, p. 21). The implication is that those who refuse to learn, and persist in serious delinquency despite its drawbacks, are unable, because of the compulsions which control their behavior and affect their judgment, to heed their own best interests, and are thus by definition maladjusted. In his account of the gang, Kobrin (1961, p. 696) makes a telltale admission. "At the age of 9 and 10, the five boys who came to constitute the core clique out of which the Eagles as a street gang ultimately emerged were known in the neighborhood by residents, agency workers, and teachers as a particularly troublesome and incorrigible lot." Such conduct is difficult to square with the notion of the delinquency of the slum areas as "the strivings of boys in a social rather than an antisocial direction" (Kobrin, 1959, p. 21). Not only the agency workers and teachers disapproved of such behavior, but also the neighborhood residents. It could not therefore be the normal response of these preadolescent boys to what their social world expected of them. Nor did it tally with Clifford Shaw's view, expressed in Kobrin's words, of the "naturalness or inevitability of violative behavior" among underprivileged youth (p. 28). These youngsters stood out from among the other children of the neighborhood as troublesome and incorrigible. They were not representative of their subculture but a special group of behavior-disturbed children. One is led to ask what kind of neglect or deprivation they had suffered. At their young age it must have been within their family lives. But we shall never know, because the Project workers who studied the gang collected no data on that score.

In a second report, the psychiatrist attached to the Project (Baittle, 1961) grouped the 16 gang members by the extent of their delinquent involvement as follows:

None	— two
Transient	— ten
Moderately severe	— four

Neither the above nor Kobrin's account of the rejection of serious delinquency by the leading group suggested that the local youth were "confronted with a vital tradition of delinquency among their peers" (Kobrin, 1959, p. 21), or that they had to "engage in delinquent activity as part of their groping for a place in the only social groups available to them" (p. 21). Indeed, the four gang members in Baittle's "moderately severe" class for delinquency later "broke away from the gang and became 'loners' " (p. 11). Considering that the group who disapproved of delinquency became the dominant faction, there must have been personal reasons for the continued delinquency of these four which were strong enough to induce them to reject the gang as a primary group.

This optional character of delinquency is further seen in a report by Jansyn (c. 1961), an unattached worker in the Chicago Area Project who worked with another street-corner group called the Dons. The latter had two main forms of behavior—the clublike, which consisted mostly of organizing dances; and the ganglike, which meant mostly fighting. Each activity became the dominant one in turn, and for each there was a different leader. In fact neither leader was ever formally chosen, or even called the leader, and he never called himself such. Thus there was no dragooning of members of the street-corner society into delinquent or any other activity. No formal membership of any body was actually recognized—the group consisted of "core" members, named such by Jansyn, owing to the regularity of their presence and the initiatives that came from them, and some scores of "supporters." Consequently membership could not be made to depend on conforming to a deviant norm. Indeed, "the gang leader . . . won loyalties merely by giving encouragement to the members in their aims, rather than organizing them to achieve these" (p. 9). Since their preferred activity was fighting, he attracted a following by his great skill therein. In this case "the leader was not interested in stealing, drinking or in boisterous play" (p. 9). But, Jansyn adds, if the group had wanted these kinds of activities, they could have chosen another core member as leader who was a skillful and habitual thief. In short, it was the street-corner society that chose the nature of its activity, and supported a leader to suit. Once again we see that Kobrin's picture of youths being forced to engage in delinquent activity in order to win a place in the only social group open to them is wide of the mark.

SHAW'S THEORY OF DELINQUENCY

Clifford Shaw himself was responsible for the discrepancy between fact and theory which dogged the Chicago Area Project. In a remarkable piece of documentation he records the careers of five brothers whose life histories and delinquencies are described, largely autobiographically, in illustration of his sociological thesis (Shaw, 1938). So that we can judge the degree to which the latter is actually borne out by the data, I shall extract its chief elements as stated in the book. "Their cases are published," he writes in the introduction, "to suggest the relationship between delinquency and the culture conflicts which often confront the immigrant family in the physically deteriorated and socially disorganized communities in large American cities" (p. x). This general formula is expanded into five propositions. The first emphasizes conflicting codes of conduct. The community situation of the family in question

> comprises a variety of social worlds and diverse codes of conduct; both conventional and delinquent forms of conduct here are fostered and approved. In the second place along with the inconsistencies in the social traditions within the community, many of these traditions are at variance with the culture, practices, and norms of conventional society at large (pp. 107-108).

The second postulate is that of direct infection from the delinquent practices of the locality: "A career in delinquency may emege as a product of the natural processes of learning and habituation under certain group influences, just as attitudes, interests, and habits of a conventional character may be formed in other group situations" (p. 102). The above wording is strangely reminiscent of Cohen's (1956) formulation 18 years later.

The third proposition derives from the different rates at which parents and children become assimilated into the host culture: "Naturally the parental control in this situation is weakened and the family is rendered relatively ineffective in developing the attitudes, habits, and interests in the child which might serve as a safeguard against any demoralizing influences he might encounter in the gangs and play groups outside the home" (p. 103).

The fourth proposition is a direct harbinger of Cohen's (1956) thesis: "To many [of the children of immigrant families] the fact that they cannot possess the things which they see others enjoy does not nullify their eagerness and determination to secure these things— even by illegitimate means when such means have the support and sanction of the groups to which they belong" (p. 100).

The gang, according to Shaw's fifth proposition, may become the overriding influence on the children: "In many instances the children belong to street crowds, play groups, or organized gangs in which the absorbing interest is in varied forms of delinquency" (p. 103).

The Martin Family

The family chosen by Shaw as an illustration of this theory of delinquency emigrated from an agricultural community, presumably in Eastern Europe, and settled in Chicago. They brought with them three children, all of whom died young; the first of the five boys who are the subject of Shaw's report was born shortly after their arrival. They had to settle in a poor part of the city, and the father worked regularly at unskilled jobs until the money he had borrowed from a relative already established in Chicago was paid back.

All five sons proved to be alert, bright boys. In adulthood they wrote autobiographies which, according to Shaw, tallied remarkably closely with the official records. All five spent a large, or the major, part of their lives up to the age of 21 in orphanages or committal institutions. They describe in detail how they got into each delinquent activity, and the conditions of their home life. In the excerpts which follow below, the boy's name as given has no significance except for reference because, broadly, they all tell the same story.

Edward Martin wrote that "Pa had liked his drinks even in the old country, but he had been moderate" (p. 168). During the four years that he was repaying his debts to his relative, he seldom touched liquor. But, "paying his last debt, Pa celebrated the occasion by getting drunk. And from that time on he continued to celebrate" (p. 170). Edward goes on to relate how the responsibility for caring for the family fell on his mother. Owing to his drunkenness the father repeatedly lost his job, but was taken back because he was a good worker. In the end he was fired for good. Not being able to pay the rent, the family had to move, and then a few months later move again, each time to worse accommodations.

Empirical sociologists such as Young and Willmott (1957) and others (see Chapter Fourteen) have stressed the importance of the extended family and permanent friendship networks for the maintenance of standards of conduct. Mr. Martin's ability to keep his drinking within acceptable limits, and his failure to do so when these sanctions were no longer operative, is a good example of this important cultural determinant of behavior. Yet it has no place in Shaw's theory of delinquency causation. He saw loss of social control rather narrowly, in the failure of the parent generation to control its children, owing to their different rates of cultural assimilation.

Meanwhile Mrs. Martin struggled bravely on, working from morning to night, going to church every day, trying to make her boys attend school, going to see the teacher, attempting to keep a tight hand on her sons. She lost control of them only because she had to leave them all day, unsupervised, while she went out to work. And considering that their delinquencies began from around the age of seven years, these could hardly be attributed to cultural conflict arising from the assimilation by the youngsters of the new pattern of life.

Nor was the mother's moral code at variance with that of the conventional society. Indeed, she would have been regarded as the epitome of virtue. But her personal life became one of continuous moral conflict. Edward recalls how, during the winter that his younger brother was born, "the house was cold at least half of the time, for lack of fuel." But when they moved to a basement flat alongside the railroad a solution presented itself. It was here, at age six, that Edward first saw the neighbors steal coal from a railroad car standing near the house. The men and women threw the coal off, then helped one another fill their coal sheds. "A lot of the kids and women living in our block would go over to the railroad tracks for coal. A whole flock would be there, twenty-five to forty." Naturally, Mrs. Martin, just having had another son, could not refuse the stolen coal. We may ask whether the communal coal-stealing was evidence of diverse codes of conduct at variance with the culture, practices, and norms of conventional society—or just sheer, grinding poverty in a neighborhood where there was casual employment but no unemployment insurance or welfare relief.

It becomes abundantly evident that the source of the Martin family's poverty and delinquency was the father's drunkenness, attested to in vivid terms by each of the sons. James pointedly attributes his and his brothers' persistent delinquencies to their father's weakness: "I think it was partly on account of him that all the boys in our family have been in prison and reform schools at times. Instead of being a good provider, he would squander almost all his money in saloons, giving only a small amount to my mother" (Shaw, 1938, pp. 221-222). What importance does Shaw give to this overriding source of hardship and distress? None. In his final chapter, headed "Analysis and Implications of the Study," there is no mention of the father's drunkenness, or of the semistarvation in which it kept the family for many years. Instead, the "specific influences" that Shaw adduces for the delinquencies of this particular family are the junk dealers, professional fences, and neighbors who purchased their stolen goods. From their availability he makes the generalization that "the careers of the brothers developed in a social world in which stealing was an accepted and appropriate form of conduct" (p. 356). He does not mention—as is evident from the boys' own accounts—that the greater part of their thefts went to support their own home. Insofar as such delinquency was accepted and appropriate in their social world, it was because a large part of that world was hungry. Even then, there is no evidence of the emergence of a delinquent subculture which developed a moral code at variance with that of the conventional society. Shaw admits (p. 355) that a very large proportion of the immigrant parents were individually moral and law-abiding. Whereas Mrs. Martin evidently asked few questions about the food, coal, and money her sons brought home to her, when she discovered some stolen jewelry in their possession she sent it anonymously to the police.

The theme of hunger, linked to their father's drunkenness, runs like a refrain through the boys' autobiographies. They would often see their mother cry when he came home drunk, and then they would cry too. The eldest, John, related that when the father was out of work and there was nothing to eat in the house, he took the boys scavenging for discarded food in the market. From that it was a short step to stealing from large food stores. Naturally, as youngsters will, they did so in groups. (Shaw saw these nine-year-olds as gangs exercising a cultural pressure.) The shoplifting was brought temporarily to an end when they were caught and sent to a juvenile detention home. John liked it there: "I always think of this joint with pleasant memories. It was quite a contrast to my home life. At home I didn't eat very often, while here I got plenty to eat" (p. 51). Other means of getting food were, first, to get up very early and steal the bread, cake, and milk left in the doorways of houses. The second was by begging. John would call at well-to-do homes and tell a hard-luck story ("the funny part of it was that, as far as we were concerned, it was a true one"). But cash was also needed to pay the rent, so that begging led to burglary. If no one answered the door, they would kick it in. As Shaw said, they progressed in the techniques of crime. At one time they would concentrate on stealing bicycles; when they grew older it was cars. Crime became a way of living for them—when they were not in some institution. In a sense it was a can't-lose game. Except for isolated experiences of cruelty, they enjoyed the institutional life ("the food was swell"); as soon as they were released, they were into crime again. Their motivation was to get enough to eat, not to win acceptance in a local gang society.

There is certainly no evidence of any gang entity in the joint stealing expeditions. Far from the Martin brothers learning their deviance from the local juvenile society, one gets the impression that

they were the leaders and organizers, and their associates just
hangers-on. On their bicycle stealing expeditions they were accompanied by a boy named Stock, who was their constant companion
during their boyhood. But Stock needed goading. Reported John:
"If he saw a new bicycle anywhere, he'd hesitate in taking it. Then
I'd have to bolster his courage for him and argue with him before
he'd acquiesce" (p. 152). Stock was certainly not a channel through
which the Martin brothers were taught their techniques. The teacher
was privation. It was survival delinquency.

In his concluding chapter Shaw is at pains to show that the
Martin brothers were normal in their mental development and personality, which seemed to be true. He then points out that their
careers in crime showed an increasing sophistication, which must
also have been true. But the third of what, with unconscious irony,
he calls his assumptions was that

> their induction into the practice of stealing, the formation of their
> bad habits of theft, their progressive sophistication in the knowledge
> and utilization of criminal techniques, and their sustained interest
> in stealing during a period of from twelve to twenty years were
> products of the varied influences exerted by the many delinquents,
> groups, and institutions with which the brothers had personal
> contact (p. 350).

Shaw makes no attempt to draw together the evidence for this
assumption. No examples are cited that the Martin brothers learned
anything, or were subjected to any pressure, or were seduced into
criminal ways, by any other delinquent group. The reason he did
not support his thesis by facts is that there were none. On the other
hand, in order to maintain this thesis, he had to ignore a massive
body of facts—the father's drunkenness, the lack of fuel and food,
the constant truancy of the boys whom the pangs of hunger forced
out onto the street. Neither was there any hint of an alternative
ideology at variance with the conventional code. The brothers simply recognized the necessity of an illegal means of livelihood, and
all five gave up their criminality in adulthood. Such loss of parental
control as there was arose from the mother's moral quandary in
being forced by the threat of starvation and eviction to accept the
products of her children's thefts. Apart from this the mother tried
to maintain a tight discipline over the family. Whereas she could
not stop their truancies, she never condoned them. Her inability
to control her sons was due to her having to work long hours on an

outlying farm. Finally, there was no hint of social grievance in the boys. The well-to-do whom they robbed were simply their prey.

A Platonic Contempt for Facts

Shaw's disregard for the facts is a time-honored epistemological practice. He was the first of a school of formula sociologists, just as Plato was a formula philosopher. And he followed the advice which Plato, through his mouthpiece, Socrates, gave to his pupil: "When I was young, Cebes, I was tremendously eager for the kind of wisdom which they call investigation of nature. I thought it was a glorious thing to know the causes of everything, why each thing comes into being and why it perishes and why it exists." But he found that he got nowhere, and, worse, that even the simple notions he had previously held about material causation were undermined. And so he gave up "investigating realities."

> I decided that I must be careful not to suffer the misfortune which happens to people who look at the sun and watch it during an eclipse. For some of them ruin their eyes unless they look at its image in water or something of the sort. I thought of that danger, and I was afraid my soul would be blinded if I looked at things with my eyes and tried to grasp them with any of my senses.

Instead he adopts the method of a priori deduction: "I assume in each case some principle which I consider strongest, and whatever seems to me to agree with this, whether relating to cause or to anything else, I regard as true, and whatever disagrees with as untrue" (Plato, the Phaedo). Likewise Shaw and his followers stuck to their formula with what Plato would have regarded as an admirable contempt for facts. We are confronted with the perplexing phenomenon of researcher workers exploding their own theories by the data they collect, yet continuing to mouth the same theory. The British sociologists of the time, who, like the Chicago school, were carrying out honest and important field work, committed the same scientific sin. Spinley (1953) describes the plight of the youth in a city slum, with his exposure to much conflict in the home and to "so many textbook causes of maldevelopment that the problem is not so much why he displays the signs of disturbance, which he does, but rather how he manages to continue as a functioning personality, as he also does" (p. 79). With all that, she ends by subscribing to the Mertonian thesis that "the slum child may be normal for his group and may be making a good adjustment in that it is the adjustment approved by his group." If she had stopped to think, Spinley would have appreciated the enormous ingenuousness of the idea that a group of maladjusted children could get on well by adopting a code of behavior. Sprott, Jephcott, and Carter (1954), in a brilliant piece of anthropological field work within a mining community, depict their two lowest cultural groups as living for the present and as anything but competitive or aspirational; but instead of relating the high deliqnuency rate within them to the equally high number of matrimonial irregularities and poorly kept homes, they quote Merton (1957) on the pressure which an anomic social order exerts to outdo competitors.

Someone ought to make a study of the compulsions of so many academics to conform to a ruling idea. Even Aristotle—no doubt under heavy political pressures—felt bound to intersperse his empirically based theories with formal obeisances to a very unempirical Soul as the source of all movement. With the sociologists, and the psychologists, of the past generation, it was partly their horror of being branded as loners and mavericks. Their insecurity as a culturally uprooted generation led them to fear cognitive dissonance, and hence to shrink from independent thinking. Partly it was their impatience to become recognized as scientists. H. A. Murray's diagnosis (1954) of contemporary psychology applied to sociology also:

> Since psychology is among the youngest and least sophisticated of the sciences, gnawing feelings of inferiority are almost universal (even normal) in our profession. As a result, many of us are harassed by relentless and importunate cravings for scientific maturity, which incline us to leap over all the tedious stages of observation, description, and classification through which chemistry and all the biological and medical sciences have passed (p. 436).

The theories of Shaw and Merton, cast in an authoritative phraseology, enabled them to offer sweeping explanations of an ever-rising crime rate. How did they get away with it? Why did no one test the formulas? The cynic might suggest that Kohlberg's (1971) finding that a mere 4 percent of people can make independent moral judgments is paralleled by a mere 4 percent even of university graduates and researchers who can think for themselves. Perhaps Shaw, Merton, and Cohen were correct in assuming that the rest just wanted formulas.

For my part I would lay some of the blame on a lack of training in the philosophy of science. Few social scientists have ever been taught to ask what knowledge is or how it is obtained. Members of the unempirical school have not advanced beyond the prescientific era of human development, when knowledge was conceived of as so many precepts. They are latter-day scholasticists. The other part of the blame I would lay on the conformity required in graduate programs on the American continent. The independent thinking 4 percent are apt to be pruned off the tree of knowledge.

EXPLANATIONS OF DELINQUENCY AS DIRECT REACTIONS AGAINST UNDERPRIVILEGE

It has been seen that the main problem of those who saw delinquency as the outcome of cultural conflicts was to show the causative links. Clifford Shaw's attempts to do this, examined earlier, were not integral parts of a theoretical structure, but rather were alternative ways of explaining the high delinquency rate of inner-city areas. Each alternative was picked up and popularized by prominent sociologists of the next generation.

These theorists did not envisage the possibility of indirect mediators between cultural factors and delinquency. The stresses which multiplied the incidence of family breakdown, drove fathers to drink and parents to abuse and reject their children were individual problems, and so outside the purview of sociology. Consequently, they assumed that the observed high delinquency rates in underprivileged areas arose from a direct reaction of the younger generation to its underprivileged position.

Some of these further developments in direct-reaction theory are reviewed in this chapter from three angles: first, their explanatory coverage—that is, the proportion of youths whose delinquency they could feasibly account for; second, the accuracy of the insights they offer into the manner in which certain social environments affect the mentality and hence the behavior of young people; and third, what residual value they may have in planning preventive programs.

DELINQUENCY SEEN AS THE OUTCOME OF CROSS-CULTURAL CONFLICT

The particular direct-reaction theory which has gained most currency in the social-work world is that of Miller (1958), who claimed that in the lower-class subculture there exist a set of moral values in conflict with those of the middle class. What the dominant culture views as reprehensible and delinquent, so the theory runs, is normal and accepted behavior in the high-delinquency area. Miller identified a number of "focal concerns" of lower-class youth which put them at odds with conventional society. Chief among these were ideals of toughness, smartness in duping others, seeking excitement by risktaking, and courting trouble.

In a social group that has been denied the education which opens up avenues of longer-term fulfillment and has not the financial resources to buy expensive and socially approved forms of toughness and excitement, it is natural that the more assertive and ambitious youths will seize upon hedonistic sources of gratification, including deviant gang behavior, which breaches law and order. Typical examples of such assertiveness are gang warfare, the obstrepterous behavior of motorcycle clubs, misbehavior at football games, and occasional semi-spontaneous youth rioting.

Formally deviant though they be, such outbreaks are comparatively safe. Either the safety comes from numbers, or the aggression is directed against rival groups rather than against outsiders. To the youth who indulges in them, there is little risk of becoming officially labeled as a delinquent, being ostracized in his neighborhood as such, or losing his employment. He can still obey what is described below as the law of least cost.

Insofar as there is any reality behind these theories of conflicting cultural norms, they represent minor divergences from a generally accepted code rather than diametrically opposed views of morality. This has been well demonstrated by Maccoby, Johnson, and Church (1958). These researchers actually started out with the hypothesis that attitudes to juvenile misbehavior would be lax in the high-delinquency, and severe in the low-delinquency area. They interviewed adults in two areas which were similar in socioeconomic status but highly contrasting as regards level of delinquency, the average annual rate per 1000 cases brought before the juvenile court in one area being 15.2; in the other 4.9. The adults were asked how serious in their opinion were various sorts of juvenile deviance, such as minor thefts from stores, damage to public property, abusive remarks, fighting, and drinking. The findings of Maccoby and her co-workers (1958, p. 44) are best quoted verbatim:

> The striking thing ... is the similarity of the attitudes in the two areas. In both areas, drinking is considered the most serious juvenile offense, fighting the least. People in the low delinquency area took a slightly more serious view of minor thefts from stores, damage to public property, and drinking than did their high-

delinquency-area counterparts; but this trend was counter-balanced by a tendency for the high-delinquency-area respondents to take a more serious view of abusive remarks and fighting.

Our findings, then, are not consistent with the point of view that the adults in a high delinquency area take a tolerant or indifferent attitude toward delinquent and pre-delinquent activities on the part of children. We see no evidence that "delinquent values" about the "wrongness" or "seriousness" of these actions prevail in the high delinquency area (p. 48).

Far from there being a general tolerance of, or indifference to, delinquent acts in the high-delinquency area, the authors observe that in such areas, "We encountered some evidence that when a family of children got a reputation of being 'bad,' the neighborhood would withdraw from the family and isolate them. Other children would be forbidden to play with the deviant children . . ." (p. 48). Maccoby and her co-workers go on to query whether even in the delinquent families "delinquent values" prevailed. They suspected that more commonly parents in delinquent families do not want to see their children become criminals. This accords with my own experience of such families. In sum, empirical evidence in the form both of systematic survey and of casework experience disposes of the "conflict of values" theory as an outsider's view generated post hoc to explain social-class differences in the prevalence of delinquency. Its authors and adherents simply had not studied lower-class moral attitudes sufficiently to appreciate how wide of the mark it was.

DELINQUENCY SEEN AS THE OUTCOME OF SOCIAL FRUSTRATIONS

The second group of direct-reaction theories to be considered are those which hinge on the concept of social frustration developed by Merton (1957). He explained aberrant behavior in sociological terms as the outcome of the plight of lower-class youth, who have neither the education nor the openings by which they can attain the success goals of an aspirational society, and are thus forced into illegitimate means of reaching them. As a follower of Merton, Cohen (1956) argued that lower-class youths, in order to deal with the "shame" which they feel from not being able to achieve high social status and the material goods that go with it, develop a hostility towards the larger society which enables them to reject its values without ambivalence. Thus becomes established a lower-class cultural pattern which virtually prescribes delinquency. "Children *learn* to

become delinquents by becoming members of groups in which delinquent conduct is already established and 'the thing to do' " (p. 12).
And "the process of becoming a delinquent is the same as the process
of becoming a Boy Scout. The difference lies only in the cultural
pattern with which the child associates" (p. 14). Cohen explicitly
denies that the child need be "different" from other children or have
"any twists or defects of personality" (p. 12). But, once again, he
does not investigate this possibility; nor does he adduce any evidence
for the psychological processes of shame, antagonism and deviance
on which his theory rests.

Cohen relies on a vivid description by Shaw and McKay (1942)
of the mischievous pranks of a delinquent gang—stealing milk bottles
from a grocery store and breaking them in somebody's hallway,
tipping garbage cans down front stairs, breaking windows, and so on.
Delinquents of a similar type whom he himself interviewed
accounted for their behavior as "just ornery" (pp. 29-30). He fell
into the trap of accepting those statements at their face value. Not
even Cohen suggests that such mischief and vandalism was the typical
behavior of the neighborhood youth. If it had been, the area would
soon have become uninhabitable. It was in effect typical of the
avoidance-excitement which is described in Chapter Seven. The
perpetrators were in no sense ordinary, normal boys, but—as I show
by abundant evidence in *Delinquency and Human Nature*—were
using an endless round of attention-dominating excitement as a
means of escape from their family worries. But to Cohen family
problems were taboo.

Cohen's explanation of delinquency as a reaction against low
status is similarly characterized at every critical stage by assumptions
unsupported by facts. He imagines a separate "delinquent subculture" (p. 28), which is even distinct from the corner-boy society. Its
youthful adherent "breaks clean with the middle-class morality,"
feels "public humiliation" at his low status, and reverts to delinquency, not as an end in itself, but as a symbolic attack on the middle-
class way of life. "The stolen dollar has an odor of sanctity that does
not attach to the dollar saved or the dollar earned" (p. 134). Such a
reaction against lower-class status demands a capacity for generalized
thinking on social issues which might be found in an intellectual
terrorist organization but is unthinkable among underprivileged
delinquent children. He sees such juvenile nihilists reinforcing one
anothers' hostility to middle-class values within a delinquent gang
whose members offer one another status "by a kind of sectarian soli-
darity." Such delinquent cults are Cohen's own creation, rendered

necessary in order to bridge the gap between his social-frustration theory and the facts of juvenile deviance. It is doubtful if a stable delinquent gang society exists among youth anywhere. Short, Tennyson, and Howard (1963) were able to locate several fighting gangs in Chicago, but not a single gang oriented to criminal activities. The typical two or three youths who consort together in a phase of delinquency because of their common motivation of excitement-seeking form only temporary associations rather than gangs with their own value system; and by no stretch of imagination can these be conceived of as closed cultist groups reinforcing one anothers' delinquent philosophy. Any such grouping would in any case be periodically broken up by arrest and committal.

Cohen's theory is at its weakest, and least supported by any kind of empirical evidence, when he tries to explain why the great majority of working-class children do not choose the "delinquent subculture"as their form of adjustment to status deprivation. He admits the plausibility of the argument that the working-class boy does not care what middle-class people think of him, but is concerned only with the opinions of his family, his friends, and his working-class neighbors. On this critical issue for his theory he can only say, "A definitive answer to this argument can come only from research designed to get at the facts. This research, in our opinion, is yet to be done" (p. 123). Cohen never did that research, but decided to make the assumption that working-class boys do care about their low status. Having thus jumped the gun of knowledge, it behooves him to explain why they choose different forms of response, including that of delinquency. He can only conclude: "The circumstances which tip the balance in favor of the one or the other are obscure" (p. 128). In contrast to this toss-of-a-penny theory I shall advance the thesis in this book that since there are powerful restraints upon the working-class youth, in the form of his standing with his family and his job prospects, against engaging in serious delinquency, so there must be powerful compulsions driving a small minority to ignore these sanctions.

It is questionable whether there is such a person as a subcultural delinquent. Cohen refers to "numberless case histories" (p. 27) but gives none and does not tell us where we can find them. For a child to qualify it would be necessary to show that he (1) had a clear perception of being trapped in an underprivileged social position, (2) decided to break free from the humiliation thereof by rejecting conventional ideas of right and wrong and attach himself to a group which saw delinquency as an alternative means of attaining status,

(3) had no family problem or personality weakness that could have been responsible for the delinquent behavior.

It may even be asked whether there is such a thing as a criminal subculture. A culture is a system of thought, skills, and precepts which has enabled a section of the human species to be successful in the struggle for survival. A subculture is a variant of the main culture which shares its major characteristics. To dignify the misbehavior of scattered groups of youths in our inner cities with the name of subculture is epistemological romanticism. If it is anything, in cultural terms, it is a by-product of culture loss.

Although also adherents of Merton's social-frustration theory, Cloward and Ohlin (1960) limit its application to those youths who, debarred from legitimate avenues of advancement, turn to highly organized illegal opportunity structures. But, as they themselves point out, these exist only when there are stable links between the criminal underworld and the "respectable" world of business and politics. Such illegal opportunity channels would be open only within certain ethnic minority groups, and therefore hardly explain the great mass of juvenile delinquency. As if to disguise the limited explanatory value of their thesis, Cloward and Ohlin divide delinquents into two main classes: those supported by delinquent subcultures, and "loners" (whose delinquencies they characterize as accidental or occasional and in any case less serious than the first type). In support of this dichotomy they quote the undisputed fact that the great majority of delinquent youths commit their offenses in groups. But because two or three excitement-seeking or unsettled youths meet in a billiard hall or amusement arcade and plan a break-in together, this does not make them members of a delinquent subculture, let alone of an organized illegal opportunity structure with links to corrupt officials and businessmen. The great majority of juvenile delinquents are thus outside the explanatory purview of Cloward and Ohlin. They likewise have little interest in the delinquency of the disorganized slum. They admit that such an environment can neither offer its youth legitimate outlets nor provide them with access to stable criminal careers; but they dismiss its crime as "individualistic, unorganized, petty, poorly paid, and unprotected," almost as if it were beneath their notice.

It remains to estimate what proportion of juvenile delinquency can be explained by the frustration lower-class youths feel in not being able to achieve the success goals of an aspirational society. Part of the answer is contained in the evidence Cloward and Ohlin themselves cite regarding dissatisfaction about promotion in the U.S.

Army during World War II (Stouffer et al., 1949). Such dissatisfaction as there was did not in the main lead to disciplinary breaches, but took the form of grumbling and cynicism. The ordinary man does not "jump out of the frying pan into the fire." Even though feeling frustrated, he does not gratuitously make his situation worse, but hangs on to what he has. In the language of social psychology, he obeys the law of least cost. The same applies to the lower-class youth. Of material goods he probably has very little, but he is normally a member of a family, with a house to live in and one or two parents upon whom he counts for emotional support. He knows, from repeated warnings, that involvement in delinquent acts will grieve and anger his parents and risk his being banished from the home. He also knows that it will be more difficult to get a job if he gets a criminal record. And he can probably tell of some uncle or aunt who has a very good job in some factory or shop and will find a job for him, provided he stays out of trouble. Thus, like the member of the armed forces who is dissatisfied with his rate of promotion, he contains whatever frustration he may feel.

How much frustration he does feel is a moot question. As a single person living at home and contributing little or perhaps nothing to his maintenance, he has more money to spend on his pleasures than most middle-class youths who are following courses of higher education. In talking with such youths the impression is not one of frustration; it is rather a fantasy picture of well-paid jobs, preferably with nothing to do all day but to press a button now and then. Their goal is not so much advancement as comfort and easy money. Not being members of an aspirational middle-class subculture, phases of unemployment have no shame for them and they are free of the anxiety of not making good. When Merton, Cohen, and Cloward and Ohlin invest them with the frustrations of unfulfilled aspirations and blocked opportunity, they are projecting their own subcultural values onto a group that does not think in such terms.

During four years spent as leader of a club in a training school for delinquent boys aged 15–18 I had the opportunity to get to know intimately over 100 of these youths. Part of my work was to counsel them regarding their future and to encourage them to read technical books. I found, to my astonishment, that few of them had ever given any thought to the future or had any vision of themselves as adults. Their concerns did not extend beyond the next few weeks and were with their personal affairs, such as going on leave or getting letters from home. Never did I hear any expression of frustration at denial of economic opportunities. Indeed, I often reflected that if only I could arouse some frustration in them, they might develop a plan to their lives. This inhibition of normal foresight is not fortuitous. During their delinquent careers, as I demonstrated in their life histories (Stott, 1950/80), these boys were under compulsions to escape from what to them had proved intolerable family situations. In order to take advantage of delinquent avenues of escape, they had to dismiss from their minds the consequences of their delinquent acts insofar as these affected their standing with their parents and their future careers. Blotting out any vision of themselves as adults was not merely a mark of their immaturity, it was a necessary part of the inhibition of consequences which gave them release for utilizing the delinquent outlet. In sum, frustration at denial of social opportunities, as hypothesized by Cohen, and by Cloward and Ohlin, definitely cannot account for the delinquencies of recidivist youths in Britain; and since human nature is everywhere the same, and recourse to delinquency is so damaging economically except for the insignificant few who can enter a criminal-opportunity structure, it is unlikely to be an important cause of delinquency among youths anywhere. After all, to a youth with normal foresight and capacity for self-control, the sensible outlet for social frustration would be participation in a political movement whose aims are to change the social order. Such a youth would obey the law of least cost in not destroying whatever of value he possesses already.

The typical form of accommodation to lack of opportunity among lower-class youths is that of lapsing into the inactivity of "street-corner society." It represents an inhibition of aspiration which is more comfortable and easier to achieve that "fighting the system." The studies of typical activities of urban Negro teen-agers reported by Himes (1961, p. 480) reveal that a variety of relatively harmless, hedonistic sources of fulfillment are open to them. Their regular way of occupying leisure time—which is by no means confined to black lower-class youths—was just hanging around in large groups. One observer made a detailed record of their leisure-time activities which affords us several instructive examples of day-to-day —one might say minute-to-minute—fulfillment, or of compensations for deprivation, as the case may be. Sometimes the bands—they are not gangs, because their membership is fluid—when they are not just hanging around,

> just wander about aimlessly, looking for something to do. Idle,
> bored, and unsupervised, they are inclined to be touchy and resent-
> ful of such authorities as parents, teachers, ministers, recreation

leaders, and policemen [i.e., of face-to-face superiors]. At night, they crowd the dance floors of recreation centers, and, by day, they listen to records in the hangouts, play their transistors, and ride about in jalopies. But mostly they just "yackity-yack." The talk, too, is aimless, full of slang, profanity, and obscenity, and about their own doings, song hits, television shows, clothes styles, Negro athletes, and so on [psychologically not aimless, but seeking self-enhancement by behaving like big guys, posing as being bad, associating themselves with prestigious fashions and personalities]. The talk, as well as the gregariousness, reveals their intense need to be accepted by peers. Almost always, also, a current of aggression runs just below the surface of this stream of talk—teasing, bantering, boasting, disparaging, blustering, threatening, cursing, playing the dozens. Occasionally, the aggression breaks through the veneer of talk into quick savage fights or delinquent acts.

The observer does not say what the latter are, but presumably they include street vandalism, molesting of passers-by, and other unruliness. The petty one-upmanship of these youths is reminiscent of the aggressive play of dog or wolf cubs, and their resentment against their status superiors, of the incipient challenge of the young adult male against the dominant old male. But just as the young nondominant animal does not go berserk or risk his skin in premature challenge, so the young human male is forced to satisfy himself with whatever crumbs of petty effectiveness fall his way. The young of both the human and of the higher infra-human species have instinctive means of accommodating themselves to their opportunities, without jeopardizing what status they have.

RELATIONSHIP OF PERSONAL TO SOCIAL CAUSES OF DELINQUENCY

It has been a pity that those who saw delinquency as a reaction against certain social conditions should have been so exercised to deny the individual variable. As if compelled to defend their territory against all rivals, these social theorists have found it necessary to fly in the face of facts about the greater prevalence of maladjustment among delinquents. The result has been an interdisciplinary warfare over the bodies of our juvenile delinquents which has led to a confusion of thought among workers in the field. This is apparent in the statement contained in the National Association for the Care and Rehabilitation of Offenders (NACRO) working party report (NACRO, 1977, p. 13), that "contemporary research seems to be

pointing to a social rather than a psychological diagnosis of delinquency." I would take exception not to the falsity of the statement
but rather to the falsity of the antithesis between social and psychological causes which makes the statement meaningless. There are no
separate social and psychological causes. Any feature of a culture
which affects the behavior of individuals can do so only by first
affecting their minds and emotions. Even those, like Cohen, who
espoused extreme sociological explanations were at pains to show
how certain social conditions could produce states of mind that
result in delinquency. The sociologist makes a study of the kinds of
social environment which are related to delinquency; the psychologist studies the mediating mental and emotional processes. They are
not bringing to light different causes but merely different stages in
a continuous causative process. It is quite logical to recognize that
most delinquents are socially maladjusted, while agreeing that, to
quote the NACRO Working Party again (p. 15), "the main reasons
for the general fact of juvenile crime and for its increase are rooted
in social conditions and in our culture." It is a question of finding
the psychological link between the culture and the individual act.

A simple answer to the apparent antithesis is that social conditions can produce the maladjustment which is the forerunner of
delinquency. Maladjustment is in the main a response to social stress.
There are indeed congenital, including genetic, factors involved, but
these usually take the form of making the individual more stress-
vulnerable. Human cultures have evolved means of protection against
potentially damaging stresses. They prescribe forms of social organization and personal conduct which regulate human relationships,
reduce health hazards, ensure adequate food and shelter, and so on.
It has become a commonplace of research that social disorganization
—the lapsing of these cultural safeguards—is associated with multiple
problems, including a high delinquency rate. The previously quoted
"Radby" study by Sprott, Jephcott, and Carter (1954) gives an
instructive picture of the relationship between freedom from "problems" and cultural intactness in an English mining community. The
authors divided its 225 families into five cultural groups, in the
lowest of which the family had succumbed under adverse circumstances to a state of disorganization, demoralization, and helplessness. Of these 25 families, 40 percent had a member of the household who was regularly in bad health or had a serious mental defect,
compared with 7 percent of the miners' families who were conscious
of and aspiring to middle-class standards. In the disorganized families
marital relationships tended to be irregular: "Husbands don't live at

home, wives go off, another man is brought in" (p. 202) and so on. The incidence of such irregularity was 51 percent, compared with only 2 percent in the high-standard families. It was indeed 9 percent among the low-standard families who were "getting along," and 4 percent among those with "respectable" working-class standards. Chapter Nine shows how the types of instability quoted result in a number of classifiable maladjustment- and delinquency-conducive family situations. In short, we can trace in detail the stages by which social disorganization generates the sorts of behavior disturbance which include delinquency. In the above 25 culturally disintegrated families, nine children (36 percent) had been before the juvenile court during the 10 years prior to the study; in the "getting along" families there has been six (13 percent); in the "respectable working class" group, five (5 percent); and in the two high-standard, aspiring groups, none.

POTENT SANCTIONS AGAINST LAWBREAKING

The social theorists who have espoused these direct-reaction explanations have noted the proliferation of delinquency in inner-city lower-class areas. They have pictured the youths who live in them as being ill-equipped to compete for the goals of an aspirational dominant culture and assume that their delinquency is the outcome of their frustration; or they observe a certain lack of respect for the property of the more fortunate, and assume a type of morality which condones delinquency. The flaw in these explanations is that any lower-class youth who gives a moment's thought to his own interests must realize that delinquency is not a solution to the frustrations he may feel (if indeed he feels any of an aspirational character); or, even if he suffers no twinges of conscience about stealing, he is made aware by his parents of the enormous social and personal penalties that are incurred by lawbreaking.

In the British working-class family, as in the American one quoted by Maccoby and her coworkers (1958), parental guidance takes the form of warnings against mixing with known delinquent age-peers, or even with members of families whose standards are lax. Certain forms of petty crime, such as shoplifting and stealing from merchandise in transit, may be "the done thing" among wide sections of certain social groups. Where such laxity obtains, deterrence is effective in the long run: the bolder or more reckless youths will need to experience punishment before they desist (Mays, 1954). Indeed, it is a characteristic of traditional cultures that in order to avoid the onus of disciplining their children, with the temporary bad feeling that it involves, parents tend to rely upon authority figures outside the family. Among the Melanesians the maternal uncle fulfilled this role, while the father remained a companion to his children. A probation officer once related to me that when he urged a mother to exercise some control over her son, she replied, "Good Lor', mister, what do you think I pay my taxes for?"

Nevertheless, in a typical working-class pattern of life the most potent sanction against deviance is the young person's need for secure membership in a family group, and hence for continued acceptance by his parents or by another adult who is filling a parental or quasi-parental role. A boy or girl only disregards the pain that lawbreaking causes his parents if he is pathologically defective in his needs for affection, or is under the influence of some powerful compulsion which overrides this need. Whereas some one-time petty delinquency is due to a lack of social learning experiences in more or less stable young people (but to a much lesser extent than sometimes supposed), persistent deviance is never merely a matter of social infection. For its understanding and treatment we have to study the nature of the abnormal stresses which induce the persistent offender to react in an abnormal manner; that is to say, to jeopardize his position in his family and his economic self-interest.

From the foregoing it becomes apparent that, once we become aware of the realities of the traditional popular culture and of the safeguards which it has developed against juvenile misconduct, we learn to see persistent lawbreaking as the outcome of influences which combine to nullify these safeguards. The typical youth or girl, even within an inner-city environment, is sufficiently buttressed against invitations from the peer society to partake in deviant activities.

RELATIONSHIP BETWEEN SOCIAL DISINTEGRATION AND DELINQUENCY

That there is an intimate relationship between the breakdown of these cultural safeguards and delinquency in the children was seen in the Radby study. It was further demonstrated by Wilson (1962) in her study of 52 families characterized as "performance-inadequate" on account of insolvency, poor hygiene, and poor school attendance of the children, which she compared with a control group of children from other families living in the same neighborhood. She found that, although the delinquency rate for the area was much higher than for the city as a whole, for the children of the performance-inadequate families it was twice that of their neighbors' children (58 as against 26 percent). This affords us a measure of the effects of extreme cultural disintegration within particular familes of a disorganized area.

One of the themes of this book is that the high-delinquency rates of inner-city areas arise from the stresses produced by a combination of poverty and cultural disintegration, and not from the direct influence of a lower-class subculture on the behavior of the local youth. The link between the helpless poverty of the disorganized area and juvenile delinquency is the breakdown of the mental health of members of the adult generation. This is demonstrated in Treger's (1976) comparison of the operation of police social-work projects in socioeconomically and ethnically contrasting communities referred to in Chapter Fifteen. The program was first developed in two white middle-class suburban communities in Illinois as a means of offering crisis intervention and intensive family therapy to the families of offenders. When it was extended to the poor mixed-race community of Maywood, half of which was black, members of the project team found themselves called upon to intervene at an earlier stage than that of the offense in order to reduce the pressures which threatened even worse calamities. A black mother attempts to set fire to her home, with herself and her three youngest children in it. Neighbors quarrel about parking a car outside; one of them physically assaults the other in the police station. In the white community for which the data are comparable, some 41 percent of the referrals to the project are on account of criminal offenses; in Maywood, only 9 percent. But in Maywood 47 percent are for family and marital problems, compared with the white community's 27 percent; and 23 percent are for mental health problems, compared with the white community's 7 percent. The disadvantaged area with a predominance of ethnic-minority families would be more accurately characterized as a higher personal-breakdown area than as a high-delinquency area (which it incidentally also was).

It is nevertheless easy to oversimplify the issue of social disorganization by seeing delinquency as arising entirely therefrom. With major uprooting of populations only one or two generations back, even the respectable urban community in the twentieth century is still a comparatively immature culture which lacks the double bracing of safeguards found in centuries-old communities. Consequently, delinquency is distributed throughout these populations. Its prevalence through the whole range of subcultures within a large city was revealed by information furnished by Glasgow probation officers in respect of my original sample of 414 boys, consisting of all those placed on probation for the first time in a single year (Stott, 1962c). The probation officers completed a schedule of cultural indications based on the categories of the previously quoted Radby study, except that the highest two of their five categories were amalgamated. Only 22 percent of the delinquents came from families in the two lowest; that is to say, who could broadly be described as having inadequate standards of management and hygiene. No less than 47 percent belong to families maintaining "respectable" working-class standards; 12 percent came from "superior" families who had or aspired to middle-class standards (the remaining 19 percent having been put on probation too recently for their probation officer to assess their families). It was thus seen that at least 59 percent of this unselected sample of delinquent boys came from homes which met the accepted standards of their culture. Their delinquency was a matter of the insufficiency of our urban culture as a whole, which offers no fender against particular shortcomings in the lives of families. That is to say, it stemmed not so much from the cultural disorganizatin of a neighborhood or of a group as from imperfections in the safeguards afforded by the Euro-American culture, especially with regard to the organization of the family.

Although juvenile delinquency is not confined to particular social or cultural groups, it is nevertheless more prevalent among those which have suffered disintegration. The reason is that stresses which tend to destroy the cohesiveness of families are more severe among them. An important part of a preventive program will certainly have to be directed towards these sources of social stress, but it cannot confine itself solely to broad community measures. A poor view would be taken of a health service that refused to care for victims of tuberculosis because it was unable to change the social conditions that made it endemic.

From the above analysis we can draw guidelines for a comprehensive approach to delinquency prevention. These consist in attacking the weak points of our culture, both as regards the defective organization of communities and as regards those parent-child relationships which are conducive to behavior disturbance. It follows also that—until such time as we can develop healthy community structures and reliable patterns of family life—we shall have to devote resources to the more immediate problems of identifying and treating the maladjusted, delinquency-prone individuals. This second aspect of prevention—that dealing with the danger spots at the family and personal level—has suffered neglect owing to the dominance of exclusively community-centered thinking.

Chapter Three
Testing the Theory of
the Subcultural Delinquent

What Shaw, Kvaraceus, Miller, Cohen, Mays, and all those who roundly declared for the emotional stability of the inner-city delinquent should have done was to take a representative sample and discover how many among them were in fact well adjusted, without constitutional vulnerability to behavior disturbance, and free of family problems. This was the methodology of two studies reported below, carried out by my former research assistant, Kara Wilson (1966). The location of the first was a housing project in an industrial region of Scotland, notorious for its high crime rate. Although containing only 10 percent of the population of the municipality, it had 37.5 percent of the criminals. The project had been formed 25 years back by the rehousing of families from the worst areas of the town. The standards of a number of the tenants remained very low and the general attitude was one of apathy and disrespect for property. Because of its bad reputation, one of the streets had had to be renamed. The gardens and open areas were in a very poor condition owing to juvenile vandalism. In short, if any urban area qualified as a disorganized area and "delinquent subculture," this project did so. If stable delinquents following the accepted pattern of their neighborhood were to be found anywhere, they would be in an area of this type.

The findings quoted earlier to the effect that "troublesomeness" in school is the best single predictor of delinquency can possibly be discounted, on Millerian lines, as mere manifestations of cross-cultural conflict; but this explanation is weakened by the findings of more than one study, that delinquents tended to be unpopular among their classmates and hence were not adjusting well even to their local "subculture." Consequently, there is reason to believe that reports by teachers of "troublesomeness" do represent genuinely disturbed behavior.

The first step was therefore to eliminate all those delinquents who showed a significant amount of behavior disturbance in school.

With the confidence that their reports are on the whole reliable, teachers were invited to answer six Yes/No questions with regard to the 42 students resident on the project who had appeared in court during the previous eleven months and were still in school. The six questions dealt with delinquency-related maladjustment. None of the students was rated favorably on all of them, so that—in order to isolate those who might conceivably be rated as having a stable personality—the students with not more than two unfavorable answers were selected for further study. In fact this criterion proved to be overgenerous: of the 13 children who thus qualified and were assessed on the full Bristol Social Adjustment Guide, 5 had scores between 10 and 19, which put them in the "Unsettled" category, and 3 had scores of over 20, which classified them as "Maladjusted." The scores of the remaining 5 children were 9, 7, 6, 3, 2—only the two last fell within the "Well-adjusted" class.

The next stage was to visit the homes of these five presumed well-adjusted delinquents. However, the probation officers in charge of two of them advised against visits as likely to exacerbate already difficult family situations. One of these was that of a girl whose mother was morally loose and cohabiting with the man by whom she had had her last few children. Both adults drank and quarreled. The girl was very neglected and, although well adjusted in school, aped her mother's sexual behavior and indulged in petty stealing. It was a typical slum-breakdown family, exemplifying culture loss rather than any sort of subculture. The other case was that of a boy whose father had just been released from a mental hospital. In addition, another member of the family had attempted suicide, so that the probation officer did not want the delicate personal relations within this family to be disturbed by the intrusion of a research worker. Because of their adverse family situations both these children were disqualified: the delinquency of neither of them could be reasonably regarded as a mere matter of conformity to the way of life of the youth of the locality.

That left three runners in the normal-delinquent stakes. It will be recalled that they had to clear two hurdles, that of an emotionally satisfactory and reliable family situation, and that of a constitutional robustness. Criteria for the latter—and also for its opposite, a constitutional vulnerability—call for some clarification. Among both the delinquents and controls of my Glasgow study of probationers a strong and consistent association was observed between behavior disturbance and a number of physical and health impairments (Stott, 1962a, 1966). The delinquents specifically were much more prone to ill health and growth abnormality than the nondelinquent controls; and in both groups those who had two or more distinct diseases were significantly more maladjusted than those with only one disease. This tendency to multiple impairment held good even in families of adequate social standard, so that its origin was held to be congenital. It served in the individual case as a measure of constitutional vulnerability to environmental stresses. (The finding that delinquents as a class are less healthy than nondelinquents conflicts with that of the Gluecks (1950), but they took their sample of delinquents from correctional schools, who would not only have been certified as medically fit but, by their robustness, would have seemed to their judges as suitable for such treatment. An interesting confirmation of the tendency of delinquents to be constitutionally at risk was the finding—among the younger members of the Glasgow sample for whom Health Cards were available— that over three times as many of the delinquents as of the controls had been in hospital during their first year of life.)

Of these three remaining delinquents, one cleared neither hurdle. His family situation fell clearly into the pattern in which the husband is throwing more burdens on his wife than she can cope with (Situation 3A, as described in Chapter Nine). In this case the boy's father was a poor provider, so that the mother had to work long hours, and the father left the discipline of their five children to her. On this subject they had had many quarrels, and the mother had deserted the home several times, only coming back for the sake of the children. The eldest son had already become delinquent and had been committed to a correctional school, on the initiative of the mother. It is unlikely that she, as the disciplinarian of the family, would have failed to make a similar threat to her other sons. The boy who was the subject of study suffered from respiratory trouble, had bad psoriasis all over his body, and was highly strung and easily upset. A little time back he had witnessed a bad automobile accident, after which he cried frequently and had nightmares. He had always been a restless sleeper, and was inclined to go into rages when frustrated. Thus, he suffered from three distinct morbid conditions apart from the lack of behavioral control, and would rank as a highly vulnerable child. In the light of so many adversities and disabilities it must seem superfluous to ask why he became delinquent. One of the few signs of behavior disturbance marked by his teacher was that of foolish pranks when with a gang. He committed petty thefts with other boys, no doubt to buy their friendship. What could have been interpreted as participation in the delinquency of a junior gang more probably reflected the emotional precariousness of his family situation and his need for human attachments.

The next candidate for normality was a 10-year-old boy whose delinquency was likewise petty stealing in company with others. His mother had various chronic stomach and kidney complaints and, with a casually employed husband and six children, must often have been on the verge of despair. She described the boy as "wild" inside the house—loud, noisy, restless, and impatient. Living in a black-spot for delinquency, the parents kept their children indoors during the dark evenings; the one night that the boy sneaked out was when he got into trouble. It sounded like an avoidance-excitement case. In my 102 cases of delinquent youths, 7 were actuated by avoidance-excitement arising from anxiety about parents' health. When one considers how typical of the underprivileged, high-delinquency area is this picture of an ailing mother with a large family and a husband who is often unemployed, one is led to suspect that the small marauding groups of prepubertal children, who are also typical of these areas, might all be seeking to escape from their family worries by substitutive hyperactivity and excitement. His teacher noted of this boy that he "started off others in scrapping and rough play"—which supports a diagnosis of incipient avoidance-excitement. Yet, with a BSAG score of only 2, he fell into the well-adjusted category. In Chapter Eight I point to the situational character of much maladjustment: separated from the provoking cause of the disturbance, the child may behave normally. In such cases general statements that the young person is normal or maladjusted mean little. All one can say is that it is during their maladjusted phases that they commit their delinquencies.

On the count of vulnerability, this boy had two congenital defects, a blocked tear duct and a severe squint. These in themselves did not categorize him as a behaviorally vulnerable child, but they are types of defects which crop up not infrequently in the histories of mentally and behaviorally handicapped children. The general tendency to multiple impairment would imply a greater risk of maladjustment with any physical morbidity, especially if the latter takes two or more distinct forms. In sum, whereas various inferences as to causation have to be made in this case, the boy was certainly not a completely well-adjusted, robust, and anxiety-free member of a local delinquent subculture.

The last of the five children who technically qualified as normal, a girl of 14 at the time of the investigation, only just made it into the category of quasi-normality. Her BSAG score of 9 contained six items indicating withdrawal. The other three indicated that she associated with unsettled types, often truanted, and was often late for school. On reaching puberty at age 13, there was a dramatic change in her behavior. She gave up playing with a younger child next door and started going around with older girls who would absent themselves from work and persuade her to truant and go into town with them. It was with one of these girls that she was convicted of shoplifting.

Changes of temperament are so frequent at puberty as to lead us to suppose that a new genetic behavior coding comes into operation then. Most often it brings a heightened need for acceptance by the peer group and an eagerness to conform to adolescent norms of behavior. The shift from withdrawal to aggressive nuisance, as occurred in this girl, was in fact a recurrent phenomenon in my year of casework with the Glasgow School Welfare Officers. Such a young person is in a more than usually acute state of anxiety if she has few natural skills in social relationships and no experience in making friends. In addition this girl had little home companionship because her father, being a long-distance driver, was seldom at home, and harsh in his discipline when he was, and her behavior towards her mother was defiant, cheeky, and untruthful. Her truancy and stealing were evidently the price she paid for the companionship of her age peers. That she was forced to find it among delinquents can be explained by her inability up to that time to make stable friendships with normal girls of her age.

On the score of vulnerability, apart from her defective social skills she had always been a highly strung and easily upset child, with abnormally developed fears, especially of dental treatment (which is also characteristic of delinquent youths).

The result of the investigation of these five residual and possibly well-adjusted delinquents from a high-delinquency area was that none of them qualified as free from family problems or as a normally robust young person following the pattern of behavior in the neighborhood. Indeed, the delinquency of all of them could more plausibly be seen as arising from a combination of their depriving and anxiety-creating home situations and their personal vulnerability to stress. It is natural that in their search for relief from their anxieties they would turn to those outlets that were available to them. In an area of social disorganization, with its high incidence of family troubles, there would be many young people seeking a temporary amnesia in daredevil exploits, so that this solution is always at hand for successive year-groups of young people. The underprivileged, socially disorganized area thus becomes one of high delinquency. So long as the curtain is not drawn back to reveal the personal lives of the young delinquents, it is easy to see them as merely conforming to a subculture of a gang. The gang—or, more accurately, the loose, unstable group of usually not more than three—is an effect rather than a cause. It is formed as the result of the coming together of those who find solace in deviant forms of excitement. Strange as it may seem, the typical delinquent is not a courageous youth; as I show in many of the case histories quoted in *Delinquency and Human Nature* (1950/80) he is beset with fears, stemming in part from constitutional impairment and in part from the emotional uncertainties of his family relationships. But the driving compulsion to escape from his tribulations nevertheless makes risk-taking attractive, and so he needs to draw courage from the egging on of companions. Many a mother has said to me that her son would never have had the courage to commit delinquencies but for the influence of the "boys down the street." Because the egging on is mutual and cumulative, a concentration of family troubles within an area will produce a relatively greater volume of delinquency than in an area where family troubles are few; hence the phenomenon of the high-delinquency neighborhood with its groups of troublesome youngsters.

The second study carried out by Kara Wilson (1966) applied the same methodology in a Scottish seaport and its environs. It was a typical working-class area, with pockets of delinquency and areas almost completely free thereform. There had been a history of petty crime around the docks, so that the findings of the study are of interest in relation to Mays's (1954) claim that the petty delinquencies of Liverpool's dockland were committed by normal boys.

The 38 schools of the area were supplied with the names of their juvenile delinquents over the previous year. Five refused to cooperate, but from the remainder, 21 children emerged as possibly stable from the teachers' completing the Yes/No questionnaire, as used in the first study. Only 7 of these qualified, by getting BASG scores of less than 10. In effect the average score of the 21 was 17—well on the way to maladjustment—showing that the teachers had erred on the side of stability. It is therefore very unlikely that any stable delinquents would have been missed. In calculating the proportion of stable among the total year's crop of delinquents, 2 had to be excluded because they committed their offenses after the end of the year. Thus there were strictly only 5 stable among the total of 70, or approximately 7 percent. Nevertheless the 2 additional cases were included in the study, since the main purpose of the investigation was to discover well-adjusted delinquents.

One of the seven residual "stable" had to be dropped from the study because the father pleaded that the mother had enough to worry about already—without, however, saying what her worries were. She had another child attending the child guidance clinic. Of the remaining six there was evidence that the delinquency of two arose directly from their family anxieties. The mother of one was in a maternity hospital for three months prior to delivery of another child; the boy visited her alone and missed her intensely. Near the end of her time there, in company with an older delinquent, he raided some railway trucks and an empty house which had already been broken into. It looked like another instance of a boy's giving way to his anxiety over his mother's health (Situation 4A, as described in Chapter Nine). The mother of the other boy, ailing and with seven children, threatened to desert the home; the boy was very upset and kept asking his father if she meant it. His delinquencies bore the character of avoidance-excitement. In the company of other boys he stole fruit, and on another occasion changed around the bottles of milk left at front doors. The latter was almost identical to the pranks cited by Cohen (1956) as the devilment typical of a juvenile-delinquent subculture. Since this boy belonged to a poor working-class family living in an ill-kept council project, his offenses could have been explained along similar lines if the personal features of the case had been ignored. The boy must in addition have suffered from some developmental handicap, since he never smiled as a baby and as a young child showed no concern at being left alone; he also had thick, indistinct speech and suffered from a "nervous tummy." In short, he showed signs of a multiple impairment which could have included an emotional vulnerability to anxiety.

The offense of two more boys was merely that on Guy Fawkes night, when boys all over Britain set off fireworks and light bonfires, these two tore some wood off a fence to feed their fires. It was hardly the mark of a delinquent subculture, even though carried out in company with other children. One of them was a nervous boy, with thick, mumbling speech, described by his teacher as reticent, seldom smiling, and "on the fringe, an outsider." Possibly the destruction of the fence was his way of trying to work his way into a group. His mate was the survivor of twins, the other having been born dead and badly malformed. With an IQ of 66 and very slow of speech, he was in a special school for the mildly retarded. His mother, a slipshod, insensitive woman, was given to making irresponsible threats in order to control her boys. The one in the present series was always hyperactive and got into unending dangerous scrapes. She complained: "I haven't got boys, I've got monkeys."

The last two of the six might well qualify as stable delinquents if minor indications of vulnerability are waived. One of them, with high fears and a history of enuresis, stole from an ice cream van, a house, and a baker in one delinquent bout with another boy. The other, with an IQ of 69 and attending a special school, stole a bicycle, in company with a boy from a high-delinquency area. However, both these boys lived in superior working-class areas where delinquency was rare. Whatever particular incitements there were to their deviant behavior, they could not therefore have been responding to the stimulations of a delinquent subculture.

RESULTS OF THE SEARCH FOR
STABLE SUBCULTURAL DELINQUENTS

The outcome of these two studies was a failure to find any children who could be regarded as "subcultural" delinquents. For all those living in the high-delinquency areas there were reasons within their family lives which could easily account for their deviance, such as it was. Moreover, the reasons tally with those adduced in the larger study of 102 institutionalized delinquents, as analyzed in Chapter Nine. Although the number of cases investigated in these two studies was small, it should be borne in mind that the original samples of delinquents totaled 112, this being reduced to 12 by the progressive elimination of those who were found to be unstable.

Perhaps the chief contribution of these studies is to provide a methodology for similar studies elsewhere, and notably where it is felt that genuine delinquent subcultures may exist. This methodology is simple and inexpensive, so that those who insist upon a purely cultural contamination, or a conflict of cultures, as the reason for the prevalence of delinquency in disorganized inner-city areas have no excuse for not verifying their theories. The only disadvantage of the methodology, as far as they are concerned, is that it entails the patient investigation of the individual cases; that is to say, looking at the facts of family life and individual temperament.

PART TWO
The Present State of Practice

Chapter Four
The Conflict of Philosophies in the Disposition of the Offender

THE CONVENTIONAL SYSTEM
OF WARNING AND PUNISHMENT

The disposition of young offenders in the legal systems of Britain and the North American continent is based on a number of assumptions about reasons for delinquency which have their origin in traditional concepts of human nature rather than in academic findings. This is not to say that these concepts can be dismissed as superstitions; it is, on the face of things, unlikely that human beings have basically false notions about how the members of their own species behave. There is therefore in these popular concepts not the same risk of massive wrongness as there is in fashionable theorizing unsupported by first-hand observation.

Traditional means of dealing with wayward children are extensions of those used for the disciplining of children in everyday life. These consist of punishments which are by and large effective, the fear of parental anger which stems from the child's need for parental love and support and the parents' appeals to the child's best interests and to the family's good name. Traditional cultures apply their sanctions indiscriminately, without thought for individual handicap or poor nurturing; the result is the banishment or annihilation of those who are unable to control their actions. The realization in our contemporary society that there are such people, who have a right to special consideration, jostles uneasily with this traditional system of indiscriminate sanctions, so that the disposition of young offenders varies inconsistently, according to whether public opinion and the individual judge lean toward the one philosophy or the other.

In the conventional means of disposition there is usually a progression of two phases. For a first offense the child will either be given a police warning or receive a more formal warning before a juvenile court or panel. There the procedure, owing to the number of cases to be dealt with, may be perfunctory, or the judge may go

to considerable pains to impress upon the offender the consequences
of further lawbreaking. Many judges feel that the court experience
will be awe-inspiring and will leave a lasting impression which will
deter the youngster. Unless the child has committed a particularly
heinous offense, the court usually dismisses him with some kind of
admonishment or by placing him on probation. This is all part of
the warning phase, and the same applies to the imposition of a fine
if its amount is nominal.

Probation has to be included in this warning phase, because
probation officers have such large caseloads that they have not the
time to investigate the stressful family relationships which are at
the root of most juvenile lawbreaking, let alone attempt to remove
or alleviate the causes of the stresses. Their work has to consist in
the main of interview contacts with the probationer. These serve
basically as periodic reminders of the possibility of committal in
the event of further offenses.

Phase two of disposition comes into operation when repeated
delinquency occurs in defiance of the warnings. This is generally
taken as a sign that the young person has been recalcitrant and
needs either punishment or training in discipline. He is therefore
committed to be detained in some form of residential institution.
Since the terms used for such institutions vary from time to time and
country to country—to be in keeping with their ostensible aims, or
just to disguise their true nature—I shall call them committal
institutions.

THE HUMANITARIAN ALTERNATIVE

Onto this old-fashioned logic of misdeed and punishment has
been grafted a humanitarian approach to disposition which derives
from the realization that the young offender is often the victim of
adverse factors in his development and upbringing. The emphasis is
on treatment rather than punishment. Attempts are made to create
a friendly and informal atmosphere at the hearing of the case, which
might include the avoidance of the words "guilt" and "conviction."
This has blurred the effect of the warning ritual.

The British Children's and Young Person's Act of 1969 was
based on this humanitarian view. The child's offense was regarded
as a form of "social disturbance," which seemed a short way of
saying that the child evidenced some form of behavior disturbance
or maladjustment brought on by social circumstances. In effect the
Act has remained largely unimplemented, partly owing to the

opposition of the judges, by no means all of whom were prepared to embrace the treatment-not-punishment philosophy, and partly because the machinery for actualizing this philosophy was almost totally lacking.

In Britain and on the North American continent these two philosophies remain unreconciled. At any one time and place, depending upon personalities and the mood of the public, one or the other takes over like two opposing weather systems. The practices of traditional cultures tend to be destroyed once they are questioned, and so we see the conventional warning/punishment strategy weakened by the newer view that the offender is the victim of circumstances. Traditional practices at least have worked in a way. But they involve harshness and a willingness to sacrifice individuals to whatever degree of deterrence proves necessary. The problem is that a viable humanitarian alternative has not been produced.

THE TREND TO HAWKISHNESS

To judge by the number of convictions recorded, there has been an intercontinental rise in the incidence of juvenile crime. In England and Wales between 1965 and 1975 it rose 70 percent for 14-16-year-old males. For the 17-20 group the rise was 140 percent. There has always been some question about the accuracy of these figures, owing to changing practices of arrest and prosecution. However, the trend has been to divert cases from the court by police cautioning in the first instance, so that the reality could be worse than the foregoing statistics suggest. During recent years there has been a comparable deterioration in the United States. Between 1970 and 1975 the arrest rate for serious offenses rose by 24 percent for boys under 18 years of age, and by no less than 40 percent for girls in the same age category. Moreover, the character of the offenses has changed to include murder, rape, muggings, and robbery of old people in their homes, which are usually regarded as the mark of the worst type of adult criminal.

The present mood is therefore one of hawkishness, with the humanitarians discouraged and on the defensive. We have therefore to consider, first, what the reintroduction of a consistent system of punishment entails, and, second, what the chances are of its success, given the limitations that a civilized community will tolerate. Even the normal means of disciplining the young practiced in traditional societies would not be tolerated today. The warning phase consisted of horrifying tales of what happens to naughty children, supported by a pantheon of supernatural punitive agents. For the defenseless waif there were the reformatory and the training ship. Physical punishment was the routine for lesser offenders of all ages; the serious offender was disposed of by transportation or execution. Short of reverting to these barbarisms, punishment as a sole means of controlling crime is ineffective.

CONDITIONS FOR SUCCESS OF THE WARNING PHASE

It is this realization that some substitute has to be found for traditional punishment that has prompted the development of the elaborate warning systems to which I have referred. The prospects of their becoming substitutes for deterrent punishment have therefore to be assessed. Psychologically, the essential feature of a warning is that, while it may evoke the fear of punishment, in itself it has no unpleasant consequences. Everything depends on whether the recipient understands it and takes it seriously. The ability and willingness of the potential young offender to heed the warnings emitted by our present legal system depend upon a number of conditions. These are considered below.

i. *The court proceedings or police cautioning are sufficiently awe- and fear-inspiring to act as a deterrent.* In the recent focusing of attention on ways of dealing with young offenders, journalists have picked up many statements which suggest that, at least in the high-delinquency inner cities, the court has lost this quality. A social worker complains that the inner London courts have become a laughing stock with many youngsters. The Metropolitan Police Commissioner has quoted the story of boys who retorted to a threat to call the police by saying, "Go ahead, call them. They can only take us in front of the panel and nothing will happen to us there anyway." New York court officials testified that deviant children have boasted openly of their ability to beat the system. Members of that city's police force voiced a disgusted cynicism owing to their inability to secure conviction and punishment in the cases they brought to court. Reasons cited were delays—sometimes running into several months—for investigation by an overworked Probation Department, with the juvenile murderer or possessor of a loaded revolver at large on parole and free to commit further crimes. Court procedure was found to be snarled up by the reluctance of witnesses to testify for fear of intimidation, and by legal

technicalities. There were complaints against judicial leniency
and sentimentalism: some judges nursed the illusion that a good
proportion of offending juveniles only needed a stern lecture.
The most bitter complaint of all was that first offenders were
let off without penalty even for crimes of violence. Coupled
with the latter is the irony of a juvenile's being able to be a
"first offender" several times a year in different districts of
New York, owing to the lack of central records (*Time*, 1977a).

These accounts of how juveniles have called the bluff of
the legal system have emanated not only from those professions
whose responsibility it is to ensure law and order but also from
social workers who are primarily concerned about the rescue of
the young offender. It is evident that the imposing warning
system built up over the past two generations is in danger of
breaking down. In terms of the psychology of learning, this is
not surprising. It is an experimental commonplace that if no
"punishment" is administered, the threat thereof will become
ineffective after a certain interval, and the behavior that was to
be inhibited reappears. Cattle soon discover the absence of the
shock when the current of an electric fence is turned off, and
young delinquents are more intelligent than cattle.

ii. *The typical young delinquent is able to control his actions, and
has the foresight to act in his own best interests.* The very facts
of court reappearance and inability to heed warnings show that
this is not the case. Many research findings have been quoted
which show a large proportion of young delinquents to be
maladjusted. Bereft of its mystique, this word means that the
affected child is unable to control his behavior, lacks foresight
as to the consequences of his actions, and indeed may have
powerful motivations which propel him into self-destructive
and antisocial behavior.

iii. *The delinquent has no aberrant motivation impelling him
toward delinquency and overriding all considerations as to his
future interests or happiness.* It is demonstrated in Chapter
Seven, with the support of case histories from an earlier work
(Stott, 1950/80), that the vast majority, at least of recidivist
delinquents, do have such compelling motivations. They seek
delinquent means of expressing their hostility against those
whom they regard as rejecting them, or put the loyalty of their
parents to the test by inviting rejection and hoping not to be

rejected. Alternatively they seek in delinquency the excitements which prevent them from thinking about their family troubles. Such compulsions assume the direction of the young person's behavior; his family attachments, the reputation of his parents, his friendships, his economic future no longer have any influence on his actions. Warnings in these terms are so many wasted words. As shown in these case studies, a delinquent may even want committal to a residential institution in order to escape from his family problems. The warning may indeed prove an incentive to delinquency.

THE APPEARANCE OF NORMALITY

Many judges insist that, except for a small minority of psychopathic or near-psychotic individuals, the delinquent is an essentially normal boy or girl. But normal children do not gratuitously get themselves into trouble time and again, incurring the sorrow and anger of their parents and risking being taken from home. The recidivist young offender must be accounted maladjusted, by the above definition. The word is shunned because it seems to undermine the whole system of warning and punishment. In fact, effective means of deterrence for the normal child depend on the correct identification of the maladjusted child, upon whom deterrent measures are of no avail.

Our failure to make a distinction between the maladjusted, who cannot be deterred, and the normal, who can, has caused deterrent measures to fall into disrepute. Proponents of the humanitarian alternative never tire of pointing to the ineffectiveness of punishment. What they should rather say is that punishment does not work on those who are incapable of foresight and self-control; that is, the maladjusted. It certainly works with the normal. And it has to be recognized that, unlike ants and bees, the human species has no instinctively built-in provision for subordinating its personal interests to the general good. The normal person, young or old, requires a framework of sanctions to ensure that he behaves in a socially responsible manner. This genetic omission has been made good by the development of the codes of behavior which every culture enforces. Remove these, and the human species reverts to the bullying of the weak by the strong, which is the general rule among other warm-blooded animals.

THE LIMITS OF DETERRENCE

As was shown in Chapter One, a large proportion of young offenders are maladjusted, even though this may not be revealed in every situation. There are nevertheless cases where the foregoing four conditions are met: a reasonably normal boy hears other children bragging about their petty delinquencies and, not having received sufficiently strong warnings from his parents, or having been brought up to attach little importance to their wishes, he falls in with their deviant ways. When children of this type are caught, it is reasonable to assume that the contact with the police and the possibility of being charged will be a serious learning experience for them and that they will "learn their lesson." It may well be, in consequence, that among youngsters living in an inner-city environment, the word gets round that the law no longer has any terrors and that the policeman need no longer be feared. For them it would seem advisable that the offense should regularly be followed by some form of punishment which will make them realize that shoplifting, petty vandalism, and other prankish delinquencies do not pay.

The effectiveness of the punishment phase of the conventional system can be measured by the proportion of youths who are reconvicted after having served a term in a committal institution. In 1972, over England and Wales, 79 percent of former reformatory trainees and 70 percent of juvenile detention center trainees were reconvicted within two years, and it is estimated that some 55 percent of the former and 40 percent of the latter were recommitted (NACRO, 1977). If these had been normal young people normally concerned for their present comfort and their future, we have to ask why the severe punishment of deprivation of liberty had so little effect on them. The only possible answer is that in the main they were not deterrable. They were not normal young people with a reasonable ability to control their behavior in their own best interests. Not only had the warning phase had no effect on them, but the great majority had proved resistant to the most severe punishment that a civilized community could impose on them.

LACK OF FACILITIES FOR INVESTIGATING THE COMPULSIONS TOWARDS DELINQUENCY

For this undeterrable group of recidivist delinquents something more than punishment must be attempted. If it is true that they are under the sway of compulsions toward continued delinquency, the obvious social strategy is to discover what these may be and seek to alleviate them. It has to be recognized that within the conventional system there is no machinery for doing so. Apart from not having the time, probation officers have not the specialized knowledge needed for identifying and treating the disturbed behavior of which delinquency is a manifestation. The number of social workers is likewise completely inadequate for an investigation of the motivation of the delinquency and of the family stresses that set if off. In a system of disposition in which casework considerations get tangled up with legal procedures directed towards the establishment of guilt, members of both professions are condemned to spend a large portion of their time waiting in courtrooms. One social worker complained in a press interview of having to attend court about twenty times in respect to one child because of procedural and administrative delays. The machinery of the law can thus deny to the child the chance of being helped.

THE HUMANITARIAN APPROACH FAILS FROM LACK OF KNOWLEDGE OF CAUSES

The means of treatment are lacking, even when some form of assessment is carried out. The head of the assessment unit at Stamford House, the London remand home, has complained that disturbed children may remain there for months because no committal institution is willing to take them. The underlying truth is that there is no systematic diagnosis of the causes of the disturbed behavior—which in these cases includes delinquency—in the true sense of diagnosis, which means achieving an understanding of the problem as a stage toward its treatment. The quandary of the assessment center is that, in terms of what is needed for the treatment of the recidivist delinquent as a behaviorally disturbed person, there is really little to choose between one committal instititution and another. Moreover, the delinquent is usually sent back into the same family situation which proved intolerable to him before committal and from which in all probability he sought to escape through delinquency. It is only to be expected that he will resort to the same means of escape again.

The humanitarian approach to delinquency has not failed; it has not yet been tried. The reason for this omission is, quite simply, that the sponsors of this approach do not know how to put it into practice. They have an ideal, but no means of realizing it. This cluelessness can reach an extreme of absurdity that would not be believed, except that it has been documented as happening. A fifteen-year-old girl is brought before the same judge of the Toronto Family Court 28 times for truancy without anything being resolved. A fifteen-year-old boy appears 22 times before the same judge before being sent to a treatment center. Of another boy, involved in stealing and damaging public property, the court psychiatrist reported that his family had been a bad influence on him—but did not say in what way. He recommended not only against removal to an institution but, incongruously, that there should be no further contact with the family! The boy continued to commit offenses and to appear in court. Section 38 of the Juvenile Delinquents Act of Ontario directs that the young offender be treated as a "misdirected and misguided child, and one needing aid, encouragement, help and assistance." But no one knows what form the aid, help, and assistance should take, it being apparently assumed that three empty words are better at hiding this awkward truth than one empty word.

CIVILIZED PUNISHMENT RATHER THAN INDISCRIMINATE PUNITIVENESS

Both in Britain and the United States the increase in the juvenile crime rate which has been the outcome of conflicting philosophies has led in certain places to a demand for "toughening up." And, indeed, where this has been put into effect there has often been a notable reduction in juvenile crime. When the Bronx courts began to sentence youths found guilty of the violent robbery of elderly people to five-to-ten-year terms, the arrests for this type of offense dropped by 40 percent. In New Orleans, with the enactment of stronger laws and the jailing of violent repeaters, teen-age homicides declined from 29 in 1973 to 5 in 1975. The threat of jail at the second offense was among the tougher measures in Memphis that brought a reduction in juvenile court appearances from 16,191 in 1975 to 14,174 in 1976, with a further reduction of 16 percent in the first quarter of 1977. The juvenile crime rate in Atlanta showed one of the biggest declines in the country, following the tightening up of the system, including the bringing of offenders to trial within ten days of their indictment (*Time*, 1977b).

It would indeed appear that in the United States the combination of a humanitarianism which lacks techniques for its realization and a legal system which gets tied up in its own niceties has resulted in a lapsing of those sanctions which keep the generality of citizens on the path of virtue. Nevertheless, the foregoing results cannot be taken as evidence for the need to revert to indiscriminate punitiveness. Rather, they show that punishment for wrongdoing should be used as the first stage in a system of prevention, designed to deter those who are capable of being deterred, and incidentally of identifying those who are not. Nor is it necessary to endorse the forms of punishment used. In a civilized society it should be possible to devise sanctions which give the offender insight into the effects of his misdoing and induce in him a greater social responsibility. Examples of these are discussed in Chapter Sixteen.

Chapter Five
Lessons from Some American Experiments in Prevention

Owing to the tangled complexity of the variables they study and the difficulty in manipulating them to get unambiguous answers, social scientists have not yet succeeded in building up a corpus of established knowledge such as has been attained by the physical sciences. Because of its lack, the way has been laid open to theoretical fashion. Fashion, by its nature, entails the denial or neglect of what has gone before. Hence the danger of swings of fashion in a field of knowledge is that the advances made by earlier generations are neglected and forgotten. No field of knowledge has been more fashion-ridden than that of delinquency. It has to be admitted that the lessons we can learn from the early studies are mainly negative ones; but they at least showed what did not work. This is an advance if it only prevents us from repeating the same mistakes.

This chapter describes four major American studies of the past forty years, so that we can profit by their failures and salvage from them certain empirical findings which represent the beginning of a corpus of knowledge.

THE CAMBRIDGE-SOMERVILLE STUDY

One of the most famous and most written-about of these early studies is the *Experiment in the Prevention of Delinquency*, known as the Cambridge-Somerville Youth Study. The thesis of its founder, Dr. R. C. Cabot, was that delinquency-prone children would respond to the influence of friendly adults, who would get to know them intimately and act as advisers and models of conduct. The "at-risk" section of the sample was drawn from some 2000 boys, aged between 6 and 12, referred by schools, social agencies, probation officers, and the police. From these were selected those whom the records suggested were the most delinquency-prone. To them were added—so that inclusion in the Study should not confer a stigma—an equal number of average, or "normal," boys. Members of the treatment group thus formed were matched for physical health, intelligence, emotional adjustment, home background, and delinquency prognosis with 325 controls who would receive no treatment.

Ten counselors were appointed, with instructions to contact the treatment (T) group children and their families and offer them guidance and friendship. Considering that the families did not request the service, the counselors met with remarkably few persistent refusals. However, a not inconsiderable number of the boys or their parents remained indifferent and relatively unresponsive over the years of the study.

Beyond this injunction to befriend and be of service to the boys, the counselors received no guidelines. The majority had in fact received training as social workers but their theoretical backgrounds were different, and no attempt was made to secure a uniformity of treatment philosophy. Owing to changes of personnel, 19 counselors were employed in all, which leads Allport in his introduction to the evaluative report (Powers and Witmer, 1951, p. x) to speak of "19 styles of approach." Each counselor had a free choice of the kind of service offered. These included—to give only a sampling—arranging medical examinations, giving tutorial help, taking the boy on outings, referral to other agencies, encouraging hobbies or participation in youth organizations, and giving general advice on family problems. About the only thing the counselors were forbidden to do was to start any local club or youth group. This ban was surprising, considering that this would have given them a natural means for frequent contact with the boys. One of the drawbacks of the treatment was the difficulty, with a caseload of 32, of maintaining friendships and a counseling role that could conceivably have much effect on the boys.

The original plan was that the counselors should maintain contact with the boys and their familes for 10 years. This was not realized, for two reasons: because of the outbreak of the Second World War some four years after the project's inception, and because of the abandonment of treatment in the case of a number of boys, owing to various causes. The average length of contact for the whole 325 in the T group was thus just under five years. Nevertheless this was a considerable expenditure of effort, and significant results should have been recorded if the method of treatment were beneficial. The actual results were shattering: the recipients of the treatment had recorded against them 114 appearances before the Crime Prevention Bureau between the inception of the project and the year following its termination; the nontreated controls made only 101 appearances. Moreover, the excess of delinquency in the treated group was owing to the greater number of repeaters. In her appraisal of the project, following a meticulous examination of the case records, Helen Witmer (Powers and Witmer, 1951) is forced to conclude that "Dr. Cabot's hypothesis [that what is needed to prevent delinquency and to foster good character development] is the presence of an adult 'friend' . . . appears to be disproved" (p. 577).

In their reappraisal of the project many years later, McCord and McCord (1959) drew attention to the similarity of its methods to those used by probation officers, social welfare agencies, and some mental health clinics. It is indeed a sobering thought that the aim of the probation officer to advise and befriend is of little value for the curbing of delinquency. This does not mean that probation and casework are valueless, but that quite a different approach is indicated. In her further analysis of the reasons for the counselors' failure, Witmer found that only 3 of those 35 boys who were extremely maladjusted benefited significantly. The project was no more helpful to those originally classified as socially maladjusted, by which term she meant the mischievous, hyperactive, aggressive boys. It is reasonable to conclude that any service or project which neglects this central aspect of delinquency is going to be equally ineffective.

Witmer noted a similar inability on the part of the counselors to influence the emotional quality of the parent-child relationships. Those boys in respect of whom it was rated as C—the worst category —benefited very little from the study. This is not surprising, since the counselors had no systematic means of diagnosing the nature of emotional stresses within the families, and, therefore, no techniques for alleviating them. Witmer's final appraisal is that, "no such generous, ambitious but professionally naive program can diminish to any considerable extent that persistent problem, juvenile delinquency" (p. 577).

From their analysis of the data, the McCords conclude that the overriding factor in the genesis of delinquency is a lack of cohesiveness in the home situation. Notably, a quarrelsome home, with or without affection, led to delinquency which began at a relatively early age. Unfortunately, the McCords progressed no further in analyzing the forms that lack of cohesiveness could take. The true nature of the stresses which drive children to seek delinquent avenues of escape will never be revealed by impressionistic ratings for affection, cohesiveness, and discipline. The most they can tell us is that parent-child relations are the key factor. But such knowledge is of little value to the therapist, for he cannot improve parent-child relations in the abstract. The particular source of weakness must be identified in behavioral terms.

THE MAXIMUM BENEFITS PROJECT

As its name implies, this project, under the direction of two psychiatrists (Hodges and Tait, 1963), aimed to give the best services currently available to a group of children referred for severe behavior problems. These included social-work, psychiatric, medical, and psychological examinations of each child, followed by case conferences at which a treatment plan was formulated. Over some three years, 179 children were passed through this program, alongside whom a matched group were left untreated. The results were very similar to those of the Cambridge-Somerville Youth Study: of the children located in the follow-up, 69 percent of the treated, but only 63 percent of the untreated, children were found to have been delinquent. The project directors reluctantly concluded that social casework, as it was conventionally offered in the United States at the time, was ineffective for the prevention of delinquency. It is not enough, they concluded, simply to provide more services of the type already existing. What are needed are "fresh innovations and techniques."

If only this final recommendation is acted upon, their study, despite its negative results, will not have been wasted. Everything depends on our ability to perfect such techniques.

THE CHICAGO AREA PROJECT

Clifford Shaw's main contribution to knowledge was his study (1942) with Henry McKay of the patterns of inner-city delinquency, along with the shifts of immigrant populations. One wave after another of immigrants settled in, and, in the course of time, moved out into better neighborhoods, but within these inner-city areas the high delinquency rates persisted. Shaw saw the social disorganization inherent in such population movements as weakening the social institutions of the parent generation, so that their control of the youth was weakened. The objective of the project of which he was the inspiration and director was thus to help local populations to rebuild indigenous community organizations, or, if such already existed, to strengthen them in their resistance to the deviance of the younger generation.

In giving evidence before the U.S. Senate Subcommittee to Investigate Juvenile Delinquency, Henry McKay (1959) listed the reasons why agencies acting from outside the communities were incapable of reestablishing the necessary control: they could not do much to change moral standards or reach delinquent groups; and in any youth facilities that they sponsored, they took the easier way out by catering to those who were well-behaved. The main thrust of Shaw's effort was therefore to stimulate the natural social reintegration of the disorganized neighborhoods by encouraging them to develop their own agencies for the welfare of youth and the prevention of delinquency. These agencies were placed under the control of the people in the area, and so far as possible their paid workers were recruited from the neighborhoods where they would work. The Project sociologists exercised only general guidance, and advisedly accepted the decisions of the local committees, even if they did not always agree with them.

In the course of two decades some 12 community committees were established in Chicago, and these had premises in the form of centers or settlement houses. The kinds of services they provided varied according to the needs of each neighborhood. They fell into three categories: recreational, incuding summer camps; the improvement of local amenities, such as safety precautions, physical maintenance, and law enforcement; and direct work with delinquent children and street gangs. Their great accomplishment, as Kobrin (1959) pointed out, is that they demonstrated the feasibility of securing the active participation of local residents in work among the local youth. Even in the most unlikely localities, capable persons of good will responded to the challenge of responsibility and, with help and guidance, were able to operate neighborhood programs. On the whole these organizations exhibited vitality and stability, and vindicated the belief of Clifford Shaw that people residing in disorganized areas can be found who have the ability to take an effective part in the welfare of their local youth.

Since no statistical records of the effects on the delinquency rates were kept, all Kobrin could say in his assessment after 25 years about the success of the Chicago Area Project was that: "In all probability these achievements have reduced delinquency in the program areas as any substantial improvement in the social climate of a community must" (p. 28). What in fact Clifford Shaw and his colleagues were aspiring to do was to rebuild a culture, with new institutions and modes of behavior with which to meet new needs and dangers. It was work for prophets as much as for sociologists.

Kobrin recognized the magnitude of the mission: "Since progress in the solution of these problems comes only slowly, permanent declines in delinquency are not expected even after years of effort" (p. 27).

It was a great pity that all this producive human endeavor—culturally or far wider import than the control of juvenile deviance—was not meticulously logged and preserved as body of experience for workers in other regions and later generations. A thousand lessons of success and failure have gone unrecorded. This applies particularly to the work with delinquents and teen-age corner groups, which was mandatory in all the local organizations. The accounts of work with the "Eagles" gang by Kobrin and of the "Dons" by Jansyn, to which reference was made in Chapter Two, show us how valuable such documentation would have been.

One is tempted to ask whether this failure to document was fortuitous. It was seen that the first-hand accounts by Kobrin, Baittle, and Jansyn failed to confirm the major tenets of Shaw's theory in more than one respect. There were two blind spots in Shaw's social perception. The first was his failure to appreciate how separation from the ancestral communities released not only the youth but also the adult generation from social restraints on their conduct. The second was his overlooking of the interpersonal stresses produced by poverty and overcrowding among people who no longer enjoyed the traditional cultural safeguards and skills needed for living under such conditions. To maintain the purity of his sociological theory he was at pains to deny the factors of emotional and personality disturbance in delinquency. Hence he failed to discern how overwrought parents breaking down under socioeconomic pressures could deprive their children of their need for the permanent security of a family, and so in turn induce in them forms of behavior disturbance which often found expression in deviance. Personal help to families in a state of breakdown thus had no place in his preventive program.

Admirable as was Shaw's aim of creating local organizations capable of dealing with the community's own problems, his exclusive concentration upon the community aspects of prevention must be accounted a negative feature of his influence. It was taken up all too literally by his followers. Martin (1961) states categorically: "*Basically, the problem of delinquency prevention is a problem of social organization or reorganization and other approaches have merit only to the degree that they contribute to such reorganization*" (Martin's italics).

This insidious dogma even lapped around the feet of the President's Commission on Law Enforcement and Administration of Justice. In a task force report to that body, Burns and Stern (1967) deprecate a case-by-case approach because of the large numbers of potentially delinquent youth to be reached and the present uncertainty of the means of identifying them. It is true that a casework approach is time consuming, but so is casework in the field of physical health. In effect, the method proposed in this book requires only a small professional commitment compared with the traditional individual and group therapies. A large amount of the time needed could be found by relieving caseworkers of the necessity of sitting around in courtrooms. And, as has been argued, the system of identification includes safeguards against incorrect identification and "labeling"—which Burns and Stern advance as a further weakness of the casework approach—because it does not lay bets on the chances of future delinquency as such, but aims to identify those children suffering from the kinds of maladjustment likely to lead to delinquency. It is the maladjustment and the home situation which are treated, and this has justification apart from delinquency prevention.

Burns and Stern rationalize their rejection of individual casework with the argument that

> to focus upon individuals and groups alone can lead one down a never-ending path of offering prevention services to person after person, while an increasing number of potential delinquents is propelled by society into the waiting line.... Major emphasis on institutional changes is probably the best and most lasting way of preventing large numbers of youth from entering delinquent careers.

There might be something to be said for such a policy—given a limitation of resources which precluded the simultaneous operation of both approaches—if the community solution were a quick and certain one. But it will be recalled that even Kobrin, who was one of the leading figures in the Chicago Area Project, did not feel able to make a confident claim that the immense expenditure of resources over some twenty years had reduced delinquency in the localities concerned; and he warned that resolution of community problems comes slowly, and permanent declines in delinquency are not to be expected even after years of effort (Kobrin, 1959). With such dubious prospects of success, to concentrate on community projects to the neglect of casework is like concentrating on the removal of the causes of wars while refusing to treat the casualties of a war in which one's country is engaged. If human beings are valuable as individuals, we have a moral duty to rescue and heal, whether they are victims of societal ills or man's belligerence.

It has to be admitted- in mitigation of the Chicago heresy—that the psychiatric and psychological theories of the time, and the techniques derived from them, were far from promising. To review their present status would require a separate volume. All that can be said about them in this book is that insofar as they imported concepts and methods derived from the data of other fields, they have the status only of hypotheses and speculations. They may possibly help us form testable concepts about delinquency, but as a priori explanations they have little value. There is no substitute for building up understanding from the direct study of the elements of the problem in which one is interested; in our case, delinquency. The dismissal from consideration of the psychological processes by which adverse environment can produce deviance has inhibited such understanding. If the necessity for more effective casework techniques had been squarely faced instead of being denigrated, the chances are that they would have been developed.

This is not in turn to denigrate Shaw's recipe for prevention. Its great virtue lay in just that aspect of sociological theory which he failed to recognize. This was the stressful and demoralizing effect of wresting people away from their circle of family and friends who can help them in emergencies but who also expect certain standards of conduct. A good example of the removal of such community sanctions was afforded by the Martin family, which was the subject of Shaw's book, *Brothers in Crime* (1938). In his home village in the old country, the father had been a moderate drinker. When he and his family came to Chicago, their only relative was the mother's half-brother, who lived on the other side of the city. For four years they must have maintained fairly frequent contact with him, since they paid off the passage money he had lent them, by installments. During this time Mr. Martin stayed off drink entirely. Apart from any personal influence which his half-brother-in-law may have had on him, he must have realized that the latter was in communication with people in their native village. From the day of the redemption of the debt and the cessation of regular contact, Mr. Martin took to drink, and—as suggested in the discussion of their case in Chapter Two—his persistent drunkenness was the prime cause of his sons' delinquencies.

In stimulating the growth of new social institutions within the disorganized immigrant areas, the Chicago Area Project would have done more than strengthen the parents' control of their children. It would have laid the foundations for a new framework of sanctions against bad behavior and demoralization which would have buttressed the standards of the older generation. Consequently, Shaw's model for intervention, which aimed to foster the growth of new organs of community action and new friendship structures within the disorganized localities, must be regarded as a fundamental—one might say, the most fundamental—strategy for delinquency prevention, even though he arrived at it from quite different premises.

A comprehensive prevention program should therefore aim both to strengthen the local community life in order to provide vehicles for the formation and expression of a public opinion in the direction of law and order, and also to provide services of family support and individual guidance. The project described by Tefferteller (1959) and discussed in Chapter Thirteen seems to provide a promising model for this two-pronged approach.

THE RECKLESS-DINITZ SELF-CONCEPT EXPERIMENT

It has been seen that one of the weaknesses of the sociological theory formulated by the Chicago group was that it failed to explain adequately how the undoubted fact of cultural disintegration affected the young generation and impelled its members towards delinquency. Reckless and Dinitz (1972) posited poor self-concept as the explanatory link. Unlike Shaw and McKay, they recognized the prevalence of family problems within the disorganized areas and the troublesome behavior to which they gave rise. What was needed to counteract this disintegration, they argued, was to provide inner-city youth with models of behavior which they would follow and on which they would build a better self-concept. The inner strengths that they would develop in so doing would then enable them to withstand the "happenstances" of their families, neighborhood, and friends. In other words, they would learn to see as unworthy of themselves the thieving, cheating, embezzlement, drug abuse, alcoholism, and other moral and legal lapses endemic in their communities.

To test this hypothesis Reckless and Dinitz formed experimental and control groups of seventh-grade (12–13-year-old) boys, half of whom had been nominated by their teachers as heading for trouble, amounting in all to 1,726. The adults whom the boys were to model themselves upon were their teachers. The latter gave them role-model lessons around the themes of the worlds of work, school, government, family, and personal relationships. Classroom discipline was centered on the concept of the rights of others. Boys who violated the code had to sit outside the classroom door until they felt ready to return and conform; they were never sent to the principal's office, because the goal was to develop in them a sense of responsibility for their own conduct.

At the end of the year, and again three years later, the effects of the training were measured by the number of police contacts, the drop-out and attendance rates, and school achievement. There were no significant differences in any of these outcome variables between the treated and the untreated groups. Reckless and Dinitz attributed this disconfirmation of their self-concept theory to the inadequacy of the training: the "medicine," as they put it, was not strong enough (p. 156).

Curiously, they do not consider the possibility that their original diagnosis was incorrect and that they applied the wrong medicine. Poor perception of the self is undoubtedly typical of delinquent youngsters, but, as I have argued elsewhere in this book, it seems to arise from feelings of not being cherished within their families. It is difficult for a boy to have adequate feelings of self-worth if those around him are neglecting him, favoring his brothers and sisters or threatening to throw him out of the home. In such cases a program designed to improve perception of the self by verbal encouragement and role playing is unlikely to have any effect. For the serious delinquent, who is constantly seeking means of diverting his mind from the traumatic insecurity of his family situation, such "training" would be grotesquely irrelevant. There is a further implication to this experiment: all the verbal exhortation to make amends that delinquent youngsters receive from judges and probation officers is similarly without effect.

Chapter Six
Recent Advances in Scottish Social Work

by Donald M. Wilson
Social Work Department, Strathclyde Region

There are many references throughout this book to changing attitudes and the inventiveness of practice on the North American continent. There has in recent years been rapid and substantial change in social work concepts in the United Kingdom and it is, perhaps, paradoxical that in Scotland, which has the most traditional of images, there has been the most radical and purposive change of all. In the field of child care (which would embrace the treatment of delinquency), the principles of change have been taken to their logical conclusion. The Probation Service has been integrated within the general structure of the Social Work Services, and, but for exceptional cases, children are no longer brought before the courts of criminal jurisdiction. It is therefore pertinent in a book of this kind to make references to these changes. There have been two milestones in the development of child-care services, which Scotland shared with England. The Probation of Offenders Act, at the turn of the century, introduced the concept of "noncustodial" care. The Children and Young Persons Act of 1937 (following the Morrison Committee Report of 1933) established the twin concepts of "care and protection" of children and the very important idea that children should be dealt with as far as possible in other than adult courts. This separation of juvenile and adult criminal proceedings was the forerunner of the present Children's Hearing System in Scotland. The Children and Young Persons Act (1937) provided for the setting up of juvenile courts which, while retaining the powers and jurisdiction of courts, were presided over by panels of three persons (normally drawn from the local community). The kernel of the concept was that these lay magistrates, being locally knowledgeable, not only would be better placed to interpret the individual needs of the child, but would be able to relate these needs to the immediately available local resources (perhaps a forerunner of present-day intermediate treatment facilities).

The Act of 1937 was in many ways "permissive" and was not fully implemented in Scotland. Nevertheless, by the implementation of the Juvenile Court (Procedure) Rules (1952) and other concomitant legislation, even greater informality was brought to juvenile procedures. Again forestalling the children's panels, the idea behind this legislation was not only to create more informality, but to simplify the language used in court and to enable parents and children to participate actively in the procedure.

By the 1950s three main themes were being actively argued: the effective separation of children from adult procedures; the effect of "labeling" on children as a result of their involvement in criminal proceedings; and the natural corollary to this, the measures for the prevention of delinquency or of progressive social maladjustment.

This summary of factors is important in the present context because the delinquency research on which this book is founded began in the mid-1950s, and it was therefore conditioned by the demands of the current situation. Notably, the Bristol Social Adjustment Guide used in these researches set out to *describe the condition* and not to *label the person*; it places emphasis on *prediction* and therefore the ability to *prevent*, and, most of all, it is concerned with the *totality of a child's needs* and recognizes the intrinsic individuality of each child, whether its behavioral patterns are conformist or not.

THE EFFECT OF CHANGE

As a result of these piecemeal developments, three distinct but often overlapping services had evolved; i.e., probation, child care, and general welfare. Because of the risk of duplication and the confused lines of demarcation, it was obviously important to reexamine their roles and how each one's scant resources might be effectively deployed. The Kilbrandon Report (1964) and the subsequent white paper made the first major reassessment and evaluation since the Poor Law Act of 1845, despite the occasional amendments which came in between and effectively separated and entrenched the three services.

Six general considerations were advanced by the government white paper, which summarized the recommendations of the Kilbrandon Report:

1. Some people with social problems cannot solve them without outside assistance and help.
2. Problem families often require advice and assistance in many directions. Consequently there was overlapping of services which dealt with only one particular aspect of the family's problem.
3. Referral of a family from one service to another caused bewilderment because of the restrictions on the functions and responsibilities of the separate services.
4. The basic skills of social work are generic; that is, common to all social workers. Specialized knowledge of one particular field is often helpful, but basically the skills and techniques are the same.
5. There was a limited number of trained social workers and, with several agencies operating, there was competition among the services for the available staff.
6. All the above meant difficulty in ensuring effective and economical deployment of workers throughout the social work field.

"In order to provide better services and to develop them economically it seems necessary that the local authorities designed to provide community care and support, whether for children, the handicapped, the mentally or physically ill or the aged, should be brought within a single organisation."

It was with these words that the white paper provided the background to the Social Work (Scotland) Act of 1968, which, when implemented in 1971, effectively created a comprehensive and unique social work service. A number of countries have elected to combine their family services and have joined the Children's Department with that of the General Welfare Department. Only Scotland has included the Probation Service and only Scotland has taken the logical step of creating a completely new and progressive channel for the total care, protection, and well-being of children.

The completely new structure of children's panels and reporter's departments was set up in April 1971 by way of implementation of the Social Work (Scotland) Act of 1968. Expectations about what the regional organizations can provide in the way of service have often outstripped their capacity to respond adequately. There have been acute staff shortages, inadequate training facilities, and problems of priority to overcome, so that by the very nature of things there have been disappointments and apparent lack of achievement. In the

middle of this period the structure of local authority was completely remodeled on a broad regional basis, and although this may not have affected the field worker, it certainly placed differing demands on management and no doubt brought unwelcome interruption of many policies which had been carefully worked out. Nor has the major act of 1968 been the final and definitive statement, for there has been a further proliferation of bills and policy statements on a whole range of social work matters (e.g., homeless families, community service facilities for intermediate treatment, and so on), and all of these have to be absorbed and adjusted to, in a period when it might have been difficult enough to make steady progress. Perhaps the sign of success is that, despite many criticisms by disenchanted organizations and persons, the service is gaining respect and the field workers themselves are in the forefront of demanding higher standards of professional practice.

THE PANEL SYSTEM

Two features of the new social-work organization are relevant to the theme of this book. The heading for Part III of the Act was "The Provision of Compulsory Measures of Care," and this provided for the setting up of children's panels and the concomitant machinery and organization for servicing them. Under this part also, the Juvenile Court was abolished, although all appeals against decisions of the Children's Panel are still subject to proof in the Sheriff Court. The term *compuslory measures* may sound rather ominous and even reminiscent of a punitive approach, and so it is important to understand that it was a carefully chosen phrase intended to cover the needs of all children whose behavioral condition or circumstances gave rise to concern. It was not intended specifically for juvenile delinquents, but embraced persistent truants, children in "moral danger," or those who were simply caught up in some family problem such as parental disunity or bad housing—in other words, any child whose personal or social well-being was in jeopardy. Although referrals still tend to be made by the established organizations such as police and schools, it is a principle that *any person* who has reason for concern can advise the Reporter to the Children's Panel. For the purpose of the Act, a child is any person under the age of 16 (or under 18, if currently subject to a "supervision requirement"). Although a criminal prosecution can still be brought against a child "where it is in the public interest," permission to do so must first be obtained from the Lord Advocate, and no court can *sentence* a child or supervised person without first seeking the advice of the Children's Panel.

During the eight years since the setting up of this structure in 1971 there has been no substantial or empirical research evaluation of the effects of the new procedures. It is brilliantly described by Martin and Murray (1976), and they are themselves currently engaged in a major evaluation. The structure has survived many of the doubts and uncertainties with which it was earlier viewed, among which was the feeling that it was "a soft option." Indeed, it may well have been, as a result of such pressure that recently (see Hansard, Feb. 14, 1979) the Secretary of State for Scotland, replying to questions in Parliament, seemed to imply that he was willing to consider extending the powers of the children's panels along what might be considered "judicial" lines. It would be a great pity if they were allowed to regress to a purely judicial process and thereby possibly lose their special and particular feature of being *a diagnostic and therapeutic agency*.

For those who are not already knowledgeable about the system, a brief description is appropriate. Only a very brief note is possible in this context, but readers are referred again to Martin and Murray (1976); also to J. H. Curran's (1977) *The Children's Hearing System: A review of research*, and, with particular reference to differences in social change, to Martin's paper to the Howard League for Penal Reform (1977), entitled "The Future of Juvenile Justice."

In brief, a children's panel consists of three "lay persons" selected from the community, who meet informally with a child and his parents in order to explore the problem which has been referred to them. The panel is served by a person called the Reporter, and his function is to decide, in the first instance, if the matter should be brought before the panel and, having so decided, to gather all the appropriate information concerning the case. This will normally mean obtaining reports from a social worker or other specialist, and the whole is presented to the panel members in advance of the actual hearing, so that mature consideration can be given to the various factors. At the hearing the chairman will disclose to the family the opinions that have been formed (without the child being present, if the matter is a delicate one) and there is then full participation, by all parties, in a discussion. At this point in time, the options open to the panel are limited. If some kind of formal intervention is indicated, the panel may refer the matter for voluntary intervention by the local social worker; may make a "requirement" for the child to be supervised, or may make a "residential requirement," which has the effect of placing the child in a List D (correctional) School. Essentially, however, the panel system is an exercise in family problem solving, and by stimulating the self-awareness of the parties involved, aims to achieve amelioration.

Figures for the referrals show that despite this ideal of cooperation with parents in order to solve family problems, the great majority of cases brought before the panels originate from the commission of an offense. Sixty-two percent of the referrals were made by the police and 26 percent by the prosecuting officer of the justice system; this compared with only 7 percent from education sources, 1 percent from child cruelty agencies, and a mere 0.4 percent from the parents themselves.

The system is gaining in respect and the principles are accepted as basically sound. Nevertheless there are major areas of concern, and these are mainly in the direction of training and resource. The panel members are initially selected from applicants who display an active interest in voluntary service and who, in their qualities of intelligence, perception, and life experience, are likely to be successful in this kind of work. The training of these good people is informal and consists of a few tutorials and some visits of observation; essentially, however, they are expected to "learn on the job," and the problem is that, after some three years' service (and just when they are developing some expertise), they are expected to "retire." The community can be justly proud of these selfless people, and one would not wish, in any way, to denigrate the excellent work they achieve; nevertheless, it is surely arguable that the most important function of a panel member is that of *diagnostic assessment* and that this calls for very particular skills in analysis, in decision making and interviewing techniques, none of which are quickly or easily achieved.

The reporters themselves are not outside this area of criticism, although perhaps for different reasons. By the very nature of their appointment reporters are drawn from the ranks of professionally trained social workers, with a leavening of legally qualified solicitors, so that they are normally equipped with the formal qualifications for the job. Unfortunately, they are expected to make immediate decisions on a great multitude of child problems referred to them daily, and not infrequently these decisions have to be based on the presenting factors and often without the opportunity for any in-depth investigation. The problem here seems to be that there is a lack of specific criteria for assessment. Although the reporter may be relied on to make an honest and reasonable assessment in the light of circumstances, like the panel members, he is heavily dependent on the availability of their support structures, which inevitably means scarce social-work support,which reflects the inadequacy of training facilities.

From the early days, when training was indeed perfunctory, there has been an increasing awareness of its importance, and individual localities have set up their own informal training programs which are no doubt now developing a more definite structure and a distinctive body of knowledge and skills. There is, however, general agreement that training facilities need to be reviewed, and perhaps there is even some agreement that there is still some confusion about what, in particular, the staff (including panel members) need to know in order to achieve competence in their function. One hopes that such examples are rare, but one certainly hears of children referred to the panel being given the same old homily of exhortation to "be good" which is reminiscent of the Criminal Court proceedings. It was ineffective then and is as likely to be so still. Perhaps, then, one of the concepts which has to be learned is that if a child is capable of "being good" in the first instance, he would not be appearing before the panel. The problem is almost always one of a negative family dynamic, and the skill required is in analyzing the family dynamic in order to lay bare the negative factors. The expertise lies in the ability to recognize these factors.

It has been frankly admitted that many of the weaknesses of the panel system stem from the inadequacy of the social-work support, and this is such a complex situation in itself that just the bald statement of "inadequate resources" fails to describe the many intricacies of the problem. The major challenge which any comparatively new organization has to face is often the level of other people's expectations and the consequent danger that it will take on just one more little burden. Of course there is a breaking point, and social workers who, in the nature of things, are always under pressure, met this situation very early on. Staff resources are daily increasing, but the problem of workload was compounded by that of professional standards. As the demands on the social work departments escalated and social workers became less satisfied with their own ability to maintain good standards of casework, there came the debate on "priorities"; that is, the question was posed: If you cannot perform all the tasks expected of you and at the same time maintain job satisfaction and adequate standards of practice, what are the priorities? This is an ongoing debate because such decisions are bedeviled by attitudes, ideologies, and, not infrequently, political expediency. It has however, been a source of satisfaction to many that, while trying to maintain not less than a minimum service to other causes, most social workers have decided (officially, or otherwise) that child care, in its broadest context, should have priority. In some ways this had a spin-off effect on the Children's Hearings, except that the older child has not benefited so directly, since the young child is naturally seen as being most exposed to danger. By far the largest area of work for children's hearings is that of the school-age child, and it would be foolish to try to suggest that all the demands made by the reporter for social background information are met or that the expectations of panel members with regard to the level of support during periods of supervision is always satisfactory. The fact that social workers have made it a principle always to be in attendance (along with the client) at the hearings, despite the fact that it makes very great inroads on their time, means that there has been a growing together in the partnership.

INTERMEDIATE TREATMENT CENTERS

This sense of partnership between panel members and social workers has brought to the fore a need for some kind of treatment, intermediate between traditional supervision and committal to a residential institution. The motivating factors were, first, the demand by panel members for more options and a greater variety of facility when faced with a child who seemed to have a need which did not readily fit into any of the current options. Then, too, the social workers themselves felt considerably under pressure as the demands upon them increased and they found that the opportunity for interpersonal casework relationships was limited. They therefore sought a wider dispersal of facilities, as support mechanisms, in order to relieve the burden. Intermediate treatment centers seemed the answer to everyone's problem.

Intermediate treatment has been in existence, as a concept, for many years and has its origins in the penal field, where the idea of something "in between" led originally to probation treatment. An extension of this was that the purpose of probation (as in the case of the original youth organizations, Boy Scouts, and the like) was that those involved should be directed into purposive pursuits, have their innate strengths developed, and be given the opportunity for productive self-expression. All this is very laudable if there is not much wrong with the youngster in the first instance. As a long-serving member of both the Probation Service and the Boy Scouts, I do not seek to minimize the value of the contribution made by these organizations. But treatment is dependent on what one is being treated for. The concept that all one needs is opportunity and encouragement to "do the right thing" may be all right for some children, but it fails to recognize the most important fact: children with individual problems require individual treatment.

It is natural that the immediate response in a departmentally structured organization is to set up yet another subdivision or department, and so in the early days of trying to provide this facility almost all social work departments throughout the country set up centralized intermediate treatment centers, to which children could be referred (and transported from the locally based social-work unit). In many ways this was a useful period of experimentation, and there are many examples of exceptionally fine pioneer work. It also had the useful effect of providing an additional service to the panels and removing one more burden from the harassed local social worker. Once again the motivation was part expediency, part an attempt to meet a need, but this need was seen in terms of traditional concepts; i.e., the provision of constructive play therapies.

There was one other aspect of the new Social Work Act which gave additional impetus to the term *intermediate*. Prior thereto, remand homes were provided in each local jurisdiction for the purpose of offering "secure conditions" for children appearing before the court, and for the additional purposes of detention as a form of punishment, or as a holding center for children committed to a correctional school and awaiting conveyance or vacancy. With the implementation of the new social-work legislation, remand homes were renamed *assessment* centers. To some extent they had to continue to act as a place of *security* because children do still sometimes require to be "restrained." But as the new act uses the term *Place of Safety*, the Local Authority Social Work Department can allocate any of its children's homes to this purpose, the special emphasis laid upon the remand home being that it should develop particular facilities for the assessment of children appearing before the Children's Panel. In Glasgow, this meant an enlargement of existing facilities. The remand home had indeed always been able to provide useful assessments for the Courts and Probation Service, but only when a child was already in custody. It was therefore now necessary to create provision for children to attend on a daily basis, have their schooling continue, and be offered interesting opportunities for self-expression, so that experienced staff could effectively use these periods for the collection of data on which to prepare assessment reports. Since the opportunity then existed for the referral of children appearing at the hearings, it was logical to extend this service to the whole social work department, for use by team workers who had children on whom they needed further evaluation or who they thought would benefit from the experience.

From such incentives—a statutory obligation, a resource for the panels, and a support for field workers—grew the present-day proliferation of intermediate treatment center projects. A list of these "official centers" is obtainable from a data bank maintained by the Scottish Federation of Boys' Clubs for the whole country, although each local authority will provide its own and develop its own policy and priorities. It is interesting, however, that the traditional voluntary organizations are so closely identified with the concept. Some of the older and established voluntary organizations have indeed developed very sophisticated techniques and facilities for child assessment. Nevertheless, it is worth noting that there is still very much an association of ideas between intermediate treatment and "play or leisure" activities, while *assessment* has been almost a by-product.

Recently, the emphasis has shifted to the provision of locally based facilities, usually within a team setting. In this way, not only can there be an ongoing continuity of contact with the social worker, who is also identified as the one visiting the home, but the child is not displaced and perhaps isolated in strange surroundings. The success of these locally inspired facilities is being daily demonstrated; at least one Glasgow social worker has had evidence of apparent amelioration in every case referred to him in the last two years, and the reporter and chairman of the local panel have placed this on record. One of the features of this local provision is the close relationship maintained with the parents, who become actively involved (not unlike a nursery playgroup situation), so that interpersonal family relationships are vastly improved and the purpose of the Children's Panel is realized (that is, to assist a family with problems to become aware and self-determined in problem solving). Intermediate treatment is therefore a logical and natural extension of the concept of interpersonal relationship therapy.

Of the formal intermediate treatment center projects there is very great variety, reflecting not only the local demands made upon them but the initiative of the staff in charge and the backing it is able to get from management in terms of resource allocation. In a few areas the development plans have progressed little further than the paper stage, and although this may in some cases reflect a lack of urgency, it is also a reflection of the rapidity of social change and the perception of local needs, whereby those involved have been overtaken by events and possibly by the realization that, in given circumstances, the centralization of resources is not always appropriate.

All these centers have similar goals; namely, to provide a comprehensive and productive leisure facility which, it is hoped, will become the setting for a general improvement in local morale. While this is an entirely laudable and worthwhile social service to a community, in terms of this book the question is where, and if, it can be demonstrated that these facilities are having an effect on the problem of delinquency. It has to be admitted that intermediate treatment exists more in the form of plans and proposals than as operating programs. Pioneer projects do, however, exist, and as an example of them can be cited that at Greenock, a semi-industrial community with a degree of multiple deprivation, some 20 miles from Glasgow. Between 1975, when it commenced work, and 1978, it has provided facilities for 117 young people, 80 percent of whom were the subject of compulsory supervision orders. There has been a very satisfactory average attendance of 85 percent. During their period of membership, 20 (17 percent) were known to have committed an offense, and 12 (10 percent) were sent for residential treatment. Considering that the area served by the center was registered for priority treatment as a disadvantaged area, this seems to be a below-average rate of relapse. Perhaps the most encouraging index of success was that the absence rates of those attending school was reduced from 55 to 20 percent, and there was also an improvement in their punctuality. Needless to say, these results as reported do not amount to scientific evaluation of the effects of intermediate treatment. It would probably be unwise to initiate such formal evaluations until the concept is buttressed by the development of improved social-work techniques for the diagnosis and treatment of family problems.

PART THREE
Understanding Delinquent Behavior

Chapter Seven
Delinquent States of Mind

THE APPARENT IRRATIONALITY OF DELINQUENCY

Our first aim in diagnosis should be to understand the compulsions which drive some children, against their own interests, to delinquency. It is a matter of studying the nature of the delinquent act and trying to understand the state of mind in which it is committed. In cases of serious and continued delinquency the existence of some irrational compulsion becomes evident when the little that the typical delinquent can gain is balanced against what he loses. But to stop at a designation of the irrationality of delinquency is of little help, and indeed—as argued in a later chapter—may induce attitudes of helplessness and pessimism. We have to try to understand the rationale behind the apparently irrational act—what advantage, in short, the delinquent hopes to get from his lawbreaking.

Whyte's (1957) motivational principle, that in general people must be presumed to intend the consequences of their behavior, serves as a baseline postulate in seeking insight into the motivation of delinquency. For example, if an illegal act is committed in a way that invites detection, we have to assume that the offender, being of generally normal mentality, intended, consciously or otherwise, to get caught. Such an inference leads us to consider what motivation he may have had for the wish. At this stage of the diagnosis we have to limit ourselves to objective descriptions of events such as would stand up in a court of law. We have to be cautious about theory-based interpretations such as "guilt feelings" or the "inferiority complex," accepting them only if they are supported by incontrovertible evidence. It was this principle that I followed in making a classification of the immediate movitations of the offenses of 102 delinquent youths consecutively committed to what was then called an approved school, reported in *Delinquency and Human Nature* (Stott, 1950/80). Five immediate motivations that constitute delinquent states of mind were identified. These are discussed below in order of their frequency.

THE IMPULSE TO REMOVAL

The most frequent motivation—present in 55 of the cases—was that of securing physical removal from an emotionally stressful home situation by getting committed to a residential school. The key indicator for this motivation is that the young person not only takes no precautions against getting caught (which could be owing to the thoughtlessness of the inconsequent child described below), but makes quite certain that he will be. Examples cited are of a youth who stole a bicycle and, instead of getting it out of the locality or out of sight as quickly as possible, rode it around until he was picked up by the police; a youth who illegally drove off a car, but, not being picked up, drove it back to the place whence he had taken it and waited to be arrested; a youth who, not being able to drive, tried to push a car away; and a youth who broke into his employer's shop the very night after his dismissal. Further instances were of boys who stole from their own homes and then ran away, this action being associated with the motive of hostility, mentioned later in the chapter. It is not uncommon for a juvenile to commit a further offense of a flagrant and obvious character during the few days between his arrest and his court appearance, as if to make doubly sure of his removal.

In a few cases the motive to secure removal is deliberate, and openly admitted. Thirteen-year-old Mary (Stott, 1966), during a phase of acute antagonism between herself and her mother, came to the school welfare officer, saying she wanted to leave home; if she were not taken away, she said, she would steal something from a shop and get put away! In her case the urge to removal was that during flare-ups with her mother, who had evidently threatened to have her removed from the home, the girl had become convinced that her mother was intent on getting rid of her. In fact she did not need to resort to delinquency owing to the intervention of the school welfare officer. No doubt she was in the midst of one of those phases of emotional turmoil that girls often go through at puberty, and her threat of delinquency was a gesture made during a period of temporary stress.

Where the young person is faced with family stresses with which he cannot cope, such as arise from a real danger to continued membership in his family or from fears about its continued existence, he can seldom admit his urge to secure removal. He may be torn between staying at home, perhaps to stop his mother from deserting or to protect her from a violent father, and an instinctive impulse to shun the source of stress. Because both courses of action are equally unbearable, he cannot face either consciously, and reveals his urge to escape only by his actions and his fantasies. In Freudian terms he represses the unwelcome thoughts. I would prefer the formulation that they are blocked from consciousness by an avoidance mechanism. Subsequently, when removed from the intolerable stress, the young person may introspect that he did not care whether or not he was caught.

The urge to removal as a motivation to delinquency should be corroborated by evidence of a similar motivation in nondelinquent behaviors. Usually, it is found that the young person has vainly attempted to secure removal by more normal and personally less damaging means, such as by trying to get into the armed forces or the merchant navy. A one-time fashionable counterpart was running away from home and finding a hippy refuge. Many attempts at removal may be quite unrealistic, or stop short at the level of wish-fulfillment, coupled with which are fantasies such as joining a traveling fair. Analogous to the impulse to removal are ruses to avoid returning to the emotionally stressful home. In a committal institution a normally well-behaved boy may commit breaches of discipline just before the date of his discharge in order to postpone it. (Cases illustrative of removal as a motivation to delinquency:* Round, p. 56; Sidley, p. 64; Elson, p. 66; Watson, p. 129; Percival, p. 136; Sharp, p. 194; Tylor, p. 251; Ross, p. 262).

AVOIDANCE-EXCITEMENT

The next most frequent motivation, present in 53 cases, was that of avoidance-excitement. The youth throws himself into a hectic round of attention-filling activities which have the effect of preventing distressing memories from reaching consciousness. Typically, he makes for the amusement arcades and billiard halls of a city. There, he becomes acquainted with other youths suffering from similar compulsions. To them, breaking into premises, taking part in hold-ups, and other high-risk forms of crime offer excellent excitement-generating possibilities.

In these avoidance-excitement cases it is not difficult to find corroborative evidence of this motivation in everyday life, because the need for substitutive attention-filling and anxiety-blocking

*Case-references in this chapter are to Stott (1950/80) unless otherwise stated.

activities is unrelenting, and dominates the whole of the young person's waking existence. There is a constant search for intense physical sensations involving movement, noise, and danger. The affected individual develops an abhorrence of sameness in physical surroundings and of any period of quiet during which his anxieties may force themselves into his consciousness. Consequently, he finds confinement within the walls of a classroom or workshop intolerable, and is impatient of any "finicky" job requiring concentration. If he is of school age he usually becomes a truant; if of working age he seeks an active outdoor job requiring little skill. Lying awake in bed is by its nature intolerable to him: the typical anxiety avoider finds refuge in sleep as soon as his head touches the pillow, and gets up as soon as he awakens.

Usually the focus of the avoidance is some traumatic event which serves as a reminder of the child's unfortunate family situation. This is exemplified by the case of *Stanley*, reported in *Studies of Troublesome Children* (Stott, 1966). His delinquency began when a younger brother was killed by a van outside the family's house. The mother, who saw the dead child soon after the accident, was badly affected and suffered what was virtually a nervous breakdown. She became intolerant of the boy and several times demanded of the school welfare officer that he be removed. He truanted regularly from school, and with a gang made excursions to distant places, committing minor delinquencies on the way. He could never stay a moment in his own home, even when he managed to avoid school with the excuse of a sore eye or similar incapacity. If, when running past a shop and some emergence of his anxiety presumably threatened, he would dive in and grab something. In a residential school, away from reminders of his insecurity, he seemed happy, with no yearning for travel. But he had nightmares of seeing a "green lady" (public health nurse) walking across the room. No doubt the public health nurse had frequent occasion to call following the accident in view of the mother's state and her numerous young children.

The motivation of avoidance-excitement may be responsible for a range of wanton pranks and abnormal behavior. *Harry*, a normally demure seven-year-old boy, would periodically, without provocation, fly at his teacher and bite her. His father was in prison for assaulting his mother. From there the father wrote letters to his own mother describing the beatings he was going to give his wife when he came out. The boy's grandmother then called on the mother and read out the threats in front of Harry. Corroboration was obtained from a moment of dreamy, absent-minded introspection that this was the memory welling up in the boy's mind which had to be dealt with by violent substitutive behavior.

A more extreme case was that of *Neil*. He resorted not only to grossly abnormal behavior but also to persistent delinquency as a means of mentally blocking the memory of the loss of his mother, who had died of cancer when he was 6. After her death the father went out drinking every night, leaving the children unattended. Three years later he remarried, but the boy refused to accept his stepmother, although she was a warm-hearted woman who was patient and tried her best with him. Even before he was of an age to be charged in court, he took to housebreaking, and received his first conviction for this offense at the age of 10. When he was 12, while playing truant, the police caught him throwing bottles at passing cars. He did not come home that evening, and his step-mother, going out to search for him, found him after midnight, soaking wet, huddled on a refuse heap. He was later charged with willful cruelty to a pigeon.

How abnormal Neil's behavior became under the compulsion to blot out a traumatic memory is illustrated by an incident that occurred when he was somewhat younger. While his stepmother was putting him to bed he asked to go to the toilet; half an hour later he was brought back by the police, having been found wandering in a public park. The unconscious avoidance remained active six years after the death of his mother: asked if he ever thought of her, his face crumpled up just as if he might cry, but without apparent emotion, and he said, "There is too much to do, there's no time to think." It would be difficult to obtain a clearer introspection of the search for incessant activity as a means of filling every spare moment of thinking time to prevent the traumatic memory from coming into consciousness.

The behavior of both Neil and Harry was stable and normal apart from crazy episodes. For understandable reasons Harry had been on bad terms with his class teacher, but in a remedial group he showed admirable powers of concentration and a determination to learn to read, so that within a year he was reading at two years above his age level. Removed to a foster home, his crazy outbursts, including the biting, ceased. Neil was described by his stepmother as a very good boy in the house. Similarly, at school he presented no disciplinary problem, and indeed his conduct was reported to be excellent. This was confirmed by his low score on the Bristol Social Adjustment Guide; the only adverse items were his truancy, damage to public property, and a certain distance from teachers, who noted that he said very little and seldom smiled. A report from a remand home ran as follows:

> During his stay here he kept himself clean and tidy. His relationships with the staff were good and he created a very favorable impression. He was amenable to discipline and generally helpful and eager to please. Full of life, he is continually on the go and always on the look-out for adventure (sic). In class he was the same brisk, bright little boy causing no trouble whatever. He worked well within his capabilities and could be relied on to do his work without constant driving.

Nevertheless, a year after his release from the period of detention in the remand home he was committed to a residential school, for theft.

If crazy outbursts superimposed on a stable personality, such as those of Harry and Neil, are not recognized as extreme devices for the avoidance of unbearable memories, they can be misdiagnosed as indications of incipient psychosis. Our committal institutions for juveniles harbor many such children who—away from the reminders of their tragic home situation—show themselves as so well-adjusted that the staff cannot understand why they ever got into trouble. But like Neil, once back among their troubles, they revert to their former pattern of avoidance, and they are soon recommitted.

Some children in the grip of pathological avoidance achieve the "repression" by attention-filling fantasies rather than by incessant activity. These are of such a realistic and detailed character, having been worked over time and again, that the fantasizer almost comes to believe them himself, and may relate them so convincingly as to deceive experienced social workers (see the case of Collins). If the fantasies are sufficiently effective in keeping the unwanted memories at bay, the child may sit quietly in class, without any signs of hyper-activity, and thus appear to negate the symptoms of avoidance-excitement. In using school behavior to estimate the extent to which delinquents are maladjusted, it has to be borne in mind that even grossly abnormal behavior can be specific to a particular stimulus-situation. (Cases illustrative of avoidance-excitement: Collins, p. 14; Blight, p. 28; East, p. 41; Nichols, p. 61; Langford, p. 62; Norman, p. 73; Banks, p. 155; Mills, p. 177; Rogers, p. 187.)

HOSTILITY

The third major delinquent motive, identified in 42 cases out of the series of 102, is hostility. It arises from the young person's becoming convinced that his parents are prepared to abandon him or get him removed from their home. A characteristic pattern of delinquency is generated, the motivation of which is to "go to the bad" and commit acts so unacceptable and likely to antagonize his parents that he makes his banishment from home inevitable. These usually begin with stealing within the family or from friends of the parents, and committing acts of destructiveness such as fire-setting or mutilating yards. The older youth will be likely to run away and embark upon a compulsive round of destructive delinquency, stealing cars and smashing them, robbing churches, and so on—all of which lasts a few days, until he is caught. While he does not usually commit obvious crimes which invite detection (for which he has not the calmness of thought) he takes few precautions, because the offenses are aimed at his parents as acts of resentment

Nondelinquent corroborative evidence of this hostility-instigated delinquency is found, first, in the young person's attitudes to those who are (or should be) nearest and dearest to him. They usually take the form of a combination of moods. One of these is "bloody-mindedness," when the child sets out to be as objectionable as possible. The other mood is a withdrawing sullenness, with refusal of any endearment or offer of friendship. It seems to depend upon the child's temperament or his circumstances whether the one or the other aspect of hostility is dominant, but both are found in varying degrees in a severely hostile child. Hostility is something more than aggressive, or acting-out behavior. A person may react aggressively to frustration. This is a manifestation of a primitive attack-response which comes into play when the person feels that he is in a position to attack the object of his frustration. (If he is not powerful enough to do so, his instinctive response is to escape.) This attack response can spill over onto any weaker object that happens to be near at the time. People resort to these attack responses more readily when they are tired or otherwise stressed, the violence of the reaction determining whether it takes the form of mere irritability or of dangerous physical attack, such as occurs in cases of child abuse. Again, aggressiveness can be a form of dominance: a more powerful individual bullies a weaker; that is to say, gets a feeling of self-enhancement from demonstrating his power and causing discomfiture.

Hostility on the other hand, has the purpose of destroying a love relationship which has proved unreliable, seen at its most intense in the fury of the jilted lover. Its value in human life is that it enables the rejected one to cut clear of an emotional attachment and to start afresh with a more promising partner. Love is killed by turning it into hate. Similarly, the hostile child goes out of his way to be hated, making himself as unattractive as he can and committing wanton acts calculated to arouse anger. He utilizes the attack response in whatever ways he can, but because he is usually not so strong physically as the adults against whom he is resentful, he also resorts to escape as a means of severing the love relationship. Thus, hostility is also a self-banishing reaction. The hostile child runs away from home, sometimes stealing the family's savings or committing some other unforgivable act. In extreme cases hostility becomes an all-pervasive emotional state, expressed against all adults because the child does not want friendship from anyone. The hostile child can consequently be identified by his behavior in school. (Cases illustrative of hostility: Martin, p. 257; Faulkner, p. 274; Newman, p. 288; Leggett, p. 291; Batchelor, p. 308; Field, p. 322; Brook, p. 338; Woodman, p. 341.)

LOYALTY TESTING

The fourth type of motivation arises from the same undermining of family security that generates hostility, but more specifically from the parental threat of disownment or "putting away" if the young person commits any further delinquencies. Before losing faith in the loyalty of the parent who utters this threat, and hence reverting to hostility, he first applies a loyalty test, in the form of the deliberate commission of a further offense. This loyalty-testing motive was recognized in 22 cases. Needless to say, many young people are able to shrug off such threats, or to heed them and desist from the delinquency. Some children—no doubt those who are anxiety-prone—take them too seriously, and cannot tolerate any doubts about their parents' ultimate loyalty. (Cases illustrative of loyalty-testing: Firth, p. 133; Weston, p. 242; Martin, p. 257; Hammond, p. 313.)

BRAVADO (FEAR COMPENSATION)

The fifth motivation is generally seen as bravado, and this word serves as a convenient name for it, without of course explaining the origin of the state of mind behind such behavior. A youth whose thoughts at the time may be far removed from deviance meets a friend who suggests the two of them break in somewhere or take a joy ride in a car. When the first youth demurs, the other taunts him with being a coward, an accusation which he cannot let pass, and he yields to the delinquent invitation. To use a favorite phrase of the

probation officer, he is an "easily led" type. A variant on the bravado theme is that the youth wants to play big with his mates, and
may get in with an older, free-spending group. He urgently needs
money in order to keep up with them or to impress others of his
own age, and so he steals—possibly from his own home—to obtain it.

It would amount to a renunciation of the quest for understanding to stop at the point of saying that such delinquencies were
merely a matter of human weakness. The youths of the type just
described—for example, Searle, Grey, Whitehead, and Eliot—were
by no means weak personalities; on occasions they were capable of
saving their money and becoming hard workers. But they showed a
group of traits, consistent with their delinquency, of showing off,
bragging, pugnacity, truculence, and —strangely—intense fears. It
became apparent that the bravado of their sort had its origin in an
attempt to compensate for a sense of inferiority derived at least in
part from the realization that at heart they *were* cowards. Whence,
then, these fears? Investigation of the cases revealed that they were
generalized and transferred fears of some element of insecurity in
their family situations, often rendered more acute by frightening
experiences in their earlier lives. Many developed a further sense of
inferiority from their doubts about their parents' concern for them.
A large part of a child's self-esteem must derive from the knowledge
of being cherished by his parents. If he is deprived of such security
by feeling himself rejected or hearing his mother threaten to desert
the family, it is to be expected that his self-concept suffers and that
he feels unwanted and inferior. Thus, even when his insecurity does
not induce generalized fears which have to be denied by acts of
bravado, the sense of inferiority may produce similar reactions. The
intense fear reactions would reveal themselves when the youth was
taken unaware, such as by the sight of blood on cutting a finger, or
on a visit to the dentist, when he did not have to pretend to be brave
before his buddies, or by his dread of thunder or of the dark. Those
in the bravado group were particularly prone to dreams of falling, of
being chased, of being attacked by snakes, and so on. In all, 21 of my
102 cases showed elements of this fear- and inferiority-compensation,
but it was never the sole motivation of their delinquencies. They
reacted to the insecure family situations which were the fundamental
cause of their fears and inferiorities also by avoidance-excitement,
bids for removal, and loyalty testing.

(Cases illustrative of bravado: Searle, p. 81; Grey, p. 91; Whitehead, p. 97; Eliot, p. 105; Stone, p. 114; Dunn, p. 125; Watson,
p. 129.)

INCONSEQUENCE

Impulsiveness—that is to say, a tendency to act without considering the consequences—is not included among the delinquent motivations already described, although it is a form of behavior disturbance associated with delinquency. There is evidence that at least some inconsequence, as I term this pathological lack of foresight, is congenital (meaning that it originates at or before birth). Apart from being between five and six times more prevalent among boys than among girls, it is much more closely associated with motor impairment than any other form of maladjustment (Stott, 1978b; Stott, Marston, and Neill, 1975); and performance on the test in question (Stott, Moyes, and Henderson, 1972) has recently been found to correlate closely with signs of neurological damage in the first year of life (Drillien, Thompson, and Burgoyne, 1980). Inconsequence must therefore be considered as making the affected child vulnerable to the conditions which are conducive to delinquency.

Many inconsequent children will get involved thoughtlessly in minor delinquent escapades. They fail to internalize the warnings their parents give them and have to learn the hard way, by experience; but their fundamental loyalties to their parents hold them back from serious delinquency.

The chief danger is that severely inconsequent children present problems of rearing and discipline from an early age which may exceed the parents' reserves of tolerance. The latter react to the source of stress by rejection, which in turn generates hostility in the child, so that a vicious circle of worsening family relationships develops (Eisenberg, 1964). The process is exemplified in the replies of parents of learning-disabled children to a questionnaire given to them by Minden (1978). They had earlier told him that what they most needed in dealing with their children was patience. In a follow-up questionnaire Minden asked them what they meant by this, and they described their reactions to their children's troublesome behavior in these terms (p. 11):

(1)   I get angry and frustrated so I hit him.
(2)   I get fed up and I yell and scream at him.
(3)   I just walk away—I just can't stand to argue with him.
(4)   I send him to his room without supper.
(5)   I'm mad at everyone and everything and my husband gets it and so do the other kids.
(6)   I begin to eat and eat and destroy myself.

(7)   I wish he were not mine and sometimes I pretend he isn't when he embarrasses me.

We see in these reactions a mixture of aggression and avoidance, and a reversion to indiscriminate attack-behavior which is vented on other members of the family. This is an aspect of the irritable-depressive nontolerance I shall discuss later as one of the characteristics of maladjustment- and delinquency-conducive parent-child relationships. Finally we see rejection expressed as a wishful denial of parenthood.

In my experience the child remains at the stage of being a "pure" inconsequent only if his parents have unusually good emotional stamina and reserves of patience. When a score for inconsequence on the Bristol Social Adjustment Guide (Stott and Marston, 1970) is accompanied by significant hostility, it can be reckoned that one or both parents have reached the stage of rejection and have destroyed the child's confidence in their loyalty to him by threats of desertion or having him put away.

Lack of foresight, in the sense that they disregarded their own best interests and the feelings of their parents, was a feature of the great majority of my sample of delinquent youths, and Roper (1951) has named it as characteristic of adult criminals. Whereas some members of both these groups may have been inconsequents by temperament, the probability is that their lack of foresight was in the main owing to their being dominated by the compulsive motivations described in this chapter. That is to say, normal thinking ahead was inhibited in favor of some need to escape from an emotionally intolerable situation or the memory thereof.

COMBINATIONS OF MOTIVES

The numbers of the cases in which evidence for the foregoing motivations to delinquency was found add up to more than the total of 102 cases, because more than one motivation was usually observed in each individual. For example, nearly half the avoidance-excitement cases also showed an urge to remove themselves from the home. This is understandable, because both these motivations are forms of avoidance, the one mental, the other physical. On the other hand there was only a small overlap between avoidance-excitement and hostility, the latter being rather an attempt to break free from the stressful situation by inviting final rejection.

Because of its element of self-banishment, hostility was associated in the great majority of its cases with the urge to removal. Consequently, since removal was associated on the one hand with avoidance-excitement and on the other with hostility, it was a sole motivation to delinquency in comparatively few cases.

A full analysis of the aforementioned five motivations by cases is given in Stott (1950/80, pp. 352–355).

EXCEPTIONS TO THE FIVE MAJOR MOTIVATIONS

From the point of view of prevention it is important to know how many exceptions there may be to these five main motivations. Only 3 of the 102 boys studied showed none of them. One was not in fact an exception: in the original study (Stott 1950/80) the motivation of hostility appears as "Resentment against Parents," so that this boy, never having lived with his parents or any parent substitute, could not be included; but he showed very strong hostility against all the adults who had befriended him, and ended up with a psychiatric diagnosis of "moral defective."

The first of the two remaining exceptions, *Rodney*, got into trouble from his desire to be reunited with his mother. She had an emotional breakdown after having been deserted by her husband, and this evidently threw him also into a state of emotional upset, during which he committed petty delinquencies. One of these was stealing a sum of money by finding, which he gave to his mother. On being taken into the care of the local authority he repeatedly sneaked home and had to be taken away again. Hearing that he was not allowed to live with his mother because her house was not in a fit state, he stole some rugs to make it more presentable. Committed to a residential school, he saved money to pay for his mother to visit him. He was not so much a persistent delinquent as the victim of administrative mishandling.

The only offense of *Edkins*, the second exception, was an indecent assault upon an apparently not unwilling girl of 8 years. His father was not only in a state of paranoia but resorted to one malicious ruse after another to make the lives of his wife and children miserable; among these were his sexual adventures in the village where they lived. Evidently in her discouragement the mother planned to give up the home, and the boy evidenced acute anxiety on her behalf by the usual symptoms of continually wanting to do her housework for her. At the age of 11 the boy had been sent to a nautical school, no doubt to get him away from the impossible home situation, and it was not long after his return that he committed the offense. Incongruously, but typically of boys who have lost faith in their mothers, Edkins conceived a fantasy admiration for his father, and in his sexual misdemeanors might well have been following the paternal model.

SUBSIDIARY MOTIVES

In addition to the two cases just described, there were five more who were prompted by other motives. These were, however, subsidiary to the five major "delinquent states of mind," and so do not rank as exceptions.

Hill bragged about his father's stealing as a docker, and liked to give the impression that he was taking after him. This was one more case of a boy's conceiving a perverted admiration for a father who ill-treated his mother. The latter ran away repeatedly, and the boy revealed his anxiety about losing his mother by doing all sorts of jobs about the house and spending his pocket money on her. His hectic deviant activities, and the way in which he fantasized about his break-ins, marked him as a typical case of avoidance-excitement.

Huntley complained that his foster mother only wanted him for his wages, and gave preference to her own son. But this jealousy was part of a general attitude of being unjustly treated. He had lost his own mother at the age of two, then had to endure five years with a harsh stepmother. Thereafter, being an attractive boy, various people befriended him, but he tested their sincerity by delinquencies after the manner of the loyalty-testing which was one of the major delinquent motivations.

Salter's parents were ailing neurotics, and he took after them, a lack of motivation, whether for work or play, being the ruling principle of his life. His two younger brothers spurned him. Nevertheless, he took part in a break-in, with them acting as the burglars and him as the look-out. He ran off and left them to be caught, but the police were able to implicate him. He had been involved in an earlier delinquency with one of his brothers; it looked as if he were desperate for their companionship. Another boy in the series stole in order to be able to buy companionship with the proceeds. In neither case, however, was this a motive in its own right, but a reflection of general affectional deprivation. *Salter*'s mother was self-centered and wrapped up in her imaginary illnesses. She had actually taken him to court for his refusal to work but had failed to get an order of "Beyond Control" against him. Such affection as the boys had had was from their grandmothers. It was a case of the conflicting maternal attachments which constitute one of the maladjustment- and delinquency-conducive patterns I shall describe later. After his mother had taken him to court, Salter evidenced a strong removal urge, and became very upset when he was rejected first by the army and then by a nautical training school. There was no other way he could secure removal from home except by committal to a residential school, and so he easily fell in with his brothers' delinquent initiatives.

Bird was another neurotic, living with a similarly neurotic, self-centered mother who spent her life imposing on her two boys. They both developed a strong attachment to a grandmother, but the latter favored the elder brother and Bird became very jealous of him. He sensed that his parents preferred his elder brother also. His delinquencies began a year after the latter went to live with the grandmother. Possibly he thought that if he got into trouble it might be suggested that he go to live with her too. But his delinquencies were of a surreptitious character, defrauding his mother as well as his friends in order to recoup himself for being kept short of money. Thus, with an unconscious removal urge as his general state of mind, there was a mixture of subsidiary motives.

Mansly was a member of a family of migrant odd-jobbers who worked from door to door, the father doing upholstery and the mother chair-caning. But the father was constantly in and out of prison, and drank all his earnings while at liberty, forcing the mother to find the means for supporting her five children. They lived in filthy common lodging houses where they paid exorbitant rents. The boy had never known toys, nor had he any means of recreation, and so he broke into an office and stole some knick-knacks, which, apart from throwing a stone at a car, was his only delinquency. He had a touching loyalty towards his mother and was a great help to her in minding the younger children. Possibly his mother-anxiety got the better of him from time to time, or his petty delinquencies were the result of the total deprivation of any other source of fulfillment.

HOW GENERAL ARE THE FIVE
DELINQUENT STATES OF MIND

Of all the 102 youths studied, it could have been maintained of Mansly alone that he stole because he coveted the objects in question, and even he was by no means free of family worries. There was certainly no case of a boy entering the business of crime for gain—

but then there was in Britain at that time no organized crime with political connections on the Cloward-Ohlin model. In four cases I suspected that the thefts were condoned or encouraged by the parents, but this was a minor factor in a sea of family problems; in two of the cases the youth's state of mind was that of avoidance-excitement, in the third an urge to removal, and the fourth was the boy who stole a carpet to embellish his mother's home. As far as the "criminal subculture" was concerned, I came to the conclusion that it was a myth: in the few cases where both father and sons were convicted criminals there were acute family problems of a classic character under which the mother broke down (cf. *Rich*, in Stott, 1950/80).

The small number of the exceptions and of unclassified subsidiary motivations serves to highlight the generality of the five delinquent states of mind, at least among the persistent delinquents who were committed to a residential school in Britain during the years following the Second World War. How far they apply in other cultures and in other times will have to be established by investigation. At least they provide working hypotheses for a preventive program which are worth putting to the test, considering that the fundamental needs of children must everywhere be the same.

Chapter Eight
On Maladjustment and Normality

THE MYSTIQUE SURROUNDING MALADJUSTMENT

The idea that most young delinquents suffer from behavior disturbance creates apprehension and resistance. To many judges it seems to undermine the system, and in any case the children brought before them appear normal enough. The rationale of probation is that most probationers are normal youngsters capable of profiting from guidance. To admit that this is not so, and that the punishments meted out by the courts may be inappropriate forms of disposition in many if not most cases, is too much like handing the whole business over to the psychiatrists.

A mystique has grown up around maladjustment, which is reinforced by the fashionable but misleading term, *psychiatric disorder*. Strictly, this means a disorder of psychiatrists, as "canine disorder" is a disorder of dogs, but of course it is not meant that way. If it implies a disorder with which only psychiatrists can deal, it is a misnomer. Rutter (1973) found that nearly 12 percent of boys in a London borough had "psychiatric disorder" according to his scale. If this is true, the prospects will always be bleak for these maladjusted children, because in the forseeable future there will never be enough psychiatrists. The inescapable truth is that the greater part of the work of the probation officer and of the social worker accepting the supervision of young offenders has to do with maladjusted children. It is their duty to try to understand the emotional problems of these children and the situations which give rise to them.

Apprehension and misconception surrounding behavior disturbance lead to attempts to pass the buck. This happens especially with community-oriented social workers and the staffs of committal institutions, who anticipate that the typical young delinquent can be cured by providing him with fulfilling leisure opportunities and a stable human environment. Their disappointments only too often turn to rejection. One of the cases quoted in the account of the Hammersmith Teenage Project (NACRO, 1978b) serves as an example of rejection arising from unpreparedness and fear. A girl was referred by her social worker, mainly because she had been suspended from school for disruptive behavior, such as lighting fires in the toilets. She presented herself as disarmingly cheerful and as enthusiastic for the Project, but proved so troublesome tht she had to be committed to a residential institution. The Project team felt that the girl had been foisted on them without sufficient background information, when "we might have recognized we were dealing with a highly disturbed girl" (p. 20). One would have thought that the fire-setting in the toilets would have given them some inkling of this. Not only were they unprepared for maladjusted behavior, but the implication is that they would not have accepted the girl if they had known! Despite the time the Project workers spent with the girl, no systematic diagnosis was made of the causes of her maladjustment. From what little information was given about her background and crazy behavior, the chances are that she was a typical instance of avoidance-excitement. The buck was duly passed, as it is with thousands of young people under the sway of avoidance compulsions.

MALADJUSTMENT NOT ALWAYS WORN ON THE COAT SLEEVE

The workers in the Hammersmith Project were evidently deceived about this maladjusted girl owing to her cheerful and normal appearance. Many maladjusted children appear like that when there is nothing to trigger their tendencies toward antisocial or other inappropriate behavior. Behavior disturbance is not a constant condition like that of a chronic illness. The *vulnerability* to stress or temptation, and the consequent tendency to react in inappropriate ways, is usually an abiding condition; but only certain forms of maladjustment, such as severe hostility or depression, are constantly in evidence. Maladjustment consists in a tendency to react in an inappropriate manner *in particular circumstances*. When the stimulus which sets off the maladjusted response is absent, the individual behaves normally. Judges have little chance of observing some kinds of maladjusted behavior from their position on the bench. If a boy is given to bragging about his exploits and, when dared by his peers, feels he has to live up to his reputation, the judge does not hear the boasting. If a boy (cf. *Searle*, in Stott, 1950/80) suffers from an inability to consider consequences, so that he responds time after time to delinquent invitations, the judge cannot see the weakness because the court is not the sort of place where such temptations are present. Unless careful inquiry is made of the delinquent's life style, he will be accounted, from his behavior in court, as a normal young person.

Even a psychiatrist, as no less a one than John Bowlby (1944, p. 7) points out, cannot reliably detect maladjustment in an interview. In his experience,

> a large number of (maladjusted) children, perhaps half, at their interview appeared fairly normal. This impression is grossly misleading in a majority of cases and if taken seriously results in disastrously erroneous diagnosis. For this reason I habitually ignore my psychiatric interviews when no positive signs of disorder have been found and base my diagnosis on the reports of the mother and teacher.

If an experienced psychiatrist can be misled by an appearance of normality, how much more can the lay person!

We may further ask how often the bench receives reports from the mother and the teacher about the offender's behavior. A journalist monitoring the procedure of a London juvenile court (Phillips, 1978) found that each case took only a few minutes. The chairman did not believe in "prolonging the agony." The principal behavior on exhibition was his own, and he could have had no inkling of the mental or emotional state of the child offender.

OVERVIEW OF THE BEHAVIORAL SYSTEM

To gird himself against the mystique surrounding behavior disturbance the social worker needs a general theoretical understanding of the human behavioral system and how it can fall into a state of dysfunction. It is a matter of recognizing the forms of behavior disturbance which most often find expression in delinquency as aberrations of universal and normal modes of response. To understand how the normal can slip into the abnormal we have first to cast a view over the nature of behavior and its value for animal organisms. It was the ability to behave which has distinguished these from vegetable forms of life. Thereby they gained enormous advantages for survival. They could escape rather than wait about to be eaten, and move around to find food. They could seek and build shelter, find mates, and learn to interact in groups for the mutual advantage. Such behavior required an accurate sensing of the features of each particular environment, and constant adaptation of their interactions thereto.

So long as the interaction of creatures with their environment remained at the level of recognizing and capturing food or moving to a sheltered spot, or mating—that is to say, responding to immediate stimuli—the behavioral system could be one of simple stimulus and response. At a higher stage in evolution, animals developed means of preferring those types of situations which would put them in a better position to satisfy these basic needs. The animal which achieved dominance within a territory over fellow members of its species got the "lion's share" of the available food and probably a monopoly of the available mates.

Human beings and the higher animals have come to value any kind of relationship which renders them more effective in the skills of living; hence the delight in accomplishment, in acquiring knowledge and understanding of the environment, in being able to bring about significant changes, to do difficult things others cannot do, to retain control of objects which may be useful, or confer uniqueness or power. This generalized effectiveness-motivation operates from infancy on, and is of supreme importance for mental development (Stott, 1961a, 1978b). I am not speaking of an instinct for effectiveness. It is rather that we can infer from observation that human beings and the higher animals normally seek to establish relationships of personal effectiveness between themselves and whatever part of their environment they feel they can influence or understand. Since this goal of behavior is universal, except when inhibited or the system is damaged, we can assume that it is part of our genetic constitution, and can therefore be called instinctive. ("Instinctive" describes a characteristic of behavior, without implying the working of an "instinct.")

The second major relationship which human beings and the higher animals seek to establish is that of social contact with members of their own species. This brings advantages in protection against predators, capturing food, breeding, and the rearing of the young. The human young have a long period of dependence upon their parents, without which they could not survive. Consequently, for them it is of vital importance to maintain a close and stable relationship with their parents or other guardian adults. We have all seen the distress of a child separated from its parents in a crowd, or on being left in a hospital without its mother. Deprivation of adult care is intolerable to the child and, if prolonged, gives rise to emergency reactions which appear abnormal or maladjusted.

Nearly all behavior, except that needed for nutrition, warmth, comfort, shelter, and reproduction, is directed towards the maintenance of these twin relationships of effectiveness and social attachment, and they are the basis of our human nature. If I henceforth, for short, refer to them as "needs," this should not be held to imply that they are some kind of entity. It is just that human beings and the higher animals have evolved in a way that ensures the continuity of these two relationships, and when, for any individual, the continuity is broken, he gets into a state of frustration or anxiety and seeks to reestablish it. We may say, then, that he evidences a need for personal effectiveness or human attachment, as the case may be. To clarify this concept we can take the analogy of a cork pushed below the surface of water. Released, the cork immediately rises to the surface again; its normal relationship to the water is reestablished. Prescientific peoples would say that the cork wanted, or had a need, to float. What actually happens is that the relationship of the cork to the water is determined by the physical characteristics of each. Similarly, the striving, as we witness it, of the human being to reestablish a relationship of effectiveness or social attachment is determined by the way in which we have evolved as organisms. In popular language, it is part of our nature, just as it is in the nature of a cork to float.

The maintenance of these basic relationships requires not only the correct interpretation of present situations; it also requires foreknowledge of the probable consequences of our acts. When we conceive a desire to act in a certain way, the mind carries out an advance rehearsal in order to ensure that we achieve what we intend without any bad effect. To use the metaphor of Craik (1943), it is as if a working model of the proposed action is run within the mind many times faster than reality. If we see that some bad consequence would ensue, we hold back, or, in psychological language, inhibit the act.

This process of advance rehearsal depends upon our knowing what the consequences of our actions are likely to be. The higher organisms have therefore evolved the means of noting consequences and storing the information against the time when they meet a similar situation. This is the process of conditioning, which makes up a large part of learning. To ensure that lessons of important events are learned, they are repeated mentally in the form of images, and this represents a method of learning which is quicker and more efficient than having to go through the actual experience many times.

In sum, for the proper functioning of the behavioral system, a double reflectivity is required. The first is reflecting in advance of the proposed act, for the maximizing of desired, and the minimizing of undesired, consequences. The second is reflecting after the act, so that one does better next time.

In fact we sometimes have to put up with periods during which one or the other of the two basic needs is not being met. An individual has to be able to tolerate a certain amount of frustration, or to be temporarily out of touch with his primary attachment-group. There may be a conflict between the two needs: an individual may have to limit what he would like to do in terms of advancing his own effectiveness because it would jeopardize his social relationships. For example, people normally avoid stealing from or bullying their friends and acquaintances. This avoidance of temptation is part of the constant inhibition that we are always exercising.

The ability to bide one's time in a conflict situation rather than resort to a solution which lands one in further difficulties is a characteristic of a person of stable temperament. The panic level of an unstable person is set too low, so that he "jumps out of the frying pan into the fire." Instead of the best, he makes the worst of a bad job. (It is no coincidence that this fundamental distinction can be expressed in traditional sayings. The latter are distillations of folk wisdom about human behavior, and the parallelism confers a measure of endorsement to the theory.)

In view of fashionable ideas about the danger of "bottling up" one's feelings, and the assumed right to do what one really wants to do, it should be emphasized that this capacity for inhibition is a normal component of human nature, upon which all social life and culture depend. It therefore does us no harm so long as, over time, the individual is able to fulfill his basic needs for effectiveness and social attachment.

Understanding of the mechanism of inhibition is important for the completion of our overview of human behavior as affecting maladjustment and delinquency. Inhibition consists of a refusal to perceive the unfavorable feature in a situation, or to recall some unfavorable event or circumstance. In popular language the slight or insult, or loss or failure, is simply ignored. When a person is upset about something, a friend will often say, "Don't let it worry you; just ignore it." Alternatively, the unfavorable feature is reduced in significance by viewing it as only a small part of one's general well-being or life goals. To do this, as we say, requires a sense of humor— that is, the ability to tolerate a setback by belittling it and "laughing it off." These devices for dealing with temporary frustration or deprivation are forms of avoidance. By avoidance we are able to control the primitive stimulus-response mechanisms of behavior in order to ensure that we respond as and when it serves our best interests to do so. And by this latter term are implied our interests as they extend into the future.

If the individual feels capable of doing so, he deals with deprivation by seeking actively to change his environment. His response is of an outgoing or attacking character. When threatened, he will attack or avoid, according to his estimate of his own strength and that of the source of the threat. The normal individual will make a judicious estimate of his chances of success, and thus minimize the risk of failure. In deciding upon his behavioral strategy he gives himself time to take account of the pros and cons of one course of action or another, calling upon his previous learning and his knowledge of the materials or persons with whom he has to deal.

There are times, however, when these mechanisms of rehearsal and foresight have to be dispensed with because immediate action is required. A person jumping over a fence to escape from the proverbial bull has no time to consider what may be on the other side. Consequently, the higher animals, including man, have evolved a special system of emergency responses which come into action in times of acute danger. These reponses are also activated at the point where stresses exceed the level of tolerance and the situation which produces them cannot be changed by the usual methods of dealing with it. The importance of these "panic" reactions for the understanding of delinquency and of other forms of behavioral breakdown is demonstrated later in this chapter.

HOW THE BEHAVIORAL SYSTEM CAN GO WRONG

Serious and ongoing deprivation of effectiveness and social attachment constitutes a state of intolerable stress such as was mentioned earlier. Our bodies and minds are attuned to cope with a degree of stress, and, indeed, a certain amount seems necessary to keep us in tone. It is constant, unremitting stress that does the damage. The amount of stress that an individual can tolerate varies with his nervous constitution, his state of health, and the degree to which he has been exhausted by cumulative stresses.

The five delinquency-generating states of mind outlined in the previous chapter can be seen as extreme forms of normal responses. Their abnormality arises from the extreme pressures and deprivations to which the youths in question had been subjected. It was seen how mental avoidance of the source of anxiety and self-banishing hostility became dominating compulsions.

The constant resort to attention-filling activities and fantasies which serve to keep the unwelcome memories out of mind also block the process of reflectivity. The youths affected by avoidance-excitement never considered the further consequences of their delinquent and irresponsible behavior. In as far as the hostility-dominated were concerned, they thought only of punishing their parents by "going to the bad." Thus, in the longer view, the delinquent's aggressive or escapist responses are ill-adaptive, since they are detrimental to his own continued happiness and thriving. His only contemporary motivation is to gain relief from an intolerable situation.

Owing to the young person's junior status in the family, the attack component of hostility is usually disguised as stealing from the parents or committing a nuisance which embroils them with neighbors. These indirect forms of attack are combined with a self-banishing form of avoidance, to become the syndrome of hostility. It is also found in nonhuman species, when the animal expects love and loyalty but senses rejection. A good example was afforded by Conrad Lorenz's dog, when it realized he intended to leave it behind. It ran amuck in the neighborhood, killing poultry and committing other nuisances, very like a delinquent youth on the run (Lorenz, 1959, p. 33).

Avoidance-excitement is typical of children who have earlier known affection and security. Those who have never enjoyed a close and stable relationships with adults develop a deeper form of inhibition, namely that of the need for affection in itself. The case of *Huntley*, in Stott (1950/80), referred to earlier, was a good example of such a child's resistance to offers of affection and an inability to believe that anyone could take a genuine interest in him. There was a large group of such boys in my series of 102 delinquents (in Stott [1950/80] cf. Martin, p. 257; Middleton, p. 59; Crowther, p. 60; Bennett, p. 64; Dixon, p. 66). They had all learned to withdraw from human association as something inherently to be mistrusted, and one could see from their life histories why they had been driven to this inhibition of fellow-feeling.

Very few cases could be pinpointed as the outcome of effectiveness deprivation. Some, feeling themselves rejected by their mothers in favor of younger siblings, regressed to the behavior level of a much younger child. They could only have done so by inhibiting the natural wish of children to keep up with their age group. *Potter* in Stott (1950/80) defeated the domineering of his father by playing dumb, which strategy he later used with consummate skill. But he had to accommodate himself to the role of the school simpleton.

Several other boys were given to bravado, which might be described as a pathological form of effectiveness arising from longstanding uncertainties about their parents' regard for them. Because, indeed, there are so many outlets in daily life for those who want to achieve effectiveness in some sphere, or, alternatively, to deceive themselves with some form of pseudo-effectiveness, few youths seem to be so acutely deprived in regard to this need as to impel them to delinquency. The insufferable deprivation was in the area of stable human attachments.

The temperamental handicap—that of inconsequence—brings us to the consideration of damage to the behavioral system, or, more accurately, to the dysfunction of its neural counterparts. Some children suffer from what seems to be a constitutional inability to inhibit a proposed action, so that they miss out that part of behavior which normally consists in an advance rehearsal of consequences. These are the inconsequent children to which I have referred. They likewise do not reflect upon the consequences of past behavior, so that they learn very slowly from their mistakes. It would be incorrect, however, to assume that they are completely unconditionable; if they were, they would be low-grade mental defectives. Tendencies to impulsiveness are also observed in a large number of otherwise normal boys, and many of these will engage thoughtlessly in petty delinquencies or be led into them by others. Whether they persist or not must depend upon the penalties attached to being caught. It was significant that none of the 102 boys committed to a residential school had inconsequence as the sole state of mind antecedent to their offenses. Although several were severe inconsequents of the bravado type, there was always some other insecurity or unease which aided and abetted their impulsiveness. This suggests that all but the most extreme inconsequents are deterrable; in any case the latter will probably be in institutions for the retarded.

We have to assume that the behavioral system, consisting of a sequence of processes, is represented by a parallel organization of the central nervous system. When any part of the latter is in a state of dysfunction we would therefore expect a corresponding dysfunction in observed behavior. In perception, at the beginning of the sequence, and in motor performance, at the end, such dysfunction is well known, but it has little direct relevance for our understanding of delinquency. Rather, we have to consider the possibility of dysfunction in the intermediate stages, those which originate and orient behavior. We can infer that at one of these stages the situation as reported by the senses is appraised by a number of criteria. These have been evolved as tests by which the creature judges whether it is in the sort of environment in which it can thrive. (I use the word "creature" to apply to all animals, and also to human beings.) Apart from ensuring one of food and drink, shelter and physical safety, the most important of these criteria are effectiveness and social attachment. We have to suppose that these means of evaluating the goodness of the environment are part of the genetic constitution of the species, and therefore embodied in genes and neural structures. We may then ask what are the results of a failure of the necessary genetic provision or of neural dysfunction.

As regards failure to apply effectiveness criteria, the results are seen in the meek, unassertive, timid child who is afaid of anything strange or apparently complicated. Since children of this type do not explore their environment or attempt to solve problems, they remain at a low level of mental development. They are usually found in settings for the retarded or the mentally subnormal (Stott, 1960b, 1961b). Because of their lack of initiative they run no risk of becoming delinquent. They are also affectionate children, which distinguishes them from the type of child described below, and they impose few stresses on their parents.

"MORAL DEFECT" AND PSYCHOPATHY

Failure to apply the social-attachment criteria is a much more serious matter. The result is a "moral defective," or what Bowlby (1944) has called the "affectionless character." Thirteen-year-old *Alec* (Stott, 1966), referred to me by the Glasgow social workers in the periodic case conferences I held with them, was a classic example.

It was not that he did not know the difference between right and wrong. He knew that adults took strong exception to stealing, but this only made him more calculating. He stole a money box from a nursery school, and maintained his denial with cool lies, until identified by several women. As a Boy Scout himself, he led a gang in breaking into a scout hut. In the course of the subsequent investigation his gambit was, "I can't understand why you're questioning me." From a grocer for whom he worked he stole whiskey and exchanged it for cakes with some boys who worked in a bakery. He also took money from the grocer's till, no doubt assuming that the loss would be attributed to someone's error. He stole repeatedly, both in and out of school and from his own home, but always escaped being charged: he was "such a nice wee boy."

He was not a constant nuisance in school. On the contrary, he was "a charming rogue," glib and plausible, and knew how to manipulate personal relationships. He even knew how to behave better after being corrected. But the teachers felt that there was always trouble brewing with him—some new act of thieving, or spitefulness to weaker children. He would brag and play the hero but he was indifferent to friendship. The personality defect from which he suffered was a lack of feeling for human attachments and consequently of the anxiety about maintaining good relationships which is the foundation of good conduct. He could not be conditioned to rectitude because there was nothing to appeal to in him: approval was no reward and disapproval no punishment.

Alec's abnormality was first noticed by his mother when he was six, with the birth of a younger brother. Towards him and the children born subsequently he was consistently spiteful. It would have been easy to attribute it all to sibling jealousy. But his not uncommon reaction towards the birth of younger siblings does not as a rule develop into "moral defect." Nor could his antisocial behavior be attributed to an unhappy home situation. The mother was not blind to his bad ways, but there was no hint of her losing patience with him. Moreover, all the six siblings were well-adjusted children, which speaks for a stable family life. It has to be assumed that the boy's condition was congenital.

Among my sample of 102 youths committed to a residential school (Stott, 1950/80), none could be classified as pure psychopaths or moral defectives. The nearest to this description, *Martin*, had been difficult from the time he was quite a tiny child, and had not been demonstrative in showing affection. He was given to wandering, and on two occasions was found, very happy, in police stations. Unlike Alec, his mother lost patience with him and favored her three younger children, and the father, with whom the boy had been on good terms, worked away from home for some years. This affectionless situation left him in a state of deep emotional conflict, which counted against a diagnosis of pure "affectionlessness." Forced to mind his two younger brothers, he ill-treated them, and within a short time they were involved in three road accidents. Cruelly blamed for these by his mother, he mentally avoided one particular incident in which a brother was injured; but he developed an obsession about seeing dead animals by the roadside. Because his mother was his only source of adult support, unsatisfactory though it was, he could not consciously reject her, and was not aware of feeling any resentments. However, he developed a classic hostility syndrome, pilfering from her money and any special luxury in the form of food she had managed to get (this was still the period of wartime shortages). To cover the thefts he told "the most fabulous tales." Knowing his parents were very set on his making progress in school, he truanted and took no interest in his studies. On beginning to work he continued to truant, and stole his mother's money to fill his pay envelope. He stole five watches from the home, as well as his sister's jewelry, and robbed anyone staying in the house. At times he could be very good to his mother, but the next day would be sullen again. Joining the army boys' service, he became homesick, and came back every weekend to see his mother instead of once a month as permitted. Then he took to deserting, and hung around the home, sleeping in the fields and raiding the larder for food. After a breach with his father which was the result of his expectation of rejection, he threw himself into a reckless round of thieving and got committed. His house master gave me a picture of a boy well in control of his emotions and capable of responsibility to the extent that he became a house leader. But, "utterly unscrupulous," he sold the other boys' boots and clothing to building workers on the school grounds, and carried out cunning extortions from new boys. On the day of his leaving he stole another boy's necktie but, in contrast to the cunning of his other thefts, flaunted it in a way that suggested his wanting his release deferred so that he did not return to his rejecting parents. If Martin had been completely devoid of the need for affection, he would not have shown the unmistakable hostility symptoms, since hostility is a highly emotional reaction against loss of love. On the other hand his apparent disregard for social attachment as a young child and his treatment of his younger brothers (which went far beyond sibling jealousy) speaks for an innate deficiency. Just to describe him as a compulsive thief, of course, explains nothing; we need to know what lay behind the compulsion.

Other cases of apparent congenital defect of personality that I was able to follow over a period suggest an answer to the problem of the origins of Martin's psychopathy. In many such, where the deficiency was in effectiveness motivation (what I have called unforthcomingness), the child who was frightened and unventuresome up to puberty thereafter developed a normal boyish assertiveness and confidence. An illiterate youth who had been described by his teachers as "too timid to learn," came along to a boys' club when he was 17 and gave a convincing display of card tricks. A similar boy, after puberty, became a keen motorcyclist. Likewise with some of the prepubertal psychopaths: a complete callousness toward the mother is suddenly transformed into tenderness. It may thus have been that Martin was a typical "affectionless character" in his early years but developed a normal need for affection at puberty. By then, however, the vicious circle of rejection and counter-rejection had soured him to the extent of once more inducing psychopathy.

THE DIVIDING LINE

In Britain there is a procedure by which a child may be "deemed maladjusted," which qualifies him for special treatment. Everywhere, psychiatrists are asked to say whether or not a child is "emotionally disturbed." We have therefore to ask whether a clear line can be drawn, dividing the maladjusted from the normal. Earlier in this chapter maladjustment was characterized, not as a constant state, but as a vulnerability to certain types of situation. Few, if any, people are invulnerable to every kind of stress or temptation; hence the legendary symbolism of Achilles' heel. The maladjusted, however, mark themselves as being vulnerable to the normal interplay of human relationships. By some original defect in their equipment for such interaction, or from unfortunate conditioning, they respond inappropriately, and often create bad situations for themselves.

The question of a dividing line between the normal and the maladjusted is further complicated in that human beings are equipped with two distinct response systems. The one consists in the judicious appraisal of a situation and of the consequences of reacting in one way or another, which has been described. It constitutes the normal behavior of an individual who is coping. The other is the capacity for emergency reaction, which is brought into play either when there is no time for the situation to be routinely processed through the mind, or when the regular repertoire of responses has failed to relieve the threat or stress. These are the typical responses of maladjustment, taking the form of blind attack or escape. They bear curiously little relation to the normal response repertoire. A mother may be kind and loving one minute, brutally attacking her child the next, and then, when she has recovered, be kind and loving again.

It is this point, where the normal adaptive repertoire is replaced by the primitive attack/escape responses, that provides us with a natural dividing line between maladjustment and normality. In an extremely vulnerable individual this point of reversion to the "panic" response system may be set so low that he is unable to control his behavior in his own best interests in most situations. He may for practical purposes be described as a maladjusted individual. With nearly all recidivist delinquents it can be said that their family lives belong to the class of stress-generating situations which are beyond their tolerance, and hence provocative of the emergency reactions. Once removed therefrom, however, and their emotions have had time to settle down, their normal repertoire of reactions may reestablish itself, and they behave like well-adjusted individuals. Should they reenter the stressful situation, there is likely to be a reversion to the emergency-reaction system, which by its nature is nonadaptive. Thus, strictly speaking, the clean division lies between alternative response patterns rather than between individuals. All one can say is that an individual is maladjusted if he is liable easily to revert to the nonadaptive emergency system and, in doing so, loses his sense of proportion and does himself and others damage.

How people can ordinarily stop short of committing serious damage is illustrated by an incident during my visit to a happy-go-lucky and poor Irish family. The father offered me some tea in a cup without a saucer, apologizing for the lack of the latter by explaining that they threw the saucers at each other. To a tea-loving Irishman the saucers, but not the cups, were expendable. Likewise, when a normally controlled person loses his temper—i.e., temporarily moves into the emergency reaction pattern—he can usually keep within the bounds of sanity.

This concept of a state of breakdown of the normal behavioral system, during which the person acts without regard for his long-term interests, helps us to clarify another problem of definition. From our everyday experience we are aware that ordinary people from time to time commit acts of theft of certain types—pilfering from employers or from automatic machines, making false tax returns, and the like. There is no reason to doubt the self-reports obtained by several questionnaire studies, in which a very high percentage of officially nondelinquent people admitted to misdemeanors. How, then, it is asked, can one speak of a special class of delinquents if we are virtually all delinquents except that we are not caught and convicted? It has often been pointed out that those who appear in the criminal statistics are the ones who get caught. The suggestion has been made that they are merely the unlucky ones; but as demonstrated in an earlier chapter, they are a special class of delinquency-prone, or perhaps we may say arrest-prone, individuals, since they are caught many times more frequently than would be predicted by chance. The difference lies in the degree of recklessness or compulsiveness. The individual who is in control of his behavior and acts with normal foresight takes good care to commit a mis-demeanor only when the chances of being caught are negligible, or where the offense is condoned and will not lead to prosecution. The delinquent under the sway of one of the compulsions described previously runs far bigger risks: his state of mind does not allow him to weigh his chances realistically, and he may even be uncon-sciously motivated to get caught. It is little wonder, therefore, that he forms a special class of arrest-prone individuals. In addition his crimes will be more heinous and more frequent than those of the normal individual.

THE CRIMINAL'S RESPONSIBILITY

When we consider the cost of crime, in terms of both money and personal distress, and the blemish it puts upon our civilization, we have to ask why no serious prophylactic measures have been taken comparable with those for the prevention of disease. It is easy to assume, in the light of so flagrant a contradiction, that people unconsciously want crime, but there is no empirical evidence of this. What we can observe is a widespread nervousness about admitting the relationship between crime and personal instability. It is feared that, if crime comes to be regarded as just another disease, or the miscreant can plead the misfortunes of his birth and upbring-ing, we can no longer hold the citizen responsible for keeping the law, or have the moral right to punish him should he fail to do so.

The present legal solution—that of excepting from the proce-dures of conviction and punishment a small number of criminals who can be adjudged unfit to plead because of their insanity—does not absolve us from the dilemma. There is a much larger number of criminals who, although formally sane, are patently undeterrable. All one can say of them is that they are unstable, in the sense that they are incapable of ordering their lives in their own best interests (which includes the avoidance of penalties).

Society's dilemma harks back to the issue of determinism versus free will. This is not the place to enter into its philosophical niceties, but something may be done to clarify the issue of criminal responsi-bility, and hence to remove the emotional barrier against penal reform which it raises, by asking the reader to accept the following propositions.

1. *Human behavior is the result of the interaction of the indi-vidual's genetic constitution and a succession of environ-*

> *mental influences which go back to conception and even before it.*

We cannot regard human beings as Nature's Great Exception. Human behavior must have its natural determinants and have been the subject of evolution just as much as the human physique.

2. *The nature of the contemporary environment is an important determinant of behavior.*

This follows from the recognition of the evolutionary value of behavior as a means of protection against here-and-now threats, and of taking advantage of here-and-now opportunities.

3. *The sanctions which every society imposes on certain types of behavior are an important element in the contemporary environment.*

By and large these sanctions are effective in deterring the ordinary man and woman. Historically, the severity of sanctions has been adjusted in order to secure general obedience to the law. The prudent individual recognizes the disadvantages of law-breaking, and chooses to be law-abiding. But—if he considers his own best interests—he has little choice. Society's sanctions are just as much a determinative influence upon him as the manner of his upbringing, his childhood friends, or the factors shaping his biological development.

4. *Individuals nevertheless show a variability in responding to these sanctions, but for no obvious reasons.*

This variability must also be attributed to natural causes, even though many of them are as yet obscure. We cannot fall back on the explanation that some people are strong-willed and others are weak-willed. To postulate a Will as the cause of individual differences is to imagine some inner entity that pulls the strings of the human marionette. And since no such entity can be identified, it is not scientifically admissible as an explanation.

5. *Human beings as at present constituted, or with the succession of environmenal influences to which they are at present exposed, are unable to subordinate their desires and impulses to the general good without a framework of rules supported by sanctions.*

It needs an exceptional individual to exercise independent moral judgment in ordering his conduct. Kohlberg and Kramer (1969) report various studies, based on the Kohlberg's six stages of moral development, which show that only some 4 percent of individuals, by the age of 25, reach the highest stage, which is that of being able to form a judgment of right or wrong based on their own reasoning. A generation earlier, Malinowski (1964) came to the same conclusion as an anthropologist working among the Trobrianders of New Guinea:

> The real rule guiding human behavior is this: What everyone else does, what appears as a norm of general conduct, this is right, moral and proper. Let me look over the fence and see what my neighbor does, and take it as a rule for my own behavior. So acts every "man in the street" in our own society, and so has acted the average member of any society through the past ages (p. 326).

Recent history has shown how shockingly criminal, by standards of personal conduct, the behavior of whole social groups can become, once traditional standards of morality are allowed to lapse. The widespread looting during the blackout of July 13, 1977, in New York City is a case in point. It was widely assumed that the police, smarting under criticisms of their treatment of earlier disturbances, were just going to look on next time. Thus, we were provided with a natural experiment in how ordinary people will behave when the machinery of deterrence goes out of action.

Given the foregoing characterization of the "man in the street," the consequent necessity of a code of behavior enforced by sanctions, and the fact that the sanctions themselves exercise a shaping influence on human conduct, we do not need to cling to the idea of an ultimate free will in order to justify punishment.

Our moral dilemma is centered on those who are undeterrable. Obviously, continued punishment of them amounts to cruelty, for it can serve no useful purpose. A further problem is that, while we can identify the crime-prone, we cannot reliably predict from among first offenders which of them belong to this undeterrable minority. At the same time, to renounce all punishment will, if the foregoing view of human nature is correct, result in the collapse of social order. Consequently, all we can do is to devise means of punishment which are sufficiently unpleasant to deter, but which have a certain educative or rehabilitative value. In this way the harm done to the maladjusted person, if harm it is, would be minimal. It follows also that for punishment of this type to be effective in identifying the unde-terrable, every infringement of the law should incur the appropriate punishment, with the fewest possible exceptions. A system of warnings and deferments merely postpones the procedure of identi-fying the undeterrable, and it is these latter who above all need help.

Chapter Nine
Family Situations Conducive to Maladjustment and Delinquency

FAMILY SITUATION AND BEHAVIOR
DISTURBANCE IN THE CHILD

It has been commonly observed by all those engaged in social work that disturbed and delinquent children tend to come from unstable or stressful families. It is not so easy to pinpoint the types of family or of child rearing which are to blame. The apparently simple answers tend to be illusory. Whereas the risks are somewhat greater in one-parent families, they are not all that much greater, and many children with both parents at home become delinquent. West and Farrington (1973) found that, apart from criminality in the parents and being a member of a large family, separation from one parent was not significantly related to delinquency. They concluded that the factor which counts most is not so much the separation itself as the underlying family problems. Children whose mothers go out to work have been shown to be less inclined to delinquency (Birkett, 1950; West and Farrington, 1973), to do slightly better at school (Fraser, 1959), and to be better adjusted (Stott, 1965) than children whose mothers do not work outside the home. We cannot therefore make the working mother a scapegoat. Nor are we justified in roundly blaming the parents of deviant children for lack of affection or failure to exercise discipline. Parents who are models of affection, patience, and common sense can have extremely disturbed and deviant children (Stott, 1966). Deprivation of mothering in the early years—of which so much was made a generation ago—by no means always results in maladjustment or "affectionless character." There is no one-to-one fit between family influence and deviant behavior in the child. And yet it remains undeniable that a large number, probably the vast majority, of delinquents come from homes which deny them the essentials for healthy emotional development.

The other side of the coin is the virtual absence of delinquency of the familiar Euro-American breakdown type in traditional communities, or in those who maintain their culture intact within an advanced industrial economy. Speaking of Jewish, Chinese, and Mexican family life, MacIver (1967) observes:

> the doctrinal upbringing in these three types of families is very dissimilar, but the common inculcation of a disciplined respect for parents is sufficient to insure a comparative absence of serious delinquency in the young. In families of these types, differences or clashes or rifts that in many American families would become trigger situations are over-ridden by the presence of fundamental loyalties (p. 76).

It is of paramount importance for a delinquency-prevention program to have a clear conception of the form these fundamental loyalties take and to be able to recognize their weakening or absence. There have been very few attempts to define such deprivation in terms of the essential emotional needs of the growing child. Glueck and Glueck (1962) postulated a factor of family cohesiveness, but—as has been seen—their conception of such was ill-defined, and they left its interpretation to the social worker. West and Farrington (1973) likewise made no attempt to identify or classify deleterious family situations, apart from ratings for failure of discipline and supervision, and for marital disharmony. These they amalgamated into a global factor of poor parental behavior. The boys in their sample experiencing the worst parental behavior were more than twice as delinquency-prone as the remainder of the sample—thus establishing the importance of the home conditions; but only some 32 percent of them actually became delinquent. And only 40 percent of the delinquents came from the worst parental-behavior group. One would have expected that nearly all the recidivists would have a background of severe family problems, but only 59 percent of them had parents in the worst group, as measured. These findings underline the need to know what it is exactly in family life that produces delinquent children.

WHY SO LITTLE PROGRESS IN IDENTIFYING DELETERIOUS FAMILY SITUATIONS?

Given that instability of the family is an important factor in the production of maladjusted and delinquent children, it is at first sight surprising that investigation has not been centered on its nature. The causes of an air or railroad accident are meticulously investigated;

we have to ask why no similar inquiries are made into the wrecks of lives. The reason for the omission lies in the hierarchy of personnel in academic research. Chief investigators do not usually spend long hours interviewing parents, let alone expose themselves to the material conditions in delinquency-rife areas that visits to the home involve. (My study of the reliability of interview data showed that interviewing a poor working-class mother in a consulting room or office usually results in minimal or misleading information, because her nervousness inhibits her memory or makes her say the wrong thing [Stott, 1957].) The time-consuming work of seeking the parents out in their home localities is given to the social-worker members of the team. Their place in the research is that of data gatherers. They are given guidelines—that is to say, prescribed variables; but since these are arrived at by the chief investigator, "off the top of his head," and not by induction from observation, they are usually borrowed from the current popular mythology. Their treatment by sophisticated statistical techniques becomes a further blurring of the real state of affairs in order to obtain significant results. The data gatherers are not expected to go through the agonizing struggle to bring order into their observations. Indeed, if any one of them, as a member of a team, attempted to so do, he or she would disrupt the course of the research.

Induction of new concepts means not being satisfied with the information that one has obtained until it provides a convincing explanation. In some cases interview after interview must be conducted before the true situation is revealed. Sometimes, as in the case of Martin (Stott, 1950/80), it is a matter of waiting for some new crisis to occur which cracks the cover-up. Often judgment has to be suspended, with the knowledge that one has not yet learned the key facts. The ability to live with such uncertainty demands epistemological stamina. A social worker who refused to meet the prescribed guidelines by insisting that the data were incomplete would soon be outside the research team. Moreover, the general run of chief investigators hanker after certainty. Many social scientists, nursing a sense of inferiority toward the physical scientists, aim at "hard" data, although their variables are of relationships between people, which cannot be calibrated like physical variables.

DRAWING TOGETHER OBSERVATIONS INTO LAWS

In my study of 102 delinquent youths I was a lone worker and hence unable to delegate the collection of the data to other people.

The result was that I was exposed to the first-hand "laboratory" experience from which insights can be generated. Personal acquaintance with the youths in the residential school, the club I founded for that purpose and in my own home, combined with visits to their parents, ensured me a rich flow of first-hand data and gave me time to discern repeating patterns of events. One such pattern of relationships was characterized by many of these delinquents wanting to do housework or buy expensive presents for their mothers. In these cases I found that the boy had some reason for fearing the loss of his mother, either from ill health or her threats to desert the family. The coupling of these two sets of facts gave me insight into the boy's basic but unadmitted anxiety, and with recurrence in other cases of the association between the boy's unnatural helpfulness and the feared loss of the mother, I was able to induce the mechanism of one kind of delinquent breakdown. In a sense the process of induction is a form of mental statistics: the brain notes, on the model of the chi^2 test, the number of cases in which an association does or does not apply. Where, for example, the boy was threatened with being thrown out of his home, quite another set of reactions was observed—that of hastening the final rejection by stealing and by behavior calculated to antagonize his parents. In this way, different patterns of maladjustment- and delinquency-producing family situations began to form themselves in my mind. As the number of cases studied grew, I was able to define the patterns more clearly and recognize possible variants which would in turn be corroborated in due course.

All these delinquency-conducive patterns could then be seen to be variations on a universal theme. The child in question was denied the security and permanent belonging in a family, which the normal child takes for granted.

It became evident, by comparison of the delinquents with their siblings, that they had some special vulnerability to such deprivation. Coupled with this was usually some traumatic incident, either in the form of physical injury or a family event, which brought the stresses to a crisis and triggered the young person's behavioral breakdown.

Interpersonal stresses exist up to a point in every family. Normally, they are recognized as danger points and, as such, are contained. Most children are emotionally robust enough to ride such stresses. Breakdown occurs when the stress, in the form of a threat to the child's security, exceeds his reserves of tolerance and adaptability—in other words, when his point of breakdown is reached. In extreme cases the child may have suffered congenital damage of a degree which renders him incapable of coping with the normal demands of life, and no part of his behavioral breakdown can fairly be attributed to the family situation. At the other extreme we find children who are able to find substitutes for difficult situations, and to do so without "going to pieces." In their case No. 150, West and Farrington (1973) describe such a family situation, which was in fact a typical example of the Situation 3A in the classification that follows and in the diagnostic worksheets in Chapter Eleven (that of the undependable mother whom the father avoids by seeking ways of absenting himself from the home). This father spent his time in pubs and used his work as a place of refuge, and there was marital conflict over his drinking. The situation remained, however, at the subcritical level for two reasons. First, the father, although discouraged about his married life, was fond of his wife and was determined that he could never leave her. Second, the boy was of stable temperament, and, deciding to get away from the home, joined the armed forces. He had no need to resort to delinquency.

THE INTERPRETATION OF INTERVIEW DATA

For the appreciation of the nature of the parent-child relationships and their effect on the child, we have two main sources of information, namely, the parents and the child. Because of their personal involvement, accounts from neither source can be taken at their face value. The interviewer has to use a system of piecing together oblique statements which are telltale of the human relationships within the family as they affect the child. A mother will seldom admit that her child is estranged from, or indifferent to, her, but may willingly admit that he is more fond of his father or of a grandparent. Similarly, a wife may not like to let her husband down by revealing his violence, but may say he has a temper.

Even more caution must be used in accepting the child's statements about his family. The truth is often the diametric opposite to the proffered account, but for this reason lends itself to a system of interpretation. The anxiety that the boy is willing to talk about is never the one which has driven him to crime. Likewise, owing to his need to keep unbearable anxieties from consciousness, a young person will never be able to divulge those which have impelled him to seek substitutive excitements, nor will he admit a rejection that hurts. As McCord and McCord (1959) found, one parent is enough to satisfy a child's attachment needs. The crisis occurs when the hitherto loyal parent weakens. In such situations the child openly blames the antagonistic parent, whom he has written off already. If this is the father, the boy is in fact worried because his mother has shown signs of yielding to the father's pressure to get rid of him. Similarly, if a boy fantasizes about the attentions he gets from a father who has in fact neglected him for years, one can safely infer that he has lost faith in his mother's loyalty.

WORKING TOWARD A TYPOLOGY
OF FAMILY SITUATIONS

It is a question of how we can bring some kind of order or scientific lawfulness into our observations about family relationships which can be made the basis for a diagnosis. Because of the infinite variety of personal traits and interactions, some caseworkers reject any attempt at classification or analysis, pointing out that every case is unique. This is true, but the uniqueness is nearly always a variant of a recurring pattern. Absolute uniqueness would preclude any advance of knowledge: there could be no generalization that could be used in subsequent cases. In effect the experienced caseworker accumulates a mass of generalized insights. If they are not formulated consciously they cannot be transmitted and hence are lost with the close of each career; new entrants to the profession, according to their varying ability to generalize, build up a new set of personal insights, which are in turn lost. Any degree of discernment of constant elements therefore represents a gain in knowledge. Ideally, the recurring indicators of stress in the child and in the family situation should be computer-stored and treated at a national or regional center to provide an objective system of diagnosis and professional training.

If such constant elements in family relationships indeed exist, it must be because of constant patterns of reaction which form laws of human behavior. Our behavioral system, in common with those of the higher animals, has evolved a number of standard modes of response which govern social relationships. A large part of their function is that of holding the group together. In our everyday lives these take the form of activities whose goal is the care and welfare of its members, and of reassurances about the permanence of group membership in the form of expressions of loyalty and affection. In human beings the basic group is that of the family. Our analysis has thus to be in terms of these emotional bonds between its members. From it we should draw our understanding of the ways in which family loyalties can break down and result in abnormal reactions in the young.

The quality of the affectional bond between parent and child can, for purposes of diagnostic consistency, be classified as follows:

1. Affectional acceptance (implying confidence in the relationship, loyalty, and a determination not to permit a breach).
2. Anxiety (fear of a breach or separation).
3. Depressive and/or irritable nontolerance (a temporary and sometimes violent rejection displacing basically affectionate feelings on the part of a person who is neurophysically exhausted).
4. Hostility (an emotional state enabling a person to break free from a love relationship which has been betrayed or threatens to be; for example, the fury of the jilted lover).
5. Uncertainty (a state of conflict arising when the relationship is felt to be unreliable).
6. Estrangement (inability to accept an affectional relationship with the other person, involving absence of group-maintaining behaviors and making life together difficult).

The next stage towards the understanding and classification of family situations is the recognition of those patterns of family relationships which signal a breakdown of essential loyalties and hence are conducive to maladjustment and delinquency. In my casework with the aforementioned delinquent youths I was able to arrive at a broad typology which was largely based on the sorts of family stresses to which they had been subjected. In my later work in Bristol I drafted out a series of descriptions of family situations which seemed, from my experience with these delinquents, to represent the chief ways in which a child could be deprived of that essential sense of security that I had detected as the missing element in the lives of nearly all of them. These were submitted to a group of family caseworkers, who met periodically with me to test the fit of the patterns, as drafted, to the cases they were handling. The result of this work was to refine the classification to the point that, with the variations inherent in every human situation, the list of descriptions seemed to be covering all the cases referred.

The result was the emergence of a number of recurrent patterns of high-risk family relationships which might serve as an aid to the understanding of fresh cases. At the same time it was necessary to guard against treating any of the model patterns as if it were an exact description of the situation within a particular family. The value of standard patterns is that they provide alternative hypotheses to be tested in seeking the cause of the child's anxiety. The behavioral forms the anxiety takes narrow down the alternatives. Stealing and provocative nuisance within the home indicate hostility, and this in turn suggests that the child feels rejected by the parents; over-helpfulness in the home suggests fear of losing the mother, and so on. The question to which the caseworker should always seek an answer is: Why does this child feel that he might be left without a home and parents who cherish him? The source of the insecurity may be of quite an unforeseen nature, but the chances are overwhelming that it will resemble in some degree one of the hypothesized patterns.

In the Bristol group we recognized the importance of the factual confirmation of every inference, and of being on the look out for features of the particular family which we could not explain (this precaution acting as a safeguard against a mechanical stereotyping of a family situation against one of the standard patterns). Often, it was a question of testing the actual peronal relationships within a family against two or three possible patterns and, while recognizing elements of each or combinations of them, deciding which pattern was the primary source of the child's insecurity and consequent deviant behavior.

It had also to be borne in mind that disturbed behavior in a child may arise, not primarily from exposure to an adverse family situation, but from his having suffered neural damage or other impairment, either congenitally or postnatally; for example, from encephalitis, injury, or severe physical shock. The effect of this may be to lower the child's resistance to stress, so that he cannot tolerate the ordinary tensions of family life. Such a child will usually be described by the parent as "sensitive," "different," or even a "nuisance from the day he was born." It may be beyond the scope of the casework intervention to probe into these more remote causes of the child's maladjustment. On the other hand, the uncovering of severe pregnancy stress, birth injury, or—in infancy—febrile illness or convulsions, may have therapeutic value in helping the parents to understand the child's behavior disturbance. A failure to realize that the child has suffered handicaps can easily cause them to react to his abnormal behavior by indignation and rejection.

THE CLASSIFICATION OF STRESSFUL FAMILY SITUATIONS

The family situations liable to produce maladjustment and delinquency fall into four main groups, according to the sort of emotional deprivations to which the child has been exposed (see the diagnostic worksheets in Chapter Eleven). These are (1) the threat of rejection and the prospect of expulsion from the family; (2) losing a supposedly secure source of affection and being left with an unsatisfactory substitute; (3) the undependability of the parents, or only parent, as a source of affection; and (4) fear of the loss of the preferred, or only parent.

Each of these major groups of deprivation or insecurity tends to be associated with different modes of reaction in the child. They therefore act as pointers to the type of emotional deprivation responsible for the delinquency.

These four broad classes of deprivation can be subdivided into the types of family situation in which they are commonly found. Along with the child's reactions, they provide the caseworker with a number of templates, or patterns, against which the situation as observed is fitted. An exact fit can, of course, seldom be achieved, because the phenomena of life are subject to endless variation. The caseworker should then give thought to those aspects of the case which the pattern chosen as the best fit does not seems to explain. This acts as a safeguard against mechanical diagnosis or jumping to conclusions on the basis of statements of the parties concerned about the family relationships.

Each of the interpersonal relations listed earlier in this chapter is expressed in a characteristic mode of behavior: genuine *anxiety*, by helpfulness and giving; *depressive/irritable nontolerance* in violent expressions of rejection or physical attack; *hostility*, in provocative acts designed to hasten a breach, together with sullenness; *uncertainty*, by hypocritical expressions of concern, combined with notable unhelpfulness, and, often, loyalty-testing nuisance; *estrangement*, by difficulty in tolerating the other person's presence.

These reactions are basic in human nature, and fail to run true to form only when the neural structures governing behavior are in a state of dysfunction, as in the case of the child innately deficient in the need for social attachment. Apart from such, the emotional equations should always come out true. The way a child behaves reflects the degree of confidence he has in his parents' affection and loyalty. If full confidence is lacking, the reason for the affectional breach has to be sought. The way a child treats his parents should be consistent with the social worker's assessment of the quality of the affectional bond between them; and this provides an objective test of the accuracy of the hypothesis.

The four main groups of maladjustment- and delinquency-conducive family situations, each comprising a particular type of deprivation, are described in the following pages. Also given are how many of my sample of 102 delinquent youths (Stott, 1950/80) were exposed to each, and their reactions to them. The youths named were members of this sample.

Despite what has been said, we cannot expect a one-to-one correspondence between the child's reaction and the type of deprivation. No two situations are exactly alike, and children differ in their temperaments and vulnerability to stress. Moreover, some children may in the course of their lives have suffered from two or more of the foregoing types of major deprivation.

GROUP ONE: THREAT OF EXPULSION FROM THE FAMILY

The threat normally takes the form of utterances by the parents that they will hand the child over to an agent of the law with a view to his being sent away to a correctional school, or of steps to do so, such as by bringing the child before the court as "Beyond Control." Alternatively, the threat is to hand the child over to the care of an absent parent or other adult about whom the child has misgivings.

In Situation 1A both parents are harsh and unaffectionate or rejecting, and are apt to ill-treat the child. Of the 11 boys of my series in this category, 10 responded by hostility, and 6 accompanied this by delinquent and nuisance attention as an ultimate test of their parents' concern for them. Seven sought means of physical removal from the parental home. No less than 5 had aggressive outbursts which verged on the psychotic. *Faulkner* (p. 274) played a game of spiraling punishment and retaliation with his parents. He extended his mischief to the world at large. He nailed up and chopped up neighbors' gates, systematically smashed a row of greenhouse windows, stuffed ignited straw up drainpipes, stole from his mother's purse and father's pockets, and finally (as he said, to end it all by getting into trouble), he broke into a neighbor's house, took some money, and spent it on a week's runaway spree.

Situation 1B is that of the set antagonism of the father against one of his children, whom he regards as the "black sheep of the family." Fearing that the other children will be contaminated, he decides to cut his losses in respect to the naughty one and get him put away. The "naughtiness" may be the result of an inborn hyperactivity or hypersensitivity, which the threats of "putting away" soon turn into hostility. The mother may be too weak or ill to defend the child, or may herself break down under the stress of the situation and turn on the boy as the source of the family troubles. All four of the boys in my series who were exposed to this paternal rejection showed high hostility, to which three added an urge to physical removal, avoidance-excitement, and delinquent loyalty-testing. These three also showed a classical symptom of anxiety over their mother, as their only anchorage to the family, in that they insisted on doing her housework for her. (The fourth was estranged from his mother, since he had been reared by a grandmother.)

Newman (p. 288) was given up for dead at birth, suffered from serious respiratory trouble in his early years, and had epileptic seizures regularly, until the age of seven. He was "a mischievous little monkey" and got many spankings from his father. But he took the beatings willingly, as a token of his father's attention. He even tried to get a little love from his father by buying him cuff links and a pipe. To me he always stoutly defended his father for sticking up for him, and denied any bad relationship.

Kennard (p. 287) similarly refused to admit any family worries, which he kept well out of mind by avoidance-excitement. "For the fun of it," he took to breaking into warehouses, "until I was caught." When eight years old he was knocked down by a truck, after which he was "a shocking nervous boy," became much more tiresome, and took to pilfering. His anxieties were redoubled by parental quarrels, during which the mother threatened to desert the home. He responded in a textbook manner, by lighting the fires and washing the floors for her.

Situation 1C is that in which the parents, although still living together, are estranged from each other, and the mother makes a son the recipient of her thwarted affection. She may use her blatant indulgence of him as a means of spiting her husband. A violent dis-like develops between father and son, with the latter openly blaming the father for the family discord. The crisis occurs when the mother's nerves break under the strain and she also turns on the boy (*Sidley*, p. 64).

Situation 1D consists of the pressure of another member of the household to have the child removed. This may be a stepparent, who has not bargained on accepting a possibly undisciplined youth into the household. The family member who is antagonistic to the boy brings matters to a crisis by saying, "It's either him or me."

In the case of *Baxter* (p. 170), a weak father gave in to the antagonism of a stepmother. The boy was one of many in my series who could have been superficially diagnosed as merely conforming to the adolescent life style of an inner-city subculture. And this was the impression he liked to give, that of a smart Cockney newsboy who had decided to take after his elder brothers and friends in their housebreaking activities. He was able to generalize about his techniques of larceny and philosophize about life with true Cockney smartness. As an excuse for allowing himself to be caught he remarked that if you threw bales of straw onto a wagon for six weeks, in the end you will throw one over the edge; even I as a psychiatrist (sic) must sometimes forget to ask one of my usual questions! He would impress a judge as a normal and intelligent youth, as indeed he was. But why the housebreaking? Not to better himself, but for "the excitement and the money"—in that order. This, and his noisiness and restlessness, suggested avoidance-excitement, and his bravado a longstanding insecurity characteristic of a further group of young gangsters described later in the chapter. For several years, from the age of three when his mother died, he was in an orphanage, where he claimed to have been ill-treated. Whether this was true or not, the separation from his parents at this early age must have conditioned him to anxiety. The four brothers played up their father by getting into all sorts of petty trouble and inducing him to pay their fines, refusing to work in his newspaper business or collecting money from his customers and spending it—as the resentful stepmother pointed out, in the confidence that they would always have their father behind them. It was classic delinquent loyalty-testing. In the end the father became as bitter against his sons as was the stepmother. Carefully concealed behind the smartness was the boy's fear of being thrown over by a father who was his only affectional prop.

Situation 1E is that of a respectable and good home, where the parents devote much time and thought to the moral training of their children. Juvenile lying and disobedience worry them as presaging a life of crime. Physical punishment is not part of their philosophy, nor do they have at their disposal the traditional pantheon of ogres, hobgoblins, and devils who devour naughty children, so they threaten instead to call in the probation officer or the policeman, who will take the boy away and put him in a school for naughty children. Parents forget the need children have to believe their parents, and if the child in question is vulnerable to anxiety, the prospect of being thus rejected by his parents destroys his faith in them and he answers by hostility. There were no cases in this category within my sample of training-school youths, partly because they are found among younger children, and partly because deviant childrem from respectable middle-class homes seldom find their way into committal institutions. But I have met several in the course of my work in the field of learning difficulties, where the hostility thus generated makes the child too disturbed emotionally to learn. The five-year-old child described elsewhere (Stott, 1978b), who deliberately dropped eggs onto the floor and stole tools from neighbors' garages, was one of them.

The central feature of Situation 1F is that of the mother who breaks down under the stresses of widowhood or separation, or from having an invalid or irresponsible husband. She has to support the family by heavy, ill-paid work, often a cleaning job with inconvenient hours, while at the same time having to manage a family of lively youngsters without the support of a husband. The more strong-minded type of woman copes in these circumstances by hardening herself into a rough-and-ready insensitivity. Some of the mothers in Situation 3A were able to do this, which their children often interpreted as lack of affection or even rejection, especially if accompanied by talk about her clearing out and leaving them or having them put away. The mother of the Martin brothers, whose delinquencies were quoted by Clifford Shaw (1938) as examples of cultural conflict (see Chapter Two of this book), affords a classic example of this strong-minded type of mother, who resorts to hardness rather than breaking down under multiple stresses.

Alternatively, as in the situation here described, these hard-pressed mothers lapse into a state of depression; but in overcrowded accommodations and with demanding children from whom they cannot escape, the depression gives way to the outbursts characteristic of the irritable-depressive nontolerance referred to elsewhere in this book. With the large number of one-parent families among lower-class blacks, this situation could account for a not inconsiderable proportion of the juvenile deviance in black ghettos. It is also the mental state of many mothers who abuse their children physically. But such acts are only the extreme expression of the temporary blind hatred that the mother feels against the child. On the occasion of quite an ordinary squabble with his sister, *Faulkner's* mother yelled at him, "Go out and drown yourself in the river. Get out, scram!" The mother may literally threaten murder, or take the child to the probation officer and say in front of him that she cannot stand the sight of him any more. Such vehement expressions of rejection amount to emotional abuse. By the time the case comes up before the family court, the mother has probably recovered her natural affections and won't hear of the child's being taken from her, but by then the damage and been done, and the child has responded by hostile counter-rejection.

All the 21 youths in Group One could be said to have been emotionally abused, in that they had faced threats of rejection and expulsion from their families. No less than 17 of them reacted by marked hostility directed against their parents, and 12 tested their parents' patience and loyalty or tried to get some kind of attention from them by nuisance. Fourteen showed that removal from the situation was part of their motivation. Only 8 evidenced avoidance-excitement.

GROUP TWO: TRANSITION FROM
LOVE TO LOVELESSNESS

The deprivation inherent in the second group of situations was that of the child's losing the preferred, or only, parent and being left with an unsatisfactory substitute. The latter may be the other parent or an unsympathetic relative.

In Situation 2A this occurs as a result of the death of the preferred parent, and in 2B as a result of the breakdown of the parents' marriage. There has been some reason, going back to the period before the loss of the preferred parent, why the child is unable to accept the one he is left with. In most cases this is because the indulgence of the deceased or absent parent has put the remaining one in a bad light, especially if he or she actively disapproved of the spoiling and thus assumed the role in the child's eyes of a withholder of good things. In some cases the remaining parent has never shown any interest in the child, and the child has learned to look entirely to the other for care and kindness.

After the loss of the affectionate parent, the child finds it difficult to accept the parent whom he has spurned, or feels unwanted by the one who has neglected or been harsh to him. Typically, the child cultivates an attitude of emotional independence, with a studied callousness against the parent or relative with whom he is living, and this "moral defect" may be extended to people in general. If the latter is his mother, a youth with this attitude will avoid contributing to her support, either refusing to work or courting dismissal from job after job, and annoying her with his spendthrift habits (*Skelton*, p. 197).

Where it was obvious to the boy that the parent he was living with was trying to hand him over to the other, he answered by a plaguing hostility which followed almost a stereotype. The boy would steal from his parents and run away repeatedly from the home, perhaps subjecting himself to privations such as sleeping out in bitter weather, while making sure that the rejecting parent could not forget his existence. *Batchelor* (p. 308) broke into his father's house twice. While on the run, the boys in this situation committed ill-concealed robberies, as if to emphasize their going to the bad. Nine of the 19 in this group reacted by a demonstrative hostility.

Thirteen resorted to avoidance-excitement, with a refusal to stay in the house more than absolutely necessary. This state was usually precipitated by a traumatic incident associated with the death or departure of the preferred parent. After *Rogers*'s (p. 187) father, with whom the boy had been on good terms, deserted the home, the mother went to pieces and led an immoral life. She killed herself in attempting an abortion. The boy had been sent to a pharmacy to get some implement, and the guilt he felt drove him to psychotic episodes in which he loudly play-acted armed robberies. *Knight*'s (p. 203) family had been a happy one until the father returned from the war in an unrecognized state of breakdown, after having had malaria and being torpedoed. He mistreated his wife, deserted her, and made a bigamous marriage, for which he was sent to prison. One day the other "wife" turned up at the home, bearing a letter from the father requesting a divorce, and the mother collapsed in the boy's presence. The boy began drinking heavily, and then ran away from home. Shortly thereafter he was convicted of armed robbery and robbery with violence. (After arrest, conviction, and a five months' delay pending an appeal, the boy received a birching.)

The most frequent motive of boys in this group—for which there was evidence in no fewer than 15 of 19—was to get themselves removed altogether from their distressing situations. When a stolen article was found in his pocket *Rogers* stole it again the next day. *Howarth* (p. 205), after serving a term in a training school, was worried at the prospect of returning to his mother.

The case of *Ferguson* (p. 161) illustrates a further standard situation (2C)—that of the foster child who has become attached to his foster mother and fears being returned to the true mother, against whom he has become emotionally indifferent. He had been with the affectionate foster mother from infancy. When at the age of eight his own mother turned up to claim him, he reacted by the avoidance-excitement type of delinquency and by nuisance designed to test his foster mother's loyalty. When the latter finally relinquished him, he made himself unbearable to his true mother, but on being returned to his foster mother punished her by a classic hostility. His case afforded one more object lesson in the dangers of ignoring the affectional attachments of children, especially of those taken into public care.

GROUP THREE: UNSATISFACTORY MOTHERS

The third group of emotionally depriving situations are those in which the mother, owing to her personality, or because another woman has attracted the child's affections, does not provide the sort of motherly affection and care upon which the child feels he can rely. Either there is no father available or he has become a background figure in the family.

In Situation 3A the mother causes uncertainties about her affection and loyalty in the mind of the child. My sample contained two main sorts of maternal failing which come within this category. The first was seen in the hard, dominant mother who treated her son with a habitual insensitivity, not only by way of harsh punishment but by routine threats to desert the family. The father is typically a chronic invalid, or of a weak personality, who leaves the discipline of the children to the mother. The children tend to look to the mild father for affection, but with his chronic sickness and ineffectiveness he does not count for much and is unable to provide alternative emotional support. In some of the cases in this subgroup the father had died or, if alive, had been neglectful, or supportive of the mother's harshness (the latter eventuality linking up with Situation 1A).

The other mothers in this category dominated their children's emotions by anxiety-creating tactics. They made a great thing of rather vague ailments that they claimed could carry them off at any time, and emphasized how utterly devoted their children were, as if determined to possess and dominate all their affections. In fact they created in their sons the most acute conflicts between obsessive attachment and resentment. In one or two cases the boy felt genuine anxiety about his mother. *Searle* (p. 81) insisted on giving his mother more than she asked for his keep; he swept the rooms and polished the furniture; she had only to express a wish for something, and he would go out and buy it for her. But more commonly the boys voiced hypocritical worries about their mothers, of a curiously similar sort: she was in financial difficulties (when she was not), or an invalid who might die at any time (when she was in good health), or she might have an accident, or some other unthinkable thing might happen to her—all of which were substitute fears masking the real fear that she would desert the home.

Because these mothers were such impossible people to live with, the fathers, when alive and dutiful enough to maintain the marriage, contrived to get jobs, such as long-distance trucking, which kept them away from the home, or had hobbies or recreations which served a similar purpose. Consequently, they were seldom present to act as fathers to their sons. The latter also sought to get away from the home, and this was an important motivation for 9 of the 12 boys in this subgroup.

It was their bravado, however, which was the most characteristic cause of their delinquencies. In its various forms it was prominent in 9. They liked to play big before their peers, but often made themselves unpopular by their bragging. Some courted popularity by clowning. Others stole from the home in order to have the money with which to keep up with a free-spending group. They resented any kind of authority, and many had lost job after job owing to their truculence and insubordination. They would tell fantastic tales, with themselves in the hero's role. Above all they were under a compulsion to prove their courage to their associates and no less to themselves. *Whitehead* (p. 97) was dared, although a nonswimmer, to jump in at the deep end of a swimming pool. Yet he was one of those boys who could only with difficulty be persuaded to sit in a dentist's chair. Intense fears were in fact another characteristic of this bravado group, to an extent that I at first saw their pose of toughness merely as a compensation for the awareness of an inner cowardice and the sense of inferiority it gave them. Some had had frightening experiences as younger children from the bombing or accidents, which no doubt contributed to their fearfulness, but others had the same intense fears, and the compulsion to deny them by bravado, without such predisposing experiences. It looked as if the uncertainties these boys had about their parents' loyalty had imbued them with vague fears, and their feelings of not being valued had damaged their self-image. This, together with their shame of being cowards in an adolescent society, induced them continually to seek compensations for their feelings of inferiority and worthlessness. Possibly the "toughness" which Miller (1958) claimed as one of the features of the lower-class adolescent life style has its origins in the small ratio of affection that overburdened ghetto mothers, stressed and deprived by lack of support from their husbands, can give their children.

Situation 3B is that in which the mother discriminates against the child in favor of her other children, and there is no effective father figure to whom the child can turn. This is the counterpart, as far as the mother is concerned, of the "black sheep" pattern (1B), in which the father rejects one of his children, and it tends to have a similar origin in the temperamental handicap of the child in question. *Ross's* mother (p. 262) described him as unaffectionate from toddlerhood and lavished her affection on his brother. The father being away in the war, the boy found a substitute in a milkman, and truanted in order to help him on his milk delivery. When he came of working age, he could not bring himself to earn money for his mother's benefit and truanted from work. Back from the war, the father promised him beatings, whereupon the boy tested him with classic delinquent attention: stealing his father's overcoat and pawning an identity card, he ran away to a seaside resort. He was beaten and ran away again, becoming this time a costermonger's mate. Shortly before, he had stolen a bicycle and ridden it around until stopped by a police car. The probation officer threatened him with "drastic court action," which was just what he wanted. Hostility and removal from home were the predominant motivations of this subgroup.

Situation 3C is that of divided maternal attachment. The child is in a state of conflict over his mother, with whom he is living, because for an important period of his life he had had a primary attachment to a surrogate mother. This is most frequently a grandmother who has cared for and loved him, or, living in the same house or nearby, has indulged him against his mother's wishes, and shielded him against her discipline. If the surrogate mother dies or her family moves, or if she loses interest in the boy as he gets bigger, the latter is thrown back on a mother towards whom he has been indifferent, and about whose affection for him he is consequently uncertain. The situation is parallel to Situations 2A and 2B, in which the child is left with the nonpreferred parent, owing to death or the break-up of the marriage.

The importance of recognizing this situation is not only its prevalence—there were 13 such cases in my sample—but the ease with which it can be overlooked. Unless careful and pointed inquiry is made about who had looked after the child, and about the people the child had been fond of at every period of his life, the influence of the lost grandmother may remain undiscovered and the breach between child and mother unexplained.

Some of the boys who had these divided maternal attachments showed the bravado which in Situation 3A was associated with uncertainty about the mother's affection. When the breach was more serious, amounting to estrangement, the boy reacted either by hostility or by behavior calculated to secure removal from the home.

It should be cautioned that the mere fact of the daily availability of a kind grandmother is not in itself a cause of divided maternal attachment in the sense used here. In my studies of slow-learning children I met several cases in which the mother and grandmother cooperated amicably in the bringing up of the child, and the child was very attached to both, with no sense of insecurity. The trouble arises when the mother has virtually left the child's upbringing to another woman, or has shown disapproval of the other's kindnesses. A typical situation is when a teenage girl has an illegitimate child who is brought up by the grandmother in her own home as if the child were her own. The young mother then comes to be regarded by the child more as an elder sister. If the mother goes out to work, as usually happens in such cases, she becomes a secondary figure in the child's life.

The primary attachment to a nanny in a wealthy family, while the mother fills her social engagements and follows her other interests, is another fruitful source of conflicting attachments. So long as the child has the alternative source of emotional security in the mother-surrogate, breakdown is unlikely, whatever other implications as regards personality development or attitudes toward women in adulthood there may be.

GROUP FOUR: THE CHILD FEARS THE LOSS OF THE PREFERRED PARENT

The immediate cause of the delinquency among the youths in Situation 4A was the mother's illness, or complications from her childbearing. In several other cases these anxieties had apparently contributed to the boys' breakdown, but in these seven it appeared as the predominant or sole immediate antecedent to the delinquency. That of *Bligh* (p. 28) began at the age of 14 years, without any previous unsettledness, when his mother was four months pregnant. He was in court three times in just over a year. *Rowledge* (p. 33) had longstanding anxieties about the chronic illnesses of his mother, for which she had been in the hospital several times. The illnesses had started from a previous childbirth, and when it became clear to him that she was going to have another child, he threw himself into a hectic round breaking into shops and factories. He was in court three times during the last three months of her pregnancy. *Tilton's* (p. 39) housebreakings coincided with his mother's stays in the hospital. He took a pride in them and entered them in his diary, such was his need for delinquent preoccupations as a relief from his anxieties.

The delinquencies of all seven were uniformly motivated by avoidance-excitement, and afforded examples of the syndrome in its purest and most extreme form. The last-mentioned boy broke out of one remand home after another, recommencing his housebreakings within an hour or two of each escape. He said he wanted "more excitement." At home he had gone out every evening to the billiard hall and skating rink, but that did not afford him enough excitement. All the boys remarked on their inability to concentrate on a job, and their dislike of reading. Three spontaneously mentioned their horror of arithmetic, and it was noteworthy how many other youths under the domination of avoidance-excitement had the same aversion; evidently the thought and the physical immobility that arithmetic requires opened a chink in their consciousness which the besetting anxiety could slip through.

One and all of them betrayed textbook signs of mother-anxiety. *Bligh* did his mother's washing and shopping for her and bought her small luxuries; *Goodman* (p. 37) did the ironing and fed the baby; *Bane* (p. 34) cleaned the house before going to work, and insisted on scrubbing the kitchen floor while his girlfriend was waiting to go out with him; *Rowledge* did the housework, cleaned the floors, ran errands, and bought his mother roses and fruit.

It has to be asked why these particular youths should find the anxiety over their mother's illnesses and pregnancies so unbearable. Nearly always, some predisposition to anxiety or earlier trauma came to light—the boy's chronic illness as a child, the insecurity-creating personality of the mother bordering on Situation 3A, being left for years with a mean foster mother during wartime evacuation, the obvious and anxiety-arousing nature of the mother's illness, and, in *Bane*'s case, hearing the doctor's opinion that his widowed mother would not get over her illness.

Avoidance-excitement was also the predominant motivation in Situation 4B—that in which parental quarreling made the boy fear the loss of mother by desertion. In seven of the eight cases there was an admission of physical assaults by the father on the mother.

About half of the youths in this group showed the aforementioned symptoms of genuine mother-anxiety, their helpfulness presumably having the aim of persuading the mother not to desert the home. In the other cases any such tendency was precluded either by the youth's overriding need for avoidance-excitement, which drove him to seek forgetfulness outside the home, or by his depression.

The longstanding stress of such an intolerable family situation reduced five of the eight to a state of irritable/depressive nontolerance such as has been noted in parents at the limit of their resources. In the training school they were depressed and moody (not to be confused with the sullenness of hostility), and they were intolerant of human companionship and liable to break out in acts of physical violence. Several of the boys in other groups suffered from this hyperirritability. (*Rogers*, the boy whose mother killed herself in attempting an abortion, admitted that he could not prevent himself from hitting other boys, although he was not aggressive by nature.) It was, however, nowhere so general as in the parental-quarreling group. The most extreme instance was *Rich*, who made no effort to get on with his peers, whom he imagined were plotting against him behind his back. When disappointed at not being allowed to go home, he became a vicious bully. It was not a matter of hostility, because he was appreciative of kindness, which would be spurned by the hostile.

Rich's family was notorious in its locality for its criminality, the father and three elder brothers all being in prison for housebreaking at the time of my visit to the home. From the records they looked like a textbook case of a chosen criminal way of life. It was not choice but breakdown. Whenever Rich's father came out of prison he set about getting a job, but then someone would ask his employer why he had hired such a man, and the fellow would be dismissed. The mother was in a state of heartbroken despondency, but so desperately anxious to get her boy home that she decked her living room out with flowers in honor of my visit. Yet she also had given up, to the extent of spending her evenings in the pub while her younger children waited outside, exciting comment by their rags. The boy himself had three good reasons for his emotional exhaustion: he would hear his parents quarreling loudly in the next room, and dreaded their coming to blows; he feared his mother would desert; and to his anxieties were added her continual childbirths. Returning on leave from the school he found her in the hospital with her fourteenth. After five days spent decorating the house to cheer her up on her return, he broke down, and he was arrested after another spate of burglaries.

Those who cling to the idea that for certain families crime is just a business or a source of part-time income are deceived by the cover-up in these cases of marital discord and violence. The boys themselves were loath to talk or even think of the tragic situation in their homes. *Mathews* (p. 67) reminisced about an idyllic home life. *Hill*'s (p. 50) parents entertained me in thier spick-and-span sitting room, and the father—who had himself just done a month for larceny—threw me off the scent by describing all the good things that came his way in his trade of stevedoring. The boy's delinquencies also lent plausibility to my initial diagnosis that here was a case of a criminal way of life being passed on from father to son. Hill was a member of a gang of six or eight who went equal shares in the proceeds of their robberies, checked up on one another's honesty in declaring their loot, and arranged alibis for each other. About a year later, when the boy was in court, awaiting trial for the rape of an eight-year-old girl, I heard of the beatings his father gave his mother, and how she would drive off in a taxi and stay away for months—only to return for another cycle of quarreling and violence. There was a similar background of personal breakdown behind every other ostensible example of a criminal subculture. This latter notion persists only because cases are not systematically investigated. Those adherents of the idea who point out that wife beating, temporary desertions, and irresponsible fatherhood are accepted by the people concerned as part of their way of life should be reminded that children's needs for a stable, loving environment transcend cultural variations.

Situation 4C, the last in this group, arises when the child is in fear of abandonment by the preferred parent. It can occur with the pending break-up of the marriage, or when—on the mother's intended remarriage—the child fears she will no longer want him in her new home. This subgroup also includes instances of the mother's proposal to have the child lodged in an institutions or with a foster mother. In those cases where the mother actually attempted to get rid of the boy or succeeded in doing so for a period, he reacted by hostility and nuisance-attention. The precariousness of the boys' situations generated avoidance-excitement. There was a mixture of genuine and hypocritical mother-anxiety, bravado, and a cool dishonesty that suggested psychopathy.

Taking this group as a whole, in which the stressfulness of the situation consisted in a *fear* of being abandoned, the predominant form of delinquent breakdown was by avoidance-excitement. It was present in 17 of the 21 cases, compared with only 5 showing bravado, 4 hostility and 2 removal.

There was a group of five boys who for the greater part of their lives had been shuttled about between institutions and foster homes. They had had enough experience of life in their own homes to feel the lack of it, or were in intermittent contact with a mother. Attempts by their mothers or relatives to claim them after a number of years were met by tiresomeness and hostility. But in some cases, the relatives having been forewarned to expect such behavior at first, the youths settled down. Among them could be observed all the usual forms of delinquent breakdown and compensations for feeling unwanted. Notable among them were paranoia and a depressive withdrawal.

THE CORRELATION BETWEEN TYPE OF FAMILY SITUATION AND TYPE OF DELINQUENT BREAKDOWN

The correlation between the types of emotional stress to which these youths had been subjected and the manner of their breakdowns was by no means perfect, owing to the overlapping and merging of the categories of stress-producing parent-child relationships, and individual variations of temperament. Nevertheless, there emerged a number of suggestive associations close enough to serve as an aid to insight and diagnosis. In Group One the threat of rejection by the parents resulted predominantly in hostility merging into loyalty-testing by nuisance and delinquency. In Group Two the transition from a situation in which the child was loved, and often indulged, into one of dubious affection and limited toleration was followed by the twin avoidance-reactions of seeking physical removal and escape through excitement, with hostility as a self-banishing reaction present in about half of the cases. In Group Three the failure of the mother to provide warm and dependable affection, sometimes highlighted by separation from a surrogate mother, generated very strong removal urges combined, according to the particular pattern of deprivation, with avoidance-excitement and hostility. Where the mother was harsh and insensitive, the longstanding doubts about her affection generated bravado as a compensation for feeling little valued. In Group Four the fear of loss of the mother, without a father to turn to, gave rise to avoidance-excitement.

In seeking understanding of the familial causes of an individual's delinquency the social worker should not be satisfied until every anomalous feature of a case has been accounted for. An unexplained reaction on the part of the child means that an important factor in the situation remains unrevealed. For example, if the only discovered source of a child's anxiety is his mother's health, and he steals from her or imposes on her shamelessly, one can be quite certain that the real source of deprivation is of quite a different character.

Let it be repeated also that the anxiety the child mentions voluntarily or talks about willingly is never that which has driven him to breakdown. The social workers who had repeatedly asked the Toronto delinquent youth, "What's bugging you?" were unsophisticated in diagnosis (Malarek, 1979).

This is not to say that all my own cases came out pat. In some I only got at the truth by the luck of circumstances. Others I had to leave with unexplained features; but at least the knowledge of which reaction to expect from each type of parent-child relationship made me aware of not having achieved a complete solution. In such cases all the social worker can do is to work with the child and his family in the hope that the essential truth will eventually come out. A neighborhood social worker is in a better position in this respect than I was with my training-school sample, because the families of the latter were spread over the whole of southern England.

PART FOUR
The Preventive Program

Chapter Ten
Identifying the Delinquency-Prone

BEHAVIORAL CHARACTERISTICS OF DELINQUENTS

It has been seen that persistent delinquents tend to show special characteristics, even within their own social class and cultural group. The success of a prevention program will therefore depend upon our ability to identify them at a pre- or early-delinquent stage. If, moreover, their key differentiating characteristic is that they have reverted to a state of behavioral breakdown in which they are liable to act in maladaptive ways, it follows that we should be able to identify them by the systematic observation of their nondelinquent behavior.

Serious delinquents form a special group in the sense that they are the particular individuals who are both more vulnerable and more exposed to the stresses liable to produce behavioral breakdown. Obviously, the most fundamental form of prevention would consist in the removal of the social conditions which, at the prenatal level, produce the vulnerability (see Chapter Thirteen) and, at the postnatal level, produce the exceptional stresses. These, however, are long-term strategies which may have to include, beside the betterment of material conditions, the adoption of new life styles; and the latter are transmitted from generation to generation with remarkable persistence.

A prevention program which aims to produce results within a measurable term of years has consequently to concentrate upon this group of the delinquency-prone. Its strategy would in the main be to identify not only the vulnerable individuals but also the situations which are bringing about their maladjustment. The situations in question are described in Chapter Nine. Since certain types of situations tend to be related to certain forms of behavioral breakdown, the type of maladjustment observed is of crucial importance. It narrows down the range of stressful situations which may be responsible and hence give us a clue as to what to look for in the child's family which may have prompted his maladjustment and delinquency. If, for example, a child is exhibiting typical hostile behavior in school, as shown by sullenness, rejecting friendly overtures, and going out of his way to arouse bad feeling against himself, we can be confident that the child has been subject to the threat, or the reality, of being rejected by the parents or the adults who stand in the place of parents. If, on the other hand, the pattern of maladjustment is one of impulsive initiatives and generally acting without thought for the consequences, but the child shows a cheerful disposition which rules out hostility, we can assume that his parents are coping with his nuisance without making threats of rejection.

Both these types of maladjustment are often included under the heading of acting out, "conduct problems," or antisocial behavior. Such terms mean essentially nothing more than that the child is a nuisance, which the teacher knows already. The hostile child is a conduct problem because he is uncooperative and can become violent or steal; the inconsequent child is a conduct problem because of his showing off, aggressiveness towards his peers, his disobedience, and his disruptiveness. These are two fundamentally different modes of behavior disturbance and have different causes. Thus, we do not get much help from a system of diagnosis which lumps them together in one broad category. Likewise, a general statement that a child is "deeply disturbed" brings us no nearer to an understanding of the nature and causes of his maladjustment.

In arguing for a differential diagnosis of behavior disturbance, Bowlby (1944, p. 6) draws a pertinent analogy with physical disease:

> Before any satisfactory work upon the causation of symptoms such as fever or rash can be carried out, an attempt at classification and diagnosis is essential. No good can come, for instance, from attempts to study the course of fever in an unclassified group of children whose one point in common is abnormal temperature. In the same way statistics and conclusions regarding the cause of juvenile delinquency will remain unsatisfactory and obscure so long as no attempt is made to classify types of delinquents and to study each type separately.

My own casework experience led me to abandon Bowlby's categories and his theories of causation, but it confirmed his point that deviant acting-out behavior is the expression of distinct modes of disturbance. I found the traditional psychiatric classification, based on the study of psychosis, of little use. It was rather a question of starting afresh by the recording of instances of behavior which in any way deviated from the normal. These had to be typed according to some concept of similarity. How behaviors are to be classified is no simple matter. To try to ape the older sciences by recording similar physical movements gets us nowhere (Stott, Marston, and Neill, 1975). Our limbs are general-purpose organs which are used in all sorts of transactions with the environment. The important thing for the understanding of behavior is the intention which lies behind it. The very purpose of behavior, as it has evolved, is in achieving certain relationships between the organism and its environment. It is therefore logical to classify behaviors by their ostensible goals.

On observing a behavior or receiving a report thereof from a housemaster, trade instructor, or parent, I consequently asked myself what the youth in question was trying to achieve. The behaviors in which I was interested were all in some degree maladaptive and sometimes highly abnormal, so that I had to seek motives apart from the everyday ones of securing some recognized benefit (which would have rendered them normal). Those consisting of the avoidance of intolerable situations and their memory, and of escape by self-banishment have already been described in Chapter Seven. In case after case, as reported in *Delinquency and Human Nature* (Stott, 1950/80) the devices used to keep the traumatic memories from consciousness were revealed in detail (see Collins, p. 14; Mills, p. 46; Langford, p. 62; Banks, p. 155; Rogers, p. 187); and evidence was also forthcoming, during interviews, of the attempts of some youths to escape physically from their situation (see Elson, p. 66; Watson, p. 129; Sharp, p. 194; Ross, p. 262); or to secure committal to an institution by hostile behavior directed against their parents (see Bennett, p. 64; Tylor, p. 251; Faulkner, p. 274; Newman, p. 288; Batchelor, p. 308).

At an early stage I was struck by how situation-specific the maladaptive behaviors were. A boy would be scrupulously honest at home and even press all his earnings on his mother, yet steal outside the home. Behavior had to be seen as directed to the attainment of different goals in different situations. Basically, therefore, the motivations were *situation attitudes*. The attempt to rate people by constant traits, such as honesty or cooperativeness, which was the standard form of personality assessment during the time of my study, was like trying to describe the sky by naming a single color. It follows that a checklist of behavioral descriptions should specify the situations in which certain reactions may or may not occur. Not to do so puts the teacher or whoever has to make the recording in a quandary, and because we resent the ineffectiveness which quandaries impose on us, this makes such checklists unpopular.

At an early stage in my search for a typology, the major delinquent motivations and the distinctive behaviors that they generated
suggested one form of classification. Because, however, the experiences of each individual youth had been different and had produced
a diversity of conditionings, and the innate strength of their reactions
and their neural stamina varied, each motivation was expressed in
rather different behaviors. One hostile boy would veer towards sullen
refusal of affection; another would act out his resentment mainly by
provocative acts and running away. Nevertheless, there was a sufficient overlap to form a core of key symptoms which could rightly be
called a syndrome. Because of this "spottiness" in the signs of any
type of maladjustment, reliable diagnosis has to draw upon a large
range of indications. Of, say, 20 possible manifestations of hostility,
a child may only show 8 or 9, and yet rightly be placed in the
"severe" category for this type of maladjustment. Parents and
teachers have often asked me at meetings, "What does it mean when
a child does so-and-so?" I have to reply that I cannot say until I
know about a large number of other things he does. Likewise, a
checklist in which the major types of maladjustment are each represented by mere two or three items, only one or two of which may
apply to the particular case, is of no use for a diagnosis which is to
be the starting point of treatment. How misleading a single indication can be is well illustrated by an experience which a fellow psychologist related to me. The court referred to him for assessment a
youth who had stolen a woman's corset off a clothesline. After
failing to find any evidence of transvestism or other abnormality,
the psychologist asked him directly: "You didn't intend to wear
them did you?" The youth's reply was, "Of course I did. It was to
keep the wind off my chest when I go motorcycling." The moral
of the story is that the type of behavior disturbance can be judged
only by the observation of a fair number of indications which have
an established syndromic validity.

BEHAVIORAL POINTERS TO DELINQUENCY

It was with the prospect of establishing such syndromes or
types of maladjustment that the first editions of the Bristol Social
Adjustment Guides were completed (Stott and Sykes, 1956). The
"Residential" edition contained those descriptions of behavior which
the staffs of institutions were able to give as characteristic of disturbed children, and the "Day-School" edition contained the same,
as reported by teachers. In interpreting the record of behavior

provided by the latter, it must be borne in mind that the school forms only a segment of a child's life. Most serious maladjustment will be available to the observation of the teacher, but there are important exceptions. The case was quoted earlier of a child who showed only a few indications on the BSAG: owing to his truancy he was seldom there for the teacher to observe, and when he was in school his blocking of the distressing memory of his lost mother took the form of a retreat into fantasy which enabled him to sit passively rather than to seek excitement.

There is no category of avoidance by excitement in the BSAG. The affected children find it difficult to tolerate the sameness of the school surroundings and having to sit still and concentrate (especially on arithmetic). Hence, the most salient manifestation of avoidance-excitement is truancy. Apart from removing them from the observation of the teacher, as in the case of the boy just referred to, truancy is not confined to avoidance-excitement. The hostile child truants as a form of self-banishment, and the inconsequent child truants because he finds it difficult to resist the invitation to do so, or dislikes being called a coward. Avoidance excitement offers a clear syndrome of abnormal behaviors in the young person's free-ranging life, but not in school.

The other important category now omitted from the day-school edition of the BSAG is that of the "moral defective" or "affection-less character." The source of the condition, it was suggested, was dysfunction of the mechanism for ensuring social attachment. In other words, the child in question does not need love or approval or acceptance, and so has no compunctions about committing acts which, if discovered, would alienate him from his human circle. But he learns by experience that discovery will bring punishment, and he is not under the emotional compulsions which render the hostile or the avoidance-driven child reckless. Consequently, his misdemeanors are calculated, and hard to pin on him. The "moral defect" of these children sometimes becomes apparent in school, and their teachers have described them to me as "just wicked," or "a really bad child." But their recognition in the day-school setting is unreliable, and apt to be confused at the secondary stage with the alienation often found among pupils who have lost interest in school. The condition was represented in the first edition of the BSAG by the *K* ("knavery") syndrome, but was removed from the second edition for the foregoing reasons. Because, however, it becomes apparent in a live-in situation, it is retained in the "Residential" edition of the BSAG.

Having arrived at indications of behavior disturbance which
have a certain validity (McDermott, 1980a, 1980b, 1981; Stott,
Marston and Neill, 1975; Wilson, 1973), the next step towards the
identification of the delinquency-prone is to ascertain which of them
are most frequently associated with delinquency. From a sample of
1,940 students attending schools in a Canadian industrial city, in
respect of whom teachers had completed a BSAG, records of the 133
who had been involved in a delinquent occurrence were compared
with those of the main body. Their scores for *underreacting* maladjustment were little different from those of the nondelinquents;
but those for behavior disturbance of an overreacting type were
two and a half times higher, and rose consistently with the number
of police involvements. Their scores in the core syndromes of the
BSAG show in greater detail the types of behavior disturbance most
associated with delinquency. Compared with nondelinquents, the
children with three or more involvements showed 73 percent more
withdrawal, 139 percent more depression, 166 percent more inconsequence, and 534 percent more hostility. Hostility is thus seen as
the form of behavior disturbance most characteristic of these delinquent juveniles. The 25 descriptions of maladjusted behavior, which
the teachers checked three or more times more frequently for the
delinquents, contained 12 hostility items and 2 of inconsequence.
The remainder were other sorts of overreacting behavior, which,
together with one of the inconsequential items, included an element
of bravado.

The items in question, given in Table 1, could form the basis of
a delinquency-proneness detection instrument. We have, on the other
hand, to take account of the feeling that the designation of a juvenile
as a potential delinquent may be a self-fulfilling prophecy, and, by
labeling him and impairing his chances of fair treatment, constitute
an encroachment of civil rights. While recognizing that prediction
specifically of delinquency may be open to abuse, we have to bear
in mind that no preventive measures are possible unless we are able
to identify the delinquency-prone. This is all the more true if, as
the studies quoted indicate, the personal characteristics of the delinquent are important. We have to recognize that such labeling and
prejudgment are at present taking place in the police practice, after
an offense has been committed, of questioning deviant juveniles
already known to them (previous conviction and association with the
convicted being good pragmatic predictors). The BSAG offers and
alternative form of early identification free of the labeling effect of
"giving a dog a bad name." It is completed by a teacher, without

Table 1

Greater frequency of maladjusted behaviors among delinquents

	Frequency Ratio: Delinquents/Nondelinquents
Inconsequence	
Shows off (clowns, strikes silly attitudes, mimics)	3.06
Borrows books from others' desks without permission	3.60
Hostility	
Will help (teacher) unless he is in a bad mood	4.31
Sometimes in a bad mood (talking to teacher)	3.36
Inclined to be moody	3.02
Seems to go out of his way to earn disapproval	3.62
Openly does things he knows are wrong, in front of the teacher	4.17
Bears a grudge, always regards punishment as unfair	3.76
Becomes antagonistic	4.80
Has uncooperative moods	3.40
Has stolen in a way that he would be bound to be found out	5.82
Uses bad language which he knows will be disapproved of	7.41
Tries to argue against teacher	3.20
Squabbles, makes insulting remarks (in relations with other students)	3.90
Nonsyndromic Overreaction	
Sometimes a fluent liar	3.62
Mixes mostly with unsettled types	3.45
Damage to personal property	13.59
Foolish or dangerous pranks when with a gang	3.05
Damage to public property	13.59
Habitual slick liar; has no compunction about lying	3.77
Has stolen within the school in an underhand cunning way	5.59
Has truanted, or suspected of truancy	10.19
Bad loser (creates a disturbance when game goes against him)	3.09
Misuses companionship to show off or dominate	3.27
Bad sportsman (plays for himself only, cheats, fouls)	3.16

From Stott, Marston, and Neill (1975).

involvement of the child in question, and only some 4 or 5 of the 109 items indicating maladjustment relate to formally delinquent acts. Thus there is no practical possibility of its use conferring a delinquent "label" unless the teacher is informed that the objective of the procedure is to pick out future delinquents, or some similar administrative indiscretion is committed. Moreover, a maladjusted child stands in need of identification and treatment on account of his behavior disturbance, whether or not this includes delinquency or the likelihood thereof. If it transpires that his maladjustment takes the form of hostility, this in itself is evidence that he is being subjected to emotional ill-treatment and is in need of help. Against such identification there can be no moral or political objection; the guilt lies upon the society which fails to identify and treat the maladjusted delinquency-prone.

It remains to describe the mechanics of a program of identification based on an assessment of juvenile behavior disturbance. Since the BSAG requires about 15 minutes of the teacher's time in respect of each student, a short preliminary screening instrument should first be used. This takes the form of six questions which the teacher answers with a "Yes" or "No," as given in Chapter Seventeen. For the whole class this takes about half an hour. The questions cover the main types of behavior disturbance, both of an under- and over-reacting type, that the teacher is likely to meet, and consequently are not focused on delinquency. The teacher would then be asked to complete a full BSAG in respect only of those students whom the preliminary screening suggests are displaying an overreacting type of behavior disturbance (questions 3-6). An independent person working under conditions of confidentiality and having no ongoing personal relationship with the student in question would score the BSAG and then apply a further template which isolates the 25 delinquency-proneness indicators. By this procedure the risk of "labeling" is virtually eliminated.

The omission of norms for these 25 delinquency indicators is deliberate. If there is a score from which a probability of delinquency can be induced, it is likely to be misused, notably by influencing the form of disposition. It is left to the psychologist or social worker engaged in the identification program to observe whether the items marked indicate a serious risk of breakdown.

Chapter Eleven
Effective Casework

INTERVENTION NEEDS A KNOWLEDGE OF CAUSES

Little reliable progress can be made in treatment without some understanding of causes. In medical science this is a commonplace. Pasteur's discovery of the part played by bacteria opened a new era of medicine. Consequently, the main thrust of medical research has been to discover the causes of diseases. Not so for the social phenomenon of delinquency: the contemporary stereotype is to dismiss the issues of causation with the statement that juvenile delinquency has no single cause, thereby implying that there is no point in giving any more thought to the matter. West and Farrington (1973) have drawn attention to the striking disparity between the money spent on social emergencies and on medical crises. Perhaps it is the social scientists' own fault. The aforementioned authors, as criminologists, criticize fashionable sociological models of delinquency causation, which can only adduce irresistible social forces. Because these forces are seen as beyond the control of the social scientist, the current mood is one of helplessness and pessimism. These attitudes neither open up further lines of enquiry nor attract research funding. They are equally unproductive when it comes to the prevention of delinquency. For effective casework we need to understand how each type of delinquency comes about. This means recognizing the motivations which drive each individual to a delinquent course of behavior,and the circumstances which provoke those motivations.

Finding that their background factors were interlocking and statistically inseparable, West and Farrington eventually also abandoned their search for causes. Their bowing-out gesture was to conclude that the reasons why some families more than others produce delinquents were "complex"—that is to say, beyond human ingenuity to solve. The real barrier to their achieving a solution was the division of function between the data collectors and the data treaters which was referred to in Chapter One. Only by observing human reactions at first hand can useful insights be gained into the processes which lead to delinquency. The study of causes has to be brought to, and over, the delinquent's own doorstep and into his haunts. It is a lengthy and painstaking type of inquiry, but so is the laboratory study of physical, chemical, and biological processes. In science there is no substitute for observation. Its comparative neglect in the field of delinquency is the chief reason for the present ineffectiveness of our treatment methods.

PRESENT NEGLECT AND INEFFECTIVENESS
OF CASEWORK

In her introduction to the NACRO (1978b) booklet on the Hammersmith Teenage Project, Lady Plowden calls, among other measures, for "better techniques of diagnosing the causes of a young person's anti-social behavior." Hers is a lone voice. Not only have such techniques been lacking, the very need for them has been ignored. In the community projects for the prevention of delinquency launched in the English-speaking world there has been a positive contempt for casework skills. West and Farrington (1973) draw a depressing picture of the state of affairs which results from the present level of social-work techniques. Reflecting upon the fate of the delinquents in their ten-year follow-up study, they write:

> Throughout this sequence of unfortunate developments, the boys and their parents experience points of contact with caring agencies. Ante-natal clinics, health visitors, general practitioners, schools, social security offices, voluntary social services, youth employment offices, and also of course police and childrens' officers, all come into the picture at some stage. None of these agencies seems able to change the course of events (p. 202).

These authors single out two important reasons for what they term "the ineffectuality of social intervention" (p. 202). The first is that the families who are most in need of help are the least likely to seek it; the second is what the authors call irresponsible breeding. The latter is too broad an issue to come within the scope of the present book. Their first point, however, is central to the procedures of any effective prevention program. These problem-ridden families cannot be left, as the saying goes, to stew in their own juices. We have to identify the children in danger and take positive measures to rescue them, for their own sakes and for the sake of society.

It has to be asked why, considering that we have probation officers and social workers, no systematic methods for the investigation of causes are in operation at the present time. Even when a case is postponed for a report of the delinquent's family circumstances what is normally forthcoming is nothing more than a sketch of the family structure, the employment and social record of the parents, the offender's school and employment history, and possibly his associates and habits. No diagnosis is attempted of the reasons for the lapse into delinquency in terms of the individual's vulnerability, the precise nature of the stresses and emotional deprivations to which he has been exposed, and his resultant state of mind.

One reason for this failure to parallel medical diagnostic practice is simply that the main body of social workers and probation officers have not had the requisite training. Even those who have been taught the skills, or who have developed them themsleves, seldom have the time to practice them. The overly large caseloads have already been referred to. Perhaps equally responsible is the excessive time that social workers have to spend in court. One London social worker reported to Melanie Phillips (1978), a *Guardian* writer, thus:

"With one particular boy, I've been in court about 20 times since Christmas. Either the case has been put forward, or he's changed his plea—administrative reasons. You go along at 10 a.m. and you can spend all day there." As the social worker in question pointed out, if the offense is a symptom of problems at home, social work help could be offered and accepted without court proceedings. This does not mean that the juvenile court can be totally dispensed with: in Chapter Seventeen I suggest what its role might be. It has, however, to be recognized that judges and lawyers are not trained to exercise the diganostic skills required for investigating the causes of the delinquency of the individual youngster or for prescribing treatment. Nor can a social worker present to a court, before the parties concerned, the confidential information or offer a professional diagnosis without possibly doing a lot of harm. Moreover, as I shall argue, the definitive understanding of the reasons for a delinquent breakdown usually emerge only as a reult of a period of work with the offender and his family. The initial investigation produces nothing but a hypothesis. It will not form an adequate basis for a legal decision as to disposition, and may be unfair both to the child and the parents.

THE CASEWORK TECHNIQUES

The first stage of the system of casework proposed in this book is that of identifying those children who are in a state of mind and emotion which is likely to lead to delinquency. Such states nearly always reveal themselves in certain kinds of maladjusted behavior, such as were described in the previous chapter. The second stage consists, as far as the vast majority of delinquent children are concerned, in the recognition of the sort of emotional deprivation from which they are suffering, and its source in the family situation. This stage is dealt with in Chapter Nine. The third stage, that of remedial action, is the subject of this chapter.

THE SOCIAL WORKER'S HYPOTHESIS

On first taking up a case, the social worker has to proceed from the diagnostic indications that are then available or that emerge from initial contacts with the offender and his family. In the course of intervention further facts will come to light, so that any action taken should be limited to whatever can be corrected later if necessary. The initial diagnosis is therefore always in the nature of a hypothesis. We have to fight against both our own pet attribution and the over-diagnosing of that which is in the current fashion.

The first orientation towards a diagnosis should come from the young person's day-to-day behavior at school or at work, and in the home and neighborhood. The nature of the delinquent act should be seen as consistent with certain aspects of the nondelinquent behavior, even though it may be markedly inconsistent with its other aspects. The next stage is an exploration of the family situation. In the course of an informal interview with the mother, preferably in her own home, the social worker will be able to pick up many indications of the family relationships. A distinction must be made between those which are openly stated—that is, "He is very fond of his father—and those which are only hinted at or implied, such as the mother's making the foregoing statement when asked about the child's affection for her.

At this point an estimate has to be made of whether or not the child has been deprived of his need for a reliable family base. Severe deprivation thereof can be confidently inferred

1. if the BSAG or direct interview with the teacher reveals strong hostility.
2. If the child, against the warnings of his parents, persists in associating with other delinquent "boys down the street."

3. if the child seeks noisy, garish leisure-time diversions in places of amusement, and—not being able to tolerate the sameness of an indoor environment—truants from school or work. An aspect of this criterion is that the child is seldom in the house, although this must not be taken as a sole indication.

4. if the child indulges in risky escapades along with other deviant youngsters.

5. If the child is given to wandering off and staying away for hours at a time.

6. if the child occasionally gives vent to inexplicable "mad" outbursts or other irrational behavior.

7. if the child steals from the home or from lodgers or neighbors, or commits wanton damage or nuisance that can easily be pinned onto him.

8. if the child is reluctant to leave the home, wants to do the mother's housework for her, mind the baby, spend money on her apart from anniversaries, and so on.

9. if the child has committed very obvious offenses, as though asking to be caught—especially committing a further obvious and flagrant offense while awaiting a court hearing.

10. if the offense is of a socially reprehensible character that no ordinary person could put down to boyish pranks; for example, arson, robbery with violence, breaking into private dwellings, major damage to property.

If any one of the foregoing criteria is met, the caseworker should then extend the hypothesis to include the type of defect in the parent-child relationship which is responsible for the deprivation. The patterns of maladjustment- and delinquency-conducive situations described in Chapter Nine are provided as a guide to this stage. They should be treated as examples of common sources of emotional deprivation which prove intolerable to the child. An actual situation may be a variant of any one of them, or contain elements of two or three. The important thing is that the social worker should form a hypothesis of how the child has been deprived of his need for secure attachment to caring adults. Needless to say, the hypothesis may have to be modified or abandoned in favor of another as the family situation becomes better known.

Progress towards a diagnosis of the reasons for a child's delinquency as they pertain to the family is facilitated by the use of the Diagnostic Worksheets for Assessing Deviant Behavior reproduced at the end of this chapter.

INDIVIDUAL CAUSES OF DEVIANCE
OTHER THAN THE FAMILY SITUATION

If none of the criteria for emotional deprivation applies, the social worker has to consider two broad alternatives. The first is that the child has lacked the social learning experiences to condition him against wrongdoing. His parents may have turned a blind eye to his petty vandalism or shoplifting because they could not be bothered to supervise his conduct or they feared the temporary bad relationship that punishment entails. On every hand one sees parents ignoring their children's misbehavior or exposure to danger, while other people look on in disgust. It is not for nothing that some preindustrial societies adopt the convention that an uncle is responsible for the child's good behavior, or delegate tribal elders to take charge once the child reaches puberty.

The second alternative is that the child may have temperamental qualities which make him difficult to discipline. The most normal of these is a strong desire for independence and personal effectiveness with which go overconfidence and, at times, impulsiveness. Such children may get into occasional trouble. The common handicap of temperament which may lead to minor delinquency is inconsequence. The child so affected is liable to respond thoughtlessly to delinquent invitations, and do so time after time. Inconsequent children are hard to discipline because they are hard to condition. The results of their actions are not impressed on their minds because they do not reflect upon them, and they act too quickly for the recall of earlier learning.

Finally, among the temperamentally handicapped are the children who have suffered damage to their behavioral system that renders them indifferent to human attachments. These are the so-called moral defectives described previously. Their misdemeanors are likely to be well covered, unlike those of the inconsequent child.

The stability of the other children in the family affords a useful clue as to whether the deviance has its origin primarily in a handicap of temperament or in the family situation. Just as a mentally retarded child can be found among a group of mentally normal siblings, so a single temperamentally handicapped child can be found in a stable family among behaviorally normal siblings. Such a child may give rise to a bad family situation owing to his tiresome ways. He may exhaust his parents nervously, or cause them to fear that his bad example will spread to the other children. The resulting rejection, in my experience, is the most common origin of the "black sheep" pattern.

REMEDIAL INTERVENTION

In medicine it is a commonplace that treatment is based on the findings of the diagnosis. The same should apply to social casework. The caseworker's overall objective is to free the young person from the state of mind which has forced him into delinquent activities. The first and main step towards the accomplishment of this goal is to remove, to the extent that it is possible to do so, the stresses which have produced it—that is to say, a threat to his permanent acceptance within his family, or a fear of losing his preferred or only parent. This general strategy should be broken up into a series of subgoals, which should be formulated in the case record so that both the worker in charge of the case and others who may be involved know exactly the stage reached in the remedial treatment.

The five delinquency-generating states of mind described in Chapter Seven therefore form the starting points of treatment. The proportions in which they may be found among delinquents who are still living in their home communities may differ from those found in a sample of youths who have been committed. The very fact that a great many of these have succeeded in getting themselves physically removed from their homes by committal makes it more probable that the removal motivation was more frequent among them. They are also likely to contain a higher proportion of young people actuated by extreme avoidance-excitement, because this motivation often results in grossly abnormal behavior. In Chapter Ten it was seen that the great majority of the manifestations of maladjusted behavior associated with delinquency were indications of hostility. Because the records in question were furnished by teachers in a day-school setting, no observations suggesting an urge to removal were possible, and much of the restlessness and misbehavior prompted by avoidance-excitement would have been included in the syndrome of inconsequence. Nevertheless, we are probably on safe ground in regarding hostility as the principal emotional state behind juvenile deviance.

THE ORIGINS OF HOSTILITY

The recognition of the nature and origin of hostility and the remedial intervention which follows from such understanding are so crucial that the social worker who masters it and nothing else will be able to make an important contribution to delinquency prevention, and the social worker who fails to understand the process will be able to make little or none. The same applies to the staffs of residential committal institutions and to professional foster parents—to which must be added that for these professions the recognition of loyalty testing by delinquency is equally essential.

Hostility must not be confused with straightforward and openly aggressive behavior, such as can occur in an adolescent struggling for independence, or in a person in a state of neural fatigue or who finds himself cornered in a position of ineffectiveness. The hostile child is more often sullen and avoiding of human contact, refusing to talk, and running off and hiding. Usually he becomes physically aggressive only when attempts are made to punish him. Then his mood of not caring about being accepted and of inviting rejection remove the restraints upon anger which ordinarily keep people's tempers within limits.

Paradoxically, hostility is the delinquent state of mind which is the most responsive to social-work intervention. The reason for this is that, although the sullenness and "bloodyminded" provocative acts by which it is expressed give the opposite impression, hostility is objectively an indication that the construed rejection and loss of love still hurt. Its aim is to kill a once-valued love relationship which have proved unreliable or has been broken by the other party. At the same time it aims to punish the unfaithful one by making him feel sorry. But hostility remains active only so long as the process is incomplete: alongside the affection-killing tactics there still lingers a desire to reestablish the relationship. The mothers of many delinquent youths have reported to me how their sons would alternate between moods of hostility and trying to be as pleasant as possible. They constantly shifted from anxiety to hostility and back again. From repeated let-downs hostility may deteriorate into a hard and constant enmity against the world in general. But as long as the affection-killing mechanisms of hostility are active, there is hope.

It is therefore of critical importance, once active hostility in a child has been recognized, to get at the situation which is generating it before irreconcilable antagonisms develop. One of the few 100 percent fits of cause and effect in the field of behavior disturbance is that found between hostility and parental behavior which undermines the child's confidence in the parents' loyalty and permanent attachment to him. Such faith can be destroyed if the preferred parent—that is, the one to whom the child looks for permanent attachment—(1) threatens to have the child removed from the home; (2) makes the child's continued membership in the family circle conditional upon his good behavior, especially in the case of a foster child; (3) threatens to desert the home and leave the child behind, or actually commits acts of temporary or permanent desertion; (4) threatens to commit suicide or talks about dying (this being a threat of deprivation); (5) yields, or appears in danger of yielding, to pressure from another member of the family, notably the other parent or a stepparent, to have the child removed from the home; and (6) as a foster parent to whom the child is attached, acquiesces in the removal of the child to the care of the true mother, towards whom the child is indifferent or from whom he is estranged.

In all the cases of hostility that I have investigated there has been one or more of the above confidence-destroying factors, or a cognate threat to the child's need for a permanent and unquestioned attachment. The converse, however, does not necessarily hold. The aforementioned threats or acts of disloyalty seem to generate hostility only in the temperamentally vulnerable child. An emotionally robust child may either not take them seriously or, if their reality is beyond doubt, take some rational step such as seeking alternative adult attachment.

THE TREATMENT OF HOSTILITY

Treatment by the social worker should in the first place consist in counseling the parents to desist from their threats of "putting away" or desertion, and to make clear their determination to keep the child within the family. How the matter is broached to the parents is a matter of tactics. A straight question as to whether the parents have uttered any of the foregoing threats will carry an imputation of blame, and may be denied. The conversation should be brought to the point where the parents make the admission voluntarily. A useful tactic is to make a general reflection, along the lines of: "Some parents tell their child that he will have to be put away if he goes on being naughty, and so give him the idea that they don't want him any more. Then the child takes it to heart and purposely does more naughty things, just to see if the parents will really have him put away." If threats by the mother to desert the home are suspected, a similar invitation to make a clean breast of them can be made, along the lines of: "Some mothers threaten to clear out and leave the family to look after themselves when they feel they are being imposed upon or the children take no notice of what she says." Well-meaning and affectionate parents nearly always respond to such openings to confession, and readily admit that they also have been holding the threat of putting them away or running off over their children.

Most threats of "putting away" and of leaving the family are made by parents either in a mood of irritation or exasperation, or because they regard them as an effective means of discipline. (One couple told me they used them rather than resort to physical punishment.) The security-destroying and hostility-generating threats are often used by well-meaning parents who are fundamentally attached to their children. Since economically underprivileged parents are subject to so much greater material stresses, they lapse more often into those states of irritable-depressive nontolerance of which threats of throwing out of the home, desertion, or suicide are a part. In short, many parents commit the sin of destroying their child's confidence in them, either from lack of imagination about how seriously their words will be taken or because they themselves have broken down temporarily owing to a combination of stresses.

The social worker has to judge whether the rejection threats stem from mere lack of imagination or from the emotional state of the parent. If it is the former it is merely a question of making the parents realize how seriously a sensitive child may take even lightly uttered threats of abandonment, and how, instead of reducing the bad behavior, they produce a reaction of an altogether more serious type. It can be depicted to them in general terms, or by relating an instance in the caseworker's experience how the child's loyalty-testing or counter-rejecting tactics take the form of what seems quite uncalled-for provocative naughtiness, such as stealing things which are needed by the parents but useless to the child; how this inexplicable bad behavior, further exasperating the parents, drives them to more vehemently expressed threats of putting away, which in turn cause a redoubling of the child's provocations. If this vicious circle of rejection threat, hostile retaliation, and more serious intention to get rid of the child has indeed begun to operate in the family, the parents will be certain to recognize it when it is described to them, and cooperate with the social worker in its unwinding. In those cases where the parents themselves are free of the emotional pressures which drive people to desperation, the mere cessation of the threats produces an immediate deflation of the child's hostility. I have in mind the case of a five-year-old boy who was stealing tools from neighbors' garages, vandalizing their flower beds, and, getting up early in the morning, would take eggs from the family refrigerator and drop them on the floor, and throw other food into the garbage pail. From the day that the cause of this abnormal behavior was explained to the parents and they ceased their threats to hand the boy over to the probation officer, there were no more such incidents.

Treatment was accomplished in one main exploratory and one short follow-up interview. Five years later I met the father again and he assured me there had been no recurrence and the boy had settled down to complete normality.

The older hostile child will probably need more positive reassurances of the parents' loyalty than the mere cessation of threats of abandonment. Instead of the habitual threats, the parents, even though continuing to get angry at the misbehavior, should be prompted to throw in remarks that they are going to make a decent man or woman of the youngster, that he or she is their responsibility, and one they are not going to pass on to anyone else, that the youngster is their flesh and blood (or whatever other folk usage expresses family cohesiveness). Such remarks should be supplemented, at a suitable opportunity, by actions which presuppose the youngster's continuing to live under the roof—making arrangements for the equipment and decoration of a special room or corner for the youngster in the home, buying a new bed or new curtains, and the like. The critical moment for positive reassurance is when the child is brought into court. This should absolutely never be at the instance of a parent; and, indeed, the legal provision for a parent to bring a child to court as "Beyond Control" should be abolished. The formal renunciation of a child which is thereby dramatically enacted seems to remain as an indelible memory that no subsequent attempts at reconciliation can efface. I have never known a youth, brought to court by a mother as beyond control, ever to be able to accept her again. In court the parents should be briefed, once they have agreed to follow the social worker's counsel, to demand in no uncertain terms that their child remain with them, and repeat their readiness to care for him until he grows out of his bad ways.

TESTING LOYALTY BY DELINQUENCY

It should be part of the social worker's strategy to forewarn the parents against the almost inevitable test of their determination to keep him that the child will impose on them. If the father has been threatening that his son will certainly be disowned if he has to go to court one more time, and the relationship between them has entered the viscious circle of rejection and hostility, it is a virtual certainty that the boy will test the sincerity of the parent's expressed change of heart by committing a further wanton offense and getting caught. If the parent can pass the "test by delinquency," by continuing to voice his determination to care for his son as his own flesh and blood, the likelihood is that the boy will then believe in his father's loyalty and settle down without further hostility or delinquency. Such loyalty tests are regularly applied by foster children on being moved to new foster parents. Their experience of being removed from one foster home to another because of their unmanageability leads them to doubt whether the new foster parents will be any more devoted to them. I have witnessed several similar loyalty tests upon a member of the staff of a residential school who has taken an affectionate interest in a boy and has put himself through a great deal of trouble on his behalf. At a time when everything seems to be going very well, the boy commits some unprovoked deviant act in order to find out whether the staff member is genuine in his liking for him. All too often the latter sees the wanton act as one of unforgivable ingratitude and will have nothing more to do with the boy. He has failed the test, and the boy is confirmed in his assumptions about the emotional insincerity of the adult world. Needless to say, he is then a much harder nut to crack, and anyone else who befriends him will be subjected to still more severe trials of loyalty. Both foster parents and the staff of residential schools should be trained to expect these delinquent tests of affection, so that they can endure them without resorting to the natural human impulses of indignation and rejection.

The foregoing strategies depend on the parents having sufficient control of their own emotions to be able to follow the counsel of the social worker. If the parents are estranged from each other or quarrel to the point that the marriage is threatened, any counseling, short of a lengthy period of marriage guidance, may be of little avail. How much of such guidance can be offered must of course depend on the caseload or on the possibility of reference to a specialized agency. The social worker will in practice often be faced with the realization that the parents, owing to their own problems, are incapable of providing a secure family base for their child. Such a conclusion should naturally be reached only after a period of work with the parents to which they have obviously failed to respond, and when the child is giving vent to more and more extreme hostility and antisocial behavior. It is at this stage that a recommendation for the removal of the child to other care should be made. Such a decision should depend not so much on the severity or persistence of the offenses as on the prospect of reestablishing for the child a secure place in his parents' affections. There is no sense in the present blind process by which the child himself determines when he should be removed, by the repetition of flagrant acts of delinquency to the point that committal becomes a legal consequence.

THE HANDLING OF CASES
OF AVOIDANCE-EXCITEMENT

The avoidance-excitement case—with its characteristic symptoms of restless risk-seeking and fantasies of such, frequenting of places of easy amusement, the shunning of any task requiring concentration (notably a dislike of arithmetic), intolerance of being within a building and consequent truancy and absenteeism, and outbursts of crazy behavior—is quickly identified by those who can read these signs. It must always be handled as an emergency. The need for consciousness-filling activity is unremitting, and spontaneous cessation of the delinquency is unlikely so long as the youngster remains in his own home, face to face with the reminders of his insecurity. It follows that the child under the compulsions of avoidance-excitement should be removed as soon as possible to a foster home or a residential school. The seven-year-old boy who was given to biting his teachers and other unprovoked violent acts returned to complete normality once he was placed in a foster home. In a residential institution the youngster given to avoidance-excitement in his home community likewise quickly settles down to normality, and learns to concentrate on his school studies or his trade. They make up a large proportion of the steady, apparently normal young people who form the bulk of those committed. They help to give the impression to people who do not know their history that the majority of young delinquents are of stable personality. With them the term becomes meaningless: constantly confronted with their family problems, they are highly unstable; away from them, with a little time to form new attachments in a new setting, they become stable. The exceptions are those who find in the residential setting some reminder of the critical episode or circumstances that they are trying to blank out from consciousness. I recall such a case, that of a handsome, well-built youth with a fine singing voice who was in constant trouble for his aggressive outbursts. He told me that he could not stand the sight of the windows abutting the recreation yard of his boarding house. He had seen some like them before but didn't know where, a typical *déjà vu* phenomenon. I inspected the windows and found them to have unusually small panes such as are seldom seen in ordinary houses. When I visited his home, the first thing I noticed was that its windows had panes of the identical type. His father told me of a quarrel the boy had had with his stepmother, in which she threw it up at him that since his mother, now dead, had gone about with other men, there was no knowing whether or not he was his ostensible father's son. The boy immediately quit the home and engaged in a hectic round of break-ins, until he was caught and committed. This case had a lucky solution, because we were able to establish by family resemblances that he was indeed the man's son, and from then on the aggressive outbursts ceased.

Taking the avoidance-dominated child out of his home gives the caseworker time to discover the sources of stress in the family situation which have prompted the avoidance-excitement. The avoidance is typically of particular memories which epitomize the defect in the parent-child relationships; but where the child's resources have been drained by long exposure to an insecure situation he may become shock-sensitive, and avoid the memory of unrelated shocks, as Collins (Stott, 1950/80) did of those of bombing and gruesome fire incidents. Naturally, the uncovering of the repressed memories is a time-consuming business, and further research is needed in order to establish its necessity. Once the youth makes new human attachments, those with the parents become less dominating, so that these, and time, may be the best healers.

THE TREATMENT OF INCONSEQUENCE
AND BRAVADO

The true inconsequent child has to be regarded as suffering from a handicap of temperament. The recognition that this is the case should induce tolerance and patience in the parents, and thus forestall the development of the vicious cycle of rejection and counter-rejection, leading to delinquency of a hostile type, which is the chief danger with this type of behavior disturbance.

The recognition of the nature of the handicap does not mean that the child's foolish and irritating behavior should be accepted as unalterable. It is a matter of patiently training him to control his impulses in one situation after another. The conditioning has to be specific to each type of temptation. Once the inconsequent youngster finds himself in a situation where he is tempted, such as being dared to commit a foolhardy act or to join in a delinquent escapade, he finds it very difficult to resist. The best form of conditioning is therefore that of training in the avoidance of tempting situations. The child should be encouraged to choose companions who are unlikely to lead him into trouble. It may be necessary to remove him from a locality in which he is likely to meet deviant associates who know how to play on his weakness.

It is important to give the older inconsequent youth who is given to bravado insight into the reasons why he allows himself to be persuaded into delinquent acts. Strange as it may seem, such youths can be deeply distressed at their repeated yielding despite their good resolutions. Because their behavior is so inexplicable, even to themselves, they begin to wonder if they are "wrong in the head." How one best explains to them why they are prone to act without considering the consequences depends on their level of mental development. They can at least be reassured that the silly impulses that spring into their minds are not in the least abnormal, because everyone has them. (The therapist will surely be able to quote some of his or her own.) It is a question of learning to resist them by some time-gaining device. Such counsel is of course useless in the abstract. The youngster should be primed with some verbal tag which neutralizes his particular temptation. If he responds to teasing by aggressive behavior, he should be taught to reply by "Sticks and stones will break my bones, but words will never hurt me." To counter a taunt of being chicken: "Go on; I'll be there to pick up the pieces," or "I'll drop you a line in jail." But mostly, with the older youth, a thorough discussion of his tendency to bravado, including helping him to introspect about how he had been seduced into delinquent and foolhardy acts, goes a long way towards helping him control his impulsiveness.

The fifth of the delinquent states of mind, that of the attempt at physical removal from the distressing family situation, is the subject of Chapter Twelve. Here I shall confine myself to the discussion of a case which serves as an object lesson in the perils of overlooking this all-too-frequent motivation. It is taken from the report of the Cambridge-Somerville Youth Study (Powers and Witmer, 1951).

At the age of eight, Peewee gained entry to a school by smashing the glass door, and being by then an experienced fire-setter and knowing how to proceed, he set some upholstered furniture on fire. Once the fire was under control, the search for the culprit began. Peewee had had plenty of time to run a fair distance, but he was found on the street not far from the scene. With his reputation as a fire-setter he must have known that he would be suspected. In fact he was "willing, almost eager, to admit that he started it." His excuse was merely that he wanted to have a little fun. No one asked whether this eagerness to get caught might have some significance. Although the boy was later placed in a special class in school, the smart-aleck answers with which he fobbed off a tester showed that he was quick-witted and hence capable of appreciating the effects of his behavior. Indeed, there were indications that he gave careful thought to them. His father constantly threatened him with "reform school," so he made repeated inquiries, from whomever he thought would know, about what a reform school was like—what kind of food you got there, how you were treated, and how far away it was— as if he were considering one as a place of abode. After several more arsons he came up with an open admission of his motivation: "I would like to leave home and live in the country. Maybe if I set another fire they will send me to the country, because the court does that sometimes." Thereupon he tried to set a fire in a coal yard, was apprehended, and sent back to the correctional school from which he had recently been released. While there he set no fires. There was no need to; his objective had been achieved.

A psychiatrist who saw the boy when he was nine diagnosed the fire-setting as "only the case of a simple-minded boy who liked to see smoke and flames. There is apparently no deeper motivation." Other evidence that he was by no means a simple-minded boy were the reasons that he gave, at eight or nine years of age, for rejecting his tutor's help in reading: "I would like to know how to write when I grow up. But not now! Now, I want to color. Do you think I am a good colorer? You can go home and tell your mother you know a boy who knows how to color."

There were indeed hints of other delinquent motivations, as there nearly always are alongside the urge to removal. Peewee's insistence on his need for fun, his intolerance of schoolwork, his disruptive hyperactivity in school, his wanton killing of pet animals, and his hair-raising fantasies pointed to avoidance-excitement. He was also a boy of high effectiveness-motivation, as shown by his refusal to be overawed by the school system into doing things he did not want to do. And a common means of creating a spectacular effect (one of the categories of effectiveness-motivation [Stott, 1961a]) is by destruction.

It would not be germane to my point to reproduce the account given of Peewee's family circumstances, except to say that they were such as would be likely to generate delinquent motivations. The case is instructive not only because of the failure of a succession of professionals to spot the motivations for the arsons—especially that to secure removal—but also for the ineffectiveness to which this lack of insight reduced them.

DIAGNOSTIC WORKSHEETS FOR
ASSESSING DEVIANT BEHAVIOR

These worksheets are designed as an aid for the social worker in discovering the causes of delinquent behavior which lie within the child's family situation. The diagnostic procedure consists of two stages.

Stage One systematizes what is known about the delinquent act or acts, the child's own perception of them and of his way of life, and his typical behavior outside and within the home.

Stage Two lists characteristic family situations (patterns of parent-child relationships) found to be conducive to delinquency. It then indicates the types of deviant and other abnormal behavior, as they emerge from Stage One, which are symptomatic of each group of family situations.

Procedure

1. Read through the descriptions of behavior or attitude in *Stage One*, underlining the items which apply to the case.

2. Review those items you have underlined. If they tend to fall within the column of a particular mode of behavior, it is reasonable to infer that the motivation indicated at the head of that column was present. Two or more motivations may be operating within the same child.

3. Turn to *Stage Two* and read through the motivations characteristic of each group of family situations. These are marked by arrows at the foot of each column. Underline those indicated from your marking of Stage One.

4. The procedure to this point directs you to various alternative family situations which may have prompted the delinquency. Choose those which, from your present knowledge of the family, you think could apply, and mark them with a query.

5. Bear these situations in mind as possibilities when again interviewing the child or a parent. In these interviews be alert for information that supports or conflicts with your provisional diagnosis. Enter such new data on your worksheets as above. The child's situation may be a combination of two or more or these patterns.

The items in Stage One also act as a guide to the information sought at the intial interview.

Table 2   *DIAGNOSTIC WORKSHEET — Stage One*
                      POINTERS TO OFFENDER'S MOTIVATIONS

Avoidance-Excitement	Removal from Home	Hostility
	Typical deviant activity	
Persistent breakings-in, robberies, etc. with associates. Group vandalism.	Obvious offenses, mostly individual, notable lack of precaution about being caught.	Stealing within home: money, or articles, the loss of which causes inconvenience.
	Flagrant offense after arrest while awaiting court hearing, or while detained pending court disposition. Arson.	Stealing from neighbors and damaging their property. Succession of flagrant offenses while on the run, usually individual. Violent crimes, arson.
	Offender's talk about deviant and other activities outside home	
For fun, excitement. Fantasizes about exploits, plans more.	Various degrees of conscious intention to secure removal. Notable lack of concern about being removed. Says he knew it would happen on repetition of offense. Search for legitimate means of securing removal.	Reluctant to talk, morose, sullen, dejected.
	Child's behavior outside home	
Frequents amusement arcade, billiard halls, or elsewhere affording constant noise, fun, excitement, sociable bustle. Searches for constant sensory stimulation (eating, drinking, exposure to weather). Shows preference for physically active open-air job needing little concentration. Engages in pranks.	May attach himself to nomadic group, hippies, cultists.	Sullen and antagonistic by phases. On bad terms with teachers and classmates. Quarrels with employer.

[continued on next page]

(Avoidance-Excitement)	(Removal from Home)	(Hostility)

Child's behavior in home and towards parents

(Avoidance-Excitement)	(Removal from Home)	(Hostility)
Restless, bored.	Stays away from home.	Moody, depressed.
Seldom in (unless tied to the home by mother-anxiety).		Alternates between good and bad moods.
Truants from school or work.		Steals, hides, destroys people's belongings, embarrasses parents.
Grimaces, sudden un-willed movements.		Flare-ups with parent.
		Runs away, often hav-ing stolen from parent.
		Malicious pranks in neighborhood.
		Truants from school or work.
		Refusal to work for parents' benefit.

↓	↓	↓
1B.	Most of Group 1.	Nearly all Group 1 except 1D.
Most of Group 2.	Great majority of Groups 2 and 3.	About half in Groups 2 and 3.
Nearly all Group 4.	Very few in Group 4.	Very few in Group 4.

POINTERS TO THE OFFENDER'S MOTIVATIONS (continued)

Loyalty Testing	Bravado	Mother-Anxiety (genuine)
	Typical deviant activity	
Episodic, individual offenses, often following parental threats to disown if repeated.	Spur-of-the-moment yielding to being dared into escapade (breaking in, driving off cars, etc.).	Insists on helping mother with housework, especially the harder tasks.
	Stealing from within home or elsewhere, to buy entry to a gang or keep up with free-spending group.	Insists on giving mother more than she asks for from earnings.
	Participation in group violence or vandalism.	Repeatedly buys mother small luxuries, presents for the home, takes her out.
		(Sometimes) wants to be always at home, near mother.
	Offender's talk about deviant and other activities outside home	All in 4A. About ← half 4B. Some 4C.
Forced confidence about parent's loyalty or softness, especially in condoning offenses or defending him if he is caught.	Admitted he wanted to play big, show he was not a coward.	**Mother-Anxiety (hypocritical)**
Alternatively, evasive.	Sometimes remorseful, thinks he has been a fool, can't understand why so easily led.	With marked absence of helpfulness, financial support: Expresses concern over mother's financial difficulties or ill-health (usually needlessly).
	Child's behavior outside home	Fears something will happen to mother (accident, etc.)
May commit offenses calculated to test loyalty of those who have befriended him.	Daring and foolish escapades and pranks with gang.	Strong in 3A. ← Some in 4C.
May run away, sleep out in bitter weather.	Hanger-on in gang.	**Anxiety over Father's Affection**
May join hippie or cultist group.	Showing off, bragging, clowning acts.	Expresses worry over father's interest in him.
	Forced pugnacity.	Gives father presents.
	Intense fears (of dental, medical treatment).	Helps father with his work, recreations.
	Truculent, insubordinate.	1B, 1E, 1F.
	Often loses jobs.	

[continued on next page]

(Loyalty Testing)   (Bravado)

Child's behavior in home and towards parents | (Antagonism to Father)

Annoying, patience-testing ways involving mother in worry, extra work, expense.

Spendthrift, and tries to borrow or cadge from parent.

Parent has to search for him away from home.

Likes to play the man towards mother.

Mock pugnacity towards father.

Expresses violent dislike of father.

Criticizes father for "shouting about," violent behavior.

Blames father for family troubles.

Plays dumb.

      1A, 1C. ⟵

Irritable/Depressive
Nontolerance

Regresses to behavior of much younger child.

Assumes or exaggerates physical incapacity.

Suicide gestures.

Depression and moodiness, without hostility.

Unsociability.

Liability to dangerous attacks on people.

↓
Most Group 1.
Some Group 3.
Very few in Groups 2 and 4.

↓
About half Group 3 (very strong in 3A).
A little in Group 4.
Very little in Groups 1 and 2.

↓
Most 4B. ⟵
Also found with acute avoidance-excitement.

DIAGNOSTIC WORKSHEET — Stage Two
FAMILY SITUATIONS

		Group 2 — Loss of Preferred or Only Parent, and Unsatisfactory Substitute
Group 1 — Threat of Expulsion from Family		

1A Both parents harsh, unaffectionate, rejecting.

1B Father regards child as the "black sheep of the family" and wants him out of the way. Mother unavailable or yields to father.

1C Father antagonistic to child because of mother's spoiling (possibly to spite husband, against whom she is estranged or hostile).

1D Pressure from another member of household to have child removed.

1E Parents use threats of putting away or handing over to authorities as a disciplinary measure.

1F In fatherless family or with irresponsible husband, mother falls into an irritable-depressive state, becomes intolerant of child, and threatens to do him harm or demands to have him taken from her.

2A After death of preferred parent, child is left with a parent or other relative who has been disapproving, neglectful, or unaffectionate.

2B As above, after the break-up of the parent's marriage.

2C Child is relinquished by loved foster mother to true mother, against whom the child is indifferent, hostile, or estranged.

Nearly all, except 1D, show Hostility.
Strong tendencies to Removal and Loyalty Testing.
1D shows strong Loyalty Testing and Removal.

Most show Removal and Avoidance-Excitement
About half show Hostility.

[continued on next page]

FAMILY SITUATIONS (continued)

Group 3 — Mother Undependable as a Source of Affection	Group 4 — Feared Loss of Preferred or Only Parent
3A Mother fails to meet child's need for security of affection, owing to her instability, harshness, or threats to desert home or abandon child. Father fails as alternative source of affection, because he is a chronic invalid, absents himself, or has otherwise become a background figures, leaving discipline of children to mother. 3B Mother or mother substitute rejects child in favor of siblings. 3C Child is in a state of conflict over mother and finds it difficult to accept her because he has formed a primary attachment to a surrogate mother. Breakdown occurs with the loss or unavailability of the latter. Most show Removal About half show Hostility About half show Bravado (especially strong in 3A).	4A Anxiety over illness or childbirth difficulties of the mother, with no alternative source of security in the father. 4B Mother threatens to desert the home, owing to marital quarrels, or does so temporarily. 4C Child fears being abandoned by mother (or father, if preferred parent) at break-up of marriage, or when the separated parent he is living with intends to remarry or to hand him over to disliked parent, foster parent, or institution. Nearly all show Avoidance-Excitement. Little Bravado or Hostility, very little Removal. Most 4B show Irritable-Depressive Nontolerance.

Chapter Twelve
Providing Avenues of
Legitimate Escape

The reader will recall that about half of my sample of youths committed to a correctional school had evidenced some urge to remove themselves physically from their home surroundings, and that the obvious nature of their offenses suggested that this was an important motive for their delinquency. This finding has important implications for a preventive program. It is surely a matter of common sense to provide legal and reputable means by which a juvenile can remove himself from an emotionally intolerable family situation without being forced to commit offenses to achieve this end. One of the reasons for the great preponderance of delinquency among boys as compared to girls is the fewer opportunities the former have for legal means of removal. A boy can no longer "run away to sea," or join the army or navy with no questions asked. For a girl there is marriage, prostitution, or running off with the ever-available married man. Until recently also there were plentiful openings for female residential employment, and the lessening opportunities for this form of self-removal no doubt explain why delinquency is increasing relatively among girls. The obvious social strategy is to provide legitimate means of escape.

We have to break away from stereotypes in designing new forms of residential care. The ghost of the reformatory still walks in the corridors of power. There will no doubt always be a need for secure institutions in which to hold the physically dangerous, and the compulsive thieves and runaways who are resistant to any form of treatment. Their committal should be made without any implication of punishment, and with the same considerations as are taken into account in committal to a mental hospital.

VOLUNTARY RESIDENTIAL SCHOOLS

In a society which accepts fee-paying boarding schools for those who can afford it, there should also be provision for residential schools in which unsettled young people, or those whose families cannot provide them with a secure and permanent base, can enroll voluntarily.

This principle of voluntary enrollment raises the issue of how we persuade youngsters and families of the foregoing types to agree to use the facility, and the youngsters, once in the school, to stay. Neither the youngster nor his family should be asked to make a definite commitment from the start. He might first be invited to visit the school with his parents, or spend the weekend or a series of weekends there. Once he begins to find playmates, and activities which absorb him and take his mind off his family problems, the chances that he will agree to stay are good. Even in a correctional school the young people are happy, provided material amenities are adequate, and they are fairly treated and have friendly relationships with the staff. Abscondments occur for particular reasons, most of which can be avoided. One of these is that some boys have formed firmer attachments to one another than to any of the staff members, so that a suggestion from a friend to run away with him is accepted out of a primary group loyalty. A second reason is that the youngster, in an unresolved mood of hostility, is determined to "go to the dogs" in order to spite parents who, in his view, have abandoned him. This calls for the continued operation of a plan of family therapy, which is discussed below. The third and most frequent reason is worry about home, such as about being forgotten and excluded from the family circle, or whether the boy's father is ill-treating his mother, or whether his mother will carry out her threat to run away. The absconder will not voluntarily express his true anxieties because, if they have proved unbearable, they will be avoided; but he will say that he is homesick or that he fears his mother is ill. To counter such worries—which often come to a head with the delay of a letter from home—each youngster should be allocated to a counselor with whom he is always free to discuss his family and who can write or phone his parents, if necessary, to make sure everything is all right at home. Once such a relationship has been established, it will be found that youngsters come and bring their letters and want to talk about their families. Contact with a counselor can be arranged in a club setting within the school or one of its boarding houses. It may be necessary to allow certain parents to make reverse-charge phone calls in order to speak with their children (but not at a prearranged time each week, since it could mean an abscondment if they fail). It should be arranged, if possible, that a youngster be accepted in a residential school near enough to his home for his parents to visit frequently and for him to go home on the weekends.

The removal of the stigma of punishment from the residential school can be effected only by making referral no longer the responsibility of a court or of any body empowered to impose other kinds of punishment. But when committal has to be made compulsory as a matter of public safety or for reasons of completely uncontrollable behavior, it should be subject to appeal for the legal protection of the child.

FORMULATION OF GOALS FOR
RESIDENTIAL TREATMENT

All other arrangements for residential treatment should be made by an appointed social agency composed of professionals in the field of child care. Removal to care other than that of the parents should be undertaken as a phase in a plan of treatment. If at all possible, the goal should be the reuniting of the child with his parents on a basis of full acceptance. If this is not possible, the objective should be to help the young person build up new human relationships of a comparable permanence. This may be exceedingly difficult in the case of a young person who has been rendered cynical about every offer of friendship owing to his being abandoned so many times before; but it has to be borne in mind that the more difficult it is to reestablish a young person in a situation where he will be permanently accepted, the more vital it is from society's point of view that the attempt be persevered with, because these cynical youngsters can become our future hardened criminals.

The treatment goal should be drawn up in a joint consultation between the social-work staff of the young person's home locality and the staff of the residential school, or the foster parents, as the case may be. It should be embodied in a reference document and reviewed annually by a formal procedure. Such a document can help ensure that a deviant young person is not simply lost sight of, or allowed to drift along in what is nothing more than a holding institution. It also serves as the recognition by society and its agents of responsibility for the child's ultimate recovery. As things are at present, the committal of a child to a residential school seems to imply a tacit relief from responsibility of the local agency until he reemerges in the community. Without such a program of treatment, meticulously monitored and integrated with the social agency of the home locality, any system of committal institutions does indeed amount to only a holding operation on behalf of society; and this is true despite the devotion of their staffs, and the incidental good they can do to some young people.

VOLUNTEER SHORT-TERM FOSTER HOMES

Temporary removal from home may indeed be necessary as a crisis measure, when relations between parent and child have reached a point where there is a danger of child abuse, or when a phase of break-ins or running away has to be interrupted to allow time for the investigation of causes. Short-term volunteer foster homes such as are used in Tampa, Florida, deserve to be widely known as a remedy which is both more economical and less inhuman than the locking up of unruly or runaway children in detention centers. The Tampa Volunteer Detention Project arose from the need to relieve overcrowding in the State's existing facilities for detention. Thirty of the youngsters considered the least dangerous were placed temporarily with families who volunteered to take them. Apart from the careful screening of the families there were formal procedures. Surprisingly aside from a few major problems, the children adjusted exceedingly well. It was consequently decided to maintain the arrangement as a regular facility for status offenders—that is to say, runaways, truants, and incorrigibles who had to be temporarily removed from their homes. It was found that these status offenders made up no less than 44.5 percent of all detention admissions.

The essence of the Tampa short-term foster home project is that the volunteer householders agree to keep one or more beds available either for specified parts of the week or at any time. They were asked to state how often they could take a child, and whether they would be prepared to accept those who smoked, wet their beds, and so on. The references, and possible police records, of all volunteers were checked; on their provisional acceptance they would attend a series of orientation sessions totaling about eight hours, after which final decisions as to volunteering and acceptance were made. The social worker responsible for placing a child with a family would contact the family each day, presumably by phone, to make sure everything was all right, and meanwhile make arrangements either for returning the child to his home or for permanent placement. The maximum stay in the volunteer home was fixed at 10 days, or less—whatever was agreed upon. The actual average stay during the initial period of the project was 6.4 days. Whereas the turnover rate for volunteers was estimated at 40 percent, it was actually only 13 percent, and some of those leaving the project did so to become professional foster parents. The runaway rate for the 1,181 children placed in the volunteer homes during the four-and-a-half month assessment period was only 5.6 percent, which is remarkable, considering that many of the children has been chronic runaways from their own homes. As a result of the success of the project, the housing of status offenders in detention centers was made illegal in Florida.

A feature of the project which may have to be reviewed if it is adopted elsewhere is that the volunteer householders did not receive any payments for the child's food or other incidental expenses, nor apparently for losses due to mischief or theft. In effect only 1.5 percent of the children stole from their temporary foster homes, and the net loss after allowing for goods returned was small. Considering that—at 1976 prices—detention in an institution was costing the Florida authorities some $30 a day per child, the saving to them was considerable. It would be so even if the foster parents were reimbursed for their outlay, which was estimated at $8 per day. Apart from the financial aspects of the project, one can surely agree with the authors of the report (Latina and Schembera, 1976) that, for a child who has revealed his distress by desperate and abnormal behavior, placement in a temporary foster home, where he will meet adults who care enough to help him, is preferable to holding him in a detention center, where he may be exposed to hardened delinquents.

The limitation of the stay to 10 days, while evidently imposed as a guarantee to intending volunteers that they will not have to keep the child indefinitely, also ensures that children will not be kept hanging about, possibly for months, in detention or assessment centers because of administrative tardiness or cluelessness. The need for quick and decisive action makes imperative a systematic procedure of diagnosis and the formulation of a treatment goal.

LENGTH OF RESIDENTIAL TREATMENT

Apart from the aforementioned emergencies, residential treatment would have its place in a well-planned system either when the parents are unwilling or are unable to provide the child with a secure family base, or when the child is imposing such stresses on the parents that there is a danger of their breaking down. There is no guarantee that either state of affairs can be put right in a few weeks, and the chances are that the resolution of their causes will take a good deal longer. There is thus no therapeutic justification for short-term committal. Considering that the final splurge of delinquency which is the reason for the young person's removal may be the culmination of years of bitterness and estrangement, even the six months which was officially favored as the normal period in the British system may often be too short for any enduring improvement to be brought about in the relations between the young person and his family. During my informal experimental work with the staff of the Kingswood Training School, near Bristol, in England, the object of which was to reconcile youths with their parents, one of the staff members made a discerning observation that summed up our experiences. This was that, all too often, no progress was visible during the first year, but from the beginning of the second year the boy and his parents would begin to get closer, and by the end of that year complete mutual trust and acceptance would be reestablished. It would seem, therefore, that if the young person has had to be removed from the home, owing to an emotional situation so adverse that the social worker sees removal as the only solution, a period of up to two years may be necessary. A stay of only six months, while appearing economical, may be a waste of public money.

"MACROFAILURE" OF THE PRESENT RESIDENTIAL SYSTEM

The second criterion for removal, given earlier—that the child is imposing unendurable stresses on his parents—reminds us that a great many children entering residential schools have a history of severe behavior disturbance. For remedial work with such children special skills are needed. Yet, according to the NACRO Working Party (1977, p. 17), "A large proportion of the staff coming into community homes are young and inexperienced. Only 15 percent of them have received any basic training, and the majority are expected to start a difficult job without even the most basic induction." It is more than doubtful that even the 15 percent who had basic training were equipped with techniques for understanding and helping the maladjusted child. Some British community schools (to give the committal institutions their latest name) reputedly refuse to take maladjusted delinquents (Phillips, 1978). Evidence of an insufficiency of those who are willing and capable of doing so is provided by the finding of the NACRO Working Party (1977) that children can be held in assessment centers for up to a year, waiting until an appropriate place of treatment is found for them.

The upshot is that our system of committal institutions— whether they be reformatories, community schools, or detention centers—are not rehabilitating the majority of delinquents placed in them. To quote once more from the report of the NACRO Working Party (1977, p. 9),

of those sentenced while under 17 who are released in 1972, 9 percent of male borstal (reformatory) trainees and 70 percent of juvenile detention center trainees were reconvicted within two years, and ... it is estimated that 55 percent of borstal trainees and 40 percent of detention trainees in this age group were re-committed to custody.

These figures led the NACRO Working Party to speak of the "macrofailure" of the present system of institutional care for young offenders.

PROFESSIONAL FOSTER PARENTAGE

One of the most worrisome aspects of a social worker's job is continually having to deal with children whose removal from the home setting is seen to be a matter of absolute necessity, without there being anywhere to place them. The chief reason for this is the failure to develop a system of professional foster parentage. Many years ago I pleaded for the recognition of a profession of paid and trained foster parents. It was objected that if foster parents were paid, the wrong sort of person would be attracted—an argument that could be used to deprive the general body of social workers of their salaries! It is cheering that at least in many parts of the United States and in some parts of Britain—namely, in the Strathclyde region, Kent, and in the city of Reading—the need to pay foster parents for the valuable social-work function that they are performing has now been recognized. Not only should foster parents be paid their due, but there should also be a scale of bonuses for the acceptance of especially difficult children. To show that we mean business, full-time one-year courses leading to a certificate in foster parentage should be instituted in every region. To have a reasonable chance of success with that problem of problems—the child who refuses to settle down anywhere—requires a body of highly trained specialist foster parents who are proof against the provocations of hostility and the testing bad behavior of those children who have lost faith in adult loyalty owing to their previous unhappy experiences. Not more than three of four children should be placed in the care of each foster parent, and of them only one should be of a sort who presents severe problems of management. The foster parents of each region should be encouraged to regard themselves as a profession akin to that of public health nurses, and have their own organization and center.

THE HOUSE OF UMOJA:
MODEL FOR A COMMUNITY SOLUTION

In a well-integrated community there is little need for publicly provided foster parents. Every family has relatives or close friends who would take in a child left parentless. Harriett Wilson (1962) noted of her sample of poor-performance families that they were cut off from relatives and had few friends. Anything that can be done to repair this social fragmentation will consequently help to solve the problem of the young person left without stable family support. The need is being met in a small way by many unofficial refuges and centers run by socially-minded individuals. Because of our preference for public delivery services, these are not seen as holding the germ of general solutions. Indeed, the provision of the public services, although necessary, tends to inhibit the spontaneous efforts of culturally uprooted social groups to reintegrate themselves by building new social institutions. Yet history shows us that through working men's clubs, chapels, temperance movements, and educational institutes, the underprivileged of previous generations have achieved a new social integration and dignity. Many such movements are afoot at the present time, emphasizing a more disciplined and restrained manner of living, and as the disintegration of families spreads, we may expect to witness a counter movement originating from those who have suffered from the emotional deprivations of having been denied a stable family background.

One project which seems to contain the possibility of real cultural innovation is described by Knopp and her co-authors (1976). Because it has to do directly with the provision of the equivalent of a family for deviant youths, I shall draw from and comment upon their account of it.

The House of *Umoja* (the Swahili word for unity), in Philadelphia, was founded by Sister Falaka Fattah and her husband, Black David, to help young black gang members. Black David was a former gang member and in preparation for the project made an on-the-spot study of gang haunts in the black districts of the city. The two of them, who were superintendents of several two-story row houses in a narrow street on the western side, offered accommodations in their own home, with their six sons, to 15 members of the South Philadelphia Clymer Street gang, all of whom were between 15 and 17 years of age.

Sister Falaka and her husband attribute the growth of gangs largely to the fact that the needs of young people are not being met by their families. They decided that what was needed was the re-creation of a family for those thus deprived. That which they offered to the youths was an adaptation of the African extended family.

Over the ensuing year Sister Falaka and Black David tutored the erstwhile gang, now family, in mathematics, economics, and Swahili, and such practical matters as preparation for job interviews. During this time none of the youths was put in jail, none wanted to go home, and seven youths had joined from other gangs. Of the original group formed in 1969, seven were in college, seven had regular jobs, and one was in jail by 1976. Members of the Clymer Street gang who did not come to the House of Umoja were among the leaders of organized black crime in Philadelphia.

The Department of Public Welfare, after initial suspicions, came to recognize the value of the House of Umoja, and now contributes funds for placements. Since its beginning Umoja has sheltered more than 300 youths belonging to 73 different street gangs. Only 10 are known to have been arrested since leaving the House. Apart from housing former gang members, it acts as a crisis center for the settling of gang wars and averting killings when quarrels erupt, and it has earned the status of neutral territory. The number of youths killed in gang wars has recently dropped sharply in Philadelphia, for which the existence of the House of Umoja is considered largely responsible.

It was some time before the police learned to differentiate between the group of Umoja youths and the local gangs, and when anything was stolen in the neighborhood they would raid the House. This was set straight after a meeting between Sister Falaka and the local police, who agreed to phone her first rather than carry out an unannounced raid. To be fair to the police, no claim has been made that the youths completely renounced their delinquent ways from the time of taking up residence. No doubt the Fattahs had to go through the usual trials of loyalty testing.

All the brothers, as the resident youths were called, earn money from odd jobs for their personal expenses and to pay nominal house dues. It is not stated in the Knopp report whether they received welfare payments, but one has to suppose they did, just as they would have done if living elsewhere. The important thing is that Umoja was not an institution from which the youths only drew benefits, but a form of extended family or affiliation group, to which they were expected to make contributions.

This sense of group cohesiveness was fostered by the adoption of an African identity. While the brothers attended regular Philadelphia schools for academic or vocational education, they had classes in Swahili and African lore in the House. The analogy of the Puritan father gathering his family around for prayers and reading from the family Bible is too close to be missed.

A large part of the genius of Umoja as a cultural innovation is that it meets the needs of socially disenfranchised black youth for personal effectiveness as well as for family attachment. In my studies of delinquent youths I often had occasion to remark upon the feelings of inferiority and worthlessness that come of being rejected by one's family. This is expressed in compensations by way of bragging, showing off, and trying to associate with older youths. Umoja gave such youths what must have been to them a totally new feeling of being accepted and cherished; and because someone else of parental status valued them, their sense of self-worth was also enhanced.

Feelings of personal effectiveness are conferred not only from status in a family group but also from status in a community and progress in its levels of esteem. In their report on the German youth riots of the 1950s, Bondy et al. (1957) point to the lack of opportunity for young industrial workers to progress in trade skills and to achieve the social status of a master craftsman. In tribal societies there is a regular progression in status from initiation to the position of tribal elder, with the addition of culturally recognized symbols of rank such as, among some New Hebrideans, the slaughtering of tuskered pigs and giving feasts, and in others the acquisition of rare Kula shells by a form of friendly barter. In many cultures, including that of the student societies of Germany up to the 1930s, status was achieved by a succession of scarifications. The unemployed black youth has no status, and no prospect of social promotions, except through gang membership and prowess in violence. Umoja gives its members prestige through a pride in their African origin. Their study of African lore might be compared to the study of the classics in upper-class British schools. Its members earn African names by their progress in learning the ethos of the group, for the help they give to each other, for the work they do to improve the house, and for community service. There are seven ranks of names to pass through before a member earns the family name of Fattah. One is reminded of the ranks earned in the orders of Freemasons, Oddfellows, and so on, and of the loyalties and codes of conduct which go with membership. Considering what scope there is in the underprivileged black populations of American and British cities, Umoja can be seen as offering a prototype for a significant movement of cultural integration.

It has been estimated (Newman, 1972) that 60 percent of all crimes are committed by members of underprivileged minority groups in the United States. Of these, probably the majority would be committed by blacks. The scope for delinquency prevention of the Umoja model is therefore large.

The problem with any cultural innovation which depends on the genius of one or two persons is how it can be replicated without losing its soul. Sister Falaka suggests that this might be done in the case of Umoja by bringing trainees in from other cities and sending them back with Fattah graduates—where they could receive the support of community funding agencies. Religious movements played a large part in the cultural reintegration of the uprooted rural poor in nineteenth-century British cities. Umoja has all the characteristics of such movements, except that it is not linked, so far as has been reported, to explicit religious beliefs. Religious groups are also providing such centers, but mostly for adults who have suffered incarceration or who have been alcohol or drug addicts. To gain the voluntary participation of unsettled and virtually homeless youths is a much more difficult proposition. Whether the established churches have the will and flexibility to undertake it and the image which would appeal to underprivileged and deviant youth, or whether new religious movements will have to be founded, only the course of events will show.

Chapter Thirteen
Biological Aspects of
Crime and Delinquency

THE ENIGMA OF DIFFERENTIAL VULNERABILITY

This chapter explores the possibility of a biological vulnerability to crime. An important objection to the explanation of delinquency solely in terms of the environment has been that, however delinquency-prone members of a particular cultural group or socioeconomic stratum may be, the majority of them do not become delinquent. It is also a commonplace observation of social workers that stresses which force some of the juvenile members of a family into delinquency leave others unaffected. It has therefore to be supposed that some children have a lower stress tolerance than others. The reasons for this differential vulnerability have been little studied.

The origins of individual proneness to criminality have been sought in the genes, prenatal and birth insult, brain damage, and early experience. The student who wishes to make a thorough study of the evidence for biological and psychophysiological factors in criminality has available the review by Shah and Roth (1974). It is expecially valuable in its plea for an interdisciplinary approach, as opposed to what they term our present discipline-oriented education, which leads to the neglect of evidence from other fields. Criminal behaviors, they point out, "like all human behavior, are determined by a very large and heterogenous array of biological, social, psychological, and other factors. Any claim or suggestion by a particular discipline to have discovered a single cause or even a set of causes underlying all this complexity would be presumptuous and, indeed, would offend scientific credibility" (p. 154). It remains in this chapter to pursue this approach by a review of more recent evidence.

THE MYTHICAL XYY "SUPERMALE"

Dramatic genetic breakthroughs tend to attract publicity, and none more than reports of a greater prevalence of males with the

XYY chromosome abnormality among criminals. It was lent plausibility because maleness is conferred by the Y chromosome in the normal XY complement. The extra Y, it was supposed, might produce a hyperaggressive male, who would be prone to violent criminal outbursts. This supposition was strengthened by the finding that XYY men tend to be very tall.

A number of studies have indeed found a significant preponderance of XYY males in prison populations, and it was invariably more marked in prisoners of above average height. The highest prevalence rate was found among mentally disordered offenders in high-security hospitals. On the other hand, more recent surveys quoted by Shah and Roth found less than the general-population prevalence of the XYY anomaly in unselected prison populations and among boys in correctional institutions. Shah and Ross conclude that there is no consistent relationship between the XYY anomaly and criminal tendencies. Moreover, their review of studies of males with the XXY anomaly (Klinefelter syndrome)—which might be regarded as an extra complement of femaleness—was also related to a greater likelihood of behavior disorders, including criminality.

The inconsistent findings of the foregoing studies can be accounted for by their having used highly selected samples of prisoners, without ascertainment of prevalence or comparable deviant tendencies in the general population. This limitation did not apply, however, to that conducted by Witkin and his coworkers (1977), who were able to use the excellent social records for the whole population of Denmark. In view of the known tallness of XYY men, they carried out chromosomal tests on the top 16 percent of the height distribution among 28,884 males born to women who were resident in Copenhagen during the years 1944 to 1947. From these 4,139 tall men tested were 12 with the XYY and 16 with the XXY anomaly. Five of the former (41.7 percent) and 3 of the latter (18.8 percent) had criminal records, compared with 9.3 percent of the chromosomally normal tall males. However, only 1 of the 5 XYY's had been found guilty of an act of violence against a person, and only 2 were habitual criminals; the other 3 had committed either one or two petty thefts. This disposed of the theory that XYY men are destined to become aggressive or serious criminals. Of the 3 XXY men, one had made a brutal attack upon his wife, but the other 2 had committed only a small number of petty thefts, without violence. The criminality of the XYY men could not be attributed to their tallness since crimnals were slightly underrepresented among the tall (normal) XY's.

The remaining possibility that Witkin and his coresearchers examined was that XYY men fell into crime, or were caught more often, owing to their mental inferiority. This explanation was strengthened by their significantly subaverage performance on the army intelligence tests administered to all Danish men when they became eligible for service, and by their having left school earlier, with lower grades, than the XY's. What interpretation to put on this finding is uncertain because "intelligence" is being questioned (Stott, 1978b) as a fundamental human dimension; and "low intelligence" is being increasingly seen as indicative of poor cognitive development resulting from impaired motivation and behavioral/emotional disturbance (Stott, 1978c). All that can be said on this count is that, to quote the final conclusion of Witkin and his colleagues, "the aberrant XYY complement may have broad adverse developmental consequences" (p. 185). Since the XXY men they studied also did poorly on the army mental test and at school, the same could be said of them. In short, both these chromosomal anomalies confer a greater liability to aberrant, including criminal, behavior as part of a general genetic inefficiency.

Genetic vulnerability to crime by way of a greater proneness in chromosomally abnormal males provides but a small part of the answer to the general phenomenon of vulnerability among the mass of delinquents. Even among the tall males selected for study, the rates per 1,000 of the XYY anomaly was only 2.9, and of the XXY only 3.9. It would have been much less among the male population as a whole owing to the above-average stature of both XYY and XXY males.

THE HERITABILITY OF CRIME
(1): TWIN STUDIES

Next to be considered are what have often been described as two types of experiment designed by nature to apportion the contributions of the genes and of the environment. These are studies of twins and of adopted children.

The methodological advantage of twin studies is that there are two sorts of twins—the monozygotic (MZ), which have an identical genetic constitution, and the dizygotic (DZ), whose genetic constitutions are no more alike than those of nontwin siblings. If there is a genetic component in vulnerability to delinquency, and its expression is not masked by the exposure of each member of a twin pair to dissimilar environments, MZ twins would be expected to show a greater degree of concordance in committing criminal acts than DZ twins.

Christiansen (1977a) reviewed eight studies of criminality in adult twins. Excluding the Norwegian demographic survey, the concordance rate averaged some 67 percent for MZ and 31 percent for DZ twins, the difference being highly significant in all studies. In the Norwegian, the rates were 26 percent for the MZ and 15 for the DZ, the difference not being significant although in the same direction. The authors of the first seven studies regarded the much greater concordance which they found among their MZ pairs as convincing evidence for a genetic factor in criminality. It is noteworthy that the Norwegian study was the only one drawn from a register of all twins born within a territory: the sample consisted of those male twins born between 1921 and 1930 of whom one or both had had a conviction. Six of the other studies relied on searches for members of twin pairs among prison populations, and the seventh almost certainly did so. Directly or indirectly these must have been derived from the prisoners' own reports, and of course they could have mentioned their twins only when they were aware of their existence. If MZ twins had been kept together longer, had continued to associate with each other more closely, or were more aware of their twin status, than DZ twins, a greater number of MZ than DZ pairs could have been reported by the prisoners interrogated. It can be calculated from Christiansen's (1977a) summary table that the ratio of MZ to DZ twins in the studies based on prison reports was nearly twice (1.07 to .57) that found in the Norwegian demographic survey. And among the studies (excluding the Norwegian study) which contained more MZ than DZ twin pairs, the MZ/DZ concordance ratio was 58 percent higher than in the studies with more DZ twins (81 percent higher if the Norwegian is included). In short, there was indeed an overall excess of MZ over DZ twin pairs in those studies based on prisoners' reports of the existence of twins; and in the studies in which this excess was present, the concordance rate was considerably higher for the MZ twins. This strengthens the surmise that the prisoners were more aware of the existence of their twins when they were MZ. If we assume that the reasons why they could report existence of an MZ twin more often are those already suggested, they would have been exposed to more similar environments and been more able to influence each other's behavior. The bias in favor of a greater MZ concordance which this selective factor evidently produced undermines the credibility of studies relying on prisoners' reports.

Christiansen's own study (1977b) utilized 3,586 unselected twin pairs from the Danish Twin Register born between 1881 and 1910, and was therefore, like the Norwegian, based on a true demographic sample. It gave concordance rates of .35 for MZ male pairs and .13 for DZ male pairs. The corresponding rates for females, although much lower, were similarly nearly three times higher among the MZ than among the DZ twins. Christiansen was the first to recognize that a truer comparison was given by taking into account the frequency of crime among each category of twin, and this he did in a twin coefficient. Since the crime rate for MZ twins was higher than for DZ, this measure reduced the difference in the concordance rates from nearly three times to only 76 percent higher among MZ males; it remained two and a half times higher among MZ females. Christiansen is insistent that the twin coefficient is not a measure of heredity, but rather of the particular combination of environmental and genetic factors associated with each type of twinning.

Christiansen points out that conclusions about heredity and environment drawn from twin studies are based on the assumption that there are no relevant environmental disparities in the situations of each type of twin, and he doubts if this condition is fulfilled. He quotes various studies showing that MZ pairs tend to establish more similar environments for each other than DZ's do; they spend more time together, choose more often the same friends, are more closely attached to and dependent on each other, choose more similar occupations, and are typically cooperative, while DZ twins are typically competitive. There is, however, a further reason why MZ twins create a more similar environment for themselves than do DZ twins, to which attention has hitherto not been drawn. It is simply that MZ twins look alike, and tend to act more alike, than DZ. If both are equally attractive, there is much less chance of one becoming the favorite of the parents and the other being rejected than if one is attractive and the other unattractive. In the descriptions of the family situations conducive to delinquency given in Chapter Nine it was seen how an early handicap which rendered the child tiresome or emotionally unrewarding to the parents could be the beginning of a parental rejection which, when openly expressed in threats to get rid of the child, produced a hostile and delinquent response. Titus Oates, the perjurer who sent many innocent Catholics to the gallows in the famous conspiracy trial of the reign of Charles II, had such an early history. His mother reported that "his Father could not endure him; and when he came home at night the Boy would use to be in the chimney corner, and my Husband would cry take away this snotty Fool and jumble him about" (Lane, 1949, p. 17). In contrast, allowances are made by everyone for the attractive child, his delinquencies tend to be overlooked, and he is given more chances—to an extent that when a really attractive youth does nonetheless get himself committed to a correctional institution, it is only after the most heinous offenses. The greater likelihood of differences in attractiveness among DZ twins could in itself largley account for the fact of their being more discordant for crime than MZ twins. These potentialities for difference in life experience and reaction thereto do not rule out the possibility that the observed disparities in concordance rates as between MZ and DZ twins are in some degree genetic in origin. They are, however, important enough to destroy the value of twin studies as natural experiments capable of apportioning the contributions of heredity and environment.

THE HERITABILITY OF CRIME
(2): ADOPTION STUDIES

The rationale of the adoption study, as the second "natural experiment" for ascertaining the contributions of heredity and environment, is that nearly all adopted children either never had contact with their biological fathers or were separated from them soon after birth. If, therefore, adoptees tend to resemble their biological more than their adoptive fathers with regard to a trait such as criminality, this—it is argued—can only be because they have inherited some tendency thereto from the true parent.

The most comprehensive and best-designed study of adoptees for the investigation of a genetic factor in criminality has been that of Hutchings and Mednick (1977). From a file of all children placed for adoption in the city of Copenhagen, they took the 971 males born between 1927 and 1941 whose biological fathers could be traced. Their critical finding was that 48.8 percent of the criminal adoptees, but only 31.1 percent of the noncriminal adoptees, had a biological father who was in the criminal register. This result was significant, at less than 1 in a 1,000 chance. It was remarkable that the criminality of the adoptees was much more related to the criminality of their biological fathers than to that of the adoptive fathers, to whose influence they were exposed. Where both the biological and natural fathers had been criminal, 36 percent of the adoptees were so also; 22 percent of the adoptees were criminal when their biological fathers only were criminal, but 11.5 percent when only their adoptive fathers were criminal.

If there were no environmental channel by which the criminality of the biological fathers could have been transmitted to their sons, the foregoing relationships would appear as convincing proof of the inheritance of a proneness to crime. The principal channel for environmental contamination is that adoption agencies often try to match the social backgrounds of the true and adoptive parents. Hutchings and Mednick recognized this, and indeed confirmed that the Danish adoption organization aimed to achieve such matching, which was reflected in a correlation of 0.22 between the social classes of the biological and adoptive fathers. Nevertheless, there remained a relationship between the criminality of the biological fathers and of the adoptees apart from social class. It is doubtful, however, whether this disposed of the effects of selective placement. The matching at which the social workers aimed would probably have gone beyond merely equating occupational group (which was the criterion used for social class). They would probably have thought just as much of placing a child in a family of the same degree of respectability as that of its true parents, the child of the ne'er-do-well with a not-too-respectable family, and so on. Within any broad occupational category, there are many degrees of "respectability." If indeed the adoption agencies did match for such, this might have been shown by a correlation between the *criminality* of the biological and of the adoptive fathers; but the authors of the study do not apply this test. It can be calculated from Hutchings and Mednick's Table 6 (p. 132) that an excess of 27 percent of the adoptees with criminal fathers had been placed with criminal adoptive fathers; conversely, 16 percent fewer of the adoptees with non-criminal fathers had been placed with criminal fathers. Likewise, proportionately fewer adoptees with criminal fathers were placed with noncriminal fathers. It is not possible to calculate the significance of this bias because of the intermediate category of "minor offenses," but it would appear large enough to suggest that a de facto matching of the biological and adoptive fathers for criminality took place.

It is surprising that Hutchings and Mednick, along with other workers who have viewed the adoption paradigm as a means of detecting genetic influences, have overlooked a further important channel of environmental transmission between the biological father and his adopted son. This is that the child was subjected prenatally to the intrauterine environment of its mother, which in turn is affected by the mother's environment. And there is abundant evidence that children born to mothers living in a disadvantaged environment suffer greater risks of mortality and handicap. Shah and Roth mention three important class-linked conditions—toxemias of pregnancy, infant mortality, and prematurity—which affect the biological integrity of the child either prenatally or perinatally. Toxemias of pregnancy have shown a prevalence of 3 percent in high-income and 15 percent in low-income groups. A woman who associated with a convicted man to the extent of having a child by him would be less likely to seek or receive the prenatal care necessary for minimizing the effects of such toxemias. As regards infant mortality, Shah and Roth quote the finding of Richmond and Weinberger (1970) that 40 per thousand nonwhite babies died during their first year in 1965, compared with 22 per thousand white babies. The British Perinatal Mortality Survey (Butler and Bonham, 1963) found that 85 percent more infants in social class V (unskilled and casual laborers) than in social class I (professional and managerial) were stillborn or died neonatally. Prematurity as measured by gestation time was 55 percent more frequent, and as measured by birthweight, over twice as frequent, in social class V than in social class I. The worst affected were the children of women without husbands, the perinatal morbidity and prematurity rates among them being even higher than among children of mothers in social class V. Probably the majority of adoptees, being illegitimate, would fall into this most vulnerable group.

Apart from its being an aftermath of prematurity (Drillien, 1964), behavior disturbance is a concomitant of social disadvantage. Among the 15,000 children followed up in the (British) National Child Development Study (Davie, Butler, and Goldstein, 1972), those of social class V were three and a half times more maladjusted than those in social class I, as measured by the Bristol Social Adjustment Guide.

Mothers of subsequently adopted children who associated with men who had, or were going to have, a criminal record would have been more likely to have been members not only of the most disadvantaged social class, but of its culturally most disintegrated section. They would therefore have been more exposed to the stresses which produce congenital damage in their offspring than women who had children by noncriminal men. Moreover, their offspring would have had a greater tendency to behavior disturbance, which would in turn have increased their chances of becoming criminals. It can also be assumed that those mothers of subsequently adopted children who consorted with crime-prone men, or were in a social group which included such, would have been exposed to emotional stresses arising from unstable and discordant relationships. Two studies, whose findings are summarized below, illustrate the effects of such stresses upon the offspring.

PRENATAL TRANSMISSION OF HANDICAP

A follow-up study from birth of a random sample of children born in the industrial west of Scotland found that mothers who had been rendered unhappy during their pregnancies by personal tensions produced children who, on average, suffered nearly twice as many handicaps as the remainder of the sample (Stott, 1973). The handicaps in question consisted of chronic ill-health, physical defects, developmental lags, growth abnormalities, and behavior disturbance, all of which were included in a morbidity score, which served as an overall measure of the noxicity of the prenatal conditions studied. The mean score for the children of the mothers who suffered these interpersonal tensions was 30.3, compared with 16.0 for all the other children. The most damaging types of interpersonal stress suffered by the mothers in question during their pregnancies were those arising from marital discord, and from being on bad terms with other members of the household or with neighbors. This finding could not be attributed to birth complications, prematurity, or postnatal influences, and was independent of social class.

The second study, covering a cohort of 1,300 Canadian children, confirmed this effect (Stott and Latchford, 1976). By the use of morbidity ratios, it was found that marital discord during the pregnancy resulted in a rate of handicap 94 percent above normal. Again, this finding applied irrespective of social class; and indeed the excess child morbidity rose to 124 percent among the adequately housed—i.e., the not-poor section of the cohort. The heightened morbidity could not have been due to postnatal deprivation because much of it took the form of physical defect, or ill-health, or abnormal behavior from birth.

These studies pointing to the massive damage that can be done to the offspring by exposure of pregnant women to interpersonal tensions make it probable that adopted children fathered by crime-prone men would have been significantly more handicapped than the children whose fathers were not criminal. Since the prenatally induced handicaps would, according to the findings just cited, have included behavior disturbance, the adoptees with criminal biological fathers would themselves have been more crime-vulnerable.

When these emotional stresses inherent in a socially unstable and stressful environment are added to the effects of prenatal malnutrition, the risks of brain damage from prematurity, neglected toxemia, and lack of prenatal care in general, we have environmental links between the criminal behavior of the biological fathers and that of the criminal adoptees which are sufficient to account for the relationship found. These sources of prenatal and perinatal insult offer an alternative explanation to that of purely genetic transmission, and render adoption studies of little value as natural experiments for disentangling the relative contributions of heredity and environment.

Congenital transmission of handicap—that is, genetic/environmental interaction up to the point of birth—explains features of several findings which make difficulties for a specifically genetic explanation. Goddard's (1913) claim that he had demonstrated a genetic factor in the deviance and other social failure of the Kallikak family has been unacceptable to geneticists because of the wide phenotypic variety—in the form of vagrancy, prostitution, pauperism, and disease, besides crime—evidenced from one generation to another. Such variety, on the other hand, is a feature of the congenital transmission of handicap.

Schulsinger (1977) encountered the same problem, in the form of a wide range of abnormal personality, when she claimed to have found evdence for the genetic transmission of psychopathy to adoptees from their biological families. The excess of behavior problems among the latter was only to a small degree accounted for specifically by psychopathy, but covered a spectrum including crime, alcoholism, drug abuse, and hysterical character deviation. And her finding is open to the aforementioned explanation of transmission by prenatal stress in a more direct way than those of Hutchings and Mednick for adoptees, since the personality disorders of the biological fathers and other relatives, such as would have been likely to produce unhappy pregnancies, was there in fact, and not inferred from the criminality of the fathers.

The well-known study by Robins (1966), often quoted as evidence for the inheritance of behavior disturbance, found that, among children who had never had a permanent home and therefore had never lived with their fathers, 50 percent of those whose fathers were sociopathic (i.e., deviant or social failures) themselves had a high rating for sociopathic personality as adults. This compared with a mere 9 percent of those whose fathers had been of stable personality.

It was overlooked that the mothers of the children of the sociopathic fathers were likely to have been harassed by their bad behavior, or to have suffered the trials of disloyalty or desertion, during their pregnancies, and hence were liable to produce behavior-disturbed children.

That social stresses can even produce congenital malformations was shown by the remarkable increases in the prevalence of such during the worst war years in Britain and during the war and the early postwar years in Germany (Stott, 1962c). The same article reports a reanalysis of Wilkins's (1960) figures for the incidence of crime by year of birth in Britain, showing that the crime rate of boys born in 1940 and 1941—the worst period of the war—was 39.3 percent above normal between the ages of 8 and 14. This could not be attributed to poor nutrition because, owing to full employment and the efficient rationing system, the British working class was better fed during the war than in the prewar period. Just as the boys in question were evidently rendered delinquency-prone by the wartime stresses experienced by their mothers during their pregnancies (living in air-raid shelters, losing their homes because of bombings, evacuation, bad news and anxieties about husbands on war service, and so on), so the finding by Hutchings and Mednick that nearly twice as many adoptees as nonadoptees had criminal records can be attributed at least in part to a greater probability of stressful pregnancy among women who have to give up their children for adoption.

Disturbed, including delinquent, children are liable to suffer from a multiplicity of diverse handicaps, the interrelatedness of which suggests a congenital origin. This tendency is shown in Table 3 in the combined sample of 818 boys placed on probation and their original controls (Stott, 1962c). Although the delinquents were much more maladjusted, it is seen that in both groups the mean

Table 3
Behavior disturbance and morbidity (ill-health and physical defect)

	Mean scores for maladjustment on BSAG	
	Probationers	Nondelinquent Controls
Healthy	16.4	6.5
One morbid condition only	19.7	8.1
Two or more distinct morbid conditions	26.9	11.0

scores for maladjustment rise with the number of distinct kinds of ill health or physical defect present. In a larger study of 2,527 randomly selected children (Stott, Marston, and Neill, 1975, p. 112), the mean scores for underreacting and overreacting maladjustment rose, with a remarkable consistency in both sexes, with each increasing numbers of types of morbidity, up to four and five.

This interrelationship of diverse behavioral and physical handicaps was characteristic of the children of mothers, in the two studies described previously, who suffered stressful pregnancies. It may be taken as the benchmark of congenital insult. A simple genetic explanation does not fit because of the wide variety of handicaps. However, this does not rule out the possibility that the vulnerability of individual children to prenatal stresses may be genetically determined. Reference is made below to evidence for such a differential genetic vulnerability in animals.

GENETIC-ENVIRONMENTAL INTERACTION

The methodology of twin and adoption studies, and of other attempts to assess the heritability of individual differences, is based on the assumption that genetic and environmental influences act independently and additively, and can be separated by the statistical partialing out of each "influence" in turn. The factors determining biological growth are not of this simple linear type. Leading geneticists (Dobzhansky, 1962, 1973) and, in the field of criminology, Shah and Roth (1974) have recognized a continuous interaction between the genetic constitution of an organism and the different environments it meets in the course of its life, with provision for alternative modes of development. A particular set of circumstances, or even a single event, may trigger a form of growth which would otherwise have remained a mere genetic potentiality. There is no constant genetic influence which produces a certain result irrespective of the succession of environments that the organism encounters. Hence, it must always be impossible to isolate or quantify separate contributions of heredity and environment. All biological phenomena, including behavior, are the product of both heredity and environment inextricably entangled. This includes differential individual vulnerability to criminal breakdown.

How this genetic component in criminal behavior is thought to operate has important implications for social policy. If we assume that it exerts a direct, linear influence which will inexorably find expression, the only hope for preventing individual vulnerability to crime is by selective breeding, which was the policy of eugenists. They attributed the social breakdown of certain families, and its continuance in successive generations, as evidence of "unhealthy stock"; and this way of thinking survives in certain quarters at the present time.

The alternative theory, which fits the facts much better, is that every individual carries genetic potentialities for defect, physical or behavioral or both, which are actualized only in conjunction with certain environmental stresses. This process of facilitation—to use its designation in experimental biology (Malpas, 1936)—is responsible for the variability in the expression of a genetic trait which was traditionally accounted for by postulating degrees of penetrance; but this was merely a case of making a label serve as an explanation.

Facilitation has been demonstrated experimentally in animals. A particular form of stress, cortisone, administered to pregnant females produces a given malformation, cleft palate, in one strain of mouse but not in others (Fraser et al. .1954). Landauer and Bliss (1946) similarly demonstrated a differential teratogenic vulnerability to insulin in chickens.

In natural populations of animals, genetic provisions for lethal defect are facilitated by crowding. In some species, when the level of population becomes dangerously high, there ensues a near-total die-off of the yearlings from stress diseases or a near-suicidal emigration from the home territory (reviewed in Stott, 1962a). The young animals in the course of their wandering often show a disregard for their own safety analogous to the inconsequent behavior typical of many delinquents. Errington (154) noted a state of behavioral breakdown—in the form of mutual intolerance and quarreling among the adults, and attacks upon their young—which exactly parallels the reversion to a breakdown state under extreme stress of human adults. It is also remarkable that the tendency in some human families for defect and behavior disorder to be perpetuated from generation to generation likewise has its parallel in the continuance of the population die-off in an animal species for up to four generations beyond the population peak (Green and Evans, 1940).

In both the field and the laboratory studies the defect-producing stresses operated prenatally (Chitty, 1952). Bruce (1960) found that the mere intrusion of a strange male mouse into the female's nesting area was sufficient to terminate the pregnancy. The effects of the exposure of pregnant women to the acute interpersonal tensions described earlier can be seen as the counterpart in humans of these population-controlling mechanisms. If the latter are to be effective, it is necessary for a large, and perhaps the greater, number of members of a species to carry a genetic potentiality for what under natural conditions amounts to self-annihilation. In some animal species the handicap is one of temperament, which, however, is corrected at puberty if the animal survives to that stage (Thompson, 1957). Such "growing out of" congenital weakness acts as a finer means of adjusting population numbers to the available food supply; and this is a common phenomenon among human children, who can grow out of not only respiratory weaknesses, but handicaps of temperament such as inconsequence and unforthcomingness. Indeed, the human species, having evolved as predators with no natural enemies to keep their numbers under control, would have needed very efficient checks to excessive population growth, and these are seen in a multiplicity of such provisions, both physiological and cultural (Stott, 1962a).

There is thus good reason to believe that the whole of humanity bears genetic provisions for defects of some kind or other, which become actualized only under those conditions of social stress which, during the tribal era of our evolution, would have resulted from overcrowding. If this is the case, it follows that selective breeding will be effective only by the virtual elimination of the human race. The practical alternative is to minimize the social conditions that generate stress breakdown in the older generation, since this—by robbing the children of their family security—renders them prone to behavior disturbance, including delinquency.

BRAIN DYSFUNCTION AND ELECTROENCEPHALOGRAPHY

The biological issue bearing on the prevention of delinquency which remains to be discussed is that of brain dysfunction. It merits consideration as a cause of at least some delinquency on two counts. The first is that many criminals and juvenile delinquents behave in the same way as individuals who are known to have suffered organic brain damage. One of the most important functions of the frontal regions, according to Nauta (1971), is the monitoring of the effects of proposed actions; the destruction of these regions produces loss of both foresight and the ability to control primitive impulses. This description fits the inconsequent behavior of delinquent youths.

The second reason for suspecting brain damage, or at least brain dysfunction, is that many persistent criminals, especially those with violent tendencies, produce test profiles similar to those of brain-damaged persons. The best known index of brain dysfunction, the electroencephalogram (EEG) tends to produce unreliable results, probably because it has access only to those parts of the brain which are near the surface. Nevertheless, a tendency to abnormal EEG in behavior-disturbed children has been reported in some studies, which are reviewed by Stevens and his co-authors (1968). Jasper and his co-workers (1938) found that more than half of the children having the characteristic syndrome of overactivity, distractibility, short attention span, extreme emotional overreactivity, impulsiveness, antisocial behavior, and poor arithmetical ability—which might be briefly described as high delinquency-proneness—had abnormal EEGs. Ellingson (1954) concluded, from his review of published studies, that 50-60 percent of children who showed the foregoing syndrome had abnormal EEGs, with 10-15 percent among normal controls. In their own study, Stevens and his co-workers found that 47 percent of disturbed children, compared with 9-19 percent of controls, had abnormal EEGs. A limitation of all these findings is that the disturbed children examined had been referred to hospitals or health clinics. No study of EEG abnormality has been made of maladjusted children as distributed within a population. It can be understood that children referred for examination would already have been suspected of abnormality on account of their bizarre behavior; while children showing the more usual kinds of behavior disturbance—often viewed as aggressiveness, antagonism, "badness," love of adventure, foolishness, and the like—would not be referred. Likewise, there is no EEG study of a representative sample of juvenile delinquents.

It is a matter of conjecture to what extent abnormal EEG readings can be interpreted as indicating brain damage. There is some evidence that they are associated with stressful environment. Stevens and his co-workers found that those of severely disturbed children frequently show improvement with the passage of time, presumably after they have been removed from their stressful domestic situations; and that, especially in maladjusted boys, a disturbed family environment from early childhood was positively correlated with amplitude abnormalities over the frontal region. They refer to the finding of abnormal EEGs in restricted cats, dogs, and rats. Perhaps EEG abnormality should be regarded as a barometer of the effects of stress upon a vulnerable individual. If the EEG registers in some measure the response to stress, a dichotomous attribution of delinquent behavior either to organic or situational causes is not in accord with reality. To regard ascertained brain dysfunction as always primary and to explore the delinquent's situation only when no such dysfunction is found in a one-sided diagnostic procedure.

NEUROPSYCHOLOGICAL TESTS AND THE
CONCEPT OF BRAIN DYSFUNCTION

An alternative method of diagnosing brain dysfunction is that of the neuropsychological test battery originally developed by Halstead and Reitan (Reitan, 1955, 1966), which aims to detect lateral (hemispheric) brain lesion. Failure in verbal tasks is held to indicate dysfunction within the left hemisphere, which is the dominant one in the great majority of males; and failure in visual, spatial, and tactual tasks dysfunction in the right, nondominant hemisphere. When the frontal and temporal lobes of the dominant hemisphere are affected there is loss of emotional control. Nonviolent prisoners tend to do significantly better on the neuropsychological test battery than the violent. Moreover, according to Flor-Henry (1974, 1976), violence in criminals is associated with dysfunction of the dominant hemisphere, whereas emotional instability and depression are associated with dysfunction of the nondominant hemisphere. This hypothesis was confirmed by Yeudall et al. (1980). in a study of a group of 25 aggressive criminal psychopaths and noncriminal depressed patients, using the neuropsychological test battery. Yeudall (1979) also found that, among a series of 101 juvenile delinquents consecutively referred to his assessment center, 86 percent had abnormal neuropsychological profiles; 60 percent showed the nondominant hemispheric dysfunction characteristic of nonviolent criminals with personality disorder. This is consistent with Flor-Henry's theory, since fewer than 10 percent of the delinquents had committed crimes of violence. It must, however, be taken into consideration that the delinquents in question had averaged 25 arrests, and, being referred, must have aroused suspicions about their mental/emotional state. They were thus an extreme group of persistent and, presumably, abnormal, delinquents. To date, no representative sample of juvenile offenders has been tested on the neuropsychological battery. Despite these reservations, the possibility of brain dysfunction of an organic nature should be borne in mind. This applies not only to those delinquents with marked neurological symptoms and/or a history of encephalitis, but also to those who show marked lack of control and a proneness to violent outbursts, those who follow stereotypic compulsions to wander, to steal senselessly, or to expose themselves, and those who have had a single epileptiform seizure (in my experience, at a time of acute family difficulties) without any previous history of epilepsy. For such assessment the neuropsychological test battery seems more reliable than the EEG. Yeudall et al. (1978) found that in a sample of 194 children assessed by both measures, the neuropsychological battery also detected as abnormal 71 percent of those with abnormal EEGs; but of those passed as normal by the EEG, 78 percent were found abnormal on the neuropsychological battery. That the latter was not overdiagnosing is shown by its correct identification of 93 percent of the maladjusted children, while finding dysfunction in only some 14 percent of the normal controls.

It may seem presumptuous to diagnose brain dysfunction by performance on tests, as in the neuropsychological battery. This would be so if the dysfunction were held to indicate organic damage, but neuropsychologists are careful to limit themselves to the detection of dysfunction. There remains the danger that those who have the disposition and care of delinquents will not make this distinction. It must therefore be insisted that dysfunction be interpreted in the literal, most parsimonious sense. Because the main function of the human brain is to monitor the environment and to modify it by behavior, any gross disorder of the perceptual-behavioral system constitutes evidence of brain dysfunction. If dysfunction is conceived thus broadly, it becomes tautological to ask whether brain dysfunction accounts for a proportion of delinquency and crime. Except for culturally condoned crime from which the perpetrators benefit, serious and persistent crime spells the social ruin of the individual. It amounts to behavioral dysfunction, which, since the brain is the originator and organizer of behavior, indicates brain dysfunction.

The confusion between brain dysfunction as a behavioral concept and brain tissue damage arises from the fact that damage to those parts of brain which govern behavior will produce behavioral dysfunction; but not all behavioral dysfunction is due to tissue damage. The typical inconsequent, and the reversion to blind hostility seen in the overstressed, meet Luria's (1968) description of the effects of frontal lobe lesion. Certainly the erstwhile loving parent who suddenly conceives a murderous hatred for his or her child, to the extent of physical or verbal wounding, can be said to "cease to follow the programs based on his (or her) intentions," (p. 149) and to replace the latter by blind instinctual reactions. Likewise, the young delinquent who becomes an obsessional wanderer or breaker-in exemplifies the replacement of rational intention by stereotypy. It is evident that the youth dominated by any of the delinquent motivations described in Chapter Seven is bypassing the appraisal of the effects of his actions, which is a function of the frontal lobes. Such behavioral dysfunction must have its counterpart in neural dysfunction—not necessarily, or even usually, as far as the delinquent is concerned, in the form of tissue damage, but in faulty neural organization. It may be conceived of as a processing, rather than a structural, problem. The most likely fault of processing would seem to be this bypassing of the outcome-appraising function of the frontal lobes which enables primitive impulses to take over control of behavior. Indeed, such simplification of response, by cutting out consideration of ulterior consequences, enables the organism to react rapidly to immediate danger. If, however, owing to intolerable stress, these emergency reactions become habitual, the main behavioral system, which ensures the adaptation of the organism to its environment, may be said to have broken down. Thus, through neuropsychology, we arrive once again at the concept of behavioral breakdown which is central to the understanding of delinquent motivation. It consists in a switch from one response system to another. Evidently, in the process, those parts of the brain responsible for weighing up the effects of actions and keeping the individual's behavior in line with his goals and intentions are put into a state of dysfunction.

VALUE OF NEUROPSYCHOLOGICAL TESTING IN PREVENTIVE AND TREATMENT PROGRAMS

Neuropsychological testing is not suitable as a screening device or as a regular assessment procedure because we cannot be sure that poor performance indicates constitutional brain dysfunction. The tests of the Halstead-Reitan battery demand of the subject an ability to understand and apply verbal directions, and a not inconsiderable ability to concentrate, reflect, and induce principles. The development of these skills depends upon the mental habits acquired in an education- and intelligence-conscious culture, and upon freedom from besetting anxieties. Children who are surrounded by confusion and disorganization in their home lives are more likely to develop here-and-now strategies for dealing with one exigency after another. Socially disadvantaged children tend to be impulsive and intolerant of problem solving, and to lack the powers of visual and aural attention and the reflectivity required to perform well on a neuropsychological test battery. Formally, the corresponding parts of their brains are in a state of underdevelopment, which registers as dysfunction. But such dysfunction is more cultural than constitutional.

The mental functioning of most delinquent and maladjusted children is further inhibited by the preoccupations of their deprivation. It was mentioned in Chapter Seven how the child who is dominated by the need to exclude painful reminders of a distressing situation from consciousness abhors thought: the calmness and freedom from external stimulus which thinking demands open a gap through which the memory of his troubles can come to the surface. With characteristic impatience he shuns anything which requires even a small amount of attention or mental manipulation. Many such youths mentioned to me their dislike for arithmetic, and Yeudall (1979) makes a similar observation. The Halstead-Reitan Category Test, which Reitan (1966) describes as requiring "fairly sophisticated ability in noting similarities and differences in stimulus material, postulating hypotheses" and so on, would be rejected out of hand by delinquents of this type. The hostile delinquent is not interested in such mental exercises because they offer no solution to his feelings of being rejected, and his motivation is towards noncompliance.

It is noteworthy that Berman and Siegal (1976) only obtained significant differences between delinquents and nondelinquent controls in those tests of the Halstead-Reitan battery—Category, Factual Performance, Speech Sounds Perception, and Trail Making—which require concentration, memory, and reflectivity. No significant differences were found in activities, such as differentiating rhythms and finger oscillation, which demand only an immediacy of response and function. It is these tests which, it could be hypothesized, would be most effective in detecting neurological dysfunction of a mechanical or structural nature.

The conditions under which delinquents, for practical purposes, have to be tested suggest the need for redoubled caution about using neuropsychological tests to diagnose brain dysfunction of a structural nature. This is well exemplified in the Berman-Siegal study, the delinquent sample for which consisted of youths serving their first sentence in a correctional school, who were tested within one week of their admission. To the emotional turmoil of the situations which impelled them into delinquency would have been added the trauma of incarceration and apprehensions about their future treatment. The latter would have been increased by the administration of the Factual Performance Test, since it involved their being blindfolded. In contrast, the nondelinquent controls were volunteers tested in their own school.

In sum, all faults of learning style and deficiences in problem-solving skills will register as dysfunction on neuropsychological tests, whether they be cultural/educational, or neurological in the strict sense of the word. Even if "neurological," this may not necessarily indicate lesion as tissue damage. Evidence has been quoted to the effect that prenatal and perinatal insult can take the form of behavior disturbances. Among the latter, temperamental handicaps such as in-consequence must have a neurological basis, but this can be a matter of neural processing. Cultural/educational dysfunction can best be distinguished from intrinsic neural dysfunction by observation of the child's response to a program of training in learning skills (Stott, 1978a). Neuropsychological tests could well be used in monitoring progress in such training. If the dysfunction vanishes, the indication would be that it had its origin in cultural/educational deficiencies or in thought-inhibiting stresses. If it persists, somatic causes have to be sought. These would include not only tissue damage, but metabolic disorders of endocrine, allergic, infective, or other toxic origin.

"LEARNING DISABILITIES" AND DELINQUENCY

The observation that nearly all delinquents have learning prob-lems has raised the issue of whether "learning disabilities"—conceived of as dysfunction of the mental processes involved in learning—may be causally linked to delinquency. The American Institute of Research (Murray, 1976; Lane, 1980) divided the various theories of linkage into two types.

The first group of theories adduces a common cause in the form of personality factors which render a child both learning-disabled and delinquency prone. These are cognate with the forms of behavior disturbance typical of delinquents and the motivations impelling them towards deviant acts, as described in Chapters Seven and Ten. The aberrant motivations consist broadly of attempts to escape, by avoidance-excitement, from an emotionally unbearable situation, or to cut free from such by means of hostility. The avoidance-domi-nated individual cannot tolerate the state of freedom from external stimuli which is necessary for application to learning tasks. Conse-quently, those under the compulsion of avoidance-excitement are, virtually without exception, poor learners; and if subjected to neuro-psychological testing would be expected to register dysfunction because of this interference with the thinking processes. As for the hostile child, since his motivation is to secure rejection by the adult world, he has a disincentive to achieve academically. Academic failure and delinquency are thus seen to share a common causation in these forms of behavior disturbance.

To these aberrant motivations must be added the syndrome of inconsequence. How it can lead a child into sporadic delinquent acts has been explained in Chapter Seven. The same lack of foresight and inability to inhibit response to distracting stimuli is typical of so-called hyperactive children, who probably account for the great majority of those diagnosed as learning-disabled. However, in the series of persistent delinquents on whom I reported (Stott, 1950/80), this personality weakness was never the sole cause of their delinquency. It would appear that family ties are normally strong enough to hold the inconsequent child back from serious delinquency. This would explain why only a small minority of the learning-disabled become delinquent.

The notion that learning failure may lead to delinquency is reminiscent of the long-standing controversy about the chicken and the egg in the strong relationship between poor school attainment and maladjustment. The latest evidence (Stott, 1981) is that the behavior disturbance is primary. Eight-year-old children with poor attainment in reading and arithmetic were no more disturbed than they had been at the age of five, before their exposure to formal learning. The awareness of failure had added no increment of behavior disturbance; or, at any rate, failing children had not allowed it to affect their general social relationships. It is reasonable to assume that awareness of failure would not generate delinquent behavior.

The second group of theories adduces a "labeling" effect: owing to the low regard in which he is held by teachers and fellow-students, the learning-disabled child is held to develop a poor self-image, for which he compensates by moving into the delinquent sphere and gaining success and esteem therein. This explanation depends on a succession of assumptions for which there is no research evidence and which general experience suggests are improbable. Notably, it is unlikely in these times that teachers will so denigrate, or fellow-students so deride, the child who is failing in school that he is forced to the extremity of seeking companionship among disreputable children, and paying the price of it in the form of delinquency. A further improbability is that the learning-disabled child will seek compensations of a type calculated to distress and anger his parents— a consideration advanced in more than one place in this book as the main reason why emotionally stable children who enjoy a secure family life do not yield to casual delinquent temptations. The principle of least cost, which is a general law of human behavior, would induce him to seek forms of compensation which do not entail throwing away the advantages he has. Such compensations may run to causing distraction and disruption in the classroom. But the most usual reaction is to come to terms with the failure by a process of accommodation: the student attaches little importance to school attainment, just accepts the fact that he "hasn't the brains," and finds innocent happiness elsewhere.

The issue is confused by disagreement over what constitutes a "learning disability" and the sanctification of the concept as a mystical entity responsible for a child's inability to learn. The modern view (Haight, 1980) is that the term covers heterogeneous impairments of the learning processes. Thus conceived, it has to include impairments of temperament, since these are undoubtedly the most important constitutional handicaps to learning (Stott, 1978a). Of these, the most responsible for poor attainment is unforthcomingness, evidenced in a yielding to fear of what is perceived as difficult or strange. It acts as a virtual guarantee against delinquency (see Chapter Eighteen). Inconsequence, on the other hand, confers a somewhat higher risk of thoughtless, casual delinquency. In short, any general statement about the relationship of "learning disabilities" to delinquency is meaningless.

Attempts to verify the existence of a common factor of brain dysfunction in "learning disabilities" and delinquency meet the same problems as those discussed earlier in the appraisal of the results of neuropsychological testing. Behavioral/emotional handicaps produce a de facto dysfunction of the mental processes involved in learning. The issue becomes, therefore, one of determining whether dysfunction is conceived of phenomenally—that is, in relation to the behavioral outcome—or structurally—implying brain lesion. It should be borne in mind that neuropsychological testing deals with the behavioral outcome, and that its structural findings are inferences. These inferences may become difficult to make if the test results are affected by dysfunction due to behavior disturbance.

In summary, we are unlikely to get beyond the general statement that learning difficulties of any sort, whether or not conceived of as "learning disabilities," are not a cause of delinquency, but can be a common outcome with delinquency of certain types of behavior disturbance and temperamental handicap. There is thus little hope of reducing the prevalence of juvenile delinquency by treating "learning disabilities."

THE PREVENTION OF VULNERABILITY

Vulnerability to behavior disturbance and delinquency has been seen to consist in a liability to dysfunction of those areas of the brain that monitor consequences and control primitive impulses. Social disadvantage is associated with a hierarchy of causes of vulnerability. The children can be affected prenatally by the stresses, both of a personal and physical nature, to which women tend to be subjected in a disadvantaged and culturally disintegrated social group; they are more likely to suffer neurological damage from prematurity and early malnutrition; during their childhoods, they are liable to suffer from continued malnutrition, insufficient sleep, and a lack of opportunities to develop powers of attention and problem-solving.

Far-reaching measures for reducing the number of delinquency-prone children would therefore include both the removal of gross economic inequalities and the development of cultural safeguards against social stress. The latter would entail the review of those factors making for instability in family life, and in particular the marital discord and other sources of interpersonal unhappiness which are massively productive of unhealthy and disturbed children. The overall goal should be to halt the transmission of handicap from one culturally disintegrated generation to the next, which is the major source of delinquency and crime.

Chapter Fourteen
Community Projects
and Initiatives

THE INSTINCTIVE BASIS OF MORALITY

Human beings have evolved as small-group animals. The isolated individual was nonviable. Because the group was vital to his existence behavior was genetically referenced to group membership and to the group's good. What has served these ends is accounted moral; that is to say, conforming to the mores, or code of behaviors, which has had survival value for groups over many generations.

The group consisted of individuals, originally tied by kinship and marriage, who knew each other by sight and heard how each conducted himself. Rees (1950) describes the control which the group exerts on its members in a rural Welsh village:

> Not only do a man's actions reflect upon himself and his household, the reputation of his relatives is also involved, and there can be no stronger sanction in the countryside than the praise and particularly the censure of one's kinsmen. A person who gains the respect of his neighbors enhances the prestige of his kin group, and they are proud to own him as one of themselves and to display his photograph in a prominent place in their homes. In the same way, a person who disgraces himself prejudices the good name of his kindred (p. 80).

Beyond the face-to-face and oral communication group there are no reference points for behavior—that is to say, no instinctive morality. As a species we still suffer from this limitation. The more remote any other group from our expereince, the less concerned we are about its welfare and the more callous we are to its suffering. The most we can hope for in the regulation of intergroup relations is that each community identifies its interests with the good treatment of neighboring communities. An integrated, or culturally organized, society is one in which individuals are affiliated with a face-to-face group and refer their conduct to it, and in which the groups themselves recognize the need for codes of morality and of law which inhibit group feuding and so ensure a general orderliness.

LOOSENING OF COMMUNITY COHESIVENESS

A salient characteristic of modern urban populations is a loosening of this group cohesiveness. This trend towards cultural disorganization has two main implications for the control of delinquency. First, local neighborhood-conglomerations lack the community organizations through which they can take action against juvenile misbehavior or bring moral pressure on the parents of misbehaving youth. Individual families, feeling helpless, lapse into apathy and concentrate on keeping out of trouble themselves. This all too often results in the attitude, "We don't mix with neighbors," or, "We keep to ourselves." Local vandalism and personal violence are accepted with a resigned tolerance; hope lies in one day getting out of the neighborhood. Second, there are many individuals, especially young people alienated from their families or with no sense of family loyalty, who lack the instinctive reference to a group for their behavior. This means that unless they belong to that tiny minority—estimated by Kohlberg and Kramer (1969) at some 4 percent—who possess independent moral judgment, they have nothing to set against their natural self-centeredness. They lack the discipline of small-group attachment upon which the human race has relied in its evolution. It is a question of how we may be able to counter this cultural disintegration, first at the community level, and second as regards socially alienated youth.

STIMULATING COMMUNITY ORGANIZATION

When traditional kinship and friendship groups are broken up by population movements, the process of regrouping occurs spontaneously, but at different rates, according to the particular skills of the incoming group and whether there is an existing community of its own culture to welcome them. Middle-class migrants are usually able to integrate themselves fairly quickly into the host community because of the means they have for entertaining and joining clubs, and the self-assurance which enables them to approach their hosts as equals. Those ethnic groups, such as the Jews, Chinese, Pakistanis, and Asiatic Indians, who bring with them a strong family tradition and code of behavior, have also been notably successful as in-comers. Those who lack a strong family unity and have a more spontaneous and extroverted life style are less successful, especially if in their homeland they relied upon senior community figures outside the family to control the young.

Our only hope, in short, is that those groups who have suffered culture disintegration will earn to respond to its stresses, not by apathy and withdrawal, but by initiatives in social reorganization. How severe these stresses can be is instanced by the story of a black mother who fled with her children from a New Jersey housing project, as told by the journalist Chet Fuller (1978). Because of the numerous burglaries, even in a locality where one would have thought there was little to steal, she was afraid every time she left her house, and afraid to stay there too. When her son picked up his paycheck for his work of bagging groceries, he had to run home because there would always be a gang of boys waiting to waylay him. The family escaped into the poverty of rural North Carolina, but at least, the son said, he did not have to fight all the time and the mother could leave her home with peace of mind. Only a few can, or would, exchange the city ghetto for the hard life of farm work to which they are not accustomed. It is a matter of how quickly the spontaneous movement of community reintegration can progress. The *Time* magazine articles on juvenile deviance in America report the beginnings of such community activity in Harlem, where the black community, as chief sufferers from the endemic robbery and violence, is increasingly supporting the efforts of the police (*Time*, 1977a, 1977b).

In general, nevertheless, the progress of community reintegration has been disappointing, not only in the black ghettos of the United States but also in the rehoused white neighborhoods of Britain. How it can be stimulated is problematical, considering that the need to form community action groups has to be felt strongly enough by the local residents to overcome their apathy and fear-generated withdrawal. Clifford Shaw's requirement that community projects should be conducted by the local residents follows logically if they are seen as part of a movement of cultural reintegration rather than as social-work exercises. When this was overlooked in a Bristol (England) project of the 1950s the residents of the housing estate chosen for its operation opposed it on the grounds that their neighborhood had been singled out as needing rehabilitation.

Shaw and his colleagues were nevertheless correct in providing advisers to local residents in the establishment of community and youth centers. It is a paradoxical truth of social anthropology that within traditional communities, in which the same families have lived for generations and everyone knows everyone else, initiatives have to come from outsiders. An insider assuming leadership runs up against the egalitarianism of nonaspirational social groups, who resent any one of their members setting himself up above the rest. Frankenberg (1957) gives some striking examples of this inhibition of initiative in a Welsh border village. Its brass band did not play, despite owning an expensive set of instruments and having adequate skilled players and two experienced conductors. But neither of the conductors could be used because a bandsman objected to being ordered about by one of his fellows. Because of the same sensitivity, the captain of the local football team could not be persuaded, as one of the villagers, to give orders to the players. In previous seasons the difficulty had been overcome by bringing in an outside captain, a West Indian Negro, from a nearby town. Following the same principle that no one of their own community should be accorded a leadership role, outside people were invited to chair village committees. Sprott, Jephcott, and Carter (1954) reported the same phenomenon in their study of an English mining community: a women's guild "had a slow and anxious committee, the members of which were in terror of being accused of getting above themselves" (p. 95).

Historically, this egalitarian inhibition of spontaneous local leadership has been overcome by precisely this device of bringing in outsiders—the itinerant minister of a religious revival, the organizer of a workingmen's association, and the formation of branches of political clubs and educational associations. But the result of the outside initiative was the creation of active local organizations. This, it appears, is the cultural process through which reintegration and remoralization occur among uprooted populations. The effect was to create new affiliation groups to which people felt themselves accountable. The key to the effectiveness of these groups as reference points for the conduct of individuals was their smallness and the exclusivity of their membership. To replicate successfully the ancient accountability to a kinship group, the new bodies—sects, chapels, lodges, trade associations, musical and educational societies, and so on—had to be composed of known persons who were respected, loved, or feared. They also had to have common aims which overrode the separate inclinations and interests of individual members.

By considering how social reintegration has occurred in the past, we arrive at a set of criteria for successful community projects. What are needed are not grandiose centers already equipped by an organ of government, with all sorts of recreational and cultural amenities—to which people drop in, or from which they drop out, as if they were shopping centers—but relatively small and enduring groups of people sharing the activities and having the same interests or social goals. We see such springing up everywhere, the tenants of an apartment house or housing project uniting for the purpose of negotiating with a landlord, making representations to a housing authority for safeguarding neighborhood amenities, church guilds which organize fetes, rummage sales, and excursions, sports followers' clubs, and innumerable other small-group activities. As an example of community cohesiveness at a germinal stage I have in mind a weekly wine-drinking party of women in a Glasgow rehousing project, which met on Tuesdays because that was the day they drew their children's allowances.

To attempt to stimulate community organizations directly around the theme of delinquency prevention would probably run into trouble for the reasons touched upon earlier: the local population chosen as the subject of the project might well resent the slur on its neighborhood, however much it were justified; and action against particular delinquents could start feuds. On the other hand, a community body formed around the other objectives might well raise the status of the neighborhood and evoke a pride in it. From there it is a short step to the growth of a code of conduct which people term respectability, upon which families will begin to model their behavior in order to maintain their good name in the community. One of the most important criteria for the respectability of a neighborhood is the cleanliness of the streets and the curbing of juvenile vandalism. Consequently, any form of community integration will place a check on youthful unruliness and delinquency.

Since degree of community organization is the long-term key factor in delinquency control, the rehousing of slum dwellers in new housing projects has done little by itself to achieve this end. In his follow-up of 1,340 Glasgow boys during the three years after they left school, Ferguson (1952) showed that the percentages found guilty of an offense from rehoused slum families (21.8), and from continuing slum dwellers (22.3) were virtually identical; while those from new housing projects not formed from previous slum dwellers was, at 6.8 percent, equal to that from the middle-class and good working-class areas.

What lack of social organization means in human terms is well illustrated by the description of a housing project in Widnes, in Lancashire, at the beginning of a Social and Community Planning Research project (NACRO and SPCR, c.1977). Its physical appearance was one of unkempt and neglected yards, broken windows, graffiti, and so much litter that the street seemed to be used as the normal receptacle for it. Vandalism was becoming normal behavior for 12-16-year-old children, and many adults were afraid of teenagers in groups and feared retaliation if they reported or rebuked children. There was no social organization, formal or informal, on the project; many tenants wanted to leave but felt themselves trapped, because the local Council would not give them accommodations in a more respectable project.

The project carried out by the local council officers and the SCPR group might well serve as a model strategy for stimulating community organization. Initially, they had to face a long-standing distrust of the Council, which was thought of as doing things to the tenants rather than for them. In order to make contact with a representative section of the inhabitants, the project team invited randomly chosen groups to discussions with them, the same groups being called together as many as three times over some two months. This enabled their members to consider propositions for the improvement of the project and to discuss them with their neighbors. Solutions proposed at one group were submitted to subsequent groups, and the final proposals were presented to general meetings. A residents' association was formed, and parents helped in a new adventure playground and day-care center. The first report of the project noted that already there was less litter in the streets.

The second report of the project, covering the first two years of its operation (NACRO and SCPR, 1978a), gives the impressions of Council officers, the police, the Residents' Association Committee, and the observations of the consultants as follows:

> Social activity on the project is increasing, friendship networks are widening.
>
> There is more confidence and less sense of being under perpetual siege.
>
> Teenagers are causing less trouble, and tenants have more confidence in dealing with trouble themselves when it occurs.
>
> The physical environment looks vastly improved.
>
> There is little visible sign of litter, broken glass, breakage and vandalism generally.
>
> More people are reported to be doing up their front yards, even in some cases paying local unemployed teenagers to do this for them.
>
> Although members of our original discussions predicted that public tree planting would not survive the attentions of local youth, the

great majority of subsequent planting has survived and is becoming established.

The police say that the estate has changed for the better out of all recognition: the beat policeman reports a "dramatic decrease in crime," and some quietening of the new families who were terrorising the neighborhood (pp. 2-3).

There are also indications that the project's specific objectives of reducing vandalism and crime by community action are beginning to be met. "Two years ago when teenagers were causing a nuisance or smashing things, nobody dared go out and tell them to stop. Now they are not afraid to, and the reasons they give are that they know the teenagers individually and they can rely on their neighbors to come out and support them" (p. 4).

The police became converted to the project and are now trusted by the adult residents. The policeman who patrols on foot countered the initial hostility by making friends of the little children, and the 15- and 16-year-olds all know him and tolerate him well. He has promoted "crime parties" to secure the cooperation of residents, and this has been another means by which neighbors have gotten to know one another.

This project might well prove one of the seeds from which widespread community action against juvenile misbehavior grows.

THE BIOLOGICAL VALUE
OF COMMUNITY ORGANIZATION

Besides stimulating the formulation of a public opinion which will induce parents to exercise a better supervision over their children and so check vandalism and other kinds of deviance, community projects such as that just described may have a more fundamental effect in reducing delinquency. Evidence has been quoted to show that vulnerability to behavior disturbance may arise from exposure of the mother to serious and ongoing interpersonal tensions during pregnancy. Among the noxious tensions observed were those with neighbors and the agents of authority. Women living in a socially disorganized neighborhood who have to tolerate the depredations and aggressiveness of the local youth, or who feel themselves harassed and bullied by the police and local officials, consequently stand a greater chance of having constitutionally maladjusted and also unhealthy children. The high level of stress in such a locality, with the prevalent mood of helplessness and frustration, is furthermore calculated to burst out in quarreling between the husband and wife, and irritable-depressive rejection by the parents of the children, paralleling the situation of "nerves" observed in animal species following a peak in population (Errington, 1954). It is also significant that Chitty (1952) attributed the wholesale dying-off of young voles following such a period of strife to "some disturbance of the hormonal balance of the mother which in some way affected the fetus." These findings offer a clue to some of the vague "broad social influences" so often quoted as the determinants of delinquency. It goes without saying that intervention of a type which has community integration as its objective will show results only in the fairly long term. But the time needed for a fetus to become a teenage vandal is much less than the whole generation we have wasted in wringing our hands over the ever-growing delinquency problem. And when it is considered that pregnancies free of interpersonal stresses also mean half the amount of childhood illness, the cost benefit to society of such community projects is incalculable.

YOUTH CLUBS AND
DELINQUENCY PREVENTION

We must not expect regular youth clubs to make a direct contribution to the prevention of delinquency, and of course that is not their chief goal. Pursuing the themes of the earlier part of this chapter, it could be argued that they will do so indirectly as vehicles of community integration. Most of the lasting friendships of life are made during youth, and as young people pass into adult life they will have formed around them a reference group by which standards of conduct are maintained. Some locus for the formation of friendships among youth is therefore valuable for the growth of structure in shifting urban populations.

A genuine club also offers its youth membership a microcosm of society within which they can develop loyalties and feelings of responsibility for the good of the whole. But to fulfill this function, a club must be small enough to allow its members to interact frequently and with easy familiarity. It must also have a stable membership who have time to get to know and develop loyalties to one another. An organization with a large and changing membership does not meet this condition, and consequently is incapable of advancing its members to the level of moral development which depends upon fellowship and obligation. A drop-in club can undoubtedly be useful as a means of making contact with youth who would otherwise shun adult society, but unless the youths thus contacted can be progressively inducted into stable clubs, their influence will be negligible.

Institutional hang-ups similar to those which have resulted in overly large secondary schools have also produced overly large youth clubs. Unless a center accommodates large numbers, a local education authority may be inclined to feel that the expenditure is not justified; but it is far better to give financial support to small clubs run in church halls or in other already existing buildings. Being forced to run a recreational institute rather than a genuine club places youth leaders in a situation of conflict. If they set out to run an orderly center with high standards, they will be tempted to get rid of unruly youngsters. Even those who are not expelled will feel on tenterhooks, and forestall an eventual showdown by leaving. Thus, the center will have failed in its social obligation to those who are most in need of adult help.

Within a small club the leader is able to notice when any member is in a suspiciously unsettled or sullen mood, and hence in need of adult support. If the member has lapsed in attendance, the leader should be aware of it and make inquiries as to the reason, which may often be quite trivial. A young person from a disadvantaged family may, from feelings of inferiority, imagine a discourtesy where none was intended, or anticipate blame for something that has happened in the club. Young people who have not enjoyed the taken-for-granted security of a stable home are inclined to such misunderstandings, and are apt to banish themselves unless they can feel confident of the enduring loyalty of an adult. Above all, the threat of expulsion must never be held over their heads. The mere possibility that the adult might reject them prompts them to get rejection in first. In a club within a committal institution, which I organized as part of my research, I insisted that no member could be expelled; in the event it turned out that this no-expulsion rule was necessary for the very existence of the club. When I had to relinquish the leadership in order to write my report, the new club leader accepted the position provided he could expel a few youths who were known in the school as troublemakers. At intervals he had to expel others, until in the end he had hardly any members left, and the club was closed.

It has of course to be recognized that, in a youth club, delinquent and predelinquent young people do present difficulties which require understanding and careful handling. It is unlikely—short of finding a rare intuitive genius, or someone with the charity of a saint—that this will be achieved unless the club leader has been trained to detect the motivations underlying deviant behavior.

The most common error made by adults working with unsettled youngsters is to expect that they will invariably respond to one's trust and efforts on their behalf. Sooner or later a test of the unconditional nature of the adult's concern will be made in the form of some flagrant misdemeanor; and indeed, the better the progress made in winning over a disillusioned child, the more likely it is that the test will be made. The adult then feels let down and is tempted to renounce further interest in the young person.

The hostile moods of many of the delinquency-prone have also to be understood. Too open an offer of friendship may be rejected as a dangerous involvement by a youth who has been let down on previous occasions. Provocative acts of mischief may be continued in order to invite banishment. A young person whose anxiety about acceptance takes the form of unreasonable demands for attention may react by some quite heinous crime if he feels that the club leader has other favorites. The leader has thus to dispense his companionship in carefully measured amounts and with scrupulous fairness, irrespective of his own inclinations.

Delinquents dominated by avoidance-excitement are seldom attracted to a youth club, because it does not offer them the constant round of hectic stimulation which enables them to keep their family problems from their thoughts. Their chosen venue will be the amusement arcades and billiard halls—at most honoring the local youth club with a raid. It is doubtful whether any youth club can meet their emotional needs so long as their family problems are unresolved or until they are able to come to terms with it. Our tactic towards a raider who is apprehended, or towards a youth who joins a club just to make trouble, should be an immediate investigation of his family circumstances in order to identify the emotional deprivations which underlie his maladjustment and delinquency.

On the other hand, a well-run club should be able to accommodate the pure inconsequent. Owing to the ease with which he can be dared or shamed into taking part in delinquent escapades, he is best kept away from delinquents who are otherwise motivated, because they may recruit him as a companion to do their risky work. He is therefore better off in a small group in which the members can build up strong loyalties to the adult leader.

A CLUB IN A COMMITTAL INSTITUTION

None of the 102 delinquents whom I studied (Stott, 1950/80) were able to maintain club membership in their home localities prior to their committal; and indeed, hardly any made an attempt to join a club. An evening spent in a club would have been "too quiet," or too much responsibility to be well-behaved would have been placed on them. Above all, they felt that their type was not wanted. Yet, in the club in their residential school, described more fully elsewhere (Stott, 1954), the same youths behaved well without an externally imposed discipline, and many of them showed a capacity for responsible leadership. It helped that they were removed from immediate confrontation with their family difficulties, and had benefited from a few months of training in disciplined living within the school. Principally, however, the club in question offered a situation which did not touch off their weaknesses. Visitors were impressed with how normal the club members appeared to be. If I had known nothing of their general behavioral breakdown in their home settings, I could have agreed with John Mays (1954), who, from his observation of boys in a similar small and personalized club in Liverpool's dockland, concluded that 90 percent of delinquents are normal young people. It is all a matter of situation-attitude; the stability and morality of the behavior of all of us depends, in the last resort, upon the framework of influences and obligations within which we seek to establish our image.

The constitution and mode of operation of the club followed from the fact that, being a research worker attached to the school but not a member of its staff, I had no formal authority over the youths, nor could I, without forfeiting their trust, fall back upon the school authority. Law and order within the club and its good housekeeping had to be delegated to the members. A chairman and secretary were elected by the membership as a whole. The chairman or his deputy for the evening was responsible for good behavior, for seeing that refreshments were made and the crockery washed, for summoning the members to clean the room before leaving, and, finally, for dismissing them at closing time. As adult leader, I never gave a routine order. This is not to say that sometimes I did not whisper a reminding word in the ear of the chairman if he forgot the time or was overlooking some persistent minor disturbance, but generally I avoided even this. If the club room was left untidy the domestic staff would be quick to lodge a complaint and this would be brought up at the general meeting which took place each Sunday or at an emergency meeting if necessary. This general assembly was the supreme authority or "parliament" of the club, presided over by the chairman, and having its decisions recorded by the secretary. I would sit at the back and generally avoided expressing an opinion.

It was, however, sometimes necessary for me to reaffirm constitutional principles when these tended to be overlooked, to exercise a discreet guidance in matters of general neighborliness, and to point out that the object of the club discipline was to serve the "public" good.

The general assembly was also the supreme court in disciplinary matters. If any member flouted the chairman's authority he could be called to account at the next meeting and the whole membership would decide as to his guilt and punishment. Conversely, any member who thought himself unfairly treated by the chairman could lodge a complaint against him. Since the assembly could dismiss the chairman by a general vote, the individual member's rights were fully safeguarded. In fact this never happened, and the haling of offenders before the assembly was also rare. That the mutual safeguards were known to exist meant that they were seldom used. The members realized that the chairman was their nominee acting on their behalf, and that they had immediate redress in case of abuse. No one could suggest that any clique were taking advantage of its position, as might have happened if there had been only periodic elections. For this reason also we always avoided appointing a committee. A committee has to be elected periodically, at comparatively infrequent intervals. Especially with delinquent boys, who tend to be very touchy when their own rights are involved, it would have been inviting accusations of unfairness if they had been disciplined by officers whom they had no personal part in electing and whom they could not dismiss.

In effect most breaches of discipline were settled out of court or before an informal meeting of the officers, called for the purpose of reasoning with an insubordinate member. Only if he refused to give an undertaking to accept the chairman's ruling in the future would the matter be brought to a "showdown" at the general meeting. As mentioned, this seldom happened; the fear of public condemnation was as great as in a tribal community.

Self-government included the choice of new members. Any boy in the school could be elected after he had been there three months. The procedure was to bring his name forward at the general meeting and, if accepted, he would be allowed to attend, on a month's trial. At the end of this period the "probationer" had to withdraw from the assembly while his permanent acceptance was discussed. If, as almost invariably happened, the vote was favorable, he was ushered in by the steward and called upon to promise to keep the club rules. The chairman whereupon shook his hand, gave him a badge, and recited a formal sentence of welcome, which was followed by an ovation from the assembly. The ceremony was always taken very seriously.

This description is given because it illustrates certain principles that could be important for the running of youth clubs in high-delinquency areas. In such areas, some alternative means of establishing leadership other than physical strength or delinquent initiative would have to be provided, and government by general assembly might be the answer. A committee could easily come to be seen as one gang attempting to dominate others. If the total membership is the effective authority, there are no authority figures to rebel against. And the knowledge that an appointed leader can be removed at any time bypasses the sensitivity felt by the underprivileged youth about being ordered about by his equals.

Exclusivity of membership would also be important, as giving prestige and fostering corporate loyalty. Every tribe or clan has to be a closed group. Likewise, a club loses its value as a source of pride, loyalty, and security if individuals can casually attach or detach themselves. Similar units of community organization are formed in all human socieities, and they have been the foundations of stable social life. They have always emphasized their cohesiveness and exclusivity by rituals, in the same way as family membership and friendship are symbolized and reinforced by gifts and endearments. Ceremony and symbols of membership are therefore important to a club.

Self-government does not imply that a youth club could function satisfactorily without an adult leader, or that the leader should take a passive role. Because of the need of youth for adult support, the leader is the pivot, and his influence is to a large extent the reason for the existence of the club. The club's success depends upon the members individually having a good relationship with him and knowing his ideas about how the club should function and what constitutes good behavior. The leader should have clear goals for the club and not hesitate to realize them. How the goals are achieved is a matter of tactics and the personal style of the individual. In some situations an unaggressive form of leadership may be the best, but the leader should remain in control of the situation and be looked up to by the members as the ultimate authority. A bland, ineffective leader who sits back to see how things will turn out will be disliked, and hence unable to exercise any influence.

CLUB WORK WITH DIFFICULT
PREADOLESCENT BOYS

In the Pre-Delinquent Gang Project, described by Tefferteller (1959), the guidelines for community work laid down by Clifford Shaw (1938) are translated into realistic and successful action. Her report would have become more of a classic than it has, but for the modern fashion among social scientists of quoting only quantitative results. The project was in fact based on that prerequisite for solid knowledge, sound observation. From their settlement house in a gang-dominated area, Tefferteller and her colleagues were able to observe gangs in formation and successive younger age groups of boys following in the footsteps of the older. They described the neighborhood parents as unaware of, or turning a blind eye to, what their sons were doing, afraid of intervening, and without any community organization through which dissatisfaction with the unruliness on the streets could be expressed.

The settlement workers decided on two main strategies. The first was to concentrate upon those members of the 8-to-13 age range who showed signs of becoming the material for adolescent gangs. The workers weaned them away from the older gangs' influence by providing them with alternative amenities and means of fulfillment, making it clear that in return certain standards of conduct were expected.

The second strategy was to help the parents establish effective control over their sons. This was done by visiting them in their homes to gain their support for a campaign to reduce street unruliness, calling them together at the first signs of trouble, encouraging them to take spontaneous initiatives to curb misbehavior, and ensuring that, through the settlement, the parents played an active decision-making role in the project.

As subjects the project workers chose five groups of boys who were attending the settlement but disrupting its program by destructiveness, restlessness, and troublemaking. They were not regarded as emotionally disturbed in a psychiatric sense; from my experience of similar types of boys of this age from rough-and-ready neighborhoods, they represented the more assertive and aggressive personalities who were modeling themselves on the tradition of dominance by violence in which they had been reared. As a close-knit group they had the makings of a formidable gang. At this stage, however, they wanted to use the facilities of the settlement and clamored to have a club of their own within it. The settlement workers did not immediately accede to the demand. They called the boys' parents together and discussed it with them, taking the opportunity to let them know more about the incipient gang that their sons were forming and leaving them to decide whether by joint action with the settlement it would be possible to let the boys have a club without its evolving into a regular gang. When the parents agreed to cooperate, it was they who were given the part of announcing the decision to the boys and the condition of good behavior attached to it.

With the boys themselves, discussions were held about the harm and distress caused by unruly street gangs. It was made clear that the group members should cease to identify themselves with such; notably, they were not allowed to adopt a local gang name, since, as was pointed out, its associations with fighting, vandalism, and stealing would label them as delinquents. This clear understanding of the adult leadership role, devoid of romanticism and misplaced egalitarianism with regard to the young, must have been a prerequisite for the project's success.

The other major factor was their clear-sighted goal of achieving community integration by involving the parents. The latter, having decided to sponsor the club, helped in the provision of suitable activities, and were always consulted at an early stage about any difficulty or new development. It was found that the parents were more willing to discuss their children's behavior in a group than individually. By meeting other parents they acquired the courage to control their own children and—although Tefferteller does not specifically make this point—must have established community expectations about control of the younger generation. The stronger of the parents advanced from mere grumbling about the gangs' depredations to openly giving their members a piece of their mind on the street. Parents learned that they need not be afraid of direct intervention, which indeed the youngsters heeded. They also found that when they were seen to be united on issues of discipline, they could enforce regulations such as the time their children came in at night.

An important feature of the settlement's work was the regular visiting of the homes. As in the case of the Glasgow School Social Workers described in Chapter Nineteen, the object of the visit was usually of a routine and noncritical nature, such as leaving messages about a trip or a new activity, or explaining some misunderstanding with a child. Other visits had to do with the child's behavior difficulties in school or in the neighborhood. The settlement workers followed the principle, in such cases, that "nothing can go ignored, and with children, nothing can wait."

Owing to the bond of confidence that the project workers were able to establish with parents, they were often asked to help in crises of employment and personal relationships. Thus they were in an admirable position to diagnose the causes of juvenile maladjustment and to counsel the parents.

The results of the project can be best communicated by quoting Tefferteller's own summary of her and her colleagues' experiences:

> As close relationships develop between families and the Settlement, and often between families themselves, the erratic, confused behavior of their children becomes more stabilized and settled. The children seem to thrive on the attention given them as the immediate adult community attempts to prescribe regularity and order. It would seem that when adults, particularly the parents, close ranks and stand together, the very ground these children travel from home to various parts of the neighborhood becomes more solid. Over and over again as we deal with these particular predelinquent groups, we find them increasingly more relaxed, more co-operative, and more accepting of adult authority. There is evidence of more purpose in the groups, new values in their thinking, and boasts about putting things over on adults begin to be replaced with plans for activities which will give them a good reputation and recognition from their families (pp. 77-78).

The general applicability of this model for community integration and delinquency prevention depends of course upon the existence of settlement houses within the disorganized and high-delinquency areas. Their establishment would depend not only on the necessary finances but on the recruitment of corps of community workers who would be prepared to give more than is demanded of regular professionals in the social-work field. Whether the famous settlement movement of the earlier part of the century could be revived and extended, or whether some new type of citizens' center could be developed, is an issue that will have to find its answer in the character of each neighborhood and the personnel available.

Chapter Fifteen
Diversion of Juvenile Offenders From the Court

THE CONCEPT OF DIVERSION

The frontispiece of a seventeenth-century treatise on juvenile delinquency, if such can be imagined, might well have shown two allegorical figures, Punitiveness and Sentimentality, tugging at a delinquent cherub and threatening to tear him limb from limb, while Reason beats her brow in despair.

We shall have to see that Sentimentality keeps her fingers out of the pot when we discuss the popular concept of diversion, which came into vogue following the publication of the report of the President's Commission on Law Enforcement and Administration of Justice in 1967. Nejelski (1976) has defined it as "the channelling of cases to noncourt institutions, in instances where these cases would ordinarily have received an adjudicatory (or fact-finding) hearing by a court" (p. 396). Since that time, diversion has attained the moral status of an Absolute Good, as if the courtroom were a place of ill repute, from which children must be kept away if possible. One of the conditions for funding under the United States Juvenile Justice and Delinquency Prevention Act of 1974 has been the establishment of diversion programs.

The humanitarianism which favored keeping children out of the courts was based on the fear that once contaminated and stamped, or labeled, as a delinquent, a child would act up to the name. Such a supposition rests on a very dubious psychological foundation. If he leaves the juvenile court with any definite impression, it is that he has done something wrong and that a number of strange adults take a serious view of it. There is nothing in empirical psychology or general experience which leads us to think that this would impress upon the child that he has been placed in a category of delinquents and must therefore behave as one. People imitate only prestigious figures. Children imitate their parents and older children. A juvenile fashion starts among the middle teenagers and works it way down to the eight-year-olds.

Such fashions are nearly always harmless. Normal children on the whole know what is good or bad for them; they do not mindlessly become delinquents because they have entered a place which is associated with delinquency. When they get into court, most are delinquents already. The fact that a proportion of them will go on being delinquents may lend some superficial plausibility to the notion that their recidivism is the result of their being "labeled." This is an example of primitive folk explanation, based on mere contiguity of phenomena, without the understanding that can differentiate between causally significant and fortuitous relations. That young toads are occasionally found all over the ground in wet weather has led people to believe that they come down with the rain. "Labeling" has no better empirical foundation as an instigator of childhood delinquency. It is equally farfetched to suggest that teachers will discriminate against those who have been in court, to the extent that this makes the children even more delinquent. The notion of the self-fulfilling prophesy popularized by Rosenthal and Jacobson (1968)—that teachers' expectations influence the performance of children in school—rested on dubious evidence in the first place, and has since been disconfirmed (O'Connell, Dusek, and Wheeler, 1974). Yet, because it was an intriguing idea, it spread so quickly that its refutation could not catch up with it, and has now become part of the labeling folklore. In sum, we are free to treat objectively and on the merits of the individual case the issue of whether or not a child should be brought before a court, without having to worry about doing him some mysterious harm.

A court procedure may have its uses. When a young person defies the efforts of social workers or the juvenile branch of the police to reform him, it may make him realize that the game is over. But—as I shall argue—the court will retain this advantage only if such punishment is meted out on a finding of guilt or breach of an order that the youngster does not feel he has been let off.

Nevertheless, in the great majority of cases where the offender pleads guilty, a court appearance may be unnecessary, besides being expensive and wasteful of the time of social workers and police. It is a matter of deciding how the goals of society with respect to a young offender can best be attained. To set up diversion as a goal may mean deflecting us from our fundamental social goals, which are to forestall the onset of delinquency and prevent its recurrence, while doing our best to rescue and educate the delinquency-prone and to eliminate those community and familial conditions which are conducive to deviance. In relation to such aims, diversion from the judicial process is not a goal but a strategy.

Lundman (1976) argues that diversion may have certain disadvantages, notably in weakening measures of deterrence. He quotes evidence that certainty of punishment is accompanied by a lowering of crime rates (Gibbs, 1968), and that more severe punishment tends also in the same direction (Chambliss, 1966). Our humanity obviously prevents us from following the logic of such findings—which in effect are self-evident—but there is a danger that the indiscriminate use of diversion may deprive us of a well-tried means of ensuring that the general run of citizens, young and old, obey the law.

Both Nejelski and Lundman point out that what is new about diversion is the name and the fashion. Diversion has always been practiced, since the police only prosecute a minority of offenders. Indeed, the function of the juvenile liaison officers of police departments, who have been operating for many years, has been that of diverters. Under the rubric of diversion have been included a wide range of youth services, including recreational facilities and vocational training, "creating changes in our social institutions so that they become more effective in providing legitimate roles for all youth" and individual counseling and treatment (Gemignani, 1972, p. 48). Diversion has thus become a synonym for prevention. In this chapter it is discussed in the strict sense of Nejelski's definition.

Nonetheless, the popularization of the concept of diversion has had the salutary effect of liberating our thinking from the bonds of conventional practices and of stimulating the search for new solutions. Some of those which seem to have a wide popularity are summarized below.

INTEGRATED EARLY-STAGE TREATMENT; A MINNESOTA YOUTH SERVICE BUREAU

The White Bear Lake Youth Resource Bureau in Minnesota (Hudson et al., 1975) is a good example of the youth services system recommended by the President's Commission on Law Enforcement and Administration of Justice as a means of providing new services and integrating those existing. The aim was not to replace those already established, but rather to facilitate more direct means of contact with youngsters needing help and to make some immediate response to their individual problems. Among these are employment, especially for young people who have had some contact with the law, and their family relationships. The Bureau has also taken initiatives in setting up a drop-in center where disturbed and alienated youths can make contact with friendly adults and from which they can be referred to other sources of help. It has also established two emergency shelters, which are used by the police as temporary accommodation for young people who are experiencing family problems. These would be largely the runaways and "incorrigibles" who would otherwise have been held in the county detention center. Considering that—as the case studies summarized in Chapter Seven have shown—a motivation to secure removal from home lies behind over 50 percent of serious delinquency, the availability of a place to run to, or to be referred to, while the family stresses are investigated should in itself be a potent means of forestalling delinquent and near-delinquent behavior. In effect it was found that 95 percent of the young people referred to the emergency homes during their first year of operation were able to complete a full year, from the time of initial contact, without further involvement with the law.

That 3,350 young people had contact with this Resource Bureau during its first three years is a measure of the scope of its operations. Of these, 62 percent came voluntarily in relation to job and employment problems. The normality implied in such a service must have been a great advantage in discovering and dealing with those young people who are headed for delinquency. If there is one trait characteristic of delinquents of all types, it is poor employability. Other sources of contact were referral by parents (7 percent), schools (6 percent), the police (15 percent), and clergy, physicians, friends, and social agencies (10 percent). Only 17 percent of the cases dealt with were strictly diversionary, in the sense that the young people probably would have otherwise been brought to the juvenile court.

There are four distinctive features of the Youth Service bureaus of the type established at White Bear Lake. First, they effect a natural integration of social services for youth; all kinds of problems are channeled through them at an early stage. Insofar as they refer young people on to other agencies for more specialized education, training, or treatment, the officers of the bureau know what is happening and where there may be overlapping, failure of service, or drifting away. Second, they are staffed to take urgent action without incurring the delays inherent in the initiation of formal treatment; and in the course of such they gain insight into the nature of the problems. Third, they are geared to take initiatives to meet local needs. Finally, their constitutions are framed so that they represent a variety of community interests. One half of the directing board of the bureau at White Bear Lake consisted of representatives of youth. It was served by 6 salaried staff and 30 volunteers.

REHABILITATION THROUGH VOCATIONAL HELP:
THE MINNEAPOLIS DE NOVO PROJECT

The Operation de Novo diversion project in Minneapolis, itself based on the Manhattan Court Employment Project, offers an intensive program of vocational training and counseling to offenders at the point when they have been charged and are awaiting trial. Candidates are carefully screened from among those young men and women, mostly in the 18-21 age range, who are unemployed or underemployed, are charged with nonviolent offenses, and are not mentally ill or chronically addicted to drugs or alcohol. If the offender is eligible and seems motivated to benefit from the training, the prosecutor is approached and asked to recommend a six-month postponement of the court hearing. For those who have committed more serious offenses, the screening takes place between the hearing in the lower and higher courts, and the judge may be asked to approve a year's postponement.

The training program consists in an intensive course on work and work-related problems. Since each staff member has a caseload of only 25, there is scope for much work with individuals. If the offender completes the course satisfactorily, the case against him is dropped. At the time of reporting (Hudson et al., 1975), 65 percent had either done so or had obtained and held a job. A follow-up six months after completion showed that only 4.8 percent (267 trainees) had been charged with new offenses. This seems a creditable result even in view of the careful screening for acceptance.

LOCAL COMMUNITY ACTION: THE BRONX
NEIGHBORHOOD DIVERSION PROJECT

The Bronx Neighborhood Diversion Project (Nejelski, 1976) offers us a model for a major cultural innovation in that an organ of the local community has taken a measure of responsibility for the control of its delinquency problem. The body in question is a "forum" of local—in this case, predominantly black and Puerto Rican—residents. From it are appointed panels of two or three local "judges" before whom cases are brought by aggrieved or disputing parties rather than before the juvenile court. Referral can be made to the court, but is hardly ever necessary. Cases are, indeed, referred in reverse by probation officers and Family Court judges. The forum deals with youths between 12 and 15 years of age. Each is assigned to an "advocate," generally a person of less than 30 years of age who lives in the youth's neighborhood. The advocate, besides counseling a youth, may make arrangements for a temporary home, help to adjust his school difficulties, or find him part-time work. Each referral is reviewed, usually every two or three weeks, by one of the forum's panels to make sure that something is being done for the youth.

The panels consist of nonprofessional members of the community who have received training in mediation and conciliation. As such they are comparable to the lay magistrates of England and Wales except for their identification with underprivileged minority neighborhoods which have a high delinquency rate. Since these neighborhoods qualify as disorganized areas in which the weakness of the community structure would otherwise have made it difficult for parents to control their children, the Bronx Project represents a perfect embodiment of Clifford Shaw's (1938) ideal. As a measure of the contrast between an indigenous community organization and one working from the outside, Nejelski mentions that in the area served by the Project none of the probation officers could speak Spanish, despite the fact that a large number of the local delinquents were Puerto Rican.

The only reservation I have against the admirable community concept of the Bronx Project is its preference for advocates of under 30 years of age. It no doubt derives from the assumption that a young adult is more aware of the problems and thinking of youths. On the other hand the older person may be able to bring to the work relevant experience of parenthood and of the ways of young people. Just as the experienced teacher recognizes repetitions of the same tricks and subterfuges which the smart alecks of successive year-groups think they invent afresh, so, over the years, the social worker learns how to interpret a delinquent's story and to discern the real problems that are worrying him, in contrast to those that he is eager to talk about.

CRISIS INTERVENTION: THE SACRAMENTO COUNTY 601 DIVERSION PROJECT

One of the cultural binds from which the diversion movement may cut us free is that of the irrelevance of formal court processing in those cases in which guilt does not have to be established, but in which the chief need is to deal with a crisis in the relations of a young person with his parents.

The Sacramento County 601 Diversion Project (Baron, Feeney, and Thornton, 1973) sprang from the realization that status offenders—the runaways, "incorrigibles," and truants which are subject of Section 601 of the Californian Welfare and Institution Code—were usually reacting to family crises which were the culmination of long-standing problems. Prior to the existence of the Project, status offenses made up 30 percent of cases brought before the prosecutor, and 40 percent of all admissions to remand homes. It was found that nearly 48 percent of such juveniles were charged with a subsequent offense within seven months, which is a measure of the ineffectiveness of the conventional procedure of charging them in court as "beyond control."

The Sacramento Project was designed to provide short-term family-crisis therapy without court processing. Its guiding principles were (1) immediate, intensive handling of cases rather than the usual routine of deferments; (2) provision of an integrated service that would retain responsibility for a case from beginning to end rather than have it passed around from agency to agency; (3) spending the greater part of the professionals' time on the early stages of a case; (4) giving special training to the probation staff involved; (5) holding periodic internal staff consultations for the improvements of crisis-handling skills; (6) offering a 24-hour-a-day, seven-day-a-week telephone crisis service; and (7) maintaining close ties with sources of referral or discovery, so that cases do not get into the legal machinery. A session with the child's family is held as soon as possible; usually this occurs in the first hour or two after notification of a problem. The session rarely lasts less than one hour and may take as long as two or two and a half hours. Families are encouraged to come back for further consultations, but the maximum number is normally five. If feelings within the family have run so high that it would be inadvisable to press for the reacceptance of the child, an attempt is made to find him a temporary refuge.

During the first nine months of the Project, 803 referrals were handled, of which only 2.2 percent had to be referred to the court. This compared with 30.4 percent in a three-month preproject period and 21.3 percent in a control group. There was a moderate but significant reduction in the number of repeat offenses—35 percent, compared with 45.5 in the control group. For repeat offenses involving criminal conduct the reduction was somewhat greater—15.3, compared with 23.4 percent, which amounts to a drop of 35 percent. Probably the best measure of the value of the immediate intervention was that the control group spent an average of 5.3 nights in detention, while the Project group averaged only 0.1 nights. In view of the dismal record of prevention projects in general (Lundman and Scarpitti, 1978), and the fact that the staff of the Sacramento Project had to develop its own techniques during these early months, the foregoing results must be accounted creditable.

One of the most commendable features of the Project was the realization of the need for new techniques. The staff members virtually had to train themselves in a field which is normally held to require a long period of professional training. Moreover, conventional therapies tend to be applied only to cases judged suitable for the method in question, and are seldom geared to crisis intervention. The staff took this training aspect of the Project very seriously, and have embodied their experiences in a manual (Baron and Feeney, 1976). It contains a neat statement by Eva Leveton of the approach to family therapy worked out by her and her psychiatrist husband, Alan Leveton. They see the family relationships or "processes" as a homeostasis arrived at by the balancing of individual roles within the family, while crises arise from its disturbance. They emphasize the need to understand how the family functions and to see it functioning. For this reason they insist on meeting the family as a whole. The course of therapy is not to have its individual members speaking to the therapist but to have them speaking to one another. The therapist is a coach helping them to do so, since they have to learn to work out their problems directly between themselves in any case. It can be appreciated that such a form of therapy would be particularly suitable in dealing with crises in which running away is resorted to as an unconstructive form of escape from tensions or as a strategy in a struggle for hegemony.

The Project received an Exemplary Status Award from the U.S. Department of Justice, and was continued, with certain changes, under the new title of Sacramento County Neighborhood Alternative Center. These alterations consisted in (1) moving the Project out of the juvenile court building into a neutral and more accessible community location; (2) an extensive use of paraprofessionals in the form of graduate student interns; (3) the extension of the 24-hour telephone service to a full day-and-night seven-day-a-week crisis intervention service; and (4) providing for short-term residential care in the form of temporary foster homes or—if the crisis cannot be resolved in three days—to the Department of Justice's nonsecure Youth Service Center. The effect of moving the Center onto neutral territory and the provision of an around-the-clock crisis service was to increase the number of cases handled by 35 percent, amounting to

1,883 for the first year of the new Center's operation. All but a very small number of cases were adolescents, with the greatest frequency in the 14-15 year-old age group, and 82 percent were white. In contrast to the usual sex distribution of juvenile deviants, 54 percent of the referrals were girls. About one third of all referrals were runaways, of whom 85 percent were girls. These figures reflect the different pattern of deviance among status offenders. Moreover, the warm California climate would enable running away to be used as a weapon against the parents by reasonably normal adolescents, without involving themselves in the hardships of the cold-weather running away plus delinquency to which the maladjusted hostile child sometimes resorts. The fact that girls made up the overwhelming majority of the runaways and other evidence suggest that the family problems which came to a crisis were more in the nature of mother-and-daughter disagreements than the deprivation of reliable attachment to a caring adult that prompts the more classical forms of delinquency. (The report of the first 12 months of functioning of the new Center shows that whereas only 37 percent of the juveniles referred lived in two-parent families, 82 percent of them were with their mothers.) We can no doubt look forward to an analysis of the types of family disagreement which produced the crises.

If my surmise is correct that the types of crises were such as could often occur between adolescents and their parents in a culture which is permissive and has few conventions about the control of the younger generation, group counseling involving the whole family can be seen to be a good method of establishing living-together rules as suggested in Chapter Nineteen. About half the cases were terminated on the known abatement of the crisis, and this probably applied to most of the 28 percent additional cases terminated by the family without reason given. Eighty percent of the families responding to a questionnaire said they would use the Center again if need be, and only 15 percent reported their experience of it as negative. The overall success rate must therefore be accounted high, considering the small number of group-therapy sessions per family. The success of the new Project as measured by the need for further legal action was even greater than that of the original 601 Diversion Project. Only 1.2 percent of the Center's referrals had to be taken to the juvenile court. The number of status offenders under formal field supervision was reduced by 29 percent, and the number placed in institutions by 59 percent. The upshot in financial terms was that the Center was able to effect savings for the Department of Justice of $82,531 for the year.

It is inevitable that a class of juveniles presenting major symptoms such as running away or being out of parental control will include a number whose problems are more serious than disagreements over the liberty an adolescent is to be allowed. Some 22 percent of referrals to the Center, and about the same proportion of those to the original 601 Project, subsequently committed breaches of the penal code. This represents 25 percent fewer breaches than in a control group, and would seem to represent the serious, recidivist delinquents among the status offenders. The true nature of their family problems will probably not come to light in group-therapy sessions. The latter work admirably in revealing points of friction within a family, but not fundamental defects in the relationships of its members to each other. For example, an interview with both parents together may amount to a cover-up operation when the cause of the trouble is severe marital discord with violence, temporary desertions and threats thereof, which one spouse is afraid to tell about in the presence of the other. Whereas, therefore, group therapy involving the whole family is quite evidently an appropriate form of treatment for explosions arising from family rivalries, jealousies, and struggles for independence, it needs to be backed up with additional casework when the problems lie deeper beneath the surface.

CONSIDERATIONS RAISED BY THE GENERAL USE OF DIVERSION FOR YOUNG OFFENDERS

The logical outcome of a policy of diversion would be the direct treatment of all juvenile offenders without bringing them to court unless some judicial decision is required. It is suggested in Chapter Seventeen that referral to the court will be necessary when guilt has to be established; when the young person or his parents refuse or fail to comply with a program of treatment, restitution, or punishment; or when the offender should be restrained for the protection of the public. Since nearly all apprehended juveniles plead guilty, and few would reject a reasonable alternative that keeps them out of court, it is theoretically feasible that in the great majority of cases the expensive and lengthy court formalities could be dispensed with.

This bypassing of the court nevertheless raises a number of issues. The first is how the legal rights of the offender are to be safeguarded, especially if the extrajudicial agency is empowered to propose measures of deterrence or restitution. For restitution there is a precedent in the imposition by local jurisdictions of fines for traffic offenses. The safeguard against injustice is the right to demand a court hearing. An apprehended juvenile should have a similar alternative to the treatment offered to him, and there should be stringent regulations ensuring that it is fairly presented to him and his parents.

The second issue is that of the discretionary powers of the extrajudicial agencies. So long as diversion is not the general method of dealing with young offenders, this means deciding which cases are to be brought to court and which are to be given the opportunity of diversion. Since the majority of offending juveniles are not brought to court at the present time but are dealt with merely by warnings, police and prosecutors already exercise wide discretionary powers. As Collingwood, Douds, and Williams (1976) put it, "The police officer is, in many respects, the single most significant decision maker within the juvenile justice system" (p. 23). If this is accepted as something that must be, it follows that at this crucial point in what happens to a delinquent youngster clear guidelines need to be established for distinguishing between casual infringements and acts which are symptomatic of delinquent compulsions.

The third issue is who should make the crucial decisions as to the type of treatment. It goes without saying that the policeman is not the right person, although the experiences quoted in the following pages suggest that he may be able to make a significant contribution thereto. Decision as to form of treatment involves, in the first place, an estimate of what has prompted the offense. Perhaps at this stage diagnosis is too presumptuous a word, and in any case—as earlier argued—even the expert's first appraisal of the facts must rank as a hypothesis to be confirmed in the course of treatment. Nevertheless, owing to the large number of juvenile offenders apprehended, someone has to place them in categories of seriousness. These should follow the standard diagnostic method of the general medical practitioner, in assuming the least serious etiology unless there are indications to the contrary or there is a failure to respond to the customary treatment. This means that—even though such a diagnosis will hold good far less often than currently supposed—the offender should be regarded as a not-too-abnormal youngster who is following the boyish, or girlish, practices of the neighborhoods, and/or has been deprived of adequate parental guidance and supervision. Where, with adequate investigation, there are no indications to the contrary, the appropriate treatment would be parental counseling, and a course of education for the youngster. Since this would impinge on his free time, it would rank as a punishment and should constitute a deterrent.

Indications suggesting that there is more behind the offense than a local juvenile tradition or lack of discipline are that the youngster exhibits maladaptive behavior in school and at home, apart from his delinquencies, or betrays other signs detailed in Chapter Eleven. Special training is needed, even for a qualified psychologist, psychiatrist, or social worker, for the reliable observation and interpretation of such signs.

The fourth consideration is our ability to provide an appropriate method of treatment for the young offender. This issue forms a large part of the subject matter of this book. It is not only a question of ensuring that the family stresses leading to delinquency are identified and alleviated, or of providing alternative human settings of an emotionally satisfying character for those youngsters whose homes have failed them; there is also the question of whether a diversion program can include penalties such as will deter youngsters who are tempted to test the limits of permissible behavior. A policy of diversion will lay its flank open to those who see a solution in more severe punishment if it amounts merely to saving the offender from the ordeal of a court hearing.

INTEGRATION OF TREATMENT AND LAW ENFORCEMENT: THE ILLINOIS AND DALLAS POLICE DIVERSION PROJECTS

The two police diversion projects discussed below demonstrate operational solutions to the foregoing issues which may prove acceptable in other jurisdictions. Although their approaches were very different, they had two important features in common. The first was that—unlike the Sacramento 601 Project—they accepted both first and repeat offenders who were formally lawbreakers, the most prevalent offenses of the juveniles accepted into the programs being theft, drug abuse, and running away. Second, the professionals responsible for selecting the cases and applying the treatment were located within the police department itself.

In the case of the Illinois diversion project, described by Treger (1972, 1975), a unit consisting of two social workers and four senior graduate students in social work was placed in the police departments of two middle-class white suburban communities with a population of some 30,000. They used a social casework approach embracing a 24-hour crisis service, short- and long-term individual counseling, marital counseling, and family group therapy. As with the Sacramento project, the emphasis was on speed of assessment and early intervention. Police, legal, and psychiatric consultants were available. There was apparently no screening of juveniles for acceptance, which was a matter of referral by police officers. Upon acceptance, prosecution of the case was deferred. The police proved to be skillful in identifying problems and providing the social workers with useful information based on their knowledge of local life styles and the local people. In one of the communities, Wheaton, juveniles made up half of the cases dealt with; in the other, Niles, 66 percent.

Comparison of the number of Wheaton Juvenile Court referrals in the year immediately before the project began and in the first complete year of its operation showed a drop of 30 percent; in the 23 of the 27 other county police departments that reported there was a rise over the same period of 36 percent. This diminution could have been due to a combination of diversion and a lessening of the number of offenses committed.

A police-social service unit was subsequently set up in Maywood, Illinois (Treger, 1976), in order to test its applicability within a community containing 50 percent blacks; with a high crime rate it qualified as a typical disadvantaged and socially disorganized area. The staff consisted of a project director and two professional social workers supervising four graduate students, with police and psychiatric consultants. They found themselves filling a much broader role than that of offering crisis intervention and family counseling in connection with the commission of offenses. Within a socially disintegrated community with many immigrants from the inner areas of a large city, their preventive work had to reach a stage further back. They provided a client advocacy service to those who were unable by themselves to draw on the facilities of existing services, thus reducing stress, preventing the compounding of problems, and forestalling law infringements. To overcome the suspicion of official agencies on the part of poor minority groups, people referred to the project were seen in their own homes. They were offered individual, marital, and family/group counseling, and referral to other needed services. No reports are as yet available of the project's effects on the crime rate of the area, but Treger gives case histories pointing convincingly to the need for immediate help to families in which one or more of its members have been reduced to a state of mental breakdown. The theoretical insights gained from work in the Maywood police-social service project have been discussed in Chapter Two.

The concept of a combination of policing and social work within a police department is spreading rapidly. At the time of writing, 40 such projects are in operation in Illinois, some of them serving more than one community, and six regional universities are using them for the field training of graduate social-work students. Experimental projects on these lines are also in prospect in Britain and West Germany (Treger, private communication, 1979).

In his appraisal of the concept of police social service, Treger (1972) mentions the fears aroused by the proposal to establish a diagnostic and treatment unit under the auspices of the police. It was thought that no police department would accept such an arrangement because it might challenge traditional roles, and that the social workers would fear losing their identity. In effect there was no difficulty in finding police departments who would welcome the project; the two chosen accepted it warmly, and it worked without role conflicts. That the project functioned at the day-to-day level is evidenced by the high percentage of clients—65.2 in Niles and 73.3 in Wheaton—who kept all their appointments.

The advantages of this integration of law enforcement and social-casework services stem from the consideration that this is the most important, and at the same time the weakest, link in the chain of offender disposition. If, as so often occurs, the police refer cases to an independent social-work department which—already overloaded with serious cases—generally takes no action—and even when it does, fails to report progress to the police department—the police are apt to become cynical about such referrals and hence to discontinue them.

Treger points to several practical working benefits of having a social-work unit right in a police department. Client problems can be discussed informally over lunch or coffee and mutual trust developed. The police, by the nature of their work, become good observers of human behavior, and could thus feed in good data to the caseworkers. Because of the day-to-day contact, referrals could not be lost sight of, and feedback would occur naturally from day to day. Finally, the existence of the social-work unit added an additional alternative to those of prosecution or the dropping of the case. Even in the event of prosecution the court all too often is at a loss to find a suitable means of disposition and weakly drops the case under one of the legal provisions for such.

The Dallas Police Department Youth Services Program (Collingwood, Douds, and Williams, 1976) was designed to cope with a state of affairs in which 75 to 80 percent of arrested youths were released without treatment or punishment of any kind. There was a re-arrest rate of 50 percent.

The project, a unit of the Police Department's youth section, was staffed, at the time of reporting, by 14 counselors, supervised by a psychologist with qualifications in counseling. Its clients were arrested youths aged 10 to 16 who would otherwise have been prosecuted. First offenders attended three hours of lectures by police officers, spread over two evenings, on the law, drug abuse, and the consequences of further illegal acts. Repeaters and those who had committed more serious offenses underwent a six-month period of training in a counseling unit. This consisted of an intake phase followed by 16 hours of training spread over four weeks. It covered three basic areas: physical fitness, with the object of increasing self-respect; interpersonal skills, notably the youth's ability to deal decently with others and to obey his parents; and study/learning skills, including remedial reading if necessary. After this month's course of instruction, the youth signed a contract undertaking to apply them to his day-to-day behavior and received "assignments" for doing so. These included observance of the rules of his home, school attendance, and achievement, and participation in constructive activities. During all three stages family counseling might be given, and the parents were advised on means of monitoring their child's activities and in the implementation of behavior contracts.

During the first full year of the Dallas project 2,282 youths were referred to the First Offender Program, of whom 69 percent participated. There were 1,084 referrals to the Counseling Unit, with 75 percent participation. Participation was voluntary, and apparently not enforced by a threat of prosecution, because those not participating were not brought before the court, but there is a hiatus in the record on this point. Because the trainee group was self-selective, comparisons with nonparticipants might not have been a valid measure of the project's success. Notwithstanding, the repeat rate for those in the First Offender Program was 9.6 percent, compared with 15.5 percent in a comparison group. For those referred to the Counseling Unit the repeat rate was 10.7 percent, compared with 50.5 percent in the comparison group. Only 2.7 percent of the youths who completed the counseling program became recidivists. A follow-up parent evaluation questionnaire showed that some three-quarters of the youths in them showed improved communication with and obedience to their parents, and between 50 and 63 percent improved in their school attendance, studied more, made better progress, and got into less trouble at school. Between 43 and 49 percent were actively participating in recreational activities and hobbies.

This record of improvement may not be acceptable to purists in the techniques of evaluation; but there is now a growing recognition that, under the conditions of real life, it is seldom or never possible to meet the rigorous criteria for matching experimental and control groups (Berman, 1978). Unless, therefore, gross bias is discernible, results such as the foregoing should be accepted as offering prima facie evidence of the effectiveness of a program. It will be noted, however, that the reduction in the repeat rate of those youths who attended the First Offender course was only moderately less than for the comparison group. For this there may be two reasons. First, a mere two evenings of lectures may not be an adequate form of treatment, even for young offenders who are normally well adjusted and in control of their behavior. If they are typical young delinquents, their powers of attention would be low, and in any case exposition unrelated to activity and practice is a poor form of teaching even for the average pupil. Moreover, having to give up a couple of evenings would not be a very powerful deterrent. It might have been better if these first offenders had been required to carry out a few hours of community service, with the addition of a quite short catechism of precept and warning. Second, a proportion of these first offenders would be serious delinquents making their debut. For the identification of such, the gravity of the offense is no indication at all. A first offender program offers an opportunity to spot the probable future recidivists, by techniques described elsewhere in this book. Merely to issue warnings and to wait and see which children heed them is a crude form of identification.

Referral to either of the programs was left very much to the discretion of the police officer concerned with the case. The most serious repeat offenders were brought before the juvenile court, so that the Counseling Unit in practice dealt with the middle range. This is the group within which it is most difficult to predict response to deterrent measures. Because of the obligation to attend courses, and other restrictions on liberty of action, the program of the Counseling Unit ranks as a form of punishment or deterrence, but of a progressive and educative character. It would therefore be an acceptable strategy for sorting out those youths who are capable of adaptation from those who are maladjusted in the sense that they cannot control their behavior in their own best interests. In order to deal with the latter a more intensive family therapy would be needed. An ideal solution might be a combination of the Illinois type of diversion program, with its emphasis on intensive family casework, with the Dallas model of training the youth in adapting to his family and school. The attractive feature of these two diversion projects was the delivery of a treatment program immediately following arrest. This is probably only possible within a single organization.

It happened in these instances that the organizations which integrated discovery and treatment were police departments. This arrangement might bring certain disadvantages if it became adopted in other cities. Whereas in Illinois and Dallas an equal partnership seems to have been maintained between the social-work unit and the police, this may have been because the social workers and psychologists concerned had clear aims as innovators. Moreover, social-work/ psychological units could become isolated in police departments and offer no clear career prospects to competent specialists. These difficulties could no doubt be overcome by various administrative arrangements. The members of the diagnostic/treatment unit could remain part of the overall social-work administration of the region but would be placed within a police department. Alternatively, a city youth department—again under the general social-work administration—could contain a number of police officers specializing in juvenile work, who would have the power to make arrests or accept youths apprehended by the main police department. The upshot is that the smooth integration of the processes of arrest, assessment, and treatment within a single organization—as in the Illinois and Dallas diversion projects—seems too valuable an innovation to be left out of consideration from an emotional reluctance to work shoulder-to-shoulder with the police. Harvey Treger (1972), of the Jane Addams School of Social Work at the University of Illinois, and Director of the Illinois project, observed that the complexity and ever-changing nature of our society call for a reexamination of the roles of all professionals. If police officers are to be called upon to be part social workers, social workers may have to be part police officers. After all, punishment and deterrence are part of the treatment.

PARALLEL DEVELOPMENT IN BRITAIN

A very similar new conception of the role of the police in preventing juvenile crime has been put forward in Britain by John Alderson, chief constable of Devon and Cornwall (1978). His philosophy of pro-active policing goes beyond preventive policing in that it "reaches out to penetrate the community in a multitude of ways." Some of these are by way of education and other means of bringing local youths into contact with the police in nonconflict situations. The police would act as a catalyst in helping communities to organize themselves, with the community constable becoming a leader in social action. Alderson's concept is summed up by the aphorism that in modern policing it is a question "not just of controlling the bad but also of activating the good." The police would work from day to day in cooperation with social, medical, and employment agencies. Rigid demarcations between different agencies would be overcome by staff exchanges, with social workers and probation officers being attached to the police force, and police officers seconded temporarily to social-service and probation departments. Alderson makes only general references to some local applications of this philosophy, but it is to be hoped that before long these will be evaluated by trained social scientists in a way that will make the experiences gained from them generally available.

Despite such excellent developments, which bring the enforcement of the law within a unified philosophy of disciplined humanitarianism, social workers should remain members of an independent profession. In whatever setting they operate, they should have their own in-service training and professional-development programs, and the means of day-to-day consultation over difficult cases. This can be ensured only if police-social workers remain members of a regional social-work adminsitration.

Chapter Sixteen
Deterrence and Rehabilitation
Short of Committal

In Chapter Fifteen it was seen that diversion usually involved some form of rehabilitative treatment which to some degree acted as a deterrent. The word punishment is emotionally loaded, but insofar as the measures in question impose some inherently unpleasant regime on the offender, such as restriction of liberty, they also rank as a form of punishment. Moreover, they are rehabilitative in that they help the offender to appreciate the effects of his action.

This chapter discusses three forms of deterrence which, it is claimed, are progressive and humanitarian because they do not inflict physical pain or injury, and do not degrade or cut the offender off from a normal life in a community. They comprise making restitution to the community in the form of work; making financial restitution to the victim; and victim-offender reconciliation.

COMMUNITY SERVICE ORDERS

As one of the earliest advocates of making unpaid work a condition of probation, Bailey Brown, Chief Judge of the U.S. District Court in Memphis, Tennessee, listed a number of what he regarded as obvious advantages of such a stipulation (Brown, 1977). These are summarized below. (1) It constitutes a practical form of atonement for the misdeed; (2) if the probationer were capable of work but were not working, it would get him used to the idea of regular work; (3) public and charitable social agencies would receive badly needed help; (4) probation would become more acceptable, since the public would see it linked with some form of punishment; (5) through the agency for whom the probationer worked, the probation officer would be able to exercise more effective supervision; (6) because of the foregoing features, some persons could be placed on probation who would otherwise go to prison.

Brown goes on to describe the program which he has implemented within his area of jurisdiction. A list of public and charitable agencies were contacted by letter, and invited to participate, but it was made clear that they could decline the services of individual probationers. The agency makes a monthly report on the work performance of each probationer. If it is poor, the latter is called before the judge and warned of the possibility of extending the period of probation with work, or of imprisonment for the original offense. The work requirement—the equivalent of one eight-hour day per week—is normally imposed for the whole two years of probation, but occasionally only for the first year. It will be noted that these work contributions—amounting to 832 and 416 hours respectively— are far in excess of the maximum of 240 hours laid down in the English Act for Community Service Orders.

During the first year of operation of the Memphis program 53 probationers accepted work service. They constituted a very high percentage of all adults placed on probation. In only two cases has it been necessary to revoke probation and impose a prison term. Twenty-one agencies, such as boys' clubs, public libraries, municipal authorities, hospitals, and various charitable institutions have participated. They have found the program acceptable to the extent of asking for more probationers, and other agencies have asked to be placed on the list. In a few instances probationers have later been employed by the agency to whom they were assigned. The generally good experiences of the receiving agencies have resulted in the court's having a more extensive list of openings than it needs.

The Memphis program was limited to adults, and Community Service Orders in Britain are restricted to persons over 17 years of age. Considering that the legal hold is just as strong for the juvenile probationer as for the adult, and that other youth training programs requiring attendance have been successful, there seems no reason why the same method of treatment should not be applied to juveniles of over 14 years of age. Programs for juveniles would certainly need more detailed organizing, but there is plenty of work for them to do, if it be only the removal of the debris from city streets and graffiti from walls, the replacement of trees in parks, and the repair of bus shelters. It would no doubt require the appointment of Juvenile Public Service Officers, but their salaries would be saved many times over once such programs were in full operation.

It does not need much Gilbertian imagination, by way of letting the punishment fit the crime, to envisage youths found guilty of slashing railway coach seats doing a year of cleaning duty in the coaches or on stations, or even helping to tend the traditional British station garden; or to imagine football match rowdies clearing up the mess left after matches. Having to spend every weekend for a year planting trees as a reparation for arboreal vandalism would be a more effective learning experience than a fine or more-or-less nominal probation. Indeed, the repetition of the treatment over a considerable period would make it, in psychological terms, a model learning exercise. It would become even more so if it were known that very satisfactory performance would be rewarded by, say, tickets to the next season's football matches, or a place on an away-match excursion.

To gain maximum early effectiveness with juveniles, a public service program would need to be launched with well-planned publicity. Deterrence gains from wide advertisement. It should also become known that all the effete methods of disposition—in the forms of admonishments, dismissal of first offenders, and fines (which have to be nominal as far as juveniles are concerned)—will be discontinued, and that punishment for any offense would be inescapable.

Such a clearcut set of consequences for wrongdoing would at least serve the purpose of separating the deterrable from the non-deterrable where no sophisticated procedure of diagnosis is in operation. One would judge that a youth who was able to fulfill his undertaking to do some form of public service while his friends attend the local football game has the ability to control his own behavior when he sees he must, and should therefore be deterrable. In contrast, the youth who fails in his undertaking is either maladjusted, in the sense that his behavioral control has broken down, or that he has some ulterior motive for misbehavior, such as getting away from a distressing family situation.

In effect the range and success of a juvenile public-service program would depend in large part upon careful choice of the youths to be admitted into it. It would probably be of little use to accept those who are showing severe hositility, unless there is concomitant treatment of the family situation. The juvenile psychopath, besides learning little from the experience, would probably be too much of a liability, as would also those whose deviance turns to arson, and offenders against the person.

RESTITUTION

Compensation of the victim for wrong done to him was a universal principle of primitive legal systems, and in civil disputes it is of course well recognized today. The remarkable thing is that it should have been lost sight of in modern criminal law. Galaway

(1977) suggests that this came about by the imposition of fines in the courts of the Norman kings, which went to the Crown. With an offender of limited means, little was left with which to compensate the victim, and so the criminal courts conveniently played down the victim's interests. The principle of restitution was rehabilitated in the 1970s in the United States and Canada, and is becoming so widely accepted that arguments need hardly be put forward in its favor. It has limited application to juveniles, because they usually are not earning the means of repayment. Nevertheless, if restitution becomes a regular part of criminal justice, it ought to be made to apply to the wage-earning adolescent and young adult.

VICTIM-OFFENDER RECONCILIATION

The principle of restitution is beginning to be extended to include the reconciliation of victim and offender. This is effected by the meeting of the two parties face to face, usually at the victim's home, in the presence of an intermediary, with the formal purpose of assessing the amount of the damage or loss and working out a plan of restitution by contributions of money or, in some cases, work.

Victim-offender reconciliation merits consideration as part of a preventive program, on several counts. Since the offender has to contribute part of his leisure time and often quite a considerable amount of money, and in addition has to face the ordeal of meeting a possibly angry victim, it ranks as a punishment which should have deterrent value. As a form of punishment it is not degrading, nor does it take the offender out of the community. On the other hand, it exposes him to social experiences calculated to awaken in him an awareness of the distress his actions can cause to other people. Not only may he find understanding and a readiness to forgive in those from whom he doubtless expected only antagonism; also, it will be harder in the future for him to dismiss from his mind any image of his victim as a human being. As a strategy for rehabilitation, the commitment to meet the victim and to repay him over a period of time calls for a self-discipline on the offender's part, which—as instanced in one of the case histories that follows—can open up for him a new source of self-worth. In short, restitution through reconciliation with the victim is an enlightened form of punishment.

A restitution-with-reconciliation program should facilitate the development of neighborhood delinquency prevention projects, by breaking down public antagonism to the criminal. Such an attitude is natural—one might say, instinctive—among the generality of citizens, in the sense that to counter a threat by attack is one of the instinctive responses of social animals.

It is of course this primitive antagonism which finds expression in the demands for more severe punishments at times of a rising crime rate or when particularly heinous individual crimes are reported. Such feelings stand in the way of progressive community programs for dealing with local delinquency problems. If the general attitude within the neighborhood is one of resentment against certain known delinquents, and yet the latter are neighborhood children, a conflict of emotions occurs which has no resolution and so results in passivity and withdrawal. Victim-offender reconciliation offers to community members a way of reforming the miscreant without fear of retaliation or feuding. Once one or two cases have been happily settled in this way, the news will travel quickly, and support can grow for progressive measures against juvenile delinquency. Victim-offender reconciliation therefore offers the prospect of community, as well as of offender, education.

Because the idea of bringing the victim and the offender together is a novel one which flies in the face of our instinctive impulses, and to many will have a flavor of impractical social idealism, I shall demonstrate its hard-headed practicality by drawing upon the reports of the Victim-Offender Reconciliation Program which has been in operation for some seven years, to the date of writing, in the Kitchener-Waterloo region of Ontario. The Mennonite* Central Committee for the Province was its source of inspiration and is responsible for its administration through a joint committee with the Ontario Ministry of Correctional Services.

Once a suitable case has been chosen, the program acts in the following way. The judge includes in a probation order a provision that the offender "come to a mutual agreement with the victim regarding restitution with the assistance of the probation officer or person designated by the probation office. If no agreement can be reached the matter will be referred back to the court."

---

*The Mennonites are descendants of the sixteenth-century Anabaptists who made themselves unwelcome by their literal interpretation of the Christian faith and their success as farmers. After being alternately invited and persecuted in several European countries, they emigrated to various parts of the American continent, where they have continued to practice their religious ideas and to be successful as farmers and business people. The Mennonite Central Committee is the relief and service organization of the various Mennonite and Brethren in Christ churches.

The officer or a designated volunteer worker then phones the victim (usually of a burglary or an act of wanton damage), and asks if he may call at the home to explain the restitution plan. In the great majority of cases the victim agrees. If he also consents to meet the offender, the latter is brought along by the worker. Although the formal business of this meeting is to fix the amount of the restitution and the method of payment, its chief value is that, by face-to-face contact with the victim, the offender learns to appreciate the distress and anger he has caused, apart from the damage done or the goods stolen. Naturally, he is liable to meet a variety of reactions, from indignation to appreciation of his willingness to make amends. In either case the experience should be an important stage in his rehabilitation.

Since its inception the Victim-Offender Reconciliation program has brought together 150 offenders and 250 victims. This considerable volume of work was made possible by a Federal Government grant under which four field workers were employed for a few months. The two case studies given below are versions abbreviated from the reports of the project team to the Mennonites' relief service agency.

Case No. 1

Joe, aged 19, and Bob, aged 18, went out for a few drinks. A few hours later, they wandered through a section of the town, damaging cars, slashing tires, and breaking windows. In all they caused damage to the property of 22 owners, including two churches.

They were charged, and each pleaded guilty. The judge remanded them out of custody while a probation officer prepared pre-sentence reports on them. It was found that Joe had a job and Bob was in grade 12 (last year of high school). They both had had problems with drinking in the past and Joe was very deeply in debt. Neither of them had any prior criminal convictions.

Partly because of these factors and also because of the large number of people involved as victims, the probation officer suggested to the judge that this might be a case in which some therapeutic gains would be made if there were a confrontation between the offenders and the victims.

Six weeks later Joe and Bob came back to court and the judge remanded them for a further month, with the stipulation that in that period, accompanied by a probation officer or a volunteer, they were to visit each of the people they had victimized, to determine the amount of damage and to ascertain how much had been recovered from insurance. Both young men found these confrontations painful. They were accompanied by the probation officer or a volunteer as they went back over the same route they had covered on their spree. They learned that they had caused a total of $2,189 damage, for which the victims had been able to recover $1,125.92 from insurance. This meant that a loss of $1,065 had to be made up. In two cases the damage done was very small and the people concerned did not want any further redress. Two others accepted offers from Joe and Bob to help repair the damage they had done. The remainder had losses ranging from $6 to $200.

After five more weeks Joe and Bob came back to court again and the probation officer told the judge what had happened. The judge punished both men with a fine of $200 and then placed them on probation for 18 months. He made it a term of their probation that they should each make restitution on an amount of up to $550, to be paid as the probation officer arranged. Both the fine and the restitution were to be paid within 3 months.

Three months later Joe and Bob had each visited all the victims and had handed each of them a check covering the amount of their loss. Joe had begun his term of probation with outstanding personal debts of almost $7,000 and no assets. Through a great deal of hard work, a lot of overtime, and the assistance of his bank manager, three months later, in addition to the payment of the restitution, this debt had been reduced to $4,000.

Following are some of the comments made by the victims when Joe and Bob paid them the restitution:

> "Thanks for coming in and clearing up your indebtedness. This is important in life. I admire you for having the guts to do it.
>
> "Hope you learned your lesson. Thanks."
>
> "Thanks, I'm glad to get the money before Christmas. It really was more, but this is okay."
>
> "Thanks very much, wish you the best, I've raised five children myself, you never know just how to cross your fingers."
>
> "Thanks, better than I expected. See the big dog I've got now?"
>
> "Thanks, never expected to see that money, I think I'll spend it in a very special way to help somebody else."
>
> "I admire you for coming in and taking care of this."
>
> "Hope you learned your lesson."

"Thanks a lot. I was young too, only some of us didn't get caught."

"Aren't you ashamed of yourself? You know this really isn't going to cover it all. Who is going to pay for all those trips to Guelph for parts? Who is going to pay when they raise my insurance premiums? I don't want anybody to go to jail, but you know I hope we don't ever have this problem with you again, or anybody else."

"Thanks, sorry that this had to happen. Do you have a good job? I didn't know what to do when I heard you fellows out there."

One of the offenders made the following remarks:

"I feel that it is good to consider doing this kind of thing again [victims and offenders confronting each other]."

"You would have to have a lot of patience to follow through on it. Some people would have said to heck with it, quit their job and collected unemployment insurance."

Case Number 2

Victims: The owners of five private homes.
Offender: George (aged 18)
Offenses: 1 count of attempted breaking and entering.
2 counts of breaking and entering with intent.
2 counts of breaking and entering and theft.

The project worker had earlier met with George and each of the victims to ascertain their willingness to participate. George had been placed on probation with the condition that he make restitution. The victim of the attempted breaking and entering declined a meeting, because he felt there was little need for it. Each of the other victim-offender meetings took on its own form.

The first was with a retired couple. After not having obtained an answer when they rang the doorbell, George and his two associates had broken in and walked into the lady's bedroom, at which time she had called out and scared them off. Although nothing was stolen, they had walked on freshly varnished steps with muddy boots and had ruined the finish. The subsequent meeting was quite cordial, although the victims told of their fear of hearing the voices downstairs, and then coming up into the bedroom. George was told that the husband was partially disabled by a stroke and the fright could have caused another, perhaps fatal, stroke; the couple also wanted to know why George was breaking into their house. The victims responded to the volunteer's assurance that George had been steadily working for the past five months, since the offense. George agreed to pay the $7 it cost to put treads on the steps, to cover the ruined varnish.

The second victim was an immigrant from Sicily who spoke broken English. Here the trio had broken in, but heard voices (which apparently came from a radio) and left without taking anything. The victim began by saying he liked people, and since he did not bother others, why did George and his friends bother him? He went on to explain that he had guns in the basement and if he had been home, "I'd have shot you."

The third meeting was with a young couple who had a small child. This was the most intensive encounter and it was obvious that the couple had been extremely upset by the incident even though the financial loss was only about $20. The wife asked many difficult and pointed questions of George. However, later in the interview, a lot of personal interest was shown in him and the earlier tense atmosphere relaxed considerably. The turning point came when she asked him why he had come to meet them and he replied, "To show you that I'm sorry." Reconciliation was furthered when the one-and-a-half-year-old daughter took a liking to George. On several occasions he held her, and later she untied her shoes so that he could retie them for her. She give him a goodbye kiss. At the leave-taking the couple indicated some interest in continuing the relationship with George and invited him to come over any time to talk if he wished.

When the worker asked George what he had learned from these encounters, he said, "the feelings people have." He said he and his friends were doing the break-ins for a bit of money and for "more or less something to do," and had obviously not considered the various repercussions for the victims.

Morris (1976) and his group of writers and researchers report a similar victim-offender program in Tucson, Arizona, run by a county attorney, as a means of dealing with certain classes of offenders without bringing them to court. The victim must of course agree to waive prosecution, but this is achieved in many cases by a meeting with the offender in the presence of the "facilitator," at which the amount of the restitution and the method of payment are fixed. After one year's operation the program has been successful in all but 9 of the 204 cases which were accepted. The cost was $304 per case, compared with $1,566 to process an average felony case. Morris and his group quote the following example of an outcome that has almost a Red Riding Hood character:

A young man stole a color television set. At the diversion hearing*
he found that his victim was an invalid woman; the television set was
one of her few links to the outside world. He was able to grasp the
full consequences of his act—he had not just ripped off a T.V., he
had materially hurt the quality of the woman's life. In addition to
returning the T.V. set, he agreed to paint her house, mow her lawn
and drive her to the doctor for her weekly checkup.

The value of a restitution-reconciliation program to juveniles
depends in large part, as with restitution in general, upon the youngster's ability to contribute from his earnings or in the form of work.
It might well be considered in cases of petty vandalism and breaking
into homes or business premises where the damage is not great. A
wider consideration is that treatment of this type depends on the
offender's ability to profit by it. That is to say, he must be condi-
tionable in the sense that he can learn to heed deterrents; and he
must be capable not only of appreciating the effects on his victims
after the event, but also of bearing such thoughts in mind at the
point of temptation. This brings us back to the issue of who is
deterrable and who is not—or, more simply, how many offenses of
the type described in the previous case studies are committed by
thoughtless youths who can be rendered capable of thought. The
case of the rampage of the teenage drinkers was probaby ideal for a
restitution-reconciliation program, because the lack of thought about
the consequences could be attributed to nothing more than the
temporary influence of alcohol.

George and his friends, who broke into a number of homes
"more or less for something to do," sound like avoidance-excitement
cases. The reason why they never considered the repercussions of
their actions were no doubt the same as the reasons why avoidance-
excitement cases in general throw every other concern to the winds.
The reactions of their parents, their job prospects, and their status in
the community are blotted out of their minds by their compulsion to
forget their domestic troubles. Until this compulsion is exorcized, no
appeal to reason or to human compassion will avail. Restitution-
reconciliation should thus be accompanied by family casework facilities. To use it alone, on the assumption that youthful housebreakers
and vandals are just thoughtless youths, is to invite disappointment.
From yet another angle, a combination of both forms of treatment
would make good sense. As pointed out in Chapter Seven, avoidance-
excitement is a situationally induced compulsion; once removed

*To divert the case from the court.

from the distressing reminders of his home troubles the affected child usually reemerges as likable and well adjusted. Visiting the erstwhile victims could provide him with a substitutive, attention-occupying activity which absolves him from the need to carry out further break-ins. But the chances are that he will have acute worries centering on his parents, which should be taken in hand at an early stage. These worries will never come to the surface voluntarily on his part because, stalling their memory, he never lets them dwell in his mind long enough to produce any sign of anxiety apart from a fleeting grimace, and the last thing he wants to do is to talk about them. He will always appear—except to those who know how to read the signs—merely as an excitement-seeking youth without a care in the world. Yet the youthful compulsions of many such young men must harden into the stereotypy of the professional house-breaker.

Chapter Seventeen
The Legal and Administrative Machinery of a Preventive Program

The legal and administrative machinery for dealing with young offenders is, by common consent—or at least by the evidence of a worsening situation—no longer effective. The reasons for its failure, amounting almost to collapse, have been examined in Chapter Four. Briefly, they stem from a confusion and conflict of philosophies—or perhaps we should say, emotionalities. One school of emotion has wanted to punish indiscriminately, without regard for the personal stresses which lead to deviance. The other school of emotion wished to save the young offender from the consequences of his actions, as more sinned against than sinning. It is apparent that we have first to get our philosophies, and our emotions, straight. This means taking the treatment of the young offender out of the political arena and giving it the independence enjoyed by medical science. It means also the building up of a corpus of established practice on the basis of what is observed to work. The text of this book has been written in the hope that it will suggest starting points for such a system of knowledge.

Above all, the machinery needs to be remodeled. Too many professionals are now wasting their time doing things that need not be done. There are not enough professionals to do what is necessary. The juvenile who requires help to free him from the forces which are driving him into delinquency gets none. The youngster who is merely testing the limits of society's discipline goes unpunished. The re-modeling must be based on the realities of juvenile crime. In the following propositions, based on the arguments of this book, I sketch out some of the dimensions of this reality.

Dimension Number One is that a large proportion—probably the majority—of juvenile offenders are in a mental and emotional state in which they are unable to heed the consequences of their actions or to control their own behavior.

Dimension Number Two is that the diagnosis and treatment of these deviance-conducive states, and of the family situations behind them, require professionals trained as specialists in family casework.

Dimension Number Three is that the average citizen, young or old, needs a framework of precept for right conduct and of sanctions against its violation. If this framework of social discipline is lacking, there seems to be no limit to human depravity. In practical terms this means a system of law effectively enforced by detection and deterrence.

Dimension Number Four is that, given our present system of public finance, one of the biggest barriers to the new legal-administrative model will be a lack of funds to support the necessary professional resources. This limitation requires that the work of every professional employed should be reviewed from the point of view of its appropriateness and effectiveness. In particular it means letting the social worker get on with a social-work job instead of waiting around court rooms.

Dimension Number Five is that youthful crime is embedded in communities. Much of it is unreachable by outside agencies. Such agencies need the help of neighborhood organizations for the development of a local public opinion against juvenile misbehavior, and, so far as is practicable, for sharing in the work of detection, deterrence, and rehabilitation. The ideal juvenile court or panel would be situated in the local community center and composed of neighborhood residents.

We now have to consider the logical embodiment of the foregoing dimensions into procedures for dealing with the young offender. These are likewise laid out in numbered sequence.

(1) On the arrest of a juvenile, a police liaison officer visits the home and reports the incident to the parents. He takes the opportunity to observe their attitude, and advises them against physical punishment or threats to throw the child out of the home on a repetition of the offense. (The reason for such warnings is that in cases where the delinquent act is the result of deep-seated hostility, or estrangement between parent and child, either type of parental action may provoke a crisis in the form of running away, wanton further delinquency, or suicide attempts.)

(2) The police officer has next to decide whether the offense is of a technical, trivial, or excusable character, such as breaking wood off a fence to feed a bonfire, stealing by finding, playing ball games on the public highway, or other similar acts not viewed by the youngster as wrong or against the law. For these types of offenses,

on first commission, he would issue a warning to the child, preferably in the presence of his parents. For a second similar offense, the officer would follow Stage 3, which follows. No kind of stealing, except by finding, would be dealt with by a warning, and "thoughtlessness" would not be held to condone any kind of vandalism.

(3) For all offenses other than those mentioned in Stage 2, the offender would be brought before some kind of panel. This could be one of a series set up by a neighborhood organization, composed, say, of three persons, one of whom could be an experienced judge, if available. The social worker attached to the neighborhood would be in attendance. (By functioning within a community of limited size the social worker would get to know the local families and their children, and would hopefully gain their confidence.) If the child admits the offense, the panel awards some penalty. This would, if feasible, include making good the damage, or compensating the victim for monetary loss. The parents should be asked to consider making voluntary restitution on behalf of their child for the sake of the family's good name, but once again they should be implored not to take it out on the child by beating him. In addition to any restitution the child would be required to attend a course of training which would include a rudimentary knowledge of the law as it applies to a juvenile's behavior and an introduction to more acceptable activities such as indoor and outdoor games and hobbies. At this stage the panel treats the youngster as if he is capable of mending his ways and needs only some educative experiences.

Where no local residents' association willing to nominate juvenile panels is in existence, the local bench of judges should take the initiative of nominating them, choosing their members as far as possible from the local residents. It would be hoped in this way to stimulate local community organization to the point that the panels can be nominated by the residents themselves.

In the event of the child's denying the offense, the case would be referred to the officially constituted bench of judges for a decision as to guilt. If they find the child guilty, he is referred back to the community panel for further action as outlined above.

Among the many advantages of having cases dealt with in the first instance by the neighborhood panel would be that, at any one hearing, there would only be a small number of cases. Consequently, each could be given due consideration, in contrast to the 15-minute conveyor-belt procedure forced on judges of large regional courts owing to the pressure of cases. Since the neighborhood social worker would probably be responsible for all the cases appearing before any one panel, the time he or she spent at the hearing would be usefully employed.

Within each neighborhood, volunteers would be sought for the running of programs of work service, restitution, victim-offender reconciliation, job training, and recreational activities. However, the offender's family problems would be left to the social worker, as described next.

(4) The neighborhood social worker (who could be the same person as the school social worker, whose functions are described in Chapter Nineteen) would have the main responsibility for the case-work. He or she would have to rely on the judgment of the police juvenile liaison officer as to whether a child's situation is critical. If it meets any of the following criteria, or if the juvenile officer has some other reason for regarding action as urgent, he would contact the social worker immediately, and the latter would investigate the case, without waiting for its hearing before a panel.

It would be important to have explicit criteria for crisis intervention—obvious though these may be in most cases—in order to systematize the procedures and guard against the personal variable. These would include the following eventualities:

a. Extreme 'parental anger, resulting in demands that the child be removed from the home, with the attendant danger of child abuse.
b. The child running away, and refusing to be taken home.
c. The child making an attempt at, or gesture of, suicide.
d. The child takes part in an escapade involving several delinquent acts.
e. The child physically attacking another person.
f. Evidence of sexual malpractice involving the child, or a girl putting herself in sexual danger.

Apart from some such crisis, the visit to the family would be made soon after the hearing, at which the parents and the social worker would meet, if they did not know each other already.

Because the interventions of the social worker have to be selective, he or she will also need criteria for sensing the gravity of the problems underlying the delinquent act. These criteria are given in Chapter Eleven and need not be repeated here.

When the social worker sees that there are severe problems in the offender's family demanding a period of intensive work, he or she will apply to the panel to have the child placed under the care of the regional social work department (on whose staff all the neighborhood social workers would be). As in the present British care orders, the child would be removed from home only when absolutely necessary. It would be made clear to the parents that if they are unwilling to accept the implications of the care order, they would be free to appeal it in the regional Family Court.

If, after investigating a case, the social worker sees that the course of training or the program of work or restitution prescribed by the panel is inappropriate, he or she would approach the panel chairman to ask that it be varied or waived. Done unobtrusively, this would maintain the association in the minds of the juvenile population of the area between wrongdoing and punishment.

It would be necessary for the neighborhood social workers to maintain close contact with their regional organization so that they have a consultation resource in difficult cases, and for in-service training. The latter could take the form of periodic seminars at which problem cases are discussed and new community developments reviewed.

(5) The grass roots of the preventive machinery would be in the local communities. A neighborhood division should ideally be of a size to make use of three or four social workers. This would allow for 24-hour crisis intervention, intensive help to families on the verge of breakdown, and staff holidays. In Glasgow one school social worker was sufficient to serve a secondary school of 700–800 pupils, with occasional service to the feeder primary schools. Since, however, the latter would have had over twice as many pupils as the secondary school, three social workers would be the minimum complement in a neighborhood served by one secondary school of the foregoing size.

An overall advantage of the aforementioned plan would be that the local community organization, both directly, by the provision of youth recreational facilities, and by delegation through its panels and the team of social workers, would have a general responsibility for curbing the level of juvenile delinquency in the neighborhood. Comparison of the rates for different neighborhoods of a region would act as a check on the amount of local effort and the type and quality of the work, and would at last provide us with the means of finding out what works and what does not work in the field of delinquency prevention.

(6) It is seen from this discussion that the bench of judges would have primarily judicial functions. These would be the judgment of guilt, giving legal force to care orders, and dealing with those

individuals who refuse to comply with conditions as to restitution or public service made by the local panels. Only the official bench would be empowered to fine or to commit, and would do so only after the neighborhood panel had failed to come to a satisfactory arrangement with the offender and his family. For treatment, such cases would be referred to the social-work organization. The latter could be represented in the judges' court by a staff member who would act as court officer. This would save the neighborhood social workers from having to attend the hearings.

It would be expected, however, that the judges would exercise a general supervision of the functioning of the neighborhood panels, and have the right to suspend any panel member who exceeds his legal powers or fails to control the amount of delinquency in his area.

PART FIVE
The School and the Deviant Child

Chapter Eighteen
Identification and Diagnosis within the School

HELPING IN IDENTIFICATION

For a systematic prevention program that is going to forestall the onset of delinquency, we need to be able to discover those children who have reached a stage of virtual behavioral breakdown and are consequently unable to heed the sanctions either of the school society or of the community. Our failure to recognize this group has led in some cases to continual inhumane and futile punishment, and in others to the renunciation of any attempt to maintain an orderly community. The first stage, therefore, in the school's contribution to the reduction of juvenile deviance is that of the identification of those who cannot either be educated in good, or deterred from bad, behavior.

The psychological and social-work services have in the main to rely upon the school to spot the early signs of deviance. It should nevertheless be recognized—in order to define the teacher's professional responsibility—that the teacher should be asked to identify, not primarily tendencies to deviance, but behavior disturbance, as something which needs attention for its own sake. Such identification can be carried out without reference to the prediction of delinquency. If the psychological service identifies and treats in the first place children who are hostile, and secondly those who are apt to be led into trouble from lack of foresight and a desire to show off, they will automatically be treating the great majority of potential delinquents. Similarly, if a social worker attached to a secondary school (see the recommendations made later in the chapter) contacts the family of a truant or of a pupil who is constantly in trouble in the classroom, he or she will at the same time be dealing with a potential or actual delinquent. Principals rightly feel that they should deal with problems of misbehavior themselves; but as soon as it is apparent that normal deterrence is not working, the case should be treated as one of maladjustment. The danger is that principals and classroom-teachers may continue to treat the young person's misbehavior as just perversity, and become increasingly incensed at it. Their ineffectiveness leads to avoidance, which takes the form of making a clinical referral as a means of getting rid of the child. Thus, referrals tend to be haphazard and are made too late. Anne Jones related her experience as a teacher at a NACRO conference (1975), "Children at Risk in School."

> A classic syndrome I have observed in every school I've ever worked in is for a student to be allowed to disrupt lesson after lesson until finally, when all the teachers are at screaming pitch, it is decided to bring in help from a specialist agency. Alas the child guidance clinic is not able to wave a magic wand, particularly when the problem has been allowed to fester for so long, and so the school decides that child guidance is no good.

It would consequently be far better for the school psychological service to initiate a systematic procedure for the identification of behavior problems. The six preliminary screening questions given in Table 3 could be used as the first stage of such a procedure. They should be answered by the teacher for all 8-year-old children, and again just prior to the delinquency peak period—that is to say, when the children are 12 or 13, whichever fits in best with the age of transfer to the next type of schooling. Those students who get an adverse rating for any one of questions 3, 4, 5, or 6 should be assessed more fully on the BSAG. If too many within any class meet this criterion, the school psychological service would have to use its discretion as to the number of students in respect of whom the teacher should be asked to complete a BSAG (with a maximum of four at any one time). It may thus be necessary to concentrate on those for whom questions 5 or 6 are marked adversely.

The indications of behavior disturbance on the BSAG as marked by the teacher are, strictly speaking, a record of how a particular child reacts to a particular situation over a short phase of his school life. The result must be seen as time- and situation-determined. In the latter are included the personality and training of the observer, who is also involved in a relationship with the child. For this reason any tendency to a permanent ascertainment of a young person as maladjusted must be resisted. Nevertheless, there seem to be a limited number of standard ways in which the behavior system can malfunction, and these can be recognized as types of maladjustment. Whether any one type will manifest itself with a particular teacher at any one time depends upon the extent to

Table 3
Preliminary Screening

1.	Is he/she exceptionally quiet, lethargic, or depressed?	Yes No	1	1 2
2.	Is he/she very timid and unventuresome?	Yes No	2	1 2
3.	Is he/she apt to be on bad terms with other students?	Yes No	3	1 2
4.	Does he/she show off, clown, or let himself be dared into foolish pranks?	Yes No	4	1 2
5.	Has he/she been involved in damage to property or showed lack of respect for other people's things?	Yes No	5	1 2
6.	Does he/she have antagonistic moods, when he seems to go out of his way to get in the teacher's bad graces?	Yes No	6	1 2

which the malfunctioning dominates the child's relations with his environment, or whether his environment touches off some element of his vulnerability. A child with an extremely unforthcoming temperament will avoid anything novel or complex, but another child may have overcome this form of avoidance, because he has learned from experience that, with the correct learning strategy, he can be confident of succeeding. A child may be unforthcoming in, say, the mathematics lesson but confident in English, or withdrawing before a very critical teacher but forthcoming with one who does not pounce on his mistakes. Similarly, a child may show hostility towards a teacher who reacts to his provocative misbehavior by rejection, or who merely reminds him of his mother, towards whom he is hostile because he has lost faith in her loyalty. However, an extremely hostile child, who is completely dominated by a mood of self-banishment, is likely to reveal his state in every human situation, by his sullen moodiness, his vehement rejection of any friendly approach, and his violent antagonism when corrected or punished. This is the type of hostile child whom it is important to identify as on the verge of delinquency, and indeed it will usually be found on investigation that he has already stolen within the home or from neighbors.

The same applies to the child who is extremely inconsequent or given to bravado. He is likely to get himself into trouble through being dared by other children who are aware of his weakness, or to injure himself by his foolhardiness or thoughtless impulsiveness. It may only be a matter of time before he is dared to take part in a delinquent escapade. When a child gets a high score for both "Inconsequence" and "Hostility" on the BSAG, the probability is that the extreme difficulty in controlling him has reduced his parents to a state of irritable-depressive rejection (see Chapter Nine), during which they threaten with convincing vehemence to have him removed from their home. The classic juvenile delinquent is one who gets a high "Inconsequence/Hostility" score, supported by "Peer Maladaptiveness" (the latter being a reflection of the same combination in relations with other children).

In sum, the completion of the BSAG by the teacher will in most cases reveal whether a young person is suffering from a type of behavior disturbance likely to lead to delinquency, and will almost certainly do so if he is in a state of behavioral breakdown in which he has lost the capacity to control his behavior in his own best interests.

A child who gets a BSAG score of 8 for "Hostility" can be reckoned to be in this state, and his parents or guardian should be interviewed as a matter of urgency in order to discover in what way he feels himself rejected or liable to be left without the support of a stable family. Hostility, as an attitude of mind in which the person refuses offers of a good relationship and seeks to bring about a bad one as a form of defense against further betrayal, arises from such fears. The hostility of which the teacher has to bear the brunt in school originates within the home. The teacher can do something to mitigate the hostility by not reacting as one more rejecting or violent adult, and by being available to meet the child's need for adult support when he is ready to accept it. In general, however, the efforts of the school at treatment or discipline will be fruitless so long as the child's domestic anxieties remain unresolved.

Statistically, proneness to behavior disturbance is a continuum: the personal weaknesses and vulnerabilities which lie at the basis of maladjustment are a matter of degree, as are also the stresses and temptations to which each individual is exposed. But when it comes to delinquency we do not have a continuum. Apart from the "testing of the system" by the not-too-unstable in order to see what they can get away with, there is a clear dividing line between those who, although having some instability or being subjected to a degree of stress, manage in general to keep out of trouble, and those who have reached this state of breakdown. The former obey a law of least cost, in the sense that they seek solutions to their problems which have the fewest bad consequences for themselves; the latter have aberrant, self-destructive motivations which they cannot control, nor can they be deterred except by a severity of punishment that is unacceptable in our present age.

Standing apart from this dichotomy are the nonconformists by temperament. It is a normal part of the development of the growing child to wish to establish his independence—insisting as a toddler on dressing and feeding himself and, in later childhood, wanting to do what he wants in his own time and not to be under the domination of adults. In adolescence conflict arises between the young person's wish for adult liberty and the parent's anxiety lest he get into trouble or forget his responsibilities. Nearly all young people arrive at an accommodation between this desire for independence and their equally fundamental need for adult support. However, some children have such a compelling urge towards independence and individuality for its own sake that all their other interests are subordinated thereto. They are often the despair of their teachers because they do not recognize the need to follow the regular curriculum of the school and may have a rooted objection to learning anything from anybody. On the other hand, if they can be persuaded to master the knowledge which makes creativity possible, they become the innovators in each generation. Their educational therapy has been discussed elsewhere (Stott, 1978b) and is outside the scope of this book. Such children have nonetheless to be mentioned here, because of the fear of liberal-minded people that any systematic attempt to secure conformance with the rules and practices of an orderly society will lead to a suppression of creativity and a subservient conformity. The individualist may choose outlets for his creativity which are disapproved or not understood, but they will usually be part of a considered life-plan. The individualist as such does not court trouble. He merely accepts, albeit often with some surprise, the trouble he is likely to encounter. Since, in short, he obeys the law of least cost as applied to his own life goals, he does not become a run-of-the-mill delinquent. Churchill, Cortes, and Napoleon were individualists of this sort who took advantage of a lucky break. Such delinquencies as they committed were incidental to their ambition, for which we cannot legislate.

THE PRINCIPAL'S OWN DIAGNOSIS

It may be that there is no school psychological service available and willing to carry out the above types of assessment, or that the service is oriented more towards mental testing or some other form of assessment irrelevant to the identification of the predelinquent. The principal has then to make up his own mind about the character of any particular example of deviant behavior.

Apart from the deviant act itself and his knowledge of the youngster and his previous deviancy, the principal has two other sources of information. The first is the use of a checklist, to be completed by the teacher, which cites a sufficient number of types of maladjusted behavior for a comprehensive view of the child's habitual reactions to emerge (see Chapter Ten). If, from such an assessment, the youngster in question appears as essentially well adjusted, so much the better: some suitable form of deterrent warning or punishment would be indicated. If the assessment reveals signs of ongoing disturbed behavior, an early interview with the parents is advisable. This provides the principal with his second source of significant information. After talking with the parents, he should be in a position to place the child in one of the four broad categories of deviant behavior that follows.

1. *The youngster has simply never been subjected to the social conditioning through which children normally learn to mind their p's and q's.* He may have been allowed to be selfish or to be a nuisance, while the parents turn a blind eye or give in to tantrums or pestering. Indications of such lack of social training in a naturally aggressive child are that he extorts excessive spending money, will not go to bed at a reasonable time, bullies weaker children, and commits rowdy disturbances and petty vandalism in the locality. Every principal must have known whole familes of such neighborhood terrors. In school, such a child will naturally attempt to carry on in the same way, but will eventually learn to heed consistent discipline.

2. *The youngster is an "independent."* This type of creative, overindependent child has already been described. He will not conform on principle, and dislikes learning from his seniors, although he has a lively, inquiring mind, or other talents of an intensely

individualistic character. Naturally, he infuriates his teachers, who may regard him as lazy or backward, and are usually only too willing to give him a bad name, which he acts up to. Einstein, who was considered mentally retarded as a child, must have been a typical "independent." Owing to their creative potentialities, children of this sort deserve special nurturing, which can be done by a member of the staff for whom the "independent" has developed a certain respect. (The independent regards nearly all teachers, especially principals, as fools, and allowances must be made for this.)

3. *The youngster is an inconsequent in the sense that he has temperamental difficulty in reviewing the consequences of his actions before engaging in them.* Speculation as to the nature of this handicap of temperament would be out of place here, except to caution against falling into all-to-fashionable assumptions about minimal brain damage. It may well be that the cerebral processes which normally ensure an advance appraisal of the effects of actions are in a state of dysfunction. On the other hand, the impulsiveness and foolhardiness may arise from the excessive strength of normal motivations. The child may be overassertive, so that he tries to dominate in play situations, and to attract attention by clowning even at the risk of punishment. Such children find it hard to resist mischievous challenges to perform dangerous pranks, and so they tend to be accident-prone. Insofar as the motivation is that of bravado—which is akin to inconsequence in its symptoms—it may be a compensation for long-standing feelings of uncertainty in the child's relations with his parents.

4. *The youngster is in a state of behavioral breakdown or is verging thereon.* The principal can pick up signs of those types of behavioral breakdown associated with delinquency. The first of these is avoidance-excitement. It should be suspected when the youngster truants repeatedly and complains that he finds school too dull or that he cannot endure being confined in a building. What he is really saying is that he needs constant excitement and sensory stimulation which will enable him to forget his family troubles. Many examples of this compulsion are given in the case histories of *Delinquency and Human Nature* (Stott, 1950/80). When suddenly reminded of a family event or circumstance, the affected child may give way to some violent outburst which can be misinterpreted as a psychotic episode. This may take the form of a sudden attack on the teacher or another child without any provocation whatsoever, or throwing something through a window. The frantic overactivity of avoidance-excitement is absent only when the child has succeeded in trans-

ferring his need for anxiety-blocking excitement into a fantasy world. Then all the teacher notices is his obdurate daydreaming, and possibly the recounting of his fantastic adventures so realistically that they carry conviction.

Hostility is another type of behavioral breakdown which it is important for the principal to be able to recognize and cope with in the absence of a specialist. In the sense in which I use this term, hostility can be reliably confirmed by its symptoms within the home. There, as in school, the hostile child will resort to provocative acts which are calculated to arouse intense indignation, his unconscious motivation being to break free from an affectional bond upon which he can no longer rely. By way of inviting final rejection and banishment and as a means of expressing his resentment, he may steal within the home or from neighbors, desecrate gardens, or start fires. He is likely to run away and be missing for hours at a time. (But by no means all running away is a symptom of hostility; it may be fear of punishment or a strategy to control a parent. Many single symptoms are ambiguous; hence the need for a consensus of indications which form a well-validated syndrome.)

The term hostility is used in everyday life to mean antagonism, and resentment against something which is regarded as an attack on the interests of a person. Thus we say that people can be hostile to an idea, because it may belittle their role or involve them in financial loss, or to an act, because it is regarded as unfair or injurious; and such hostility is of course directed against the person from whom the threat originates. These are specific hostilities, limited to the object of the resentment, and do not extend to the person's general social transactions. Likewise, children can become hostile to some specific treatment in school, without all their human relationships becoming dominated by hostility.

Where, on the other hand, a child is seen to be dominated by a general hostility, this almost invariably originates from his home life. It must be the same elemental reaction as that directed against specific injury, but it becomes generalized because it arises from the deprivation of a need which is fundamental to a child's existence— namely, that of secure and unquestioned attachment to a parent or other adult to whom the child looks for support and protection. Without intending to do so, even well-meaning parents who think they are providing their child with a secure and stable home may be inducing in him feelings of being rejected, to which he responds by hostility. How the principal, the teacher acting in a pastoral role, or the school social worker can help such parents is discussed in Chapter Nineteen.

Chapter Nineteen
The School's Liaison with Parents

THE CASE FOR THE SCHOOL SOCIAL WORKER

At the NACRO (1975) conference on the part that the school could play in the control of deviance, there were forthright expressions of opinion about whose job it should be to counsel parents. Teachers objected that it should not be theirs, because its very magnitude would stop them doing their real job, which is to teach. Educational psychologists had been found to be "so overworked that they are hard to catch." The prospect of help to parents appeared bleak. Summarizing the discussion, Gavin Scott pointed to the need in every school for a trained specialist in behavior problems and parental counseling.

In September 1945 the Glasgow City Education Committee, on the recommendation of a subcommittee appointed to report on juvenile delinquency in the city, appointed three school welfare officers to three secondary schools on an experimental basis. The experiment turned out to be perhaps the only delinquency-prevention project whose formal success has been reported. The results are given in Table 4 for 1944-5, the last preexperimental year, and for the two following years, when the experiment was in operation. It is seen that, during the preexperimental year, attendance rates in the three schools (designated A, B, and C) were significantly lower than for the city secondary schools as a whole, but by the end of the second experimental year had nearly reached the average. The total number of students convicted of what, in Scotland, are called crimes (indictable offenses, in England; and felonies, in the U.S.A.) was more than halved in the second experimental year, compared with that prior to the beginning of the experiment (dropping from 148 to 65 court appearances), whereas for all Glasgow children it rose by some 6 percent over the period (Cunnison and Gilfallan, 1951). In view of this result the Education Committee progressively built up a service of school welfare officers. Unfortunately, the experiment got little publicity, and no similar services were instituted in Britain.

Table 4
*Effect of Glasgow School Welfare Officers in increasing
school attendance and decreasing delinquency*

School	1944-5	1945-6	1946-7
	Attendance Percentage		
A	80.5	83.8	86.9
B	81.0	86.0	87.6
C	82.3	86.9	87.4
All-Glasgow average	85.4	87.3	88.3
	Delinquency Total		
A	37	33	11
B	65	52	24
C	46	45	30
All-Glasgow totals (ages 8-16 years)	2,266	2,540	2,406

It was my privilege to conduct a series of case-study seminars
with the Glasgow school welfare officers some years later (Stott,
1966), during which I came to appreciate the many advantages
which their position gave them in dealing with behavior problems.
Being members of the school staffs and meeting teachers in the staff
room, they could pick up indications, in the form of teachers' comments about students, that enabled them to sense trouble early;
and since they had an office in the school, students could seek them
out to discuss their problems. Moreover, the school welfare officer
was able to get to know and to win the confidence of those families
of the neighborhood whose younger members were likely to run
into trouble in school. Being attached to the school, he or she was
also at hand to deal with the stresses and crises of adolescence as
they arose.

The great majority of cases of juvenile deviance and behavior
disturbance can be handled by a school social worker, provided he or
she follows certain clearly defined principles of diagnosis and treatment—a competence in which does not require more than the equivalent of basic social-work training. Nevertheless, some of the cases will
be of a complex nature, for the handling of which the social worker
may need to consult with colleagues; and even the basic principles
which apply to the majority of cases need constantly to be reinforced
by liaison with a more specialized psychologist or social worker.

Each school social worker should therefore be a member of a case conference to which the more difficult cases can be referred. Through the sharing of experiences in diagnosis and treatment, such conferences would also provide valuable in-service training.

It was a great pity that, during the fiscal economies of the 1960s, the Glasgow education authority destroyed the whole rationale of their school welfare service by having two secondary schools share an officer. Thereupon, the officer became nothing more than a visiting social worker, instead of a member of a school staff. Moreover, because there was always more than enough liaison work with parents to be carried out in a single school, only a half service was henceforth provided. Apart from the reduction of juvenile crime, a service of school social workers following the original Glasgow plan would bring hard benefits by way of relieving teachers of many behavior problems and helping unstable pupils to get through a difficult phase of their lives without irretrievable harm. Behavior problems in the classroom waste teaching time and, by imposing stress on teachers, impair their health, so that an on-the-spot means of dealing with them would raise educational standards. By reducing the number of unemployable adolescents and, later, adults, it would raise a nation's productivity. The appointment of social workers to the staffs of all secondary, and eventually to all large primary, schools in inner-city areas, would be a social investment of immense profitability.

During the early 1970s school social workers were appointed in a few other parts of Britain, and the Centre for Information and Advice on Educational Disadvantage has performed a useful service in reporting the experiences gained (CIAED, 1978). There was consensus as to the advantage of having a social worker who could devote the whole of his or her time to the needs of a single school. The preventive possibilities of such an arrangement, in detecting trouble long before a case would normally be referred to the district social-work organization, were remarked upon in particular in connection with the Haringey project. The following factors in this project's success were identified: immediate help in crises, regular liaison with outside supportive services, quick feedback of information and advice to the teacher, willingness of disturbed children to relate to the school social worker as an impartial person, the social worker's acting as a go-between in cases of involvement of a student with the police, resolution of cases of school phobia and school refusal, reduction in the number of suspensions, and providing a ready means of internal referral available to the school pastoral staff.

A service of school social workers would involve less expense than might at first appear because, once established, it could take over the work of the existing educational welfare officers and, with suitable in-service training, absorb their personnel. With their function officially limited chiefly to checking on nonattendance, this latter service has long been undervalued. Very often its members, calling at the homes as they do, are the first resource that a mother turns to in cases of family difficulty. The mention of the help that the welfare-officer member of the social work support team in Ellesmere Port (see the CIAED booklet) gave in cases of bereavement is typical of this unrecognized humanitarian role of the educational welfare officer (EWO). When it is considered that truancy must be accounted danger signal number one in the identification of the delinquency-prone child, and that any professional who has gained the confidence of parents is in a key position for sensing family problems, the home-visiting experience of the present body of EWO should be given higher status and incorporated in a school social-work system.

The CIAED reports are of equal value for the frankness with which they deal with the difficulties incurred in introducing school social workers. In some of the projects they met opposition, on the one hand, from the established district social workers, and, on the other, from those teachers who already had pastoral responsibilities. The detailed causes of such frictions were unimportant. The mistake made, in one project especially, was to introduce a whole team, consisting of a school-based social worker, a teacher-counselor, and a school welfare assistant, with the support of a prestigious committee which included the principal of the secondary and of the primary schools in the "pyramid." This must have made the existing pastoral staff members feel that they were being undervalued, or even superseded. The lesson seems to be that only one school social worker should be attached to each school, or at least to each staff-room unit. It is a fact of social psychology that a group of departmental colleagues who are members of a general common room feel constrained to associate together during refreshment breaks or other social activities. (For one to break away from the group in order to mix with other colleagues would incur the risk of being thought stand-offish.) The effect on the other members of the common room, however, is to make the group—in this case the social-work team—look like a clique. Naturally, this arouses animosity, or at least a feeling that they are not part of the general fraternity.

COUNSELING PARENTS

The purpose of an interview with a parent should be twofold. It should give both parties an opportunity to pool their information as a basis for understanding how the misbehavior has come about. And it must work out a common policy of remediation. According to the diagnosis of the cause of the problem, this will consist in measures for the alleviation of the child's anxieties or for the exercise of more effective discipline. These two objectives should be proposed to the parent as a sort of agenda for the interview and for those which might follow.

Parents will often come along feeling guilty and anticipating blame. Even if the interviewer agrees that they are blameworthy, it is important not to say so, but rather to sympathize with their difficulties. Any suggestion of blame destroys the basis of equal partnership needed for continued cooperation, since an unpleasant or unrewarding relationship will be avoided in the long run. Above all we have to resist getting into depth psychology by asking parents to examine their true feelings towards the child or, worse still, to delve into their own childhoods to find explanations for their affectional or disciplinary shortcomings. Such probing puts the parent in a position of inferiority—one might say, of being psychologically bullied—which destroys the equal partnership between the parent and the counselor.

Ideally, the counselor and the parents should come jointly to an understanding of the reasons for the child's deviant behavior. The former may nevertheless have to provide information, based on analogous case experience or research findings, which help the parents to see the problem in a new light. The notes below follow the four broad categories of on-the-spot diagnosis described in the previous chapter. Insofar as suggestions for the handling of the child are included among them, they must be taken as supplementary to, or as summaries of, the notes on treatment in Chapter Eleven.

SUSPECTED LACK OF DISCIPLINE

When it seems apparent that the misbehavior is the result of a failure of discipline on the part of the parents, it will seldom be of any avail merely to exhort them in general terms to exercise better control. In my critique of the use of "defective discipline" as a research variable, I pointed out in Chapter One that such can never be accounted a prime cause of deviance. It is nearly always the result of some anxiety that a parent has about upsetting the child, and so losing the child's love or provoking an aggressive reaction. Sometimes these anxieties reflect deep-seated weaknesses in the parent-child relationship such as are described in Chapter Nine. Until any such anxieties are revealed—and this is a matter for the professional case-worker—the counselor should act on the assumption that the discipline-inhibiting anxiety originates merely in the loss of confidence that many parents feel about exercising discipline.

One central truth should be impressed on these parents who fear that they are not strong enough to control their children, or that any punishments they use will result in forfeiting the child's love. This is that ultimate loss of control and loss of love occur only when the child no longer believes in the permanence of the parent's interest and loyalty. The counselor should say this time and again, until it sinks in, and give examples of how some parents (not necessarily those being interviewed) unwittingly destroy their children's faith in them by threatening to have them "put away," or that they themselves will leave the home.

In short, parents who, in their relations with their children, speak and act upon an assumption of this permanence need have no fears in exercising discipline. This principle is reinforced by research findings quoted by Bealer, Willits, and Maida (1971) in an instructive chapter entitled, "The Rebellious Youth Subculture—a Myth." Although children are so insistent upon their adherence to peer opinion, when it comes to the crunch it is the regard of their parents that they value. Parental disapproval is more feared, in the last resort, than peer disapproval. The reason why the typical adolescent can expostulate so vehemently against parental restrictions and old-fashioned parental ideas is that, sure of their concern for him, he does not have to consider the risk of losing their loyalty.

The counselor may have to help the parents work out a way of getting along with their adolescent children. Here apply three principles which are characteristic of all stable human groups. The first is that there must be a leader. A leaderless group consumes itself with quarreling. Among all social animals the mature generation assumes this leadership. In the modern human family it is ideally shared, in their different spheres, by the mother and father. The second principle is that every member has an obligation to make life bearable and rewarding for the other members. Teenagers, taken up with their struggle for independence and self-expression, often forget that their parents also have the right to a bearable and rewarding family life.

Their very uncertainties cause them to overdo the pressure and make their parents' lives a misery. The third principle is that of group loyalty—in the case of the family, maintaining it as a viable economic unit and preserving its good name.

When the counselor senses that these conditions are not being fulfilled, it might be suggested to the parents that they discuss with their children the making of a Living Together Contract. In explaining the "bearability principle" the parents could point out to their son or daughter that he or she is living in their home and enjoying physical support and many other amenities, and that they would not wish it otherwise. But the home has to be a home and not a hell. If any one member constantly breaches the bearability rule, the family will sooner or later come to ruin, because there is nothing so damaging to the human organism as unmitigated stress. As regards the maintenance of the family's good name, especially in avoiding involvement in delinquent activities, it may be pointed out that this is a common interest of all its members. In particular the ability of the younger members to find the right friends depends on it.

Many parents find it hard to make a distinction between critical threats to the family's reputation, which are going to hurt them all, and the ephemeral dictates of custom, as regards, for example, the length of a youth's hair. There have been times when, unless a man belonged to the 10 percent of the population which could afford a wig, he had to wear his hair long. The counselor might have to point out to the more rigid kind of parent that long hair, provided it is clean and well-tended, can be beautiful.

With the younger child, who is still at the stage of recognizing only his own immediate interests, the parents might be advised to apply the principles of behavior modification. One method of doing this is to give the child his allowance, in daily installments, for his good behavior during the day. Because getting him to bed may be a source of friction, the day should be accounted over only when he is tucked in for the night. If the child misbehaves during the day he forfeits a nickel or so of the daily allowance, care being taken never to deduct the whole of it for any offense unless it be a heinous one. If the child makes a real effort to make amends, the possibility should be open of canceling the forfeit. If the child does not care about his allowance, he might be allocated a limited ration of TV viewing time each evening, which similarly can be forfeited. In operating such a plan the parent should make clear to the child the types of behavior which could lead to forfeits. If it is misbehavior with boys in the street, then he should get a minimum nickel or two each day that no untoward incident occurs, independently of his conduct in the home. If the parent reacts against such an arrangement as being a form of bribery, it may be pointed out that, by definition, bribery consists in an inducement to arrange some illegal or unfair advantage or evasion of punishment. Rewarding a child for good behavior is no more bribery than paying a person for satisfactory work. In any case it may be pointed out that, for the preadolescent child, what is right is what he is rewarded for, and what is wrong is what he is punished for. It is better to secure acceptable behavior by rewarding the good than by punishing the bad.

THE INDEPENDENT CHILD

The child to whom doing his own thing, right or wrong, is the most important consideration in life is always difficult to manage. Except that the effort to do so may try the parents' patience and possibly cause a rift between them, leading to their turning on the child in a mood of irritable-depressive rejection, the management of this sort of child would be outside the scope of this book. The short answer is that—provided there is no other source of behavior disturbance—the overly independent child can be treated for what he is, that is, basically stable. I have made some observations on his educational treatment, elsewhere (Stott, 1978b), which amount to an insistence upon his mastering the rudiments of scholarship and so building his creativity on a foundation of knowledge. Just as the discipline of learning will never stifle this creativity, so the disciplining of his behavior will not dampen his spirit, but keep his experimentation and enterprise within acceptable bounds.

THE INCONSEQUENT CHILD

Mere impulsiveness—that is to say, acting without taking time to consider the consequences—may have several quite distinct causes. The overly independent child may sometimes act in this way because of the compelling power of his need to deal with his environment in a unique or spectacular way (which is an aspect of his high effectiveness-motivation). He will distinguish himself from the neurologically impaired inconsequent by his capacity for concentration when it suits his purpose. Likewise, the child from a happy-go-lucky lower-class background may be impulsive because he has lacked training in weighing consequences. He distinguishes himself from the "neurological" inconsequent by the speed with which he can acquire the skills of attention and concentration in a suitably planned educational program. The child who is given to bravado, the symptoms of which are somewhat similar to those of inconsequence, may be suffering from long-standing uncertainties about his parents' concern for him.

The history of the child, as given by the parents against the norms of behavior to which they are used to in their social environment, should reveal the gravity of the temperamental inconsequence. If it is exhausting the parents' resources and there is a danger that the stress to which they are subjected may cause rejection of the child or risk destroying their marriage, the medical control of the condition by drugs should be considered. However, the indiscriminate use of drugs, as widely practiced on the American continent following a diagnosis of "hyperactivity," works against genuine remediation (Stott, 1978b). The aim of the latter—hard as it may be to achieve—should be to train the child to control his impulses, while safeguarding him as far as possible from situations which discover his weakness. If allowed to run wild in a neighborhood such boys tend to get picked up by delinquent associates. There should never be a letting up on discipline on the grounds that it seems to have little effect. The conditioning of the inconsequent is always slow, and has to be painstakingly established in one area of temptation after another, with the hope that he will not be taken unawares by an unusual situation against which he has received no conditioning. For extreme cases the protected environment of a residential school would be indicated.

An important aspect of the treatment of the inconsequent is the recognition of the weakness both by the affected young person himself and by his associates. As a boy of this type gets older, he himself may be mystified as to why, despite his good resolutions, he repeatedly responds to an invitation to join a delinquent escapade. Deeply discouraged, he begins to suspect that he is "going off his rocker," and this suspicion is confirmed when he is referred to a psychologist or psychiatrist. There is a marked sense of relief and gain in self-respect when insight is given into the reason for his being so easily led. It might be explained that irresponsible and bizarre impulses to action are continually presenting themselves to the minds of all of us—the counselor or other adviser will certainly be able to quote examples from his own experience—but that a moment's thought brings the realization of their danger. It is just this moment's thought that is lacking in the inconsequent. Once the youngster sees this, some ritual for reflection might be suggested. What is needed is a response of a tangible nature upon which the process of conditioning can be concentrated. The most effective would probably be to advise him to think of someone he would be ashamed to face if he yielded to the temptation.

When an inconsequent child is being egged on by others who relish his pranks and dangerous clowning, they also could be given insight into the nature of the weakness and asked to help by giving reminders when they see that danger or irresponsible behavior is imminent. It would not be inappropriate, if they fail to do so, to make them share in restitution to an aggrieved party or in the repair of damage to public property.

THE HOSTILE CHILD

It is remarkable how many hostile children come from what look like, and in fact are, stable families. The reason is that many well-meaning and affectionate parents try to frighten their children into being well-behaved by empty threats of "putting them away" or of calling in the police or the probation officer, not realizing that they may be taken seriously or that they undermine the child's faith in them. That not more children react by counter-rejecting hostility or delinquent loyalty-testing may be accounted for by differences in temperament. The emotionally robust, with a low anxiety level, are able to shrug off the threats; it is the constitutionally anxious who are vulnerable to them and take them seriously to the extent that they imagine themselves likely to be expelled from the family circle. When the counselor suspects that threats of this nature are being used as a means of discipline by overconcerned parents, a simple explanation of their mistaken policy along the foregoing lines will usually suffice to solve the problem. Once the parents discontinue the threats, and replace them by assurances that, however naughty a boy is, he is still their son and they are going to stick by him, the hostile behavior will usually vanish with surprising speed, because the emotional necessity for it has gone also.

THE EXCITEMENT SEEKER

If the counselor has a case of acute avoidance-excitement to deal with, it should be referred to an experienced psychologist or social worker for a thorough investigation of the nature of the situation from which the child is attempting to escape. A mere half hour in a psychiatrist's consulting room, from which a diagnosis of deep disturbance, neurotic character structure, or prepsychosis emerges, is no substitute for such an investigation. Several hours are needed in which to observe the dangerous areas of memory that the child is avoiding, going over the recent family history with the parents, and then re-interviewing the child for evidence of the amnesia. (Many cases are given in detail in *Delinquency and Human Nature* [Stott, 1950/80].) If the child's behavior is so bizarre or unpredictable as to arouse apprehension, he should be lodged away from his home, preferably with a family who is prepared to give him plenty of attention-filling activity for a few days.

Apart from the acute case of avoidance-excitement, there is some evidence (see Chapter Three) that many petty acts of delinquency are attempts by children to forget sources of worry concerning their parents, such as illness or lightly threatened desertion of the home. The counselor should work on the principle that there is no such thing as an act of casual delinquency without a cause other than boyish high spirits or a desire for adventure.

A telltale symptom of family anxieties, paradoxically, is over-helpfulness in the home or wanting to give the mother more money from earnings that she expects. Such unnatural and excessive virtue may spring from the young person's fear that the mother will carry out her threats to desert the home. A normal child shows a healthy distaste of household chores. Often a child reduced to a near-intolerable state of anxiety by threats of being "put away" or by the fear of the mother's desertion will alternate between moods, in his hostile phases, of "bloodymindedness" and of refusal to remain within the home and in his phases of anxiety, of overwhelming his mother with love and help. The young delinquent who is "a golden boy at home" is by no means an uncommon phenomenon.

HOW MUCH CAN BE EXPECTED OF COUNSELING?

The diagnosis and counseling outlined in this and the previous chapter may be compared to that of the primary-care physician with regard to illness. The treatment has in some degree to be exploratory, resulting either in cure or the narrowing down of the possible causes of the trouble. Indeed, what is proposed may be appropriately termed a system of primary care for behavior disturbance. Should counselors wonder whether they are qualified to treat behavior disturbance at any stage, let them reflect that specialisms based on an extensive body of treatment experience do not yet exist, and that teachers and the staffs of correctional schools are engaged in the day-to-day handling of behavior problems as part of their duties. The counselor's safeguard is to work in partnership and agreement with parents, using measures which seem to suit the case and are in accord with common sense and what is acceptable in the culture.

In the majority of cases the primary-care measures outlined should be effective, provided the cooperation of the parents can be obtained and maintained. Once they have been given insight into their child's misbehavior, their affection and common sense, combined with the natural resilience of children, may do the rest. If improvement does not come fairly soon, this would be an indication for seeking more expert help from the regional social-work organization. It may nevertheless have to be faced that no such resource is available, in which case the counselor is in the position of having to do the best in the circumstances, like a missionary providing medical services to a remote tribal community.

Nor must the therapeutic effect of the counselor's efforts on the staff of the school be overlooked. The anxiety bred of helplessness and frustration easily turns to rejection. I have had to peruse many principals' reports on delinquents which begin with expressions of affection and seeing good in the boy, with a resolve to keep trying with him, but at a later stage characterize him as a hardened crook and demand his removal from the school. It is not the child but the principal who has changed. There is nothing like action to banish anxiety. The fact that there is someone, in the person of a counselor —or principal or pastoral worker—who is working on a plan of rehabilitation should prevent this emotional reversion to rejection, which amounts to a renunciation of responsibility.

Chapter Twenty
The Tone of the School

WHAT MAKES A "GOOD SCHOOL"?

What makes for a good or poor moral tone in a school is a difficult subject which, in these days of preference for hard data in research, has attracted few scholars. We have, however, in the observations of Sir Alec Clegg (1962) the kinds of insight which form the basis of knowledge. Although he modestly makes no claim to have discovered all the "tricks of the trade" by which some principals are able, without much resort to punishment, to achieve a tone in their schools which ensures an orderly and happy community, the points he makes are probably those which matter most. His examples show that, where discipline in the school is lax and the staff slack and demoralized, the amount of delinquency outside the school is great; and, conversely, when the internal tone and standards of conduct and dedication of the staff are high, the amount of delinquency outside the school is minimal.

Clegg does not dogmatically enunciate a formula, but the elements of one can be extracted from his descriptions of a "blackboard jungle" in the form of a secondary school, and of the measures taken by a new principal to cleanse the Augean stable. When the new principal took over, a large number of students were regularly coming late. Boys smoked openly in the playground and girls secretly in the toilets. There were regular thefts of bottles of milk, dinners were taken without payment, and stealing was commonplace and went undetected. The building and fixtures were willfully abused. There was gross impropriety between the sexes; 16 boys and 1 girl appeared before the juvenile court in the first term, and 1 girl attempted suicide. The staff played bridge before school and during the lunch hour, without any supervision of the students' lunch, and a regular group left the building immediately at the close of school. Caning was ruthless and incessant, but ineffective.

The new principal reestablished tone in the first place by the simple remedy of effective supervision. The toilets and grounds were carefully policed, and tardiness was reduced to insignificant proportions by the use of student monitors. Parents were invited to cooperate in dealing with the more serious instances of deviance and to ensure punctuality and cleanliness. Lunch-hour abuses were stopped by having the staff take their lunch with the students, and student-staff relationships were improved by a variety of school clubs, excursions, and supervised lunchtime dances. The result was that, after five years, the school in question, which had been among those with the highest delinquency rate in the county, was among the group with the very lowest.

What emerges, as a first precept, from the foregoing is that efficient policing is more important than harsh punishment. The ordinary citizen, adult or juvenile, will flout the law so long as there is little chance of being caught. In my own school experience it was noteworthy how a thorough and publicly conducted investigation had a miraculous effect in putting an end to the type of misdemeanor in question, even though the culprit was not caught. The knowledge that there would be an investigation raised the stakes high enough to deter potential wrongdoers.

The second element in the principal's success, as reported by Clegg, was his visible concern for every student as an individual, especially for those in the lowest tracks. His dedication to the happiness and purposefulness of the school was evidenced in his positive attention to detail, and this would have evoked a reciprocating responsibility from the staff and student body.

The "school factors" which Clegg discerned have been amply borne out by a study conducted by the British school inspectorate, published in *Ten Good Schools* (DES, 1977). From 50 secondary schools nominated by inspectors over England and Wales, 10 were chosen for study; they represented contrasting neighborhoods, and type and size of school. The inspectors set out to discover—by direct observation and communication with principals, staff, and students— what it was about the schools that made them so successful. They identified a number of common features.

First, the staffs aimed to create a learning environment which was rewarding for every student. This meant paying special attention to the understanding of learning difficulties, and providing a varied curriculum which allowed a measure of success to all. Learning was regarded as important, and students recognized the dedication of the teachers and responded accordingly. Teaching was by mixed-ability groups, albeit in some of the schools within broad age groups (tracking of necessity discourages all but those in the top tracks).

Second, care for each individual student was not only recognized as an ideal but ensured by carefully organized systems of academic oversight and pastoral care. The principals of the smaller schools made a point of knowing every student by name. When the size of the school precluded this, it was broken up into sections by broad age groups which, from the point of view of teacher-student relations, became separate schools.

Third, close links were maintained with parents, both with respect to their children's progress and to secure their understanding of the policy of the school. Such links included visits by members of the staff to the home, or arrangements by which parents made staggered visits to the classroom.

The fourth factor was the leadership of the principal in ensuring clarity of aims, sound discipline, good teaching, and attention to the welfare of every student. This, as the authors of the report point out, was the key factor from which all the other virtues sprang.

The Vulnerable Child Scheme at Bicester in the English Midlands (CIAED, 1978) demonstrates the possibility of improving the tone of a school community through the measures advocated by Clegg and the English inspectors. Although, historically, Bicester is a small market town, it has been converted into a typical area of social disorganization by the establishment of an army depot of a special character. It is, namely, the base for that section of the army designed to supply rough, unskilled labor, to which recruits of the lowest educational level are drafted. It is also the base to which are returned those servicemen who have proved unsuitable for work overseas. The effect of this concentration of low standards and failure is a large proportion of problem families, together with frequent changes of school for the children. In addition an army ordnance depot employs 8,000 civilians, mostly on unskilled repetitive work, who have been attracted from other parts of Britain by the offer of publicly provided housing. Called "white immigrants" by the native Bicesterians, they are the counterpart of the poor European immigrants whom Shaw and McKay (1942) studied in Chicago. In the words of the field officer to the project, "Principals tell of widespread marital breakdown, alcoholism, wife and child battering and vandalism in the community at large, with truancy, violence, emotional disturbance and under-achievement in school" (p. 19).

This situation was tackled by the appointment of a teacher-coordinator, who had special qualifications and many years' experience in the education of maladjusted children. His brief was an open one, defined only by the injunction to work with all available agencies in helping families with problems. The strategy used was notable for its use of existing personnel. The coordinator carried out

an intensely practical form of in-service training by visiting classrooms and advising teachers on the management of disturbed
children, in this way developing a team of remedial and special-
education teachers as agents of the project. In addition a small
number of other teachers were given posts of special responsibility
for the care of "vulnerable" children, and part-time remedial
teachers were appointed to teach basic skills at the primary level.
Regular lunchtime interdisciplinary meetings were held at the local
health center, and case conferences to discuss individual children
were held with educational psychologists, social workers, and educational welfare officers.

Probably the most telling aspect of the project was the development of a favorable teacher-climate within which children who had
become apathetic or defensive found that they were valued. It was
recognized that the anxieties which such children cause to teachers,
and the teachers' consequent rejection of them as nuisances, had
been an important negative factor in the situation. This was overcome by the teacher-coordinator's working personally in classrooms.
One senses an atmosphere of dedication to the educational and social
needs of individual children, which must have been appreciated by
the children themselves and by their parents.

This strategy produced positive results. There was a reduction
in the number of suspensions for unmanageable behavior and a vast
reduction in juvenile-court cases. The court sittings most recent to
the writing of the project report could be cancelled for lack of cases!
Remaining problems are, first, the constant arrival of secondary-age
students from other areas, where they have received no such individual attention to their needs; and, second, the threat of cuts in teaching staffs, which would reduce the amount of attention that can be
given to problem students and their families.

DIFFERING SCHOOL-DELINQUENCY RATES

Alarmingly different delinquency rates have been noted for
schools serving similar neighborhoods. In Tower Hamlets, a predominantly working-class borough of London, Power, Benn, and
Morris (1972) found that the annual delinquency rate per 1,000
boys aged 11 to 14 in its 20 secondary schools ranged from 6 to 77,
and the "batting order" of the schools hardly changed over two five-
year periods. These large and consistent differences were not attributable to size of school, age of buildings, or being single-sex or
mixed, nor did they reflect the delinquency rates for the districts

from which the schools drew their students. The investigators could offer no explanation except to call it a "school factor"; that is, it reflected something about the individual schools. In the study of the same phenomenon by Rutter (1973), discussed earlier, behavior disturbance was found to be associated with a high teacher- and -student turnover, and the proportions of the latter being given free meals and being born of immigrant parents. He does not suggest that these are causes of the high rate of behavior disturbance in some schools. It was in effect also high in these schools among the pupils who were not given free meals or who were children of native parents. Like Power, Rutter is unable to identify any feature of the schools in question which might account for their having so many disturbed children.

In the West-Farrington study (1973), the six nonacademic secondary schools to which the great majority of the boys in their follow-up sample proceeded showed delinquency rates varying from 2.6 to 9.0 percent. They found that the conviction rate showed a close correspondence with the number of boys who had been rated as "troublesome" in their primary schools. The secondary school in which the greatest proportion were convicted had received over four times the proportion of "troublesome" boys. Hence, powerful selective factors must have been operating, through the degree of choice that the parents and the secondary-school principal were able to exercise. Evidently, also, the primary-school principals tended to steer the more stable boys into the less rough schools, and the less stable into the rougher ones.

In the light of this careful analysis, it may often be unjust to blame a school or principal for a high delinquency rate, and more thought has to be given to the part that the school can play in its reduction. A further telltale statistic from the West-Farrington study helps to clarify the position: the proportion of those boys earlier rated as troublesome who became delinquent was very similar in the high-delinquency schools (57 percent) and in the low-delinquency schools (50 percent). In other words, none of the schools was able to do much to check the delinquent proclivities of the boys with ongoing behavior problems. This is understandable, because these problems would be the outcome of a vulnerability, possibly going back to before birth, and exacerbated by family stresses. But there exists a zone of the mildly unstable and thoughtless who, together with the large number of individuals who base their conduct on what their neighbors do, would be responsive to a good tone in a school and take advantage of a poor one. Parents who are keen on education and on good standards of conduct would try to avoid sending their children to a school with a bad reputation, while the negligent or uninterested parent would not care. Thus, there develops a vicious circle. This is not completely to exonerate the school and the principal, since the preponderance of disturbed children which some schools collect may reflect the standards that the principal and the staff have sought to maintain over the years.

THE MILLSTONE OF VASTNESS

To maintain good standards the principal has to be the leader of a genuine community whose influence extends to every member. He has to know what is going on, and can at least recognize every individual as a member of his school. It is a commonplace of anthropology that the members of a tribe sense a bond of humanity only towards fellow tribe-members. Their moral obligations are limited to these few hundred persons. Even in a so-called civilized society, spontaneous personal honesty is restricted to those with whom the individual has face-to-face relationships. There is little compunction about robbing an impersonal state or a large industrial organization. These elementary truths of human nature were forgotten when the vast comprehensive schools were built. The emotional and moral well-being of the majority was sacrificed to the supposed academic needs of the few.

Eventually, the folly of these mammoth institutions may be recognized and steps taken for their dismemberment, as has been done with the large mental-deficiency insitutions on the American continent. Meanwhile, the only thing we can do is to try to create within them natural communities of a size that the instinctive make-up of the human race can tolerate. The principals of the 2 large schools—of 1,350 and 1,500 students—among the 10 selected by Her Majesty's inspectors for study recognized this problem and overcame it by breaking them up into subcommunities, or "villages" of manageable size, each with its own de facto principal. In these schools also pastoral care was well organized, and the staff devoted a great deal of time to liaison with parents and social agencies.

THE ORGANIZATION OF PASTORAL CARE

The danger is that pastoral care, without explicit procedures, may become an empty formality. One hears tales of the tutorial system being nothing more than the teacher appointed to act as tutor sitting with a class for 20 minutes each day while the students do their homework and he or she marks papers. Another lesson we can learn from anthropology is that the only way of ensuring that an activity is carried out is to embody it in a ritual. How best pastoral care can be implemented can only be arrived at by a pooling of experiences. The following suggestions are therefore made as points for discussion.

The first of these suggestions is that pastoral care and academic oversight should be combined in the same staff member, who would also have regular teaching duties, but be allowed adequate time during the school day for the pastoral work. The staff member should have the care of the same group of students throughout their time in the school. The combination of pastoral and teaching duties—which would presumably be shared by most of the staff—would do much to overcome the territorial frictions which have been noted as an endemic weakness of pastoral care (Watkins and Derrick, 1977). If guidance workers or counselors are full-time specialists, as in American and Canadian schools, the remainder of the staff tends to resent their freedom from teaching duties, and barriers of communication arise. These guidance workers have in addition tended to concentrate on advising upon choice of courses in large high schools which offer multiple options. Whereas these functions would be within the pastoral teacher's province, the more urgent needs are oversight of academic progress and social adjustment. Moreover, part-time involvement in pastoral work places a natural time limitation upon the amount of social work that can be covered; hence, the presence of a school social worker would be welcomed rather than resented. The latter would receive intimations from the teacher exercising pastoral functions that particular students are "under the weather," which would lead to the investigation of the causes by regular social-work procedures, including interviews with the parents and visits to the homes. Such a division of function should remove all reasons for territorial friction, provided the school social worker is a full-time member of the school staff and not shared with other schools.

Second, the teacher undertaking pastoral work should run some kind of out-of-school activity, ideally in the form of a club, within which it would be possible to get to know and to exercise a personal influence over his or her flock. In addition to their indoor activities, all school excursions and even sports might well be organized through such clubs, and a group of such clubs, covering all age groups in the school, could form the traditional "house" of the English school system. No doubt many similar solutions are in existence already, merely waiting to be reported for their more general adoption.

The third suggestion is that the pastoral teachers or tutors should be the persons responsible within the school for implementing the proposal of the British Warnock Committee (1978) that students should be assessed three or four times during their school career. In fact the pastoral teacher could systematize his information about the social and education progress of the students under his care by asking subject teachers at least once a year to complete the six short "Yes/No" questions given in Chapter Eighteen, with possibly a further question inquiring whether the student is making the best use of his capabilities. Such a procedure should ensure that none is left in a state of educational and emotional neglect.

THE CRISIS OF ORDER IN
NORTH AMERICAN SCHOOLS

The quandary of the North American school is that of a community without effective sanctions against bad behavior. The sanction most routinely applied—suspension from school—only legitimizes the time off that the truant or the malingerer takes anyway. The result has been that behavior has to be tolerated which seriously interferes with the teaching function of the school, imposes stress on teachers, and gives an unrealistic impression of what is acceptable in a civilized society. If ever there was a situation which could be rectified by effective deterrents efficiently enforced, surely this is one.

A press report of the state of affairs in a secondary school of 2,000 students in an Ontarian town may be taken as typical of the latest wave of unruliness. The principal complained of an increase in wall graffiti, profanity, disrespect for teachers, fighting in the halls (even among the girls), drinking, and drug use. The noticeable increase in fighting occurred, according to the principal, because more students stayed inside during the winter weather! What did the principal do about it? He gave the school a talking-to. If he is quoted correctly, he said, "I spoke to the students because I felt things were sliding down and it was time to straighten their outlook" (Globe and Mail, Dec. 9, 1978, p. 5). Such threat-posturing, as the ethologists would term it, may produce a temporary fall in the disorder level; but learning theory, and the experience of life, tell us that signals not followed by any punishment soon exhaust their effect.

The obstreperousness of the adolescent is no latter-day problem. The Cook in Chaucer's *Canterbury Tales* describes how the apprentices of that time got together in gangs for gambling, which led to their robbing their masters' tills. In his *History of London*, Noorthouck (1773) relates how "the licentiousness of the populace, who drew in the London apprentices to join them, produced such alarming riots in 1595, that it was judged expedient to proceed against these dangerous insurgents by martial law" (p. 140). All traditional cultures have built-in provisions for the control of the adolescent and young adult, taking such forms as a religious reverence for the old men, as among the Chinese and the Australian Aborigines, or initiation followed by a prescribed progression in rank and an order in which people may speak—the whole enforced through the magical powers exercised by the senior generation. Only the Euro-American Western civilization has lost the means of control. And control is necessary because it is uneconomical for each new generation of young people to have to learn afresh that disorder threatens its own interests, aspirations, and even liberties. The students of a disorderly secondary school are deprived of opportunities for study, are forced to endure degrading surroundings, and go about in fear of their persons and their property.

Having made the diagnosis, what is the remedy? Surely, the same as that for disorder in any place of public assembly, which is to evoke the machinery of the law. If the educator can no longer be a policeman, the policeman may have to do a turn of duty as educator. In other words, society's officially constituted forces of law and order should be used for the strengthening of school discipline. This can be done, as I shall explain, with sophistication and without show of force. To those who react emotionally against such a solution I can only suggest that they reexamine the solidity of their objections in the light of the threatened collapse of our culture. In effect, police backing for the discipline of the school could be arranged with fewer entries by the police onto school premises than at the present time.

The instructor of a woodworking class in a Glasgow youth center once consulted me about the disorderliness he had to suffer from his 15-18-year-old students. It originated from their being required (rather unwisely) to attend an educational course during the first part of their evening, before being allowed to take part in its recreational side. I suggested to him that he announce to the class that each of them was to be accorded five "lives," and that they lost one for each instance of misbehavior. Only those with some lives left would receive his signature of attendance. All he had to do, on the appearance of any disorder, was calmly to scan the leaders and write down their names, as having forfeited lives, in a notebook which he kept open on his desk. I impressed upon him that it was important to be so judicious in taking away lives that in effect a student would hardly ever be deprived of his evening's recreation; and when he observed an erstwhile rowdy, who already had some lives in forfeit, resisting the incitement of his buddies, to restore to him one of his lives. A few weeks later the instructor waylaid me at the entrance to the university to tell me that the scheme had completely solved his problems of discipline.

The foregoing graduated warning system could be applied, with certain modifications, in secondary schools. Since it would be well to concentrate on major breaches of discipline, there should perhaps be only three, and not five, lives to lose. Those students who are in forfeit would be kept informed of the tally by a weekly computer notification or posted list. Lives lost would be restored after three or four months, so that a student has an opportunity to start again with a clean slate after a period of good behavior. It should also be possible for a life to be restored for a period of notably cooperative or constructive participation in the life of the school. The great advantages of this staged warning system are twofold. It leads inexorably to punishment, unless the youngster desists from the undesirable behavior. Also, it gives the high-spirited or potentially mischievous youngster time to think of the consequences of what he is doing. Only the extreme inconsequent would fail to get the message. An analogous system, involving loss of points, is operated by some traffic authorities.

On losing his third life a student would be arrested and charged by the police in the ordinary way for insulting words and behavior, disorderly conduct, intent to do bodily harm, possession of drugs, or being drunk in a public place, as the case may be. Since he would have the opportunity to plead not guilty in court, there would be no need for appeals against the forfeits themselves. Ideally, such an appeal would be made in the first instance to a community-elected panel on the Bronx model (see Chapter Fifteen), on which the parents would have substantial representation.

If there is a diversion program in operation in the local jurisdiction, probably the great majority of those arrested would elect to follow the prescribed course of training rather than incur prosecution. The training might be modeled on that of the counseling unit of the Dallas police diversion program, also described in Chapter Fifteen.

It consists of physical training, interpersonal skills, and adjustment to family and community discipline. Such a course might be planned to last six weeks, for eight hours per week, during the offender's out-of-school time. To avoid the personal unpleasantness which entry of the police into the school might cause, the arrests would normally be carried out in the offenders' own homes by police juvenile liaison officers. This would give the latter a chance to explain the nature of the young person's misdemeanors to his parents and seek their cooperation.

If a youth fails to be deterred by such a program of correction and education, the chances are very great that he must be considered maladjusted. Very mild sanctions deter the average citizen, provided the means of detection and enforcement are good. My prediction is that, if at the inception of such a three-lives program, it were given good advance publicity, it would hardly ever be necessary to put it into operation. The complete transformation of the life of the school would earn it the enthusiastic support of the parents, the community, and the great majority of the students.

Chapter Twenty-One
Overview of Theory and Practice

THE POINTS OF ATTACK

This book is about the prevention of delinquency. It is no simple matter to prevent something from happening, when its causes go back biologically to before conception and culturally to the loss of age-old traditions; and when we further have to include the relationships of the child with his parents from birth, the influences of his peers and teachers, and sicknesses, accidents, bereavements, or deprivations which render him prone to breakdown. Where to start? Many children are born emotionally vulnerable to stress, or are reared in a disorganized community, or with less than satisfactory parents, or in a broken home, or in no home at all—but few of them become seriously delinquent. There must therefore be particular events and circumstances that administer the final blow leading to delinquency. This reasoning suggests that the most effective preventive measures will be those directed against the immediate antecedents. It is they fortunately which, once recognized, are most within our ability to control.

If we could remodel whole human societies we would of course attack those fundamental weaknesses in our civilization that make children vulnerable or deprive them of the centuries-old cultural safeguards against emotional abuse. We would reinstitute small communities within which every individual cherishes above all his own good name and the standing of his family. In the shorter run I believe that much can be done to help the most disorganized population groups to achieve a true community entity. Some promising beginnings in this direction are reported in this book. As we develop our skills in cultural rehabilitation, we should be able to eliminate a great deal of our present maladjustment and misbehavior. As we reeducate future age groups of teenagers in those skills of human relationships which will enable them as adults to stay married and to provide a secure growing-up place for their children, we shall have fewer emotionally abused children. As we replace the present fashion of emotional self-indulgence (the assumed right to do or say whatever one has a mind to), we shall reduce the number of personal crises.

Notwithstanding this necessary cultural therapy, the most pressing need is for a program of rescue for those children who have been reared, and for some time will continue to be reared, in delinquency-conducive homes and social environments.

Such a program has two aspects. The first is that of identifying and treating the delinquency-prone child. The second is the study of the antecedents of deviant acts as seen in the state of mind and family circumstances of the already delinquent; and, from the insights gained, the taking of the appropriate steps to halt their delinquency. Such a program could not be left at the level of pious exhortation, so that a large part of this book has had to be taken up with the exposition and discussion of techniques for identification and treatment, such as I hope will be of use to practitioners in the field, including teachers and administrators.

WHY SO LITTLE PROGRESS IN PREVENTION?

Objectively, it is remarkable that I should need to write such a book. I had to ask myself why—considering the extent of the problem and the cost of dealing with it—an advanced civilization such as ours had not long ago found the means of identifying and treating those children who were at risk long before they became delinquent. When any new disease, especially of childhood, is identified, it immediately becomes the subject of public interest and of expert and expensive research. Delinquency and its companion, maladjustment, are among the most prevalent disorders of childhood. The youngsters in question do not get the same facilities as those with physical disorders: they are processed through a perfunctory legal machinery and given a pretense of treatment which leaves the majority unaffected, and some in a worse state than before.

Why, then, has there been so singularly little progress in this field of childhood disorder? Why so little planning of preventive programs and virtually no development of techniques? Fundamentally, I think the answer to these questions is that, whereas medicine could draw upon established biological and physical sciences, and medicine itself became an applied science, the study of juvenile deviance and other behavior disorders could call upon no corpus of knowledge about human behavior. Medicine is founded on research into the causes of diseases. There has been little genuine investigation of the causes of delinquency. No agreement can be found on the subject, and it is therefore not surprising that there is similarly no agreement about preventive measures. I find myself, therefore, having to hazard a statement of the causes of delinquency such as form the rationale of the preventive measures which I propose.

THE NEGLECT OF OBSERVATION

The upshot is that I have had to devote a larger part of this book to theoretical issues than I intended. It has meant in the first place reviewing evidence from formal research. But statistical findings are incapable of interpretation without the sort of understanding that comes from an observation of the nature of things and processes, such as physical scientists have done in the laboratory. And just as the laws of science were induced by observing that certain effects followed regularly from certain conditions, so, through similar observations of regularities in the preconditions for delinquent acts, we should be able to develop the concepts which amount to an understanding of their causes.

This induction of concepts from observation—which forms the foundation of every science worth the name—has been skipped by delinquency specialists. Becker's (1963) was a lone protesting voice, and his stricture is worth quoting at length:

> The most persistent difficulty in the scientific study of deviant behavior is a lack of solid data, a paucity of facts and information on which to base our theories.... [Studies of deviant behavior] are, on the whole and with a few outstanding exceptions, inadequate for the job of theorizing we have to do, inadequate in two ways ... there simply are not enough studies that provide us with facts about the lives of deviants as they live them. Although there are great many studies of juvenile delinquency, they are more likely to be based on court records than on direct observation.... Very few tell us in detail what a juvenile delinquent does in his daily round of activity and what he thinks about himself, society, and his activities (pp. 165-166).

Our quest for causes demands that we study what is happening at one stage after another of a long process of events. Each stage requires different techniques and many years of painstaking work. No individual can hope to cover even those which are currently open to our observation, and of course the determinants go back endlessly into history. For my part I have concentrated my efforts on the later stages of causation. My method was to try to understand what prompted individual youths to commit delinquent acts. I sought data and explanations that made sense in human terms; that is to say, drawn from our knowledge of human emotion and mentation.

HOW DO CERTAIN SOCIAL CONDITIONS PRODUCE DELINQUENCY?

The prevailing school of thought over the past two generations has concentrated upon only one aspect of causation, that of cultural influences upon inner-city youth. There is no question about the importance of cultural determinants; I would go so far as to say that they are pivotal, in the sense that they control the extent to which other determinants come into play. Far from downgrading cultural influences, I see them as being of a more fundamental character than that postulated by the dominant school of criminological sociologists.

An explanatory bridge has to be built between the individual delinquent act and certain social conditions clearly conducive to delinquency. We need to be able to understand, still in human terms, why there is so much more delinquency in underprivileged areas of our cities, even though their inhabitants are far less poor than peoples in other cultures whose children do not become delinquent; why a population rehoused in modern accommodations continues to show the same high rate of delinquency as that of the slum from which it came; why some children in underprivileged, high-delinquency areas do not become delinquent; and why some become so despite their privileged surroundings.

My studies of the family circumstances of delinquents gave me insight into these social aspects of deviance which are not revealed by demographic studies. I was able in addition to see the linkage between intrafamilial stresses and disruptions, and findings from two other fields of knowledge. The first of these was social anthropology, which showed to what extent standards of behavior depend upon the integration of the family into a community by kin and friendship ties. The second was field biology, which portrays the same kinds of physical and behavioral breakdown in animal populations under stress as can be observed in the form of delinquency, crime, feckless-ness, child neglect and abuse, and sexual promiscuity in culturally disintegrated sections of human populations. Since this book is primarily about preventive measures, I shall have to refer those who are interested in these wider biological aspects of abnormality to other reading (Stott, 1962b). Suffice it to say that I came to see adverse social and cultural conditions as determinative at two stages:

congenitally, they activate psychological and biological potentialities for malfunction, which in one form or other are inherent in the human species; postnatally, they impose a degree of stress upon the individuals thereby rendered vulnerable, which induces behavioral breakdown. It is not a matter of competition of statistically derived factors for slices of the variance, but of processes which interact and provide the conditions for other processes.

MISCONCEPTION OF CULTURE

Before I can progress in my discussion of causes, I have to draw from the field of social anthropology in order to lay bare the cavalier use of the word *culture* and its derivative, *subculture*, in the delinquency literature. The ability to pass down knowledge, skills, and forms of social behavior from generation to generation is one of the distinctive characteristics of the human species, and this is what cultures amount to. Our instinctive programming is an incomplete guide to action: it prescribes the general character of the goal to be achieved or of the need to be met, which the individual has to supplement from the transmitted precepts of his culture. This applies particularly to social behavior. Some animal species, notably the bees and ants, are genetically programmed to altruistic service of their community. Humans are only partially so. To make possible the organized life of communities, they have had to adopt elaborate rules of conduct which formed part of the transmitted culture. The resulting mores became a recipe for success, since it conferred survival advantages on the population adopting them. The criminological sociologists have ignored this criterion of success in their use of the word culture. To them any state of affairs within a population is called a culture of a subculture, whereas *cultural disintegration* or *culture loss* would be the more accurate terms. It is a misuse of the word to dignify the delinquent behavior of groups of youths with the name *subculture*. The street corner society of city adolescents is a social phenomenon of dubious survival value either to themselves or to their culture as a whole.

The foregoing discussion is more than one of semantics. The elevation to the status of a culture of the way of life of underprivileged sections of the population which have become disintegrated and disorganized from migration and economic stress, with its corollary of cultural clash, generated pessimism about the possibility of reducing the volume of delinquency, short of effecting fundamental cultural change. This is not to imply that major social changes are not needed in themselves or that humanity should not look forward to the establishment of a system of social justice in which there are no longer any underprivileged and culturally disintegrated strata of the population. It is rather that major changes come about as people address themselves to the anomalies and contradictions which a traditional culture inevitably accumulates in a changing ecology.

CRITIQUE OF THE CHICAGO CREDO

Having made these sweeping accusations, it behooves me to substantiate my polemic. The theories against which it is directed go back to the writings of the famous Chicago sociologist Clifford Shaw. With his associate, Henry McKay (1942), he documented the high delinquency rates in the inner-city areas which received wave after wave of immigrants. With good reason he attributed them to social disorganization, but when it came to explaining the processes by which this produced delinquency, he forgot the need for evidence and reverted to a credo. One of its articles ran that parents were less able to control their sons because their own social institutions were weakened. Youngsters then established their own social groups, in the form of gangs, to which delinquency was the passport. The Chicago group curiously failed to elaborate on the subject of parental social institutions. These were apparently held to include the family, although there are few explicit references thereto; and they ignored the greater risk of disruption of family life under the combined stresses of poverty and of isolation from the ancestral community. The family remained a blind spot in their thinking, and indeed also in that of the sociologists who reiterated their theories. As for delinquency being a condition of entry into the gang, first-hand studies by Kobrin (1961) and other members of the Chicago Area Project staff showed the opposite to be nearer the truth: serious delinquency was actually discouraged by the leading gang members.

The second article of Shaw's credo was that within the inner-city areas there developed a powerful alternative system of values which was in conflict with those of the conventional morality, and supported and sanctioned delinquency in the young. Yet the very case histories he quotes, and the famous autobiographies of the Martin brothers, which he makes the subject of a book (1938), show these to be a moral compromise into which the poor were forced for lack of food and fuel and secure accommodation. Shaw never produced any evidence of a deviance-vindicating philosophy of life in the high-delinquency areas, and the existence of such is contradicted by other studies.

The third part of Shaw's credo was that, in the low-income areas, crime was one of the means by which people attempted to meet the social and economic values idealized in our civilization. Again, no evidence is quoted to show that underprivileged youths think in such broad terms; and there is again contrary evidence that typically they seek expression in here-and-now satisfactions quite unrelated to social aspiration.

Thus, at each critical point, the theories of Shaw and his Chicago school remain at the level of unsupported generalizations which later empirical studies have refuted. Nonetheless, their formulae were repeated, with little variation, by Merton (1957), Miller (1958), Cohen (1956), and Cloward and Ohlin (1960). They no more quoted any pertinent evidence for the particular formula that each selected for amplification than did Shaw and McKay. The technique of persuasion has been that of the endless repetition of these elegant but groundless theories, and the sorry thing is that it worked to the extent of dominating sociological thinking about delinquency for two generations.

THE METHOD OF FIRST-HAND STUDY

In my own case the circumstances of my entering the field forced me into the methodology advocated by Becker (1963). At the time, soon after the end of the Second World War, that I was appointed by the Carnegie United Kingdom Trust to make a five-year study of delinquency, I had no previous experience in the field. I did not know enough about the subject to frame hypotheses for a formal experiment; all I could do, consequently, was to try to learn some of the realities of the problem by getting to know intimately a large number of delinquents. This entailed my living among them, helping them with their family problems, and, in doing so, getting to know their parents and becoming acquainted with the localities in which they lived. In this book I have had no need to lay all my case data before the reader, because a large part of it is contained in my report to the Carnegie United Kingdom Trust, a second edition of which was recently published (Stott, 1950/80). My method was rather similar to that a detective would use in attempting to solve a crime. I made a detailed study of the nature of the delinquent act and tried to piece together the state of mind that prompted it. Then, by relating this to the boy's life in his home locality—his associates, haunts, job history—and getting a picture of his family life and the quality of his relationships with his parents, I tried to see how the delinquency-conducive states of mind arose.

Because, even over five years, there are limits to the data that one can collect, I had to confine my own to these later stages of delinquency causation. This did not mean that I was unaware of the broader social determinants. Indeed, my knowledge of criminal families and of the ways of thought and attitudes to crime of their various members enabled me to appreciate the groundlessness of the notion of a criminal subculture. At the same time I saw how hardship and the lapse of traditional social ties can create stresses which tend to fragment the family and make delinquency more likely.

Of particular interest to me was the link between the kinds of things that can happen to families—illness and death, unemployment, failure of a marriage partner to meet responsibilities, separation of parents and children, moving out of the home neighborhood—and the breakdown of personal relationships within the family. The child only too often becomes the butt of parental quarrels, jealousies, and personal breakdown in the form of depression and hostility. Whether attacked, rejected, threatened with banishment from the family, forced to witness discord which threatens the family's continued existence, or rendered anxious by an ailing mother struggling against unequal odds and threatening to desert, the child of the under-privileged, stress-ridden family finds himself deprived of what—apart from the sheer physical means of existence—a child needs most, the affection and permanent presence of caring adults. The threatened loss of this basic security forces the child, in turn, to resort to emergency responses which are all too often maladaptive, in the sense that they worsen rather than alleviate his emotional deprivation. In *Delinquency and Human Nature* (1950/80) I show that delinquency is part and parcel of these maladaptive pseudo-solutions. Looked at in detail, the delinquency even of inner-city youth is not a viable way of life that offers opportunities for social betterment; it is a form of self-destructive behavioral breakdown.

DELINQUENCY AND MALADJUSTMENT

It was necessary for Shaw and the schools of sociologists who followed him to deny forthrightly any connection between delinquency and maladjustment. To admit the connection would have brought their theories down in ruins, opening up new areas of empirical inquiry which would have revealed a totally different state of affairs from that so neatly delineated in their formulations. It has therefore been necessary for me to quote in detail the results of several studies showing that young offenders tend to be troublesome and maladjusted apart from their delinquent acts. Lest these findings be discounted as merely reflecting the conflict of values between middle-class teachers and working-class children, it must be mentioned that more than one study shows the typical juvenile delinquent to be unpopular and rejected even among his peers. His portrayal as a normal young person adjusting to the demands of his inner-city subculture is a theory-dictated figment. That there is an important individual factor in delinquency is demonstrated by the fact that even in high-delinquency areas only a minority get involved in serious delinquency. At the same time the greater absolute volume of delinquency is spread over areas which cannot be described as disorganized or as harboring delinquent subcultures.

WHAT HOLDS BACK THE ORDINARY YOUNGSTER FROM DELINQUENCY?

If this personal factor is not a delinquency-proneness seen in the child's general behavior as maladjustment, we have to ask why the majority of essentially normal, high-spirited youngsters in all localities are able to resist the temptation to have some fun or to obtain petty luxuries by delinquent activities. The proverbial "boys down the street" are everywhere. Why do the majority spurn their invitations? The answer lies in the child's need for attachment to a caring adult. To the normal youngster his secure place in his family is not something to be lightly gambled with. He knows that involvement in a delinquent escapade will anger and grieve his parents; it will mean the loss of valued friends in return for associates whom decent young people shun; it will also impair his chances of employment. He may be feeling bored, or frustrated at his lack of economic opportunities or inability to get a job (although the few who think this way are more likely to join a political organization than hit out blindly by deviant acts). But a moment's thought will make him realize that the odds are stacked against a delinquent solution to his discontent. He obeys the law of least cost. That is to say, in a state of conflict he chooses the alternative which causes him the least pain. He does not jump out of the frying pan into the fire.

The ordinary youngster has in effect so much to lose when he does commit a delinquent act that we have to ask, as the first question we put to ourselves in our inquiry into its causes, why the foregoing restraints have lost their hold on him. It may be that he belongs to one of those very few families whose reputation can sink no lower and whose senior members are criminals. It may be that the child has no family or parent figure whose affection he values, or that he suffers from a rare constitutional deficiency of the need for human attachment. But for the serious delinquent in general— as I think I have demonstrated in *Delinquency and Human Nature*— some overriding emotional compulsion forces him to forget or flout the wishes of his parents and to ignore his own interests.

DELINQUENT STATES OF MIND

What the nature of the compulsion may be in the individual case is revealed by objective signs. These are seen in the delinquent acts themselves and in the child's everyday, nondelinquent behavior. One should be able to discern a consistent pattern of motivation running through both. From my study of 102 delinquent youths I was able to identify five main states of mind which caused them to seek a delinquent solution to their anxieties. What at first sight looks like a love of adventure or having fun with a group of other boys or girls mostly turns out to be the seeking of excitement as a means of banishing the memory of a distressing family situation. Alternatively, or along with this avoidance-excitement, as I have termed it, the youngster may aim to secure physical removal from the home, by repeated offenses which earn him committal to a residential institution. Other delinquent states of mind were those of hostility—a deliberate "going to the devil" as a means of self-banishment when the youngster feels himself rejected; delinquent loyalty-testing, in response to threats of being put out of the home; and finally bravado, as a way of compensating for doubts about being valued and wanted. The telltale indications of each of these delinquent states of mind tend to corroborate one another, as do the syndromes of diseases (although we must not take the analogy with disease too far). Their recognition should be among the basic skills of the social worker, child psychologist, and psychiatrist. They may even account for much of what looks like casual petty delinquency.

THE FACTOR OF DISCIPLINE

This does not mean that lack of discipline is never a factor. Given the opportunity and the stimulus, the ordinary youngster—or, for that matter, adult—will lightheartedly indulge in forbidden or illegal acts, provided no penalty is incurred. Likewise, many parents are inclined to condone the petty deviant behavior of their children by "turning a blind eye" or saying, "boys will be boys." Such children, and their parents, "learn their lesson" once they become involved with the juvenile justice system.

The same applies to the mildly inconsequent youngster, whose impulsiveness and thoughtlessness may be too much for the parents' resources of vigilance and control. One involvement with the law is usually enough to steer the impulsive child away from illegal acts. The failure to heed consequences which is typical of the persistent young delinquent or adult criminal can be traced to the dominance of one or more of the emotional compulsions mentioned above.

The social worker should also bear in mind, before blaming the parents for a failure to exercise discipline, that very occasionally one meets the type of child, instances of which I have described elsewhere, who suffers from a constitutional defect of temperament, in that he lacks the normal child's need for attachment to an adult (Stott, 1966). Such juvenile psychopaths, as these young incorrigibles are sometimes called, defeat all discipline, since there is nothing to appeal to in them. The term became fashionable at one stage, and the condition was overdiagnosed. Fortunately, it seems to give way with the onset of puberty to a heightened need for adult support and affection. Although for five years I was in a situation where possible adolescent psychopaths would have been directed to my notice, I never found one, only those who had become callous and embittered from ill-usage.

Apart from psychopathy, the reasons for a gross lack of control should be sought in a correspondingly serious defect in the parent-child relationship. In other words, the social worker has to discover why the youngster is prepared to jeopardize his family security or why the parent is unwilling or afraid to exercise discipline. If mutual affection and loyalty have given way to estrangement, attempts at control will break down, or, if persisted in, degenerate into harshness and cruelty. If, feeling rejected, the child reverts to hostility, he will go out of his way to commit mischief, as a means of bringing the situation to a crisis. Doubts about parental interest or fear of loss of the parent whose affection he has valued may induce him to commit delinquent acts in order to secure removal from the anxiety-fraught situation. In these circumstances he no longer has any incentive to obey his parents or avoid their displeasure. Likewise, if his form of escape is anxiety-blocking excitement, this will cause him to forget that wrongdoing may endanger his family membership.

In short, a failure of parental control which cannot be rectified by counseling is a by-product of affectional breach or of the feared loss of the valued parent. It goes with delinquency, rather than being a direct and major cause of it.

We have to assume nevertheless that the tradition of family discipline within a culture has some effect on the incidence of behavioral breakdown. In the analysis of the states of mind in which delinquent acts are committed, it was seen that at a certain point the child resorts to spurious immediate solutions, such as giving vent to his impulse to spite or punish his parents for their supposed or real rejection of him, and running away physically or mentally from the source of his anxieties. This breakdown point will occur at an earlier stage of exposure to stress if the child has never learned to control his behavior and the unbridled expression of his emotions. If, on the other hand, he has been conditioned to self-control because it met with parental approval while lack of control was disapproved, and if he has always been presented with models for self-control in his parents' behavior, it is reasonable to suppose that he will develop powers of resistance against breakdown. Moreover, the stresses which confer a risk of breakdown will be fewer in a family where the parents exercise self-control. This must be one of the reasons why the delinquency rate is low in cultures which emphasize restraint.

WHY DELINQUENTS USUALLY DO NOT APPEAR MALADJUSTED

To many people the maladjustment of the general run of delinquents is hard to accept. In court they look normal enough to the judge, and they seldom display symptoms of psychosis or gross abnormality. The answer to the paradox is twofold. First, acts which are by definition maladjusted, in that the individual goes against his own best interests, are extreme forms of normal reactions—those of avoiding what is stressful and anxiety-creating, expressing resentment against deprivation or disloyalty, or proving to oneself and one's friends that one is not a coward. These reactions go beyond normality when the individual's lack of control is such that he does himself damage—in other words, when he ceases to obey the law of least cost. Second, the disturbed emotional states characteristic of a delinquent phase do not, except in extreme cases, hold the child permanently under their sway. They are activated by the stress of particular circumstances. A maladjusted phase may be brought on by the witnessing of a parental row, the fear of a mother's desertion, being discriminated against as a "black sheep," or the threat of removal from the family. It will not be provoked in a courtroom, where it can be witnessed by the judge. And so long as the tendency to antisocial or self-injurious behavior remains unactivated, no interviewer, however skillful, can be certain of detecting it.

INDIVIDUAL VULNERABILITY

Some children remain unprovoked and maintain their stability under conditions of acute emotional deprivation and anxiety that drive others to a state of behavioral breakdown. There appears thus to be a differential factor of individual vulnerability. My own studies suggest that it is related to the stresses, predominantly of an interpersonal character, to which the child's mother was exposed during the pregnancy—which also explains the multiple handicaps of the problem family.

BREAKDOWN *AS THE ONSET OF AN EMERGENCY BEHAVIORAL SYSTEM*

The term *breakdown* is used in an exact sense: it is the point at which a person's capacity for judicious control of his behavior is superseded by an emergency response system of which panic is the best recognized manifestation. It comes into operation in the face of mortal danger or when deprivation is so massive and long-standing that the resources of accommodation become exhausted. It is a breakdown in the sense that the regular procedure for thinking ahead to the consequences of behavior are put out of action. This is the typical state of a child rendered emotionally disturbed by the stress of an acute threat to his family membership—a threat that he cannot cope with, and from which he has to flee physically, or the memory of which he has to block, because it has become intolerable. Since this panic-button system is a regular part of the human behavioral repertoire, it might be described as normal; as are its lesser manifestations, such as when people get irritable or lose their tempers. But in its extreme forms, which include uncontrolled aggression, ill-considered flight from the source of stress, and a variety of bizarre devices for fighting off intolerable thoughts and memories, it becomes abnormal, maladaptive, damaging to others, and self-destructive. This is the state of otherwise affectionate parents who physically abuse their children, or that of the young person who commits major delinquencies against his own best interests. Either the abusing parent or the delinquent child can move out of the breakdown phase and resume normality. It is then difficult for observers to believe that he has not been so always, and to condemn him as cruel or incorrigible. The delinquent in one of these phases of behavioral breakdown will be undeterrable by the usual resources of punishment, not because he is willfully perverse, but because the mental processes by which people weigh their longer-term interests —which include the avoidance of punishment—have been put out of action.

NATURE OF THE FAMILY STRESSES PRODUCING DELINQUENT BREAKDOWN

It was seen that delinquent states of mind are the outcome of stresses which have become unbearable to the individual, given his particular degree of vulnerability. The next step is to pinpoint the nature of these stresses. When I asked myself this question with regard to each of the family situations of the earlier-mentioned delinquent youths, a common feature emerged: nearly all of them, by some type of breach or threat, had been deprived of that secure attachment to a caring adult which is an instinctive need of child-hood. My subsequent casework in Bristol confirmed this induction. The principle has to be stated in terms which bring out the unquestioned and unconditional nature of the bond between parent and child. Its continuance must never be made to depend on good behavior which the child may not feel confident of delivering, nor put in doubt by family disruption or irresponsible talk.

There are many variations of the ways in which the child may suffer deprivation of this need, and I have tabulated a number which tend to recur in case after case. These sources of undependability fall into four main groups. The first covers those situations in which the child faces a threat of rejection and possible expulsion from the family. In the second the child has lost the preferred or only parent and is left with an unsatisfactory substitute. The third group consists of those in which the mother is not a dependable source of affection and care. In the fourth, the child fears the loss of the preferred parent. Exactly how many categories of breach of affectionate relations may be listed depends upon where the line is drawn between categories and subcategories. The important thing is to exemplify the main principle, so that the caseworker learns to recognize the critical fault in a child's relations with his parents which has constituted deprivation for him. Unless the cause of the child's breakdown can be traced in such terms, casework is likely to be ineffective.

OTHER REASONS FOR DELINQUENCY

It will be asked what proportion of instances of delinquency have their origin in this loss, or threatened loss, of a secure family base. From my analysis of the 102 cases reported in my Carnegie work I was able to find only a few understandable exceptions (these have been discussed in this book); but this was in a series of recidivist delinquent youths. Among younger delinquents one is more likely to come across—but even then, rarely—the child described as a "moral defective" because he seems not to value adult attachment or affection and hence feels none of the loyalties that might deter him from wrongdoing.

Apart from membership in a small ethnic group linked by family ties, for whom preying on the outside world has become a family tradition and a livelihood, I feel confident that we shall never find instances of continued delinquent acts of a reprehensible nature committed by an emotionally normal young person who enjoys the secure and responsible affection of an adult. The concept of criminal opportunity put forward by Cloward and Ohlin (1960), which assumes the existence of a well-organized underworld with links to a corrupt judiciary and administration, has little relevance to the general problem of juvenile delinquency. And as far as the less-organized and less-disciplined underworld of our big cities is concerned, it has yet to be shown that those who get sucked into it are really stable youngsters from stable families rather than the emotionally deprived, who are willing to pay any price for adult support. Some of the delinquent youths I have described were members of this less reputable underworld, and they were no more stable than the rest. For practical purposes there is no such thing as delinquency merely for the prospect of gain, and the same applies to a love of adventure or a weakness for pranks.

We may indeed find rather more ordinary youngsters committing offenses in these times, when the use of drugs and alcohol has become prevalent among teenagers. Deprivation of his drug arouses in the addict the aforementioned panic state and hence causes him to inhibit all consideration of consequences. The influence of alcohol on some temperaments is to produce a recklessness which can be defined as a temporary dissociation from consequences.

Since young people can come under the influence of alcohol merely through fashion or experimentation, we are likely to have an increasing number of temperamentally normal adolescents who commit delinquent acts while in this state of dissociation.

To such cases we have to add those youngsters who feel free to commit delinquent acts because they are able to dominate their parents and hence have no anxieties about the continuance of parental support, and the quasi-normal inconsequents who can be led on by more confirmed delinquents. There is thus a marginal zone of stable or quasi-stable delinquents within the distribution from normality to maladjustment.

THE IMPORTANCE OF DETERRENCE

How wide this zone may be depends upon the effectiveness of deterrence. Maladjustment was defined in this book as the inability of a youngster to control his behavior in his own best interests. This includes the inability to heed punishment. Conversely, normality is defined for our purpose as an ability to control one's behavior when it pays to do so. Ordinary individuals, juvenile or adult, are inclined to promote their self-interest over that of their fellows, and in so doing, to test the boundaries of permissiveness. Precisely because they are sensitive to their own interests, they are deterrable. We cannot, moreover, rely upon the independent moral rectitude of the man, woman, or youngster in the street. They take their moral standards from those around them. What they can get away with, even if not right, can at least be winked at. Hence, we need a consistent system of deterrence which leaves few loopholes. This implies that there should be enforcement of the law by efficient detection and effective punishment.

PUNISHING THE UNDETERRABLE?

We have nevertheless to face the fact that a large proportion of delinquents—at any rate at the time of the commission of their offenses—are not deterrable. How, then, do we square this with a system of justice in which the ordinary citizen has to reckon on punishment if he commits an offense? Part of the answer is that such a system serves the valuable purpose of separating the deterrable from the nondeterrable. If a young offender repeatedly walks out of the courtroom, having been given nothing but warnings, he may be either calling the bluff of authority or genuinely incapable of controlling his behavior. If, on the other hand, he persists in his deviance despite punishments which make inroads into his leisure time and possibly his spending money, he is likely to be in the nondeterrable class, and so identify himself as a young person in need of casework help.

The other part of the answer to the apparent inconsistency of punishing the undeterrable lies in the type of punishment used. If it does not arouse bitterness or resentment—as physical pain or incarceration may be reckoned to do—and does not impose a senseless treadmill of routine work, little inhumanity will be involved. It must of course impose a regime or a forfeit upon the offender to which he would not ordinarily submit, or it would not be punishment. In effect, any course of treatment of the maladjusted offender would meet this criterion. It might be compared to the restrictions imposed on an invalid to help him recover from his illness.

NEW TYPES OF PUNISHMENT AND
METHODS OF TREATMENT

Several innovative courses of training, of which I have given examples as possible models for adoption, meet humanitarian criteria for punishment, and they have either already demonstrated their success or give promise of doing so. Probably their most important feature is that they show the young offender how to function more effectively and with a greater sense of personal satisfaction. They include improvement of work habits and skills either at school or in employment, the ability to get along with family, friends, and teachers, and physical exercise as an introduction to recreational activities. Last but not least, they provide young offenders with an opportunity to meet caring adults and to realize that the whole adult world is not against them.

Restitution by work or monetary payments, and organized service to the community are additional types of educative punishment that should be extended to juvenile offenders. A recent innovation is to bring the offender face to face with his victim. This is done with the formal purpose of deciding upon the amount and form of the restitution. More important, however, are its social objectives. Being confronted by the victim, usually in the latter's own home, is calculated to make all except the most hardened psychopath appreciate that the personal harm for which he is thoughtlessly responsible far outweighs the satisfactions he gets from his delinquencies. The effect on the victim is to mellow feelings of hostility and punitiveness insofar as he sees the offender as a misguided, likeable, or unhappy youth. Such victim-offender reconciliation could play an important part in neighborhood programs for dealing with delinquency. If it is known that the young offender, once apprehended, will be dealt with as a member of a family might be who has been guilty of some misconduct, local residents will be less reticent about reporting them.

HANDLING OF DELINQUENCY PROBLEMS BY LOCAL COMMUNITIES

Passing to the wider social aspects of delinquency prevention, we have to appreciate, but not get discouraged by, the forces of disorganization and demoralization which are everywhere at hand in our society. In high-delinquency neighborhoods, the helplessness of the residents about the danger of molestation and damage to property leads to a passivity and a noninvolvement that encourages further lawlessness. The remedy suggested by social innovations such as one in the Bronx, New York, is that of decentralization. The enforcement and administration of the law, like the programs of deterrence and rehabilitation, become a neighborhood responsibility. Residents' organizations are encouraged to nominate youth panels before whom the local juvenile miscreants are brought in the first place. There, if their offense is admitted, they are allocated to some program of reeducation and restitution, with a right to appeal to a central juvenile court if guilt is denied or the punishment decided upon by the panel thought too harsh.

Social-work and police juvenile units could also be organized on a neighborhood basis to work closely with residents' youth panels. Since the area served by a secondary school and its primary feeder schools might form a convenient neighborhood for this purpose, a social-work unit with, say, a staff of three or four could also serve as school social workers and be centered within the schools.

Such a decentralized control of juvenile deviance would have many advantages. It would place responsibility for law and order, and the intactness of local amenities, on the local residents, so that they would be encouraged to report juvenile wrongdoers and join as volunteers in programs of training and restitution. The neighborhood police, juvenile officers, and social workers would be able to work from a knowledge of—and, ideally, with the cooperation and trust of—local families, including those whose junior members are the troublemakers. Whereas now there are often delays of weeks or months before a young person's family problems are treated—if they are treated at all—an area social-work team, as in some pioneer projects in the United States, would be in a position to intervene in crises within hours, and deal with serious ongoing problems within days. Finally, social workers and police juvenile officers would be saved the present monstrous amount of time they waste in waiting in central courts and having to reappear again and again owing to adjournments on legal issues.

THE ROLE OF THE JUVENILE COURT

The establishment of neighborhood organizations for the handling of juvenile deviance would also render the contribution of the central bench of family court judges many times more effective. The present superficial processing of a succession of cases ranks equally as a means of wasting judges' time with that of keeping social workers hanging around courtrooms. A central juvenile court would be needed to establish guilt when it is disputed and to give legal backing to the treatment measures of the neighborhood panels. Its judge might in addition be given the responsibility for ensuring that the neighborhood panels work efficiently and fairly, with powers to reorganize them if necessary. By the keeping of careful records of progress within each neighborhood, the effectiveness of various forms of treatment could be compared. The neighborhood social-work units would, however, remain responsible to a regional administration, in order to provide them with expert consultative help and ongoing in-service courses for the improvement of their professional skills and the communication of successful experience.

THE TONE OF THE SCHOOL AS
A FACTOR IN LOCAL DEVIANCE

The school is a focal point from which good or bad influences radiate. The perspicacious first-hand observation of Sir Alec Clegg and the English inspectorate (1962) shows that there is a close connection between the tone of a school and the external deviance of its students. The widely disparate student delinquency rates in schools serving similar areas are hard to interpret from statistical findings; but the upshot seems to be that once a school begins to get a bad name, standard-conscious parents avoid choosing it for their children, so that it is left with a residue consisting of the neighborhood's maladjusted and neglected children, and recent immigrants.

The degradation of such schools then becomes cumulative, until some dedicated and energetic principal takes over, who insists on meticulous supervision extending to every corner of the school premises, and makes determined efforts to stamp out bad behavior by the tracking down and punishment of offenders.

THE LACK OF EFFECTIVE SANCTIONS
AGAINST MISBEHAVIOR IN SCHOOLS

My acquaintance with the at-that-time strap-happy educational system of Glasgow confirms the research of Clegg in showing that corporal punishment is not only signally ineffective, but amounts to senseless cruelty perpetrated against the maladjusted. The problem is that with this punitive crutch knocked away, schools find themselves without the means of controlling the merely thoughtless, obstreperous, assertive, or easily led. On the American continent the dearth of sanctions against misbehavior has led to an ostrichlike idiocy: students who don't want to attend anyway are punished by suspension. I have proposed a system of graduated warnings which, when used up, would be the signal for the police arrest of the miscreant and his being dealt with by a neighborhood panel along the lines described earlier. Those who jib at using the police to reinforce the discipline of a school should reflect that the alternative is all too often a sink of disorder which ill-prepares the rising generation for life in the wider community.

IDENTIFICATION AND PRIMARY CARE
OF THE DELINQUENCY-PRONE

There are many positive things that the school can do, apart from ensuring the orderliness which allows teaching and learning to be safe from interruption. At the technical level it can help the psychological services to carry out periodic and systematic screening by which the maladjusted—and thereby also the delinquency-prone— can be identified and helped. Through the counseling of parents by a school social worker, or, for lack thereof, with the principal or teacher acting in a pastoral capacity, I believe that the greater number of family problems leading to delinquency can be resolved. If not, they can at least be recognized as needing expert treatment. A service of school social workers could become a system of primary care for the maladjusted and delinquency-prone, analogous to that of the family physician.

THE PERSONAL INFLUENCE OF THE TEACHER

Probably much more than what they glean from the media or from general hearsay about the ways of the world, young people form their system of values from the feelings of respect and admiration, or otherwise, that they conceive for individual members of the senior generation. The personal influence of the principal and the teaching body may therefore be the critical factor in establishing standards of conduct. Modeling needs loyalties, and primary loyalties are developed through ongoing face-to-face relationships. For teachers to be able to influence their students, it follows that the school must not be too large, or should at least be broken up into subcommunities. Although it will always be hard to establish statistically, these human truths about good and bad behavior make it probable that very large schools induce the same kind of moral anonymity as is characteristic of a large city. One may further reflect that if the teaching profession is a vehicle through which standards of our culture are transmitted, teachers have an awesome responsibility. After all, no one knows a teacher better than his students. Neither his virtues nor his vices, his diligence or laziness, dedication or indifference can be hidden from them. (The woman teacher is excluded only grammatically, owing to the clumsiness of "his or her.")

FOREBODINGS ABOUT THE DECAY OF RESTRAINT

What kind of morality, then, should we display before the younger generation? At a British Columbia educational convention a few years back I listened to the platform speaker, a young psychiatrist, winning the applause of his teacher-audience as he expounded his philosophy around the catch phrase, "It's me." And that justified anything. If you felt like doing something, you did it. There is a danger that this latter-day atavism may be the undoing of our culture. The Marquis de Sade formulated it in more sophisticated terms, as the right of each individual to follow his natural instincts wherever they might lead him; and in his own life he gave many practical demonstrations of what forms such self-indulgence could take.

An offshoot of this philosophy is the fashionable notion that whatever a person feels strongly, he has a right to express. There is even an idea, based on a popular but fallacious psychology, that any kind of restraint in the expression of feelings is harmful because of some dire effect which follows from their being repressed or bottled up. In no human society or group can "saying what you think" be tolerated, any more than can the right to injure other people physically. Every culture insists upon restraints which serve to minimize friction and render stable relationships possible. In our schools we should teach our students that their friendships, their family life, and their future marriages can have no permanence without restraint of word and deed. In terms of sociobiology restraint has to be seen as the complement to the genetic constitution of the human species. Behavior dictated purely by instinct entails an enormous wastefulness of life, as is seen in infra-human species. Human nature, on the other hand, has evolved within a framework of controls upon the exercise of instinctive behavior. This is what cultures are mostly about. We pay for culture loss in lives and handicap. To throw restraints aside as inherently evil would be to expose humanity to the stresses and cruelties of animal existence. That this is a matter of biological reality and not just old-fashioned moralizing is shown by a recent finding: a marriage rendered intolerable by discord doubles the chances of producing an unhealthy or behavior-disturbed child. A civilization which cannot establish rules for harmonious married life is on an accelerating downhill slide, each generation being less stable, having an ever-greater number of unhappy marriages, and from them, ever more maladjusted and delinquent children.

POSSIBILITIES OF DELINQUENCY REDUCTION WITHOUT INCURRING ADDITIONAL EXPENSE

Even though they would yield a very high financial return to the community, new approaches to delinquency run the risk of being rejected because they are liable initially to impose budgetary burdens and be deemed inflationary. It is anomalous that similar investments made with a view to increasing efficiency in the private sector are seen as creating employment and adding to the strength of the economy. The paradox becomes all the sharper as productive processes become more advanced, since most of the unfilled consumer needs are those for services which can best be supplied by public authorities.

It is beyond the scope of this book to suggest how this economic contradiction might be resolved, but in drafting a program of reform it has to be faced as one of the realities of the situation. The strategy of the sagacious reformer is to stagger new measures so that the most profitable of them are introduced first, in order that taxpayers can see early budgetary savings and eventually become reconciled to the new policy as a whole.

We have to ask ourselves therefore where the most immediate budgetary savings are to be found in the program outlined in this book. The first and most important would lie in the use of effective diagnostic and counseling techniques by the existing body of social workers. At present, social work, including probation, is merely a holding operation, sometimes described as picking up the pieces after the damage has been done. It is not so much prevention as post-vention. Analysis of the states of mind in which delinquent acts are committed (given in Chapter Seven) affords us a measure of the extent of the increased efficiency which these techniques make possible. Physical removal from an anxiety-creating home situation was seen to be the sole, or one of the chief immediate, motivations in 54 percent of the cases of serious, persistent delinquency. Avoidance-excitement was such in 52 percent. Allowing for the overlap of these motivations, 75.5 percent of the youths in question were found to be seeking relief from their troubles by delinquent escapism. To these we have to add those whose motivation was hostility and/or delinquent loyalty-testing without evidence of escapist motivations. They amounted to a further 17.6 percent, bringing to 93 percent the proportion of delinquent breakdowns attributable to these major motivations stemming from a breach in the affectional bond between parent and child. The remaining motivations were no less related to family circumstances or the lack of a family.

It is not, of course, claimed that the casework techniques described in this book would eliminate serious recidivist delinquency (which is our main problem): the limiting factor is the proportion of home situations which are capable of being mended by casework intervention. Some of them are not unstable, nor are the parents unaffectionate; it is just that the latter are creating an impression of rejection and instability by unthinking and irresponsible threats or actions. In others there are real weaknesses, which can neverthe-less be kept below the danger level if the parents are cooperative and they can be given insight into how their child's faith in them is being undermined. Appropriate counseling by itself should fail only when the parents remain uncooperative or when the situation is past mending; and this is the point at which removal to other care is indicated. What proportion of the parents of serious delinquents fall into each of these three categories must depend partly on locality and socioeconomic level, and general estimates would be hazardous. What can be confidently affirmed is that sophisticated counseling of the parents of those children identified as delinquency-prone should reduce the amount of serious delinquency very considerably. I am tempted to say by half, but that may be stretching credibility in advance of the experience gained by demonstration projects. Such an estimate may not appear so unrealistic when we consider the enormous reductions in the prevalence of diseases, once their causes have been understood. And the difference between the new techniques proposed and the almost total lack of technique which is the position at present is that they are designed from insights into the reasons for delinquency gained by many years of first-hand study. If the reader considers this an arrogant claim, let him reflect upon the lack of other first-hand studies. A person who looks inside a box is more likely to have an accurate idea of what is inside it than someone who tries to infer is contents from external measurements. It must be added that the utilization of this knowledge of causes depends upon the existence of an adequate casework service staffed by suitably trained professionals. Nevertheless, existing services using these techniques should be able to show significant reductions in delinquency rates.

PRESENT MONEY GOBBLERS IN THE SYSTEM

The categories of no-cost reform next to be considered involve the elimination of the money-gobbling features of the present system. The most obvious of these is the time social workers spend in juvenile and family courts. It is not only a matter of repeated attendances for purely legal reasons: the court procedure itself is redundant in those cases—forming the great majority—in which guilt is admitted. In the time available a judge simply cannot review the circumstances of a case in a way which reveals the reasons for the offense. It is a polite understatement to say that the attempt to do so in a few minutes is a waste of time. Diagnosis, and the treatment which it indicates, are matters for skilled social workers, who should be freed from the legal rituals to give them time to be in fact social workers. To convince the public and our legislators on this point, studies should be made of the time they (including probation and police juvenile officers) spend in and around courtrooms.

The second money gobbler is the committal institution. Its ineffectiveness as a means of rehabilitation has been demonstrated by well-known follow-up studies. We have first to ask how children at present get committed. All too often it is because a child is thought to have deserved it because of his continued offenses. We get anethetized to the follies we live with: this criterion for committal is no more logical than it is for a doctor to refer a patient to the hospital as a punishment for having made a certain number of visits to his office. Apart from those cases where a child has to be detained for his own or the public's safety, removal is justified only when it becomes apparent, after social-work investigation and the appropriate counseling effort, that no headway can be made in giving the child the kind of security in his home life that he needs. This has to be a social-work decision taken on the basis of objective criteria. There is a second element of folly in making committal contingent upon number of offenses. So long as it is known that committal can be achieved in this way, some children will persist in their delinquency as a means of securing removal from a distressing home situation. Thus, we have the paradox that what is meant to be a deterrent acts as an incentive to delinquency.

The obvious alternative is to provide legal means of getting away. A large number of committal institutions could be converted into voluntary boarding schools or vocational colleges. There should in fact be a reduced need for places in residential institutions, for two reasons. First, since the use of more efficient casework techniques should have the effect of alleviating the home difficulties of many children to the extent that they become bearable, far fewer will be desperate about leaving home. Second, the professionalization of foster parentage will have the effect both of making a greater number of foster homes available and—by the training of foster parents in the care of more difficult children—increase the number who can be successfully managed by such means. In terms of our balance sheet, foster parenting is a far more economical way of caring for children who have to be removed from their homes. A rough calculation of the staff needed for institutional care suggests that it amounts to one per child; a professional foster parent should be able to cope with three or four, and in some cases six. Beside this, there is saving on the cost of maintaining the fabric and services of the building.

The third money gobbler is the repair of wanton damage. In the Strathclyde Regional Council of Scotland, covering a population of some 3 million people, this amounted for the year 1977–8 to over $10 million. Of this, glass breakage alone accounted for over $2 million; and vandalism in the form of other kinds of deliberate destruction, some $1,200,000. The grand total would employ several hundred social workers. Not the total amount could be saved, but here is a source from which considerable funds might become available to pay the salaries of extra social workers who would be needed in a sophisticated prevention program.

THE SOCIAL WORKER'S CASELOAD

The all-embracing principle governing the financing of a prevention program is; the earlier, the cheaper. It provides the justification for the larger social-work force which early identification and treatment would require. Excessive caseloads are self-defeating. The objective of casework intervention is to remove the critical stresses which are forcing the child into delinquency. This inevitably means a period of intensive work with the family. To leave this half done—as a diagnosis that cannot be followed through, or by not giving parents time to be reconciled with their troublesome child, or not making arrangements for the child's removal when the crisis cannot otherwise be resolved—means a waste even of the time that is spent on the case. It is like partly stopping a hole in a sinking boat: the boat sinks just the same. Ideas about what constitute effective caseloads have consequently to be revised. Below is given a model for a family caseworker's week:

Two new cases per week, involving for each a 2-hour interview with the parents, plus one-half hour with the child, one-half hour to study reports of the offense, and one hour to write up case notes and complete a form on symptoms for computerized records (which see below) .... 8 hours

Four recently accepted cases still the subject of counseling, each involving 1 hour of parental interview, one-half hour with the child, 1 hour for making treatment arrangements, one-half hour for completing records .... 12 hours

Continued further supervision of eight cases, one hour, including writing up of record .... 8 hours

Travel .... 4 hours

Weekly consultation with supervisor or casework seminar .... 2 hours

Attendance at neighborhood panel or juvenile court . 2 hours

Total .... 36 hours

The above gives a workload of 14 cases, assuming that the cases requiring further supervision are followed up weekly. Some may need less time than this, but allowances have to be made for contingencies. The foregoing number may therefore be taken, for staffing purposes, as the maximum for optimal effectiveness. Anything larger would be subject to the law of diminishing returns. Two new cases per week may seem small, but the interviewing of parents is very exacting. My experience is that if two such are attempted in a day, the interviewer loses the freshness of mind needed to piece together the clues to the motivation of the deviant behavior. Moreover, adequate time must be allowed for making case notes. (Apart from their value as records, the writing up of the latter provides a ritual for thought about a case.)

How many additional caseworkers would be required to operate an effective system of diagnosis and counseling is not only a matter of conjecture but need not be our present concern. The number for which provision will be made in the budgets of the future depends on the results of the experimental implementation of the program in representative localities. If these are convincing, we may expect a change in official concepts of social casework—from one of a face-saving administrative resource when something has to be done about a deviant child, to that of a high-priority public service on a par with the health services. It is sufficient to note that even a service with caseloads small enough to allow of intensive work with families would still be a less expensive form of treatment than residential care. Evidence before the Presidential Commission on Law Enforcement and Administration of Justice showed that a caseload of 15, as operated by the California Youth Authority, cost less than half that of institutionalizing the children concerned.

THE IMMEDIATE CALLS ON
THE NATIONAL BUDGET

The outcome of this consideration of the finances of the proposed prevention program is that the first stages towards its implementation would require relatively modest calls upon a national budget, such as could never justify its rejection on the grounds of expense. Itemized, these expenditures would have to cover the following:

1. Professional training and retraining programs in family casework and school counseling.
2. Demonstration projects in representative neighborhoods, for the evaluation of the effectiveness of family counseling

based on systematic diagnosis of the reasons for delinquency, coupled with a crisis-intervention service.

3. Community projects for the control of local vandalism and
   other bad behavior.
4. Development through experimental projects of the concept
   of "communal policing," including the establishment of
   police social-work facilities.
5. Experiments in new forms of disposition of the young
   offender, involving diversion from the court and the use of
   progressive forms of punishment such as restitution, public-
   service conditions of probation, and training in life skills.
6. A national advisory center staffed by social workers and
   sociologists trained to act as consultants to local community
   projects.
7. A computer center for the storage and analysis of casework
   data for the improvement of diagnostic and counseling
   skills.

REFERENCES

Alderson, J. (1978). *Communal Policing.* Exeter, Devon and Cornwall Constabulary, Force Headquarters, Middlemore.

Baittle, B. (1961). Psychiatric aspects of the development of a street corner group: an exploratory study. *American Journal of Orthopsychiatry* 31, 703-712.

Baron, R. and Feeney, F. (1976). Juvenile diversion through family counseling. Washington, D.C.: Office of Technology Transfer, National Institute of Law Enforcement and Criminal Justice, Law Enforcement Assistance Administration, U.S. Department of Justice. Superintendent of Documents, U.S. Government Printing Office. Stock No. 027-000-00371-

Baron, R., Feeney, F. and Thornton, W. (1973). Preventing delinquency through diversion: The Sacramento County 601 Diversion Project. *Federal Probation* 37, 13-18.

Bealer, R.C., Willits, F.K., and Maida, P.R. (1971). The rebellious youth subculture—a myth. In R.E. Muuss (Ed.), *Adolescent Behavior and Society: A Book of Readings.* New York: Random House.

Becker, H.S. (1963). *Outsiders: Studies in the Sociology of Deviance.* Glencoe, Ill.: Free Press. London: Collier-Macmillan.

Berman, P. (1978). *Report to the U.S. Office of Education.* Prepared by the Rand Corporation. Washington, D.C.: U.S. Government Printing Office.

Berman, A., and Siegal, A.W. (1976). Adaptive and learning skills in juvenile delinquents: a neuropsychological analysis. *Journal of Learning Disabilities* 9, 583-590.

Birkett, N.T. (1950). Juvenile delinquency in the City of Aberdeen in 1948. Master of Education Thesis, University of Aberdeen.

Bondy, C., Braden, J., Cohen, R., and Eyfesth, K. (1957). Jugendliche stören die Ordnung. Munich, Juventa Verlag.

Bowlby, J. (1944). Forty-four juvenile thieves. *International Journal of Psychoanalysis* 25, 1-57.

Brown, B. (1977). Community service as a condition of probation. *Federal Probation* 41, 7-9.

Bruce, H.M. (1960). A block to pregnancy in the mouse caused by proximity to strange males. *Journal of Reproduction and Fertility* 1, 96-103.

Burns, V. and Stern, L. (1967). The prevention of juvenile delinquency. In *Task Force Report: Juvenile Delinquency and Youth Crime.* President's Commission on Law Enforcement and Administration of Justice. Appendix S, 361-4. Washington, D.C.: U.S. Government Printing Office.

Burt, C. (1925). *The Young Delinquent.* London: University of London Press.

Butler, N.R. and Bonham, D.G. (1963). *Perinatal Mortality: First Report of the 1958 British Perinatal Mortality Survey.* Edinburgh: Livingstone.

Chambliss, W. (1966). The deterrent influence of punishment. *Crime and Delinquency* 12, 70-75.

Chitty, D. (1952). Mortality among voles (microtus agrestis) at Lake Vyrwy, Montgomeryshire, in 1936-1939. *Philosophical Transactions of the Royal Society of London.* B. 236, 505-552.

Christiansen, K.O. (1977a). A preliminary study of criminality among twins. In S.A. Mednick and K.O. Christiansen (Eds.), *Biosocial Bases of Criminal Behavior*, pp. 89-108. New York: Gardner Press.

———. (1977b). A review of studies of criminality among twins. In S.A. Mednick and K.O. Christiansen (Eds.), *Biosocial Bases of Criminal Behavior*, pp. 45-88. New York: Gardner Press.

CIAED. (1978). Booklets on school social work and similar projects. Centre for Information and Advice on Educational Disadvantage. 11, Anson Road, Manchester M14 5BY, England.

Clegg, A.B. (1962). The role of the school. In *Delinquency and Discipline*. London: Councils and Education Press.

Cloward, R.A. and Ohlin, L.E. (1960). *Delinquency and Opportunity: a theory of delinquent gangs*. Glencoe, Ill.: Free Press.

———. (1963). The prevention of delinquent subcultures: issues and problems. In W.R. Carriker (Ed.), *The Role of the School in the Prevention of Juvenile Delinquency*. Washington, D.C.: U.S. Dept. of Health, Education and Welfare.

Cohen, A.K. (1956). *Delinquent Boys: The Structure of the Gang*. Glencoe, Ill.: Free Press.

Collingwood, T.R., Douds, A., and Williams, H. (1967). Juvenile diversion: the Dallas Police Department Services Program. *Federal Probation* 40, 23-27.

Conger, J.J. and Miller, W.C. (1966). *Personality, Social Class and Delinquency*. New York: Wiley.

Craig, M.M. and Glick, S. (1968). School behaviour related to later delinquency and non-delinquency. *Criminologica* 5, 17-27.

Craik, K.J.W. (1943). *The Nature of Explanation*. Cambridge: Cambridge University Press.

Cunnison, J. and Gilfallan, J.B.S. (1951). *Third Statistical Account of Scotland*. Glasgow: Collins.

Curran, J.H. (1977). *The Children's Hearing System: A Review of Research*. London: Her Majesty's Stationery Office.

Davie, R., Butler, N.R., and Goldstein, N. (1972). *From Birth to Seven: Second Report of the National Child Development Study*. London: Longman and National Children's Bureau.

DES (Department of Education and Science). (1977). *Ten Good Schools*. London: Her Majesty's Stationery Office.

Dobzhansky, T. (1962). *Mankind Evolving*. New Haven: Yale University Press.

———. (1973). *Genetic Diversity and Human Equality*. New York: Basic Books.

Drillien, C.M. (1964). *The Growth and Development of the Prematurely Born Infant*. Edinburgh: Livingston.

———, Thomson, A.J.M., and Burgoyne, K. (1980). Low-birthweight children at early school age: a longitudinal study. *Developmental Medicine and Child Neurology* 22, 26-47.

Eisenberg, L. (1964). Behavioral manifestations of cerebral damage in childhood. In H.G. Birch (Ed.), *Brain Damage in Children: Biological and Social Aspects*. Baltimore: Williams and Wilkins.

Ellingson, R.J. (1954). The incidence of EEG abnormality among patients with mental disorders of apparently non-organic origin: a critical review. *American Journal of Psychiatry* 111, 263-275.

Errington, P.L. (1954). On the hazards of over-emphasizing numerical fluctuations in studies of "cyclic" phenomena in muskrat populations. *Journal of Wildlife Management* 18, 66-90.

Ferguson, T. (1952). *The Young Delinquent in his Social Setting*. London: Nuffield and Oxford University Press.

Flor-Henry, P. (1974). Psychosis, neurosis, and epilepsy: Development and gender-related effects and their etiological contribution. *British Journal of Psychiatry* 124, 144-150.

———. (1976). Lateralized temporal-limbic dysfunction and psychopathology. In H. Steklis, S. Harnad, and J. Lancaster (Eds.), *Origins and Evolution of Language and Speech*. *Annals of the New York Academy of Science* 280, 777-797.

Frankenberg, R. (1957). *Village on the Border*. London: Cohen and West.

Fraser, E. (1959). *Home Environment and the School*. London: Scottish Council for Educational Research and University of London Press.

Fraser, F.C., Kalter, H., Walker, B.E., and Fainstat, T.D. (1954). Experimental production of cleft palate with cortisone, and other hormones. *Journal of Cellular and Comparative Physiology* 43, suppl. 237-259.

Fuller, C. (1978). Poor U.S. Blacks live in despair. *Toronto Globe and Mail*. Reprinted from the *Atlanta Journal*, Oct. 4, 1978.

Galaway, B. (1977). The use of restitution. *Crime and Delinquency* 23, 57-67.

Gemignani, R.J. (1972). Youth Services Systems. *Federal Probation* 36, 48-53.

Gibbs, J. (1968). Crime, punishment and deterrence. *Southwestern Social Science Quarterly*, 515-530.

Glueck, S. and Glueck, E.T. (1950). *Unraveling Juvenile Delinquency*. Cambridge, Mass.: Harvard University Press.

———. (1962). *Family Environment and Delinquency*. Cambridge, Mass.: Harvard University Press. London: Routledge and Kegan Paul.

———. (1968). *Delinquents and Non-Delinquents in Perspective*. Cambridge, Mass.: Harvard University Press.

Goddard, H.H. (1913). *The Kallikak Family: A Study in the Heredity of Feeble-mindedness*. New York: Macmillan.

Green, R.G. and Evans, C.A. (1940). Studies on a population cycle of snowshoe hares on Lake Alexander area. I, II, III. *Journal of Wildlife Management* 4, 220-238, 267-278, 347-358.

Haight, S.L. (1980). Learning Disabilities—the battered discipline. *Journal of Learning Disabilities* 13, 452-458.

Hansard Parliamentary Reports. London: Her Majesty's Stationery Office.

H.M. Inspectorate for Schools (UK). (1977). *Ten Good Schools: A Secondary School Enquiry*. London: Her Majesty's Stationery Office.

Himes, J.S. (1961). Negro teen-age culture. *Annals of the American Academy of Political and Social Science* 338, 92-101.

Hodges, E.F. and Tait, C.D., Jr. (1963). A follow-up study of potential delinquents. *American Journal of Psychiatry* 120, 449-453.

Hudson, J., Galaway, B., Henschel, W., Lindgren, J., and Penton, J. (1975). Diversion programming in criminal justice: the case of Minnesota. *Federal Probation* 39, 11-18.

Hutchings, B. and Mednick, S.A. (1977). Criminality in adoptees and their adoptive and biological parents: A pilot study. In S.A. Mednick and K.O. Christiansen (Eds.), *Biosocial Bases of Criminal Behavior*, pp. 127-141. New York: Gardner Press.

Jansyn, L.R., Jr. (c.1961). The structure and dynamics of a street corner group: II—Leadership, structure and behavior. Chicago: Institute for Juvenile Research, Department of Public Welfare, State of Illinois. Mimeographed report.

Jasper, J.H., Solomon, P., and Bradley, C. (1938). Electroencephalographic analyses of behavior problem children. *American Journal of Psychiatry* 95, 641-655.

Kilbrandon, Lord (Chairman). Children and Young Persons, Scotland. Edinburgh: Her Majesty's Stationery Office.

Kobrin, S. (1959). The Chicago Area Project—a 25-year assessment. *Annals of the American Academy of Political and Social Science* 322, 20-29.

———— . (1961). Sociological aspects of the development of a street corner group: an exploratory study. *American Journal of Orthopsychiatry* 31, 685-702.

Kohlberg, L. (1971). Moral education in the schools: a developmental view. In R. E. Muuss (Ed.), *Adolescent Behavior and Society: A Book of Readings*. New York: Random House.

———— and Kramer, R. (1969). Continuities and discontinuities in childhood and adult moral development. *Human Development* 12, 93-120.

Kvaraceus, W.C. and Miller, W.B. (1959). *Delinquent Behavior: Culture and the Individual*. Washington, D.C.: National Education Association.

Landauer, W. and Bliss, C.I. (1946). Insulin-produced rumplessness of chickens. *Journal of Experimental Zoology* 102, 1-22.

Lane, B.A. (1980). The relationship of learning disabilities to juvenile delinquency: Current status. *Journal of Learning Disabilities* 13, 425-434.

Lane, J. (1949). *Titus Oates*. London: Andrew Dakers.

Latina, J.C. and Schembera, J.L. (1976). Volunteer homes for status offenders: an alternative to detention. *Federal Probation* 40, 45-49.

Lorenz, K. (1959). *Man meets dog*. London: Methuen, p. 33.

Lundman, R.J. (1976). Will diversion reduce recidivism? *Crime and Delinquency* 22, 428-436.

———— and Scarpitti, F.R. (1978). Delinquency prevention: recommendations for future projects. *Crime and Delinquency* 24, 207-220.

Luria, A.R. (1968). The complex mechanisms of psychological processes. *Impact of Science on Society* 18, 141-156.

Maccoby, E.E., Johnson, J.P., and Church, R.M. (1958). Community integration and the social control of juvenile delinquency. *Journal of Social Issues* 14, 38-51.

MacIver, R.M. (1967). *The Prevention and Control of Delinquency*. New York: Atherton Press.

Malarek, V. (1979). Young and bitter in the Year of the Child. *Toronto Globe and Mail*, Feb. 3, p. 10.

Malinowski, B. (1964). *Argonauts of the Western Pacific*. London: Routledge and Kegan Paul, p. 326.

Malpas, P. (1936). The incidence of human malformations and the significance of changes in the maternal environment in their causation. *Journal of Obstetrics and Gynecology of the British Empire* 44, 434-454.

Martin, F.M. (1977). The future of juvenile justice. *Howard Journal* 16, 78-89.

———— and Murray, K. (1976). *Children's Hearings*. Edinburgh: Scottish Academic Press.

Martin, J.M. (1961). Three approaches to delinquency prevention: a critique. *Crime and Delinquency* 7, 16-24.

Mays, J.B. (1954). *Growing up in the City.* Liverpool: Liverpool University Press.

————. (1962). The influence of environment. In *Delinquency and Discipline.* London: Councils and Education Press.

McCord, W. and McCord, J. (1958). The effects of a parental role model on criminality. *Journal of Social Issues* 14, 66-75.

————. (1959). *Origins of Crime.* New York: Columbia University Press.

McDermott, P.A. (1980a). Hierarchical and discriminant analyses of syndromic profile patterns on the Bristol Social Adjustment Guides. *British Journal of Educational Psychology* 50, 223-228.

————. (1980b). Prevalence and constituency of behavioral disturbance taxonomies in the regular school population. *Journal of Abnormal Child Psychology* 8, 523-536.

————. (1981). Patterns of disturbance in behaviorally maladjusted children and adolescents. *Journal of Clinical Psychology* 37.

McKay, H.D. (1959). *Juvenile delinquency.* Hearings before the Senate Subcommittee to investigate juvenile delinquency of the Committee on the Judiciary of the United States Senate. Part 2. (Community Programs in Chicago and the Effectiveness of the Juvenile Court System.) May 28 and 29.

Mednick, S.A. and Hutchings, B. (1977). Some considerations in the interpretation of the Danish adoption studies in relation to social behavior. In S.A. Mednick and K.O. Christiansen (Eds.), *Biosocial Bases of Criminal Behavior,* pp. 159-164. New York: Gardner Press.

Merton, R.K. (1957). *Social Theory and Social Structure.* Glencoe, Ill.: Free Press.

Miller, W.B. (1958). Lower-class culture as a generating medium of gang delinquency. *Journal of Social Issues* 14, No. 3, 5-19.

Minden, H. (1978). Evidence before the Senate of Canada Subcommittee on Childhood Experiences as Causes of Criminal Behaviour. No. 17, Hall, Quebec. Queen's Printer for Canada.

Morris, M. (Ed.). (1977). Instead of prisons. Syracuse, N.Y. Prison Research Education Action Project.

Murray, C.A. (1976). *The Link between Learning Disabilities and Juvenile Delinquency: Current theory and knowledge.* Washington, D.C.: U.S. Government Printing Office.

Murray, H.A. (1954). Toward a classification of interactions. In T. Parsons and E.A. Shils (Eds.), *Toward a General Theory of Action.* Cambridge, Mass.: Harvard University Press.

NACRO. (1975). *Children at Risk in School.* London: National Association for the Care and Rehabilitation of Offenders.

————. (1977). *Children and Young Persons in Custody. Report of a Working Party under the Chairmanship of Peter Jay.* London: Barry Rose.

———— and SCPR (Social and Community Planning Research. (c.1977). *Vandalism: An Approach through Consultation. Interim Report.* London: NACRO.

———— and SCPR (1978a). *Vandalism: The Cunningham Road Improvement Scheme. Second Report.* London: NACRO.

NACRO. (1978b). *The Hammersmith Teenage Project*. London: NACRO.

Nauta, J.S.H. (1971). The problem of the frontal lobes: A reinterpretation. *Journal of Psychiatric Research* 8, 167-187.

Nejelski, P. (1976). Diversion: the promise and the danger. *Crime and Delinquency* 22, 393-410.

Newman, J. (Ed.). (1972). *Crime in America*. Washington, D.C.: U.S. News Service and World Report.

Noorthouck, J. (1773). *A New History of London including Westminster and Southwark*. London: R. Baldwin.

O'Connell, E.J., Dusek, J.B., and Wheeler, R.J. (1974). A follow-up study of teacher expectancy effects. *Journal of Educational Psychology* 66, 325-328.

Phillips, M. (1978). Nicked in the bud. London: *The Guardian*. Four articles, June 13-16.

Power, M.J., Benn, R.T., and Morris, J.N. (1972). Neighbourhood, school and juveniles before the courts. *British Journal of Criminology* 12, 111-132.

Powers, E. and Witmer, H. (1951). *An Experiment in the Prevention of Delinquency*. New York: Columbia University Press.

Reckless, W.C. and Dinitz, S. (1972). *The Prevention of Juvenile Delinquency*. Columbus, Oh., Ohio State University Press.

Rees, A.D. (1950). *Life in a Welsh Countryside*. Cardiff: University of Wales Press.

Reitan, R.M. (1955). Certain differential effects of left and right cerebral lesions in human beings. *Journal of Comparative and Physiological Psychology* 48, 474-477.

————. (1966). A research program on the psychological effects of brain lesions in human beings. In N.R. Ellis (Ed.), *International Review of Research in Mental Retardation* 1, 153-218. New York: Academic Press.

Richmond, J.B. and Weinberger, H.L. (1970). Program implications of new knowledge regarding physical, intellectual, and emotional growth and development and unmet needs of children and youth. *American Journal of Public Health* 60, 23-67.

Robins, L.N. (1966). *Deviant Children Grown Up*. Baltimore: Williams and Wilkins.

Roper, W.F. (1951). A comparative survey of the Wafefield Prison Population in 1948 and 1949. *British Journal of Delinquency* 1, 243-270.

Rosenthal, R. and Jacobson, L. (1968). *Pygmalion in the Classroom*. New York: Holt, Rinehart & Winston.

Rutter, M. (1973). Why are London children so disturbed? *Proceedings of the Royal Society of Medicine* 66, 1221-5.

Schulsinger, F. (1977). Psychopathy: Heredity and environment. In S.A. Mednick and K.O. Christiansen (Eds.), *Biosocial Bases of Criminal Behavior*, pp. 109-124. New York: Gardner Press.

Shah, S.A. and Roth, L.H. (1974). Biological and psychophysiological factors in criminality. In D. Glaser (Ed.), *Handbook of Criminality*, pp. 101-173. Chicago: Rand McNally.

Shaw, C.R. (1938). *Brothers in Crime*. Chicago: University of Chicago Press.

———— and McKay, H.D. (1942). *Juvenile Delinquency and Urban Areas*. Chicago: University of Chicago Press.

Short, J.F., Jr., Tennyson, R.A., and Howard, K.I. (1963). Behavior dimensions of gang delinquency. *American Sociological Review* 28, 411-428.

Spinley, B.M. (1953). *The Deprived and the Privileged.* London: Routledge and Kegan Paul.

Sprott, W.J.H., Jephcott, A.P., and Carter, M.P. (1954). The social background of delinquency. Unpublished report lodged in Nottingham University Library.

Stevens, J., Sachder, K., and Melstein, A. (1968). Behavior disorders of children and the electroencephalogram. *Archives of Neurology* 18, 160-177.

Stott, D.H. (1950 and 1980). *Delinquency and Human Nature.* Dunfermline, Scotland: Carnegie U.K. Trust. 2nd edition, Sevenoaks, Kent: Hodder and Stoughton. Baltimore: University Park Press.

————. (1954). A club in an approved school. *The Boy* 27, 108-119.

————. (1956). *Unsettled Children and Their Families.* London: University of London Press. New York: Philosophical Library.

————. (1957). The reliability of data on early life. *Case Conference* 4, 67-74.

————. (1960a). Delinquency, maladjustment and unfavourable ecology. *British Journal of Psychology* 51, 157-170.

————. (1960b). A new delinquency prediction instrument using behavioural indications. *International Journal of Social Psychiatry* 6, 195-205.

————. (1960c). Should we "segregate" the slow-learning child? *The Slow-Learning Child* 7, 15-20.

————. (1961a). An empirical approach to motivation based on the behavior of a young child. *Journal of Child Psychology and Psychiatry* 2, 97-117.

————. (1961b). IQ Changes among educationally subnormal children. *Special Education* 50, 11-14.

————. (1962a). Cultural and natural checks on population growth. In M.F.A. Montagu (Ed.), *Culture and the Evolution of Man.* New York: Oxford University Press. Also (1969). And in A.P. Vayda (Ed.), *Environment and Cultural Behavior.* New York: Natural History Press and American Museum of Natural History.

————. (1962b). Delinquency and cultural stress. *British Journal of Social and Clinical Psychology* 1, 182-191.

————. (1962c). Evidence for a congenital factor in maladjustment and delinquency. *American Journal of Psychiatry* 118, 781-794.

————. (1963). Delinquency proneness and court disposal of young offenders. *British Journal of Criminology* 4, 37-42.

————. (1965). Do working mothers' children suffer? *New Society,* Aug. 19.

————. (1966). *Studies of Troublesome Children.* London: Tavistock Publications.

————. (1969). Personality and adjustment. In J.F. Morris and E.A. Lunzer (Eds.), *Contexts of Education.* London: Staples Press.

————. (1973). Follow-up study from birth of the effects of prenatal stresses. *Developmental Medicine and Child Neurology* 15, 770-787.

————. (1974). *The Social Adjustment of Children* (Manual to the Bristol Social Adjustment Guides). Fifth Edition. Sevenoaks, Kent: Hodder and Stoughton.

————. (1977). Children in the womb: the effects of stress. *New Society* 40, 329-331.

————. (1978a). *Helping Children with Learning Difficulties.* London: Ward Lock. American edition: *The Hard-to-Teach Child.* Baltimore: University Park Press.

Stott, D.H. (1978b). A critique of Jensen and Eysenck. *Australian Psychologist* 13, 29-32.

————. (1981). Behavior disturbance and failure to learn: a study of cause and effect. *Educational Research* 23, 163-172.

Stott, D.H. and Albin, J.B. (1975). Confirmation of a general factor of effectiveness-motivation by individual tests. *British Journal of Educational Psychology* 45, 153-161.

Stott, D.H. and Latchford, S.A. (1976). Prenatal antecedents of child health, development and behavior. *Journal of the American Academy of Child Psychiatry* 15, 161-191.

Stott, D.H. and Marston, N.C. (1970). *The Bristol Social Adjustment Guides* (Rev. ed.). Sevenoaks, Kent: Hodder and Stoughton. Toronto: Dominie Press. San Diego: Educational and Industrial Testing Service.

Stott, D.H., Marston, N.C., and Neill, S.J. (1975). *Taxonomy of Behaviour Disturbance*. Sevenoaks, Kent: Hodder and Stoughton. (Distributed by Brook Educational Publishing Ltd., Box 1171, Guelph, Ontario. N1H 6N3.)

Stott, D.H., Moyes, F.A., and Henderson, S.E. (1972). *Test of Motor Impairment*. Guelph, Ontario: Brook Educational Publishing Ltd.

Stott, D.H. and Sykes, E.G. (1956). *The Bristol Social Adjustment Guides*, 1st ed. London: University of London Press.

Stott, D.H. and Wilson, D.M. (1977). The adult criminal as juvenile. *British Journal of Criminology* 17, 47-57.

Stouffer, S.A., Suchman, L.C., DeVinney, L.C., Starr, S.A., and Williams, R.M. (1949). *The American Soldier: Adjustment during Army Life*. Vol. I. Princeton: Princeton University Press.

Tefferteller, R.S. (1959). Delinquency prevention through revitalizing parent-child relations. *Annals of the American Academy of Political and Social Science* 322, 69-78.

Thompson, W.R. (1957). Influence of prenatal anxiety on emotionality in young rats. *Science* 125, 698-691.

Time. (1977a). July 11, 16-18.

Time. (1977b). December 12, 54.

Treger, H. (1972. Breakthrough in preventive corrections: a police-social work team model. *Federal Probation* 36, 53-58.

————. (1975). *The Police-Social Work Team*. Springfield, Ill.: Charles C. Thomas.

————. (1976). Wheaton-Niles and Maywood Police-Social Service Projects. *Federal Probation* 40, 33-39.

Warnock, M. (Chairperson). (1978). *Special Educational Needs: Report of the Committee of Enquiry into the Education of Handicapped Children and Young People*. London: Her Majesty's Stationery Office.

Watkins, R. and Derrick, D. (1977). *Cooperative Care*. Manchester: Centre for Information and Advice on Educational Disadvantage.

West, D.J. (1969). *Present Conduct and Future Delinquency*. London: Heinemann.

————. (1973). "Are delinquents different?" *New Society* 26, 456-458.

———— and Farrington, D.P. (1973). *Who Becomes Delinquent?* London: Heinemann.

White, R.W. (1959). Motivation reconsidered: the concept of competence. *Psychological Review* 66, 297-333.

Whyte, W.H. (1957). *The Organization Man.* New York: Doubleday.

Wilkins, L.T. (1960). *Delinquent Generations.* London: Her Majesty's Stationery Office.

Wilkinson, D. (1955). *Land of the Long Day.* London: Harrap. Toronto: Clarke Irwin.

Wilson, H. (1962). *Delinquency and Child Neglect.* London: Allen and Unwin.

Wilson, J.A. (1973). Adjustment to the classroom. 1. Teachers' ratings of deviant behaviour. *Research in Education* 26-33.

Wilson, K. (1966). *The Stable Delinquent.* Unpublished monograph.

Witkin, H.A., Mednick, S.A., Schulsinger, F., Bakkerstrom, E., Christiansen, K.O., Goodenough, D.R., Hirschhorn, K., Lundsteen, C., Owen, D.R., Philip, J., Rubin, D.B., and Stocking, M. (1977). XYY and XXY men: Criminality and aggression. In S.A. Mednick and K.O. Christiansen (Eds.), *Biosocial Bases of Criminal Behavior.* New York: Gardner Press.

Yeudall, L.T. (1979). Neuropsychological concomitants of persistent criminal behavior. Paper presented at the annual meeting of the Ontario Psychological Association, Ontario.

Yeudall, L.T., Fedora, O., Fedora, S., and Wardell, D. (1980). A neurosocial perspective on the assessment and etiology of persistent criminality. *Australian Journal of Forensic Sciences.*

Yeudall, L.T. and Fromm-Auch, D. (1979). Neuropsychological impairment in various psychopathological populations. In J. Gruzelier and P. Flor-Henry, *Hemisphere Asymetrics of Function in Psychopathology.* Lausanne, Elsevier.

Yeudall, L.T., Tuokko, A., and Tuokko, O. (1978). *An Exploratory Study of the Incidence and Type of Brain Dysfunction in Elementary School Children.* Final Progress Report. Det. of Neuropsychology and Research: Alberta Hospital, Edmonton, Alberta.

Young, M. and Willmott, P. (1957). *Family and Kinship in East London.* London: Routledge and Kegan Paul.

Index